Patricia Unterman's
Food Lover's Guide to San Francisco

PATRICIA UNTERMAN'S

Food Lover's Guide to San Francisco

PHOTOGRAPHS BY BARBARA LUCAS

CHRONICLE BOOKS

SAN FRANCISCO

Text copyright © 1995 by Patricia Unterman.

Photographs copyright © 1995 by Barbara Lucas;
photograph on page 215 copyright © 1995 by Sydney Goldstein.

Library of Congress Cataloging-in-Publication Data available.

Text design & production: Margery Cantor

Cover art: John Mattos

Printed in the United States of America.

ISBN 0-8118-0759-2

Distributed in Canada by Raincoast Books, 8680 Cambie Street, Vancouver, B.C. V6P 6M9

10 9 8 7 6 5 4 3 2 1

Chronicle Books
275 Fifth Street
San Francisco, CA 94103

TO TIM AND HARRY

ACKNOWLEDGMENTS

This book is the product of over twenty years of reviewing restaurants, shopping, and cooking in the Bay Area with maniacal passion. Many, many, many thanks go to Tim Savinar, who trouped with me everywhere, and to Harry Savinar, who grew up in restaurants.

Niloufer Ichaporia King gleefully trekked through every ethnic market and neighborhood with me and graciously contributed endless time and knowledge. Anne Haskell, my former cooking partner at Hayes Street Grill, collected and worked wonders on many of the recipes. Special thanks to Laurie MacKenzie, an expert on the Mission and Latin American culinary arts; Yoko Tahara, my guide to Japantown; Yanek and Mary Chiu for my Chinese cultural education during hundreds of meals in Chinese restaurants here and abroad; Bruce Cost for his unfailing generosity and expertise on San Francisco's Chinatown; Lin and Kien Nguyen for Vietnamese shopping and eating; Gordon Wing for his help with Oakland's Chinatown; Stephen Singer, Bruce Cass, Pam Hemenway, and Denise Lurton Moullé for their expertise on wine and wineshops; Tim Savinar for his intimate knowledge of bars (though his list would have been different); Barbara Mendelsohn for her insight into Pacific Heights and everything else in life; and Howard Karel for his willingness to go anywhere, anytime. Special appreciation to Alice Waters for advice, teachings, a lot of great meals together, and a higher vision. Thanks to Paul Johnson and Andy Powning for making the fish and produce charts; Bobbie Lucas for her upbeat energy and images; to Laura Shapiro for advice on writing and a trip to India; Wendy Lesser for help with the introduction; and big thanks to Paula Tevis, the best editor and assistant a writer could have.

I have referred often to two books: *Cook's Marketplace: San Francisco Bay Area Sourcebook* by Sherry Virbila, (101 Productions, 1982, a forerunner of this book); and the exhaustive *Cafe San Francisco: A Guide to the City's Coffee-house Culture* by James M. Forbes, a self-published book.

Special thanks go to the kitchen crew at the Hayes Street Grill for their unfailing support and generosity over the years, and to my partner Dick Sander, whose humanity and sense of fun teaches me to keep things in perspective.

—Patricia Unterman

CONTENTS

Out of Town

Indexes

Specialty Indexes

The *Food Lover's Guide to San Francisco* was written both for visitors and for residents who want to explore the culinary landscape of their own city. Anyone who loves to travel knows the value of a guidebook that dovetails with his or her own passions and sensibilities. An intuitive writer can open up a seemingly impenetrable place and foster a deeper level of understanding and pleasure. Some travelers I know argue that arriving cold in a new place, completely open to any adventure, is provocative, but this argument does not convince me. If we travel to expand our senses and broaden our minds, then setting off unprepared and untutored lessens the scope of our experience. I like to know in advance where to find the qualitative best—especially when it comes to my personal passion, food—and I'm willing to go to the ends of the earth for a taste of the extraordinary.

These thoughts ran through my mind as I was sitting outside a small but famous coffeehouse in Rome called St. Eustachio, drinking the best caffè latte in the world. What if I had gone to Rome and missed this coffee? It wouldn't have been a disaster (you don't know what you haven't tasted), but I shudder to think about it. I went to St. Eustachio on the advice of an émigré Roman whose taste I trust, and whom I interrogated before I left home. As a result, my sense memory of Rome has been changed forever. I went to this cafe every morning and had not one, but two of these coffees, and I can still taste them, so strong, so rich, so sweet, so fragrant. Now I have a new standard by which I judge every other coffee, for better or worse.

For the last twenty years I have been developing my sense of taste as a restaurant critic (fifteen years at the *San Francisco Chronicle* and at magazines before that), and as a cook both at home and in San Francisco at the Hayes Street Grill. But what I really am is an eater, someone who loves food of every kind, but with an almost obsessive discrimination. Such openness combined with unrelenting critical consciousness seems like a paradox; being a connoisseur suggests a narrowing of taste. But eating something gorgeous, humble or high as it may be, floods me with pleasure. Looking for sensuous food has been an unending quest. I admit it: I eat, therefore I am. Sounds frivolous (I can hear Descartes turning over in his grave), but by extension, I taste, I buy, I cook, I feed, I nourish to enrich the lives of the people around me and, taking this line a step farther, I support the causes that nourish every human being. As far as I can see, the better the eating, the happier the person, if even for a moment. My idea of a better world pretty much hinges on wanting all people to have a good meal when they are hungry.

Since I am an enthusiastic user of guidebooks myself, I thought I would contribute to the genre from my own little piece of the earth, San Francisco and environs, and pattern it after a book that has been the source of hundreds of wonderful eating experiences for me, Patricia Wells's *The Food Lover's Guide to Paris* (Workman). Reading that guidebook and plotting a course from it sends a thrill down my spine, second to actually being in Paris. Wells writes about not only restaurants in every neighborhood, but bakeries, cheese stores, butchers, open markets, and the whole complicated tree of French culinary life, with an intelligent, personal, sensual voice. I can only hope to come close.

I am not sure I could have written a similar survey of San Francisco, or any American city (except New York), ten years ago because there simply wasn't that much to write about. Our Bay Area culinary resources have grown over the three decades I have been surveying them, however, and now I firmly believe that Northern California represents the most exciting and energetic food system in America—indeed, one that is equal to any in the world.

While Paris, Rome, and Hong Kong may be meccas for great eating, San Francisco has become a culinary crossroads where ethnic cooks and ingredients, especially from Asia, enrich our own indigenous products and cooking style. The mild Northern California climate supports an enormous variety of fruits, vegetables, and herbs. Our location on the edge of the Pacific assures a supply of fresh seafood. The cool fog and protected hills and valleys make for fertile wine country. But even more interesting has been the development of artisan producers, some of whom have learned from European techniques, others who use traditional American methods to get a superior product. We have a vital organic farming movement here, not only in produce but in meat, poultry, and dairy, and an efficient distribution system that delivers these foods to consumers. Furthermore, the Bay Area has become a large enough market to support importation from all over the world. The products we don't make ourselves we fly in. This bounty attracts an ever more sophisticated food community and an influx of people who come here to eat, work, and live within it. San Franciscans never cry about coming home from a trip. They have too many pleasures right here.

ABOUT THE CATEGORIES

Even I was surprised by the ethnic diversity of the city as I started marching through the market streets of each neighborhood. The discovery of new ingredients (new at least to me) made me want to cook with them, and many meals were inspired by finds from my wanderings. Hence the recipes and tidbits of information that relate to the neighborhoods or to products.

The book is divided into chapters that explore loosely drawn neighborhoods in the city plus some important centers of good eating outside the city. While not every one of the following categories is represented in every chapter, the restaurants always are, because they, more than any other culinary institution, excite our desire to explore.

RESTAURANTS

Each chapter starts with a very personal selection of restaurants that I have enjoyed over the years, for one reason or another. Sometimes a restaurant is included because it makes one dish I adore or because it provides a useful service to its neighborhood or because it feels good to be sitting in it. A very few have been included because of the importance of their role in the city's dining-out consciousness (though not necessarily mine), and I felt I had to say a few words about them. You'll just have to read the entries. Unlike Zagat and newspaper reviews, I am not providing a rating service. The very fact that a restaurant appears in the book means that it is interesting and the entries tell why. After fifteen years of assigning stars and thereby pigeonholing restaurants against my inclinations, these writings come from the heart. Something has grabbed me in all of these places.

There are so many restaurants in the city now that you almost don't need to reserve in advance, especially if you go at a slightly off hour. The weekends can be tougher at the most popular dinner houses, but unlike many European restaurants that will not seat you without a booking, whether they're full or not, San Francisco restaurants want to find you a table. Even without reservations, it never hurts to drop by if you can be flexible. Some parties don't show up for their tables, maddening and discourteous behavior though it is, which allows the maître d' to fit you in. The American appetite tends to be spontaneous (unlike that of Europeans, who all eat at certain hours), and many restaurants cater to this free-spirited dining by serving at the bar, cocktail tables, and counters. You can get a good taste of expensive restaurants without spending an arm and a leg, by ordering a glass of wine and a few appetizers from a perch at the bar. This impromptu seating also works nicely if you are eating alone. In San Francisco's competitive atmosphere, restaurants want only to accommodate.

CAFES

You can always get something to eat in coffeehouses in San Francisco, but the food service is usually informal, requiring you to order at a counter. Some cafes put out stunning snacks, sandwiches, and light fare, but the draw of cafes is that you can sit, think, talk, write, or read over a beautifully made cup of coffee.

BARS

What are these doing in a food lover's guide? Ask my husband, who considers an ice-cold martini, or a perfectly balanced margarita swirled in ice and served "up" as important sustenance. Many restaurants have bars and are included in this category for their pub identities—their buzz—not their kitchens.

DELICATESSENS/TAKE-OUT

With more and more members of the household working, and little time left for shopping and cooking, a good delicatessen can be a godsend. Semi-prepared food requiring a minimum of last-minute cooking can greatly improve a meal served at home. The best delicatessens, no matter what their ethnic origins, prepare or import foods that are difficult to make at home, even if you had the time. How many of us have the equipment or patience to air-dry Peking duck, cold-smoke salmon, or make fresh sausages? Delicatessens also sell food to eat on the spot, though usually there are no places in the stores to sit.

Does the tremendous proliferation of bread bakers relate somehow to the demise of the pastry shop? Are people turning away from cake to eat bread? I think so, seeing the scores of different kinds of fresh breads delivered to stores from bakeries all over the Bay Area, many of which have their own retail outlets. Of course, San Francisco has had a long tradition as the sourdough bread capital, and few artifacts represent San Francisco to the world as vividly as a crusty, chewy loaf. Several historic sourdough bakeries crank out thousands of fresh loaves every morning, having bought up many of the smaller operations, so those left remain vital.

Pastry shops, on the other hand, struggle. Perhaps because restaurants have such strong pastry kitchens, people eat their desserts out and don't buy them for home. Pastries are so labor-intensive and perishable that shops almost can't charge enough to stay in business and put out a good product.

ICE CREAM/CHOCOLATES

The ice cream parlor is disappearing like the pastry shop, and even simple ice cream scooperies seem to be diminishing. There are no great ones like Bertillon in Paris or Vivoli in Florence. San Franciscans buy their ice cream in the supermarkets and eat it at home. We have some wonderful local chocolate makers, though these, too, are under siege. The one-item specialty store depends so much on location, and location can be so expensive, that running a specialized operation becomes a precarious balancing act. Chocolates can be found in gourmet food halls in department stores and other outlets, allowing the chocolatiers to expand their production.

I have seen Russians cry at the bounty in American supermarkets. They cannot believe that so much food can be under one roof, waiting to be piled into carts. As convenient and tempting as supermarkets may be, I find that I shop in them less and less. I turn to specialty stores, Chinatown stores, and farmers' markets for fresh food, and try to use paper products and disposable goods as little as possible. To meet the challenge, the supermarkets try to be all things to all people. They have large deli counters, cheese sections, and their own bakeries. But too often the quality level is so low that the food is not worth buying, even at the cheapest prices. The rock-hard warehoused fruit in towering pyramids in the produce department is tasteless, and the shelves are filled with overpackaged processed food, often quite expensive, that almost is not really food at all. The good general markets included in this book make an effort to carry better fresh food and more of it than the gigantic chains. They often have independent butchers and carry some organic produce and meats. They take daily deliveries from local bread bakeries and local dairies, and feature goods from small producers.

ETHNIC MARKETS

Many of the items I buy at ethnic markets are essential for my general pantry, necessary to the eclectic cooking style so many of us have developed over years of travel and ethnic eating. Visits to these markets are as close as you can get to a trip to another country, and a pastime that I find stimulating. Seeing the juxtaposition of ingredients and figuring out what to do with them puts me in a mood to cook. Ethnic markets often have a deli component that makes them invaluable if you've decided to cook an exotic meal and you don't quite know how to prepare everything.

PRODUCE

If any kind of shopping has blossomed over the last five years, it has been produce. Invigorated by the influx of Cantonese, then Vietnamese immigrants, who buy, grow, and sell a huge variety of vegetables and herbs, and by the increasing demand for organic produce, availability and quality improves every year. People get turned on to fabulous tomatoes or sautéed pea shoots in restaurants and want to get their hands on them. Organic produce has moved from natural foods stores (still the major outlet for it) into general produce stores and even onto some supermarket shelves. Farmers' markets have proliferated so that almost every local community has one. Our growing season is year round, so even winter markets have wonderful things. As our diet shifts toward eating more fruits, vegetables, and grains, farmers and retailers are rising to the occasion, bringing greater and greater variety to the market.

MEAT AND POULTRY

The personalized butcher counter is making a comeback even as people turn to eating less meat. When they do, they want smaller and fussier cuts for use in recipes in which the meat is not the main ingredient. Organic beef and small-farm-raised pork and lamb are more and more in demand. Everyone has gone chicken crazy, and the production of these birds has become specialized, with the popularity of more flavorful, relatively freerange birds at a peak. Cooks are discovering quail, poussin, squab, pheasant, and other smaller birds, and the best shops are carrying them. Chinatown has always sold more flavorful chickens and birds of every sort, but specialty poultry is nudging red meat over to the side in all butcher cases.

Even though people are eating more and more fish in restaurants, they don't cook it at home. I don't know which comes first, the paucity of good fish markets or the lack of retail demand, but finding pristine fish remains a challenge. Chinese fish markets are an excellent source for fresh fish, but you have to know what you're doing. The smell emanating from the fish departments in supermarkets is enough to make you walk by quickly, and very few butchers know how to buy and handle fish and shellfish. The fact is that there are only two or three non-Asian fish markets in the whole Bay Area that I trust.

Cheese is everywhere but great cheese almost nowhere. Like every small specialty shop, the independent cheese store faces the two-headed dragon of perishability and small purchases. Though some supermarkets have huge cheese sections, the cheese suffers from mass buying and indifferent handling, the same way produce does. We have one great cheese store in the Bay Area and a lot of places like delicatessens and natural foods stores, where you dependably can find a favorite cheese.

WINES AND SPIRITS

The small, personally run wineshop is under siege from discounters, just the way the independent bookstores are from huge chains. The market for high-end wines seems to be softening as a generation of collectors in their late forties and fifties realize that they have to start drinking up if they are to outlive their cellars, and potential young buyers seem to be in love with beer. Even so, we have some famous, ground-breaking importers in the Bay Area, with some retail outlets for their interesting wines, and the abundant supply of excellent West Coast wines keeps wine shelves full everywhere. As this book is geared toward the qualitative, I include the wine shops where the service, understanding, and knowledge of wine lead patrons to unusual and well-made bottles from all over the world.

COOKWARE AND BOOKS

Cookware chain stores and small cookware shops are everywhere in the Bay Area, but my favorites are Asian, stocked to the rafters with handsome crockery and elegant cooking utensils for a song. Every Asian market street has one or two "Kitchen Friends," and I have stocked my cupboard at them with a bazaar's worth of unmatched pieces, all of which miraculously seem to go together as needed. As for cookbooks, the best ones hold up over time, making used cookcook sections in bookstores a valuable resource. The Bay Area's best independent bookstores often have a broad selection of both new and used books, although the two bookstores that were dedicated to cookbooks alone have closed, alas.

By using the indexes you can quickly scan all the recommended bakeries, butchers, coffeehouses, and so forth, in the individual subject listings. Restaurants are cross-referenced alphabetically by nationality and by price, among other groupings. But my main impetus was to explore the city neighborhood by neighborhood, so that if you found yourself in a certain part of town you'd immediately know where the good food is.

My companion and guide during much of the research, food anthropologist Niloufer Ichaporia King, told me that when she visits her eighty-two-year-old mother in Bombay, her greatest pleasure is starting a walk in the middle of the city and wending her way outwards through layers of neighborhood, observing, tasting, smelling, buying this and that as she goes. I have done that with this city on a spontaneous basis over the years, one spot leading to another, but with this book my research became more methodical. People who like to visit parks, monuments, and museums to get a feel for a city have the Michelin Guide. For those of us who learn about culture through food, this book should be of some help.

FISH AND SHELLFISH

	JAN	FEB	MAR
Angler (Monkfish) (East Coast)	x	x	
Cabezon, Rockfish, Lingcod (local)	x	x	x
Catfish (aquaculture)	x	x	x
True cod (East Coast, Alaska)	x	x	x
Flounder, Petrale (local)	x	x	x
Pacific halibut (local, hook & line)			
Northern halibut (Alaska, Canada, East Coast)	x	x	x
Mahi-mahi (both hemispheres)	x	x	x
True snappers (opaka, onaga, Gulf snapper)			
Salmon (local)			
King salmon (Alaskan)	x	x	x
Sand dabs, rex sole (local)	x	x	x
White sea bass (Channel Islands)			
Swordfish (California)			
Swordfish (Hawaiian)	x	x	x
Trout (aquaculture)	x	x	x

APR	MAY	JUNE	JULY	AUG	SEPT	OCT	NOV	DEC
							x	x
x	x	x	x	x	x	x	x	x
x	x	x	x	x	x	x	x	x
							x	x
							x	x
		x	x	x	x	x		
x	x	x	x	x	x	x	x	x
		x	x	x	x			x
		x	x	x	x	x	x	
	x	x	x	x	x			
								x
x	x	x			x	x	x	x
		x	x	x	x			
				x	x	x		
							x	x
x	x	x	x	x	x	x	x	x

	JAN	FEB	MAR
Tuna (both hemispheres)	x	x	x
Spearfish, ono (Hawaii)	x	x	x
Opah (local)			
Dungeness crab (local)	x	x	x
Blue crab (East Coast)	x	x	x
Lobster (East Coast)			
Mussels (Northeast)	x	x	x
Oysters	x	x	x
Scallops (East Coast)	x	x	x
Spot shrimp (Santa Barbara)	x	x	x
White shrimp (Florida, North Carolina)			
Squid (Monterey)			
Squid (San Pedro)	x	x	x
Manila clams (Pacific Northwest)	x	x	x
Spiny lobster (Pacific)	x		
Crawfish (Louisiana, Oregon)			

APR	MAY	JUNE	JULY	AUG	SEPT	OCT	NOV	DEC
			x	x	x	x	x	x
						x	x	x
				x	x	x		
x	x						x	x
x	x	x	x	x	x	x	x	x
				x	x	x	x	x
x					x	x	x	x
x					x	x	x	x
					x	x	x	x
						x	x	x
x	x	x	x	x	x	x	x	
	x	x	x	x	x	x	x	x
x								
x	x				x	x	x	x
							x	x
x	x	x	x	x	x	x	x	

(from Paul Johnson, The Monterey Fish Company)

SEASONAL PRODUCE CHART

A MONTHLY LISTING OF FRUITS AND VEGETABLES

This list focuses on California-grown produce at its best, which is at the beginning of its growing season, although many items are available over a period of months or year round. Everything listed here should be available at farmers' markets or in good produce stores. Please note that growing areas do change from year to year, though the towns listed in parentheses have been primary sources for particular crops over the past several years. An asterisk indicates a personal favorite.

JANUARY

Arugula, mizuna, baby red mustard (Bolinas)
Savoy cabbage (Pescadero)
Baby bok choy, Napa cabbage, lemongrass (Fresno)
Baby turnips, White Rose and red Irish potatoes,
  Bloomsdale spinach (Clovis)
Purple cauliflower (Esparto)
Seville oranges (Porterville)
Meyer lemons, allspice tangerines, Page and Kinnow
  mandarins, Lavender Gem tangerines (Fallbrook)
Morro blood oranges, kumquats (San Diego)

FEBRUARY

Carrots, turnips, fennel, leeks, gold, red, and Chiogga
  beets (Watsonville)
Green garlic (Santa Cruz, Bolinas, Guinda)

Choy sum, baby gai choy, gai lan (Gilroy)
Yellowfoot mushrooms (north and central California
  coast)
Chandler strawberries* (Santa Maria)
Rangpur limes (Santa Cruz)
Pomelos, Minneola tangelos* (Fallbrook)

MARCH

Baby lettuces, mâche, pain du sucre chicory, lavender
  and chive blossoms (Watsonville, Sonoma)
Treviso radicchio, Catalognia chicory (Guinda)
Young escarole, red and green chard (Pescadero)
Flambeau and Easter Egg radishes, salad Savoy (Santa
  Maria)
Dandelion greens (Bolinas, Watsonville)
Mustard greens (Capay)
Sorrel (Escondito, Guinda)
Navel oranges (Livermore)
Star Ruby grapefruit, Fortune and Dancy tangerines
  (Fallbrook)
Rhubarb, hothouse grown (Oregon, Washington state)

APRIL

Asparagus* (Delta)
English shelling peas,* sugar snap peas (Half Moon
  Bay)
New-crop Hass avocados* (Southern California)
Spring bulbing onions with tops, snow peas (Fresno)
Fiddlehead ferns, morel mushrooms (Pacific
  Northwest)
Japanese cucumbers, scented and opal basils
  (Watsonville)
Fava beans (Stockton)
Baby summer squashes, baby corn, baby Japanese
  eggplant (Selma, Vista)

Chervil, red Russian kale (Pescadero)
Meyer lemons (Fallbrook, Santa Cruz)

Young yellow waxbeans, Blue Lake beans, *haricots verts*
  (Vista)
Red onions, green almonds, loquats, Thai basil (Fresno)
New-crop creamer,* Bintji, yellow Finn, ruby crescent
  potatoes (Guinda)
Summer squash, red and gold zucchini, crookneck,
  sunburst, pattypan (Fresno, Santa Rosa)
Tartarian, Rainier, Bing* cherries (Suisun, Santa Clara,
  Gilroy, Smith Flat)
Royal Blenheim apricots* (Winters, Brentwood)
Cantaloupe (Imperial Valley)
Valencia oranges (Fallbrook)
Local field-grown rhubarb (Pescadero)
Red and black currants (Sebastopol)

Early Girl tomatoes* (Coachella)
Sweet 100 and Sungold cherry tomatoes (Capay,
  Winters)
German fingerling and red potatoes, pickling
  cucumbers (Bolinas, Fresno)
Baby Blue Lake beans* (Palo Alto)
Romano beans (Fresno)
Walla Walla onions (Washington)
Sea beans, or pousse pied, a seashore succulent
  (Oregon)
Red and white fraises des bois, red and gold raspberries
  (Watsonville)
Olallieberries (Stockton, Fresno)
Boysenberries, loganberries (Winters, Palo Alto)
Montmorency sour pie cherries (Smith Flat, Placerville)

Santa Rosa plums,* Firebrite* and White Snow Queen
nectarines, peaches, including Red Haven, Babcock,
Regina, and Early O'Henry* varieties (Brentwood,
Fresno)
Green Perlette seedless grapes (Delano)
Yellow and red watermelon (Imperial Valley)

JULY

White, yellow and bicolored* corn (Brentwood)
Heirloom tomatoes, including Golden Jubilee, Yellow
Taxi, Brandywine, Green Zebra, Marvel Stripe, Great
White, Purple Calabash and yellow and red plum and
pear cherry tomatoes (Capay, Palo Alto, Winters,
Davenport, Healdsburg)
New-crop red Italian garlic* (Pescadero)
Long beans, Armenian,* Jordanian, and lemon
cucumbers (Capay, Stockton)
Jacobs Cattle, Lima,* speckled butter, fresh cranberry*
and French horticultural shelling beans, Black-eyed
and Crowder peas, okra (Fresno, Watsonville)
Garlic chives, summer savory (Pescadero, Bolinas)
Plums, including Wickson, elephant heart, Satsuma,*
and Mariposa varieties (Placerville, Vacaville, Santa
Rosa)
Red and green Thompson seedless grapes, Champagne
grapes (Fresno)
Wild blackberries* (Sonoma)
Italian butter pears (Walnut Grove)
Asian pears (Brentwood, Sebastopol, Guinda)
Melons, including Charentais, Sharlyn,* Crenshaw,
ambrosia,* pink and green honeydew (Guinda,
Fallbrook, Brentwood)
Gravenstein apples* (Sebastopol)
Blueberries* (Oregon)

Chanterelles* (Oregon)

Peppers and chilies, including red, green, gold and
  yellow bell, jalapeño, serrano, long hot sweets,
  cubanelle, Aconcagua, corno di toro,* Gypsy,
  cheesecake,* and lipstick pimientos (Stockton,
  Winters, Fresno)

Red torpedo onions (Capay, Stockton)

Globe, Chinese, and Japanese eggplant (Fresno)

Figs: black Mission,* Kadota, Adriatic, and brown
  Turkey (Stockton, Maywood, Chico)

Bartlett pears (Lakeport)

Italian and French* prune plums (Vacaville)

French butter pears* (Walnut Grove)

Concord, Italian Muscat grapes (Fresno)

MacIntosh, Mutsu, Jonathan apples (Sebastopol,
  Capay)

Pumpkins, including Sugar pie, Baby Bear, White
  Cheesequake, French Red, winter squash, including
  delicata, sweet dumpling, red kuri, buttercup,
  butternut, acorn, blue Hubbard, banana, hokaido
  (California)

Red* and white* Belgian endive (Santa Rosa)

Brussels sprouts (Pescadero, Half Moon Bay)

Tomatillos (Capay, Stockton)

Red, gold, and white pearl onions (Central California)

Chestnuts (Northern and Central California)

Cape gooseberries (Graton)

Pineapple quince (Stockton, Santa Rosa, Reedly)

Granny Smith, Rhode Island Greening, Ozark,
  Hawaiian Gold, Rome Beauty, Orange Cox pippin,
  Royal Gala,* and Fuji* apples (Smith Flat, Sebastopol,
  Capay, Redding)

Huckleberries* (Oregon, Northern California)
Seckel, Comice, and Bosc pears (Northern and Central California)
Pomegranates (Dinuba, Stockton, Woodland)
Medjool and khadrawi dates (Walnut Grove, Coachella)
Varietal grapes including Chardonnay, Pinot Noir, Sauvignon Blanc, Gamay Beaujolais, Zinfandel (Napa)

OCTOBER

Small loose artichokes,* fennel (Watsonville)
Many greens including red and green chard,* spinach, collard, kale (Central Coast)
Celery root (Fremont, Watsonville)
Cauliflower and broccoli, including Venetian, purple, and Romanesque varieties, leeks (Central Coastal Areas)
Broccoli Rabe* (Salinas, King City)
Russet, purple Peruvian, yellow Finn, and Yukon gold* potatoes (Washington, Oregon)
Garnett and Jewell yams, sweet potatoes, Japanese sweet potatoes (Livingston)
Black trumpet, porcini and matsutake mushrooms (Pacific Northwest)
Gourds, decorative corn (Stockton)
Fuyu and Hachiya persimmons (Aptos, Santa Cruz, Santa Rosa)
New-crop Mission and Non-pareil almonds (Guinda)
New-crop walnuts (Hartley)
Cranberries (Michigan, Massachusetts)
Passionfruit* (Carpenteria)
Golden Delicious, Spitzenberg, and Sierra Beauty apples (Philo, Sebastopol)
Crab and lady apples (Placerville, Hairston)
Sapote, feijoa (Fallbrook)

Cardoon (Salinas)
Curly endive or frisée (Santa Rosa, Watsonville)
Baby turnip greens or rapini (Santa Maria)
Parsnips (Lamont)
Jerusalem artichokes (Watsonville)
Turnips and rutabagas (Fresno)
Uncured Manzanillo olives (Central Coast)
Late-harvest Granny Smith apples (Smith Flat)
Winter Nellis pears (Reedly)
Pepino melons (Graton, Santa Maria)
Fairchild tangerines (Coachella)
Orlando tangerines (Orosi, Fallbrook)
Kumquats (Thermal)

Hedgehog mushrooms (Central Coast)
Green, red, and Dutch Flat cabbage (Central Califonria)
Black Spanish radishes, carrots (Watsonville)
Beets (Oxnard)
Red Russian kale* (Pescadero)
Mixed winter braising greens, including chard, tat soi,
  kale, and mustard (Central California)
Dried shelling beans including cannellini, cranberry,
  tongue of fire, flageolet, French horticultural, and
  scarlet runner (Central California)
Wreaths and garlands of cedar, redwood, noble fir,
  juniper, and mistletoe (Pacific Northwest)
Blood oranges (Porterville, San Diego)
Satsuma mandarins,* oro blanco (a pomelo-grapefruit
  hybrid), pomelo (Orosi, Fallbrook)
Limequats (San Diego)
Fresh Barhi dates (Indio)
Kiwi (Chico)

—Compiled by Andy Powning, Greenleaf Produce

Chinatown

CHINATOWN

RESTAURANTS

GOLD MOUNTAIN

Kinson Wong, who owns both the R & G Lounge (with partner Joe Ling), the hottest restaurant in Chinatown (see page 51), and Gold Mountain, recently decided to extend this vast Chinese teahouse and dim sum parlor from its second- and third-story dining rooms to street level in the modern Ocean City building. Gold Mountain opened with a bang, but every second-floor operation in this building has had a problem getting people upstairs. The new ground floor dining room packs them in: The high-quality dim sum are as good as ever.

A dizzying variety of dim sum, noodles, and soup flows out of the kitchen. An armada of carts negotiating a sea of round tables ferries treasures like pleated dumplings filled with Yunan ham, shrimp, and vegetables decorated with minced carrot; translucent half-moons filled with shrimp, black mushrooms, and greens; and curly-edged dumplings filled with pungent Chinese chives and shrimp. Some of the carts have propane-fueled griddles for heating pot stickers or thick rice noodles studded with barbecued pork. Soup carts divided into four compartments distribute bowls of

644 Broadway (between
Columbus and Stockton),
San Francisco
Tel: 296-7733
Open daily 8 a.m. to
9:30 p.m.
Price: Inexpensive
Credit cards: AE, MC, V

steaming *congee* (rice porridge) flavored with salt pork and thousand-year-old egg. Sticky rice topped with sweet Chinese sausage comes in glass bowls that are overturned on your plate to form a perfect mound. From the dessert carts come tiny egg custard tartlets with crusts that melt in your mouth.

In addition to the food wheeled to your table, soup and noodles can be ordered from the kitchen. Rice wine-cured chicken vermicelli in soup brings good chicken stock and white noodles with a huge portion of thick-sliced velvety chicken that you dip in a fresh ginger and green chili puree. When you can get a beautiful, clean, satisfying lunch like this in less than five minutes (at the current price of $3.50), it proves that the Asian notion of fast food far outstrips ours.

In the evening, when a full menu goes into effect and the carts are garaged, the dining rooms become less like a train station and more like a restaurant, but I love Gold Mountain at its busiest. The dining rooms roar as hundreds of people come and go, turning this teahouse into a crossroads of Chinatown life.

HING LUNG

674 Broadway
(at Stockton),
San Francisco
Tel: 398-8898
Open daily 8 a.m. to 1 a.m.
Price: Inexpensive
Credit cards: MC, V

Very Cantonese and unique to San Francisco, Hing Lung turns out thousands of bowls of white rice porridge called *congee*, or sometimes *juk*. It is kept hot in a gigantic sunken vat at one side of a wildly active glassed-in kitchen at the entrance to the restaurant. You can watch the porridge being ladled out into saucepans and brought to a rolling boil, at which time it is poured over finely shredded ingredients waiting in deep serving bowls, cooking them instantaneously. Cilantro, ginger, and green onions are a given, along with such things as "sliced hard head," a trout-like fish and my favorite, though not always available. (One time, on a take-out order, Hing Lung substituted chicken on me. Oh, the disadvantages of being Caucasian!) First-timers feel confident with Sampam porridge seasoned with bits of shrimp, fish, lettuce, and peanuts, but the cognoscenti go for the sweetest, most velvety pork liver, kidney, tripe, and meatballs in Hing Lung's famous pork giblet porridge. I wouldn't try this dish in very many places, but when my surgeon/Chinese dining guru was gobbling his up I snatched a few bites. The pork giblets were impeccable—like silken foie gras.

The long oblong doughnuts you see on every table, translated as "fried bread," are yeasty, airy, crisp, and unsweetened. People tear them up and throw them into the *congee* or, better still, into bowls of lightly sweetened or salted warm soy milk. The doughnuts also come warm, wrapped in a sheet of rice noodles, cut into sections, sprinkled with sesame seeds and a gingery soy sauce. Wonderful!

The other specialty, pearly rice noodles, is made from a thin batter poured onto an oiled canvas in a rectangular steamer. Bits of that amazingly sweet pork liver, barbecued pork, and shrimp, just to name a few foods, are cooked right into them. The sheets are then folded over, cut with a scissors, and sauced with a mixture of soy, ginger, and peanut oil.

Hing Lung is a madhouse on weekends, but the turnover in the large, cheery, utilitarian dining room is rapid, the wait never too long. People from all segments of San Francisco's Chinese community come here. The owner of my Telegraph Hill cleaners, a city vice-mayor, my most elegant Pacific Heights friends, their Hong Kong nanny, and all the Chinatown chefs getting off the late shift rub elbows at Hing Lung.

I can see why. *Congee* is a restorative. Hot, soothing to the stomach, easy to eat, Hing Lung's superior version is as good for breakfast as it is at midnight, though the place turns out hundreds of bowls for lunch as well. *Congee* is not served after 3 p.m., when Hing Lung switches to its miraculously cheap and generous dinner menu. The *congee* returns to the menu late in the evening, ready to get people home with a full, but not heavy, stomach.

HOUSE OF NANKING

919 Kearny Street (between Jackson and Columbus), San Francisco
Tel: 421-1429
Open Monday through Friday 11 a.m. to 10 p.m., Saturday noon to 10 p.m., Sunday 4 to 10 p.m.
Price: Inexpensive
No credit cards

Peter Fang and his wife Lily have personally operated this hole in the wall from the day it opened. The lines out the door have only gotten longer and the dining room, crammed with nine tiny tables and a counter with a dozen stools, more cramped. Lily seats people so close to each other that they have to mind their elbows and hold onto their plates when tables are moved to allow others to get up and sit down. But you're so hungry by the time you get a seat, and, I suppose, psychologically primed for the experience, that everyone goes for it, grumpily or not. For some, the ridiculous conditions become part of the reason for eating here. I have also noticed that once the unusual, tasty, vaguely Shanghai-ese food starts coming out, people forget their discomfort, start joking with the strangers next to them, and leave the cafe happy, especially when they see how low the check is.

Peter Fang's cooking is nothing if not original. His primary goal is to keep prices about as cheap as they can be, and his next is to please the palates of the mostly young, Caucasian crowd that loves the place. Western broccoli, not Chinese broccoli, white mushrooms, not shiitakes, and enough garlic to satisfy a Sicilian have been incorporated into the style. However, since the restaurant is so amazingly small, with all the cooking, prepping, and dish washing done right in front of the counter, there is absolutely no place to store anything. So shopping is done sometimes two or three times a day in Chinatown, where a savvy buyer can find the highest possible quality-to-price ratio.

What sets House of Nanking apart from any other Chinese greasy spoon is Fang's culinary imagination. What he does under these conditions, frankly, is phenomenal. Each week or so he comes up with a new idea that is communicated to regulars by word of mouth. Most recently it was a platter of ethereal chicken dumplings wrapped in wonton skins, topped with dry-fried onions, chopped fresh Bing cherries, ground peanuts, and a light, clean, gingery sauce. I prefer to order dishes that use less-expensive ingredients here and forgo such creations as scallops stir-fried with thin slices of sweet potato, banana, and snow peas and sprinkled with toasted sesame seeds, which might have succeeded with better scallops (and have been twice as expensive). However, the regular menu is made up of successful dishes that do work on a shoestring budget, like true Shanghai dumplings made with raw bread dough, fried, then steamed and stuffed with vegetables. I like the tender chicken breast slices sautéed with long slices of zucchini and a resonant sauce made with Tsing-tao beer. For starters, crisp deep-fried pancakes stuffed with shrimp and vegetables napped in a salsalike mix of diced cucumber, green onions, and peanuts get a meal off to a good start. I also like the clear Nanking fish soup seasoned with lots of coarsely ground black pepper. It wakes up the palate without filling up the stomach. Vegetable dishes like rich Szechuan-style eggplant, simmered in a spicy brown sauce and tossed with broccoli flowerets and snow peas, are as substantial as a main course. Ice-cold Chinese beer is plunked down on the table without glasses and tastes all the better for it.

I have to admire Peter and Lily for not expanding, because the magic of the place depends on all its quirks. They have freshened House of Nanking a bit by tiling the walls, hanging schoolhouse lamps, installing new sheet metal around the kitchen, and hanging a little TV at one end of the counter. These much-needed improvements don't ruin the grunge look at all. In fact, you feel that at the current nonstop level of business they have only stemmed the tide of wear, tear, and grime for the moment, keeping House of Nanking just a little ahead of its most authentic and beloved state of encrustation. But what this amazing success boils down to is Peter Fang's gentle, generous spirit and sense of fun. This little place deserves those lines out the door. It has earned its cult status.

IMPERIAL PALACE

919 Grant Avenue (between Washington and Jackson), San Francisco
Tel: 982-8889
Open Monday through Friday 10 a.m. to 10 p.m.
Price: Inexpensive
Credit cards: AE, D, MC, V

When the marvelous Lichee Garden (see following review) burned down and took three years to reopen, some of its cooks and managers went off to other operations. This influence is recognizable at Imperial Palace, where people order magnificent crispy chicken, plates of sparkling fresh steamed greens, and platters of fillet of pork with Chinese sweet rice vinegar, which have the pedigree of the Lichee Garden versions. But Imperial Palace has a personality of its own, inherited in part from its former identity as the fanciest restaurant in Chinatown. Vestiges of its former swank remain in richly carpeted and paneled dining rooms decorated with Ching Dynasty paintings and late-nineteenth-century plates and vases. With its chic little bar in the front, perfect for a pre-dinner martini, and about half the number of tables that currently are jammed in the dining rooms, you can see how Imperial Palace once worked as an elegant Chinatown hideaway. In its current incarnation prices are incredibly reasonable and service can be dismissive, but there is some very good eating to be done.

From the Chinese menu order velvety slices of black cod, crisply pan-fried and seasoned with a relishlike mince of Chinese black beans, fresh chilies, garlic, and ginger. Insist that the waiter bring you the soup of the day, always a rich double chicken and pork broth with chicken feet and pork meat at the bottom. The mustard greens with threads of Yunan ham are lovely, especially with a crispy chicken. Preserved vegetable with fried bean curd brings golden brown tofu in a haunting sauce of pickled greens and hot red chilies.

At lunch, during the frantically busy dim sum service, people order from menus because there's no room in the dining room for carts. The dim sum chef is from the estimable Fook Yuen on the Peninsula. Some of his unique and tasty creations include spicy pork and peanut dumplings; a pan-fried curly-edged dumpling filled with shrimp and Chinese chives; plates of deep-fried black cod strips; glutinous rice–flour puffs stuffed wih sweet-and-sour ground pork; and juicy pork dumplings wrapped in fried bread dough. *Yee min*, noodles first fried, then braised with Chinese chives and enoki mushrooms, take on an astoundingly tender texture, and noodle pillows topped with stir-fried meats and vegetables are perfectly crisp and greaseless.

The only drawback here, beside the roaringly loud dining rooms, is the difficulty of eliciting the best dishes from the waiters if you don't speak Cantonese.

LICHEE GARDEN

Lichee Garden earned a reputation as the city's premier home-style Cantonese dinner house when it opened fifteen years ago, becoming the forerunner of the new generation of upscale Hong Kong–style restaurants like Flower Lounge. Early on it offered high-quality ingredients in a comfortable, though not formal, environment. As a result, Lichee Garden appeals to middle-class Chinese families and practically everyone else who lives nearby in North Beach, Telegraph Hill, and Russian Hill. They come in for meals of glistening spareribs, crispy chicken, radiant green vegetables, and creamy

1416 Powell Street (between Broadway and Vallejo), San Francisco
Tel: 397-2290
Open daily 9 a.m. to 9:30 p.m.
Price: Inexpensive
Credit cards: MC, V

tofu cakes in thin gravy—the Chinese equivalent of meat and potatoes (or in the case of San Francisco, pasta and salad). Lichee Garden also has taken on the role of the Chinatown family club, with birthday, anniversary, marriage, and New Year's parties all celebrated here.

Much of the popularity of Lichee Garden can be attributed to the soulful cooking of chef-owner Chak Siu, who has been with Lichee Garden since it first opened. His wife Annie Siu is the maître d'. Everything that comes out of his kitchen has the heartiness, the savoriness, of food you could eat every day. He is famous for his crispy-skinned chicken and the house-special pork spareribs, thin slices with bones lightly battered, deep-fried, and tossed in a piquant sweet-and-sour sauce. I adore them. From a list of amazingly cheap dishes written in Chinese (you'll have to ask for a translation) comes a huge platter of fried tofu, bone-in chunks of satiny black cod, and wilted iceberg lettuce seasoned with pickled greens, a dish you pile onto rice and slurp up, bowl after bowl. Pan-fried noodles here have the much-prized "taste of the wok" (for 50¢ extra), which turns chicken-and-black-mushroom chow mein into a crispy pillow slathered with chicken, baby bok choy, and mushrooms. The noodles cook so hot and fast that they caramelize slightly, skirting the edge of burning in the way that barbecue does, taking on a special flavor that only comes from the fire. The wonton soup is also a dream, boasting rich, clean stock and noodles stuffed with sweet-flavored shrimp and pork. The new dim sum lunch service is excellent and ridiculously cheap. I don't know how these highly competitive Chinatown restaurants can do it, but Lichee Garden's dumplings boast the sweetness of fresh shrimp and other high-quality ingredients.

The spacious dining room has the aura of a resonant old Hong Kong cafe with wooden chairs and wainscoting, a celadon-green carpet, and lots of small square tables interspersed with large round ones—the perfect configuration for a restaurant that accommodates two cultures with single-minded integrity.

ORIENTAL PEARL

Unlike many Chinatown restaurants where low price is the most important consideration, Oriental Pearl's goal is to offer a civilized dining experience as well as authentic food for a still-reasonable tariff. When out-of-town visitors want a top-notch dinner spot in the heart of Chinatown, I always send them here, as do many well-informed concierges. I tell my guests to start with a house special chicken meatball—one for each person at the table—a delicate bundle wrapped in a gossamer pancake made only of egg whites, tied with a Chinese chive. Inside is an ethereal forcemeat of finely chopped chicken, shrimp, black mushrooms, fresh water chestnuts, and Virginia ham. Another must is a dish called *pei pa* tofu, spicy golden-fried dumplings of bean curd in a lush, hot sweet-and-sour sauce. Tofu Soup brings a peppery broth spiked with toasted garlic and cilantro leaves, an exciting background for lots of sweet, fresh shrimp. *Chiu Chow* marinated duck braised with aromatic Chinese spices and served with a dipping sauce of vinegar and red chilies reminds me of a duck stew, but don't expect the crisp skin of Chinese roasted duck. However, the spectacular spicy braised prawns, first battered and deep-fried, then sauced in a hot, chili-flecked sweet-and-sour syrup on a cloud of crackling fried rice noodles is all about crunchiness. Even simple vegetables like slightly bitter mustard greens taste different here, set off by tiny slivers of Virginia ham. The crisp-tender stalks refresh the palate at the end of the meal, almost like a sip of strong black tea. If you have room, order a plate of

760 Clay Street (at Kearny), San Francisco
Tel: 433-1817
Open for lunch 11 a.m. to 3 p.m., dinner from 5 p.m. to 9:30 p.m.
Price: Inexpensive to moderate
Credit cards: AE, DC, MC, V

Oriental Pearl's elegant chow mein, made with the thinnest noodles quickly and cleanly tossed with slivers of chicken breast, shiitakes, green onion, and bean sprouts —a stellar preparation of an often pedestrian dish.

People travel across the city for a glass pie plate of Oriental Pearl's "house special noodles," (*yee min*), which are first deep-fried, then braised with Chinese chives and enoki mushrooms so that they achieve a miraculously soft, silky, yet elastic texture. It's hard to stop eating them.

This comparatively small Chinatown restaurant also puts out an accomplished tea lunch, which is ordered from a menu rather than being brought around on carts. This means that each item will emerge fresh and hot from the kitchen, though the tea lunch draw of immediate gratification is lost. The impeccably fresh shrimp and pork dumplings in all their various forms are certainly worth a wait. Be sure to try the scallop and shrimp dumplings, the rustic taro leaf packets filled with sticky rice and pork, the fantastically crisp taro balls, and the cigar-shaped egg rolls of exceptional crunch. Finish with crisp thin pancakes filled with red bean paste.

PEARL CITY

641 Jackson Street (between Kearny and Grant), San Francisco
Tel: 398-8383
Open daily
8 a.m. to 10 p.m.
Price: Inexpensive to moderate
Credit cards: AE, D, MC, V

A spot for very inexpensive, rustic dim sum in huge portions, this teahouse is almost unapproachable on the weekends, although unrelenting competition in price and quality from other dim sum houses in Chinatown have somewhat diminished the crowds during the week.

Some of my favorites here are sticky rice–stuffed taro packets, more moist and savory than most; vegetarian rolls wrapped in crisp deep-fried tofu skin; and coarsely chopped *sui mai*, which are noodle-wrapped cylinders of pork and shrimp barely bound together. The best dumplings come in translucent wheat-gluten wrappers filled with chopped greens, garlic chives, and a little bit of pork. They have a delightful fresh flavor. Little accommodation is made for non-Chinese speakers here, but the authentic food at fantastic prices allows adventurous choosers to shrug off any unexplained surprises. The women bearing the trays and carts want only to lighten their loads.

R & G LOUNGE

631 Kearny Street (between Sacramento and Clay), San Francisco
Tel: 982-7877
Open daily 11 a.m. to 9:30 p.m.
Price : Inexpensive to moderate
Credit cards: AE, MC, V

My most recent meal in the newish upstairs dining room made me want to come back the next day. R & G Lounge started in the basement with family-style seating (small parties ended up sharing large tables), but the pristine seafood and vegetables streaming out of the kitchen at bargain prices made it more and more crowded. Connoisseurs who wanted live lobster, spot prawns, and fish pulled from the tanks were elbowing out regulars who ate the aromatic five-spice oxtail stew or other terrific Cantonese lunch specials for $3.50. Befitting R & G's growing reputation as the premier Chinatown seafood house, a quiet, carpeted upstairs dining room was opened with an entrance around the corner on Commercial Street. Lined with Japanese screens, which give the room the illusion of being flooded with natural light, the room has a peaceful and restrained decor. Pop music plays ever so softly, and a video monitor hanging from the ceiling soundlessly runs the soaps during the afternoon. (This practice reminded me of a meal I had in a restaurant in Estonia during which a video monitor showed a woman giving birth, also with the sound off.)

The food at R & G is excitingly good. Start with a specialty like salt-and-pepper-fried whole shrimp, so crisp and lightly battered in the proper balance of Sichuan pepper and sea salt that you devour the thin shells and head meat along with the bodies. Or get live spot shrimp from the tank cooked two ways—the heads salt-and-pepper roasted, the bodies steamed—to appreciate their exquisite freshness. Flounder gets a two-way treatment, too. The tiny dorsal bones are salt-and-pepper fried and taste like the best potato chips, while the fillets are steamed with vegetables. I am partial to the whole steamed flounder slathered in ginger, green onions, threads of pork, and shiitakes—one of the best preparations of this local fish I have tasted. I love oxtails so much that I ask for them in the upstairs dining room. Gently aromatic with star anise, they cook in a clay pot with iceberg lettuce leaves, onions, and a sauce that is absolutely luscious over rice.

We coaxed the best dish of the year from our loquacious waiter Raymond (who wore a name tag engraved with a happy face) by asking him what vegetables he had. He ran them down—asparagus, spinach, bok choy, Chinese broccoli—finally mentioning *yin choy*, a spinachlike leaf with a purple center, called *amaranth*, or Chinese spinach. He suggested we have it cooked with two kinds of egg: salted and thousand-year-old. Well, I'm telling you, it was a destination dish. The eggs added richness and texture to the amazingly tasty, juicy greens. Don't be put off by the exotic ingredients: Order this dish. For dessert, Raymond insisted on bringing us cool, barely sweetened coconut pudding, really a tender gelatin, scattered with red beans, ending the meal brilliantly. I can't wait to get back to this restaurant to explore further. R & G has only gotten better since it first opened six years ago, and who knows how high it will reach?

CAFES

Every time I enter this serene haven in the form of a traditional Chinese teahouse I wonder why I don't come here more often. I spend a tranquil half hour or so sipping small cups of refreshing and invigorating tea and walk out a new person. Everything about this teahouse works against daily stress and soothes a person back into civilized existence. I don't know why this place has such a strong effect on me, because I am not a tea drinker or even someone who likes to linger in coffeehouses, but the minute I sit down at one of the Tea Court's antique square tables and the tea master takes a look at my face and suggests a certain brew, I know that my life will improve.

Most recently he suggested a light herbal tea called "silver needle," aptly named for its soft, furry pointed leaves, with two (not three, not one) chrysanthemum flowers in the pot. He set a kettle of water to simmer on a special heater at the table and, when the water reached the right temperature, which he could tell from its sound in the pot, he half filled the tea pot, then poured out the first brewing of tea, then rebrewed and finally served us our first cup. We continued to add water to the pot to drink four more small covered cups of tea. Time flew by, and I felt as if I had just taken a small vacation.

On other occasions I have had strong espressolike tea in thimble-sized cups, and medium-bodied *pu-erh* ("po nay") tea after lunch across the street at Lichee Garden. Each infusion gets a different pot, a different cup, and undergoes a different brewing process. You can learn as much as you want from the eager teachers in the shop, or you can just enjoy your tea. The people who run this charming cafe are friendly and sensitive to their customers' desires.

1411 Powell Street (between Broadway and Vallejo), San Francisco

Tel: 788-6080

Open daily 11 a.m to 6:30 p.m.

Credit cards: MC, V

The room evokes old China. Dark, polished wood tables and shelving, jade-green Chinese silk insets in the burnished maple walls, a marble floor, wooden lanterns, and a beautiful antique tea counter look like they were all airlifted from some pre-Revolution Shanghai tea-house. If you're in the neighborhood drop by and see what it was like to be a mandarin.

LEE'S FRENCH COFFEE

1310 Stockton Street (between Broadway and Vallejo), San Francisco
Tel: 391-6868
Open daily 11 a.m to 9 p.m.
No credit cards

A sugarcane juice–extracting machine sits in the open window of this Vietnamese coffeehouse. An operator takes thick stalks of fresh sugar cane and puts them through the spiked rollers. A sweet white juice comes out into a pitcher of ice. Ask for limes—absolutely essential—and squeeze at least a half lime into each glass. You will have the most wonderful tropical drink you have ever tasted. Slow-dripping Vietnamese coffee, stirred with the sweetened condensed milk that awaits in the bottom of the glass, is another reason to stop by Lee's. Depending on the weather, have this sweet, rich Vietnamese coffee iced or hot.

BARS

LI-PO

916 Grant Avenue (at Washington), San Francisco
Tel: 982-0072
Open daily 2 p.m. to 2 a.m.
No credit cards

Like its sister street-level bars nearby, Bow Bow and Buddha, Li-Po was a historic haunt for seamen visiting the Barbary Coast. With a golden Buddha enshrined in a cave behind the bar, and an entrance that looks like it leads to a temple, Li-Po still provides an atmospheric haven. The women bartenders are welcoming and pleasant, but tough. You pay for each drink as it's served. Although the liquor and beer selection is generally unexceptional, the bar does stock a number of good cognacs, brandy, and Scotch whisky.

DELICATESSENS/TAKE-OUT

JANMAE GUEY

You can buy glistening barbecued ducks, pork ribs, slabs of pork, and chickens at any number of places in Chinatown where you see them hanging in the windows, dripping onto steam-table trays of prepared foods. Janmae Guey is one of the oldest and most well established of the barbecue houses, with a brisk turnover. I take my duck home, cleaved through the bones, and serve it with mango salad and rice. Other people eat their roast pig on the premises with a bowl of noodles and soup in the tiny dining room. You can catch a glimpse of the whole pink pigs, hanging downstairs, waiting to be roasted.

1222 Stockton Street
(between Broadway and
Pacific), San Francisco
Tel: 433-3981
Open daily 8:30 a.m.
to 6:30 p.m.
No credit cards

NEW HONG KONG NOODLE COMPANY

For want of a better category, I put the Hong Kong Noodle Company here. This small shops sells only noodles: fresh, long, and of every width, in one-pound packages. These are tender egg noodles that cook up in boiling water in about a minute—ready to be stir-fried with meat and vegetables, served cold in peanut sauce, or put into soups. If you want the freshest Chinese noodles, pick them up here. Wonton skins fill the other half of the refrigerated case. They come in rounds for *sui*

874 Pacific Avenue
(between Stockton and
Powell), San Francisco
Tel: 433-1886
Open Monday through
Saturday 8 a.m. to 5 p.m.
No credit cards

mai (a dim sum) and pot stickers, and squares for won-tons and dumplings. The thickness of the skins deter-mines their use: thin for deep-frying, medium for wontons in soup, thick for pot stickers. There are also packages of egg-roll skins. The noodle dough here is smooth and elastic, easy to separate, but always tender, with good flavor. Just seeing the stacks and stacks of skins inspires me to make wontons or dumplings, everyone's favorite food. The skins are so versatile, they can be filled with cheese to make Russian *vareniki* or with meat for *pelmeni*; layered with onions and deep-fried to make northern Chinese green onion cakes; or stuffed with all sorts of different ingredients for egg rolls. The only other item sold at this shop are eggs by the flat, which seems a bit odd since the eggs have already gone into the noodles.

BAKERIES/PASTRIES

MEE HEONG PASTRY COMPANY

1343 Powell Street
(between Broadway
and Pacific), San Francisco
Tel: 781-3266
Open Tuesday through
Friday 7 a.m. to 6 p.m.,
Saturday and Sundays
8 a.m. to 6 p.m.
No credit cards

Lots of busy Chinese bakeries are sprinkled throughout Chinatown, most of them full of people eating the lightly sweetened, egg-rich Chinese pastries and drinking tea, but I like this bare little place because of their 35¢ sponge cakes, each wrapped in a piece of parchment. These indi-vidual airy, free-form cakes with puffy tops are so light and tender they practically dissolve on your tongue. They can be soaked and served with macerated fruit or served plain with tea and fresh lichees or mango. While the selection of pastries at Mee Heong remains small, they have a distinctive handmade, not machine-made, quality. In fact, you can see the baker in the back at all hours of the day, cutting and shaping pieces of dough on a large wooden table.

MEE MEE BAKERY

Not only are the fortune cookies baked here fresh, crisp, and delicious, but they can hold your very own messages. As you can imagine, the potential for fun cannot be overstated. Even if you settle for precomposed fortunes, the big bags of cookies make for an inexpensive and much-appreciated present for kids. For adults who might appreciate a bag of cookies with risqué messages, Mee Mee always has them on hand.

1328 Stockton Street (between Broadway and Vallejo), San Francisco
Tel: 362-3204
Open Monday through Saturday 8 a.m. to 6 p.m.
No credit cards

ETHNIC MARKETS

CHINA HERBS AND NATIVE PRODUCE COMPANY

From the front, Alan and May Lai's store does not look like the biggest herbal dealership in the Western world, but inside, this building is a warehouse of Chinese dried goods and herbs for all purposes. A huge variety of dried shiitakes from Korea and Japan, seeds, nuts, bitter almonds (really apricot kernels), and dried dates and figs are all easily recognizable laid out on tables in the skylit space. More exotic items like different grades of shark's fin, sea cucumber, and birds' nests are kept like jewels in drawers. Bins of red beans, soybeans, and the Chinese version of black-eyed peas (the mature seeds from Chinese long beans) are but a few of the high-quality dry goods that fill every nook of the store. Don't

622 Broadway (between Stockton and Grant), San Francisco
Tel: 788-2963
Open daily 9 a.m. to 5:30 p.m.
Credit cards: MC, V; $30 minimum

The market streets of Chinatown rival Hong Kong's in their frenzy, smells, and crowds. Chinatown can seem daunting to the uninitiated shopper, but there is no more exciting area in which to buy food in the city. You can find excellent raw materials here in the way of fish, poultry, shellfish, pork, and vegetables for any style of cooking, and of course anything you might need for the Asian pantry. The great shopping blocks are between Broadway and Pacific on Grant Avenue, and Broadway to Washington on Stockton Street, with growing activity on Powell. A scattering of good Chinese markets have jumped over Broadway into North Beach, as have a number of good Cantonese restaurants. Broadway itself between Stockton and Columbus offers a number of stores selling produce and groceries. You don't hear much English, although almost everyone does speak it, and the shops and stores want only to move their merchan-

dise, so don't be shy about asking for what you want. The prices can be very good, but it takes a keen eye to find the best things. One store can have tables of beautiful baby bok choy and moldy water chestnuts. Another will have piles of tiny pea shoots, yet another mangoes and apricots. One of the fish markets will have local rockfish still gasping for breath; another, exquisite live spot prawns swimming in a tank. At first you think the same things are being sold everywhere, but certain places have special things, and those things

seem to move around from place to place. I approach shopping in Chinatown the same way I do at a farmers' market: I go with empty baskets and cloth bags slung across my shoulder and an open mind instead of a specific shopping list. That way I can walk around and pick up the best things available at six different stores. Once you start shopping this way, you will find it boring to shop in the supermarket where everything is available whether in season or not, and where the emphasis is on packaged, not fresh, living foods.

leave without buying a bag of Jae Jae Ginger Drops (hot, cleansing, better than Clorets) or Japanese Super Lemon Drops, which start out tart and end up sweet. A walk up and down the aisles discloses a realm of goods that Westerners never imagine.

MAY WAH SHOPPING CENTER

Compared to the complete and expansive May Wah on Irving, the Chinatown May Wah seems cramped, but it still carries an enormous variety of fresh foodstuffs and groceries. Shoppers will always find good-quality walnuts and pecans, pickled greens in crocks, garlic shoots, and thick, flat-stemmed Chinese chives in the produce section along with all the Southeast Asian herbs, since the May Wah company is owned by a Vietnamese family. This store happens to be one of the few places anywhere in the city to find clear-eyed fresh sardines and mackerel,

1230 Stockton Street
(between Broadway
and Pacific),
San Francisco
Tel: 433-3095
Open daily 8 a.m.
to 6:30 p.m.
No credit cards

May Wah piles its elegant purple-and-green-leaved Chinese spinach, or amaranth, on sidewalk tables to attract buyers. A huge bunch costs $1.29 and will easily serve four. This cooking technique works for big bunches of long-stemmed watercress, pea shoots, or regular spinach as well, although you don't need to cook these vegetables as long.

In a large wok or casserole with a cover over high heat, heat the oil. Add the garlic, ginger, salt, and chili flakes, optional. Cook over high heat until the garlic just starts to color, about 1 minute. Then add the amaranth. Toss the leaves in the aromatics and add 1/2 cup water. Cover. Lower heat to medium and cook for 5 minutes.

Check the pot or wok for water. If completely dry, add 1/4 cup more. Cook 5 minutes longer. Taste for tenderness and serve.

Serves 4

BRAISED AMARANTH

1 tablespoon vegetable oil
2 garlic cloves, minced
1 tablespoon minced, peeled
 fresh ginger
1 teaspoon kosher salt
1/2 teaspoon dried red chili flakes
 (optional)
1 large bunch of amaranth, stemmed
 and washed, but not dried
1/2 to 3/4 cup water

a red-fleshed fish not typically used in Cantonese cooking. Slices of Smithfield ham and exotics like frozen river fish from China are among the hundreds of items that May Wah stocks. You could spend hours just wandering down the aisles marveling at the culinary diversity.

METRO

641 Broadway (between
Grant and Stockton),
San Francisco
Tel: 982-1874
Open daily 9:30 a.m. to 6 p.m.
No credit cards

A Shanghai grocery like Metro is a foreign store in Cantonese Chinatown. The neatly arranged Metro shelves are filled with northern ingredients like the salty dried Smithfield hams from Virginia used in many Shanghai dishes; all sorts of Chinese seaweed; salted and cured bamboo shoots in beautiful reed and leaf packages; jars of sweet fermented-rice pudding in the refrigerator case; jasmine and short-grain rice; jars of Lan Chu brand sauces from Taiwan; and excellent peanut oils. Panther brand oil, sold in yellow gallon tins, is absolutely clean in flavor and superb for deep-frying since it has such a high flash point. Many Western as well as Chinese restaurants use this oil for their fryers. A whole section of Metro is devoted to Chinese *Shaoxing*, or rice wines, and liqueurs. One of the most surprising is *kuei hau chen*, a lightly sweet and haunting wine made from grapes infused with osmanthus (a relative of jasmine), which reminds me of Sauternes. It is lovely chilled and served as an aperitif—especially at $5 a bottle—or instead of vermouth in an icy vodka martini as Bruce Cost does at his Berkeley restaurant, Ginger Island. Aged rice wines, the oldest continually made wine, taste like sherry and come in handsome celadon jugs. At Metro you can find all the jarred, bottled, or cured ingredients you need to prepare practically any Chinese recipe, in one of the most pleasant shopping environments in Chinatown. The merchandise in this spacious store is organized logically, and friendly clerks (most of whom happen to be older women) will be happy to help you find anything you might need.

PRODUCE

The same woman owns both Kum Luen and another, slightly higher-quality produce store with outdoor tables directly across the street on the southwest corner of Stockton and Broadway. Western fruits like apricots and peaches, always several varieties of mangoes, bunches of the striking purple-leafed amaranth (a Chinese spinachlike vegetable; see page 59 for a fabulous preparation of it), asparagus, Chinese chives and chive flowers, and whatever else is in season at good prices will be placed closest to the sidewalk, just as in Hong Kong. When expensive fresh lichees are in season in the early summer, Kum Luen will have them.

1265 Stockton Street
(between Broadway and
Pacific), San Francisco
Tel: 989-4668
Open daily 7:30 a.m.
to 6 p.m.
No credit cards

SUN YUEN TRADING COMPANY, INC.

This grand corner market on the North Beach side of Stockton lays its most tempting produce outside on tables in front and along the sides of the store, protected by a red and yellow canopy. If you see piles of tiny purple amaranth leaves, huge bunches of watercress, or some hard green mangoes, you'd better grab them because an hour later they might be gone. The water chestnuts are plump and fresh, and there is always a table of special seasonal fruit of fairly good quality at loss leader prices —like Santa Rosa plums, oranges, or white peaches. I am attracted by Sun Yuen; it's always busy, the produce looks appealing, and the lightning-fast clerks behind the registers smile. Inside, the store is stocked with Chinese dry goods of all sorts, including candies, cookies, and everything you need for red-cooked pork (see page 513): rock crystal sugar, star anise, dark and light soy sauce, tangerine peel, rice wine. The sheer volume and variety of the inventory gives the store its color.

717 Vallejo (at Stockton),
San Francisco
Tel: 989-0937
Open daily 8 a.m.
to 6:30 p.m.
No credit cards

1210 Stockton Street
(between Broadway
and Pacific), San Francisco
Tel: 989-2350
Open daily 7 a.m. to 6 p.m.
No credit cards

This old Chinatown produce store lures buyers from the steady stream of foot traffic on Stockton with open-air tables piled with Bing cherries in season and the prettiest baby bok choy. This shop specializes in winter melon, sold by the chunk, that lovely huge white-fleshed melon that tastes so good in rich chicken broth. Mangoes at the best Chinatown prices and net bags of fresh lichees, worth every cent of their $7-per-pound price, always catch my eye. Leafy greens like big bundles of watercress and thick-stemmed mustard greens always look good here. If you need watercress, Chinatown produce stores have the best and biggest bunches for the cheapest prices. The Chinese sauté it like spinach, so buyers expect the bundles to be huge.

MEAT AND POULTRY

KWONG JOW SAUSAGE COMPANY

1157 Grant (between
Broadway and Pacific),
San Francisco
Tel: 397-2562
Open Monday through
Saturday 9 a.m. to 6:00 p.m.,
Sunday 9 a.m. to 5 p.m.
No credit cards

On one side of this specialty store hang long, skinny Chinese sausages and slabs of sugar-cured Chinese bacon (cook it with fresh fava beans or in sticky rice) dangling from strings; on the other is a refrigerated case of good-looking fresh pork, including hard-to-find spareribs and slabs of fresh bacon—just what you need to make luscious red-cooked pork (see sidebar, page 513). When you walk into this immaculate shop, the smell of rice wine and curing pork makes you want to get cooking.

Basically a wholesaler with a tiny retail storefront, Man Sung only displays a few of the poultry items it sells. But this is the place to go for fresh chickens and chicken parts. Chinese shoppers insist on free-range chickens and bought them long before the mainstream market caught on. These hormone-free chickens are raised for flavor and tend to be lean, but oh so tasty. Be sure to specify Petaluma chickens at Man Sung; they are specially raised by the Petaluma Poultry Company for the Chinatown market. Take home a whole bird complete with head and feet, appendages that greatly enrich a stock. Birds with head and feet attached are called Buddhist chickens and may be sold because of an exemption granted by the U.S. Department of Agriculture, which otherwise requires that they be removed. Since these Buddhist chickens are bled, a method of killing required by Jewish law, they are also sold in kosher butcher shops.

Man Sung also sells Pekin ducks from Reichardt duck farm in Petaluma. These ducks do not have huge breasts, so they roast up quickly and stay moist, especially when bathed in an aromatic Asian marinade.

The California history of the Pekin duck, a mallard crossbred in China thousands of years ago, began in 1880 when a Yankee clipper ship, on its way to the East Coast from China by way of South America, docked in San Francisco. Somehow a dozen Pekin ducks in its cargo disappeared and ended up at a small poultry farm in the middle of the city. In 1901 Otto H. Reichardt bought the stock and moved the operation to Petaluma, where the duck farm, still in the family, raises over a million ducks a year, supplying most of the West Coast.

1116 Grant Avenue
(between Broadway and
Pacific), San Francisco
Tel: 982-5918
Open daily 7 a.m. to 6 p.m.
No credit cards

MING KEE GAME BIRDS

1122 Grant Avenue
(between Broadway and
Pacific), San Francisco
Tel: 391-8287
Open Monday through
Saturday 8 a.m. to 6 p.m.,
Sunday until 5 p.m.
No credit cards

The word must have gotten out about Ming Kee, because there are signs in the window that ask tourists not to take pictures of the fluffy live hens, quail, squab, and partridges crowded into cages behind the counter. Chinatown women come to the ordering window, point at a handsome brown hen, and watch as the clerk grabs the bird by its feet, pops it into a heavy brown paper bag with holes in it, staples it shut, and puts it into a thin plastic bag for carrying. The shoppers walk off with the live birds, just as if they were carrying bags from the supermarket. Some French cooks I know tell me it's no big deal to kill a chicken, bleed it and pluck it, fry the blood (*sanguette*), and use every part of the bird in cooking, but I can't imagine doing it myself.

For the faint of heart, freshly butchered birds, vacuum-packed in plastic, fill a small refrigerated case in the store. Expensive black-skinned chickens used for restorative broths (surprisingly their feathers are pure white) and superb quail and squab can be found here. In the spring, game-bird eggs are available, a rare delicacy, especially squab eggs, which sell for $50 a dozen.

NEW HOP YICK MEAT

1145 Grant Avenue
(between Broadway and
Pacific), San Francisco
Tel: 989-0247
Open daily 8 a.m. to 6 p.m.
No credit cards

You can identify this shop by the crisp-fried pork rinds in the window. While New Hop Yick mostly sells wholesale, the retail counter displays a sample of its wares: nice-looking market steaks at $5.79 a pound, freshly ground beef, veal, an unending supply of hard-to-find never-frozen pork ribs, and fresh pork of every cut. If you're produce shopping in Chinatown and want to make a Western meal with meat, New Hop Yick is Chinatown's most complete meat market. On the other side of the store, crisp, freshly rendered pork rinds smell so good that you have to have a nibble, the potato chips of pork products.

FISH

This relatively new fish store lays its freshest fish on tables of ice at the front, open to the sidewalk, so you notice them when you walk by. If brilliant blue crabs are in they will be wiggling around in boxes on the street. I usually return to this market after a perusal of several others to buy bright red local rock cod, about two pounds each, with clear glassy eyes, blood-red gills, and firm flesh. You tear off a plastic bag and use it as a glove to pick up your fish by the gills (the slits by the head). A genial counterman weighs it ($3.50 a pound), then scales, guts, and takes out the gills, leaving you with a beautiful whole cleaned fish. I preheat the oven to 450° F, put the whole fish seasoned with salt and pepper in a pan, fill the cavity with sliced fennel, lemon slices, sprigs of rosemary or Chinese aromatics like ginger and green onions, cover it with a piece of aluminum foil, cut slits in the foil, and bake it for about 20 minutes. The fish comes out of the oven moist and firm, with the glorious chewiness that comes only with the freshest of fish cooked whole this way. These rockfish make an easy and very spectacular meal.

The Dragon Market carries red-fleshed fish like mackerel, not often seen in Cantonese markets, along with salmon, tiny pomfret, and yellow China cod. Price determines quality. The cheap cleaned and beheaded sand dabs will be flabby. The fresh whole sand dabs at three times the price will be excellent. The selection here is different from the other fish stores in the neighborhood, so it never hurts to take a look.

1145 Stockton Street (between Jackson and Pacific), San Francisco
Tel: 433-0403
Open daily 8:30 a.m. to 5:30 p.m.
No credit cards

FOUR SEA SUPER MARKET

1100 Grant Avenue (at Pacific),
San Francisco
Tel: 788-2532
Open daily 8 a.m. to 6 p.m.
No credit cards

Unusual items appear on and off at this fish store on the corner of Pacific and Grant, like a wooden crate of live blue crabs and live spot shrimp with long, balletic whiskers in a tank at the back of the store. One time I saw live moray eels swimming around in a tank, detoothed. I try not to look at the bins of huge live frogs and live hard-shell and soft-shell turtles near the front window. They remind me too much of pets I had when I was a kid. The fresh, but not live, spot prawns at $8 a pound, if available, are a very good buy.

NEW LEE SANG FISH MARKET

1207 Stockton Street
(between Broadway and
Pacific), San Francisco
Tel: 989-4336
Open daily 8 a.m. to 5 p.m.
No credit cards

Fish markets seem to come and go, and you have to make the rounds of a number of them to find the treasures. New Lee Sang currently has a source for the freshly caught whole rockfish so beloved by the Cantonese community. When these local rock cod have just been pulled from the water they have a firm, chewy texture much prized by lovers of truly fresh fish. Tables of whole fish—some stiff from rigor mortis, some still gasping—have been sighted here first thing in the morning. These whole fish are more expensive than the fillets of local snapper sold everywhere from Fisherman's Wharf to Safeway, but less expensive than live fish netted from tanks. The difference in flavor and texture of just-killed fish may not be to everyone's taste, but once you start appreciating the firmness and sweetness of the flesh, you can't go back. I started ordering live rockfish in Chinese restaurants with Chinese friends and have become an addict, so I always look for the fish with the stiffest bodies and the glassiest eyes. New Lee Sang also regularly carries fresh raw shrimp.

Jean-Pierre Moullé, the downstairs chef at Chez Panisse, is a hunter, gatherer, and fisher, both on the water and under it. He knows how to cook everything from the sea, including seaweed. One day at his house he cooked a white sea bass in rock salt, and it was the most succulent fish I ever tasted. Here is his recipe. It works for any whole fish with scales, such as a small salmon, sea bass, or local snapper. I used a beautiful green-skinned lingcod, and this method of cooking made it taste extraordinary. The fish is so delicious, moist, and aromatic, it needs no sauce, though you could put extra-virgin olive oil infused with lemon zest on the table.

Preheat the oven to 500° F. Stuff the inside of the fish with the herbs. Choose a baking pan just large enough to hold the fish. Cover the bottom with a 1-inch layer of rock salt. Lay the fish on top and cover the entire fish with more salt. The fish should be completely mounded with the rock salt. Depending on the size of the fish, bake for 20 to 30 minutes. (My lingcod was 3 1/2 pounds and I cooked it for 25 minutes.)

Remove from the oven and let rest for 10 minutes. Break the salt crust. Gently remove the fish from the pan. Lift off the skin. It should peel very easily. Serve the whole fish at the table. Be careful to brush off all the grains of salt.

Serves 4

WHOLE SALT-ROASTED FISH

One 3- to 4-pound whole lingcod,
    snapper, or sea bass, cleaned and
    with scales left on
6 to 8 fresh herb sprigs such as parsley,
    thyme, oregano, rosemary
10 pounds coarse rock salt

SAN FRANCISCO HONG KONG MARKET

You shop for fish in Chinatown just like you shop for vegetables, by popping in a bunch of shops to see what looks best. A perusal of this fish market with a cement floor and the fish laid out on metal tables covered with crushed ice might net you clear-eyed whole rockfish, farmed sea bass, pomfret, all sorts of whole local flatfish (flounder, sand dabs, rex sole), conch in the shell, live frogs, and huge abalone.

1136-38 Grant Avenue
(between Broadway and
Pacific), San Francisco
Tel: 986-8410
Open daily 8 a.m. to 6 p.m.
No credit cards

COOKWARE AND BOOKS

CHONG IMPORTS

838 Grant Avenue,
Empress of China building
(between Clay and Washington),
San Francisco
Tel: 982-1432
Open Monday through
Thursday 10 a.m. to 8 p.m.,
Friday and Saturday until 9 p.m.,
Sunday noon to 8 p.m.
Credit cards: MC, V

A huge space filled with all sorts of both rare and affordable treasures makes the trip downstairs worthwhile. Chong has elegant antique Chinese bowls in the shapes of fruits—quinces and melons—at $450 each, and teapots in the shape of a pig with tiny thimble-sized cups for $15. Lotus-shaped teapots with lotus seeds rattling in the tops, packets of Chinese vegetable seeds, and a lot of Chinese tableware make up a small fraction of the stock. Regular Chinatown shoppers drop by just to see what might have come in—like large and very inexpensive glass jars for pickling.

GINN WALL

1016 Grant Avenue (between
Jackson and Pacific),
San Francisco
Tel: 982-6307
Open Monday through Saturday
10 a.m. to 6 p.m. (closed
Thursdays), Sunday until 5 p.m.
Credit cards: MC, V

This Chinese hardware store is filled with Chinese cooking essentials, from woks of all sizes to the utensils used to cook in them. Cleavers and knives, huge stockpots and steamers, marble mortars and pestles—the building blocks of an Asian kitchen—are all here at nontourist prices. A section of paperback Chinese cookbooks at the front of the store, including Shirley Fong-Torres's instructive guide to Chinatown, will inspire you to start cooking. But you don't have to be a Chinese cook to use a wok.

The wok's versatility as a cooking tool makes it an excellent and inexpensive addition to any kitchen. In mine, I steam vegetables, fish (on a glass pie plate), and tamales on top of a beautiful and inexpensive bamboo basket insert. I also use the wok for deep-frying. Its efficient shape makes a small amount of oil go a long way. The oil heats quickly and recovers its temperature after food is dropped in it, which makes deep frying easy.

Try frying fresh corn chips or whole sand dabs in it. Heat a couple of inches of olive oil in the wok until a piece of bread dropped into the oil turns golden. Dip the sand dabs in buttermilk, then in seasoned flour. Carefully slide them into the oil and cook until brown and crispy, about 4 minutes, depending on the thickness of the fish. Cook just a couple at a time so that the oil surrounds each fish and they do not touch. I serve one of these hot, crisp fish with a little green salad as a first course.

T A I   Y I C K   T R A D I N G   C O M P A N Y

I'm a pushover for celadon, that mysterious gray-green color the bay becomes on certain overcast days. At Tai Yick, a store packed to the rafters with Chinese pottery and porcelain, you can buy a whole set of celadon plates, cups, saucers, and flat bowls at Crate and Barrel prices, though you may have to sort through piles of dishes in a cluttered corner to find them. Celadon china always looks elegant and is particularly beautiful with fish or dark green vegetables served on it—colors you might find in the sea. Fresh fruit on celadon also is stunning. Deep Chinese soup bowls in all sorts of ornate patterns are stacked next to simple blue and white china decorated with cheerful brush-painted fish. Dark brown, glazed terra-cotta casseroles for all of $4.50 are suitable for both serving and cooking in the oven or even on top of the stove. You can bake potato gratins in them or heat up stews, and handsomely present them on the table where they will stay hot. Several sizes come with glazed covers. Finally, for fans of cracked-glaze porcelain, Tai Yick has all sorts of vases and planters, some huge, in mustardy yellow and celadon green.

1400 Powell Street
(at Broadway), San Francisco
Tel: 986-0961
Open daily 9:30 a.m.
to 6:30 p.m.
Credit cards: AE, MC, V

YING COMPANY

1120 Stockton Street
(between Broadway and
Vallejo), San Francisco
Tel: 982-2188
Open Monday through
Saturday 9:30 a.m.
to 5:30 p.m.,
Sunday 10 a.m. to 5:30 p.m.
No credit cards

A small, narrow street-level store dedicated to Chinese table and cookware, the Ying Company has a full array of electric rice cookers, woks, and steamers. I drop in to see what specials are stacked up on a table, like tiny terra-cotta dipping-sauce dishes at three for $1, bamboo skewers in three different sizes, or glazed brown clay dishes for both cooking and serving. Some prices are great, others a bit high, but those in the know always pop in to see what the loss leader will be that day. Sometimes the narrow aisles are so jammed you can't get to the back of the store

Civic Center
& Hayes Valley

CIVIC CENTER & HAYES VALLEY

RESTAURANTS

HAYES STREET GRILL

I must be completely up front about this sixteen-year-old fish house across the street from the Performing Arts Center, because I am an owner and kitchen presence there. So, instead of trying to give my own place a qualitative description, I will tell you what we do each day from the point of view of a chef.

The first thing in the morning, the grill chef has a chat with the fish man (Paul Johnson of Monterey Fish) to find out what looks good that day, and we base our daily menu on this. The Hayes Street kitchen is divided into three areas: a pantry or salad station, the mesquite grill, and a sauté station. We divide what we order among the three, so that big meaty fish like wild Alaskan king salmon or buttery swordfish come off the grill, while pan-fried Hama Hama oysters, petrale sole with chanterelles, or braised sea bass with artichokes are under the sauté chef's jurisdiction. The grilled fish comes with a pile of french fries cooked in peanut oil, our trademark, and a choice of at least four sauces and salsas. From the salad station comes our signature fresh crab "slaw" or a Mexican-style scallop cocktail with warm corn chips.

320 Hayes Street (between Gough and Franklin), San Francisco

Tel: 863-5545

Open for lunch Monday through Friday 11:30 a.m. to 2 p.m.; dinner Monday through Thursday 5 to 9:30 p.m., Friday and Saturday until 10:30 p.m., Sunday until 8:30 p.m.

Price: Moderate

Credit cards: AE, DC, MC, V

The whole menu benefits from the stunning array of seasonal produce we get directly from the farm of an erst-while employee (Pomponio Creek) as well as from Greenleaf Produce, an organic produce broker. Collabora-tively the cooks figure out what dishes to make to create a balanced and tempting menu. We use an international mix of recipes with the unifying theme of fish and seafood. Above every other consideration, we want the freshness and pristine quality of the fish and the produce to speak for itself. Though preparations may be Thai, French, Italian, American, or Mexican, they are always simple, allowing the ingredients to shine.

We opened the Grill because there simply wasn't a good place to eat before the opera, ballet, or symphony. My partners and I wanted such a place ourselves, so we created a restaurant that cooks unfussy food, which is casual enough to serve before a performance, but sub-stantial and tasty enough to be a main event. We drew inspiration from old San Francisco grills like Tadich and Jack's, which have always featured local ingredients in straightforward presentations, but we took the grill concept a step farther by seeking out more sophisticated ingredients and cooking them in a modern style.

The Hayes Street Grill's walls are covered with auto-graphed photos of the artists who use the restaurant as their club. We used to have bentwood chairs and worn wooden floors, but we remodeled and installed ban-quettes, chairs with upholstered seats, and carpeting, making the restaurant less noisy. The original brass coat hooks along the walls remain, as does our founding philosophy of cooking only the food we would serve at home to our families—dressed up a little—with a relig-ious dedication to wholesomeness.

At Hayes Street Grill, we use fresh-picked blue crab for this salad, which can be purchased at Monterey Fish Market (see page 545). During local Dungeness crab season, cook a live crab yourself and pick out its meat to use in this recipe, making it extra special.

1 tablespoon sherry vinegar

1 tablespoon shallots, minced

1/2 teaspoon kosher salt

Freshly ground black pepper to taste

3 tablespoons olive oil

2 medium heads Belgian endive

1 small head radicchio

1 1/2 cups (8 ounces) fresh crabmeat

1/4 cup fresh chives, minced

1 tablespoon fresh lemon juice

In a small bowl, combine the vinegar, shallots, salt and pepper. Whisk in the olive oil. Set aside.

Separate the endive leaves, stack them, and cut them into thin strips lengthwise with a sharp knife. Core the *radicchio* and cut it into thin strips as above.

In a large bowl, combine the crab, endive, *radicchio*, and chives. Toss with the lemon juice, then toss with the vinaigrette and serve.

Serves 4 as a side dish

HEARTLAND CAFE

This casual little cafe with a completely open kitchen and some choice tables outside on Market Street currently is cooking homey American food. The chef-owner is Rob Zaborny, a nurturing sort from the Midwest who happens to be a genius at pickling and preserving. Don't leave Heartland without picking up at least one jar of his corn relish, spicy pickled beets, or fresh fruit preserves. He has that Eastern European knack of balancing vinegar, sugar, water, and aromatics to make the perfect brine.

The menus are dotted with American favorites like buttery crusted chicken potpie, and California classics like salads with grilled fish or chicken. But my favorite meal here is weekend brunch because it starts with large cups of full-bodied coffee made with Roma Roastery beans, and Heartland's incomparable dried-cherry scones, warm from the oven, buttery, and so delicately

**1772 Market Street
(between Octavia and
Gough), San Francisco
Tel: 863-3516
Open for dinner
Wednesday and Thursday
5 to 10 p.m., Friday and
Saturday until 11 p.m.; for
brunch Saturday and
Sunday 10 a.m. to 3 p.m.
Price: Moderate
No credit cards**

textured they melt in your mouth. These two items alone would be worth a trip across town, but save room for huge smoked salmon and asparagus omelets, eggs with delicious grilled turkey sausages, home-fried potatoes, and a plate of Zaborny's own made-from-scratch baked beans. The portions are ample and the prices extraordinary, especially when you consider all the gems that just seem to appear at the table—like those warm scones. This chef's generosity, his "motherliness," in the best sense, makes a visit to Heartland a sustaining experience.

Zaborny has told me that he plans to turn the cafe into an international tapas bar somewhere down the line, but promised me that the dried-cherry scones would still be prepared, one way or another. And wait till you try his spicy, ethnic dishes.

SCONES WITH DRIED SOUR CHERRIES

2 cups all-purpose flour
2 teaspoons baking powder
1/4 teaspoon salt
3 tablespoons plus 2 teaspoons sugar
2/3 cup dried sour Michigan cherries
1 cup heavy whipping cream
1 teaspoon butter, melted

This scone recipe from Rob Zaborney at Heartland Cafe is a winner: easy to make and delectable. You can purchase dried sour Michigan cherries at Nuts About You (page 92). Dried Michigan cherries are plumper and moister than the Washington State variety.

Preheat the oven to 400° F. In a large bowl, sift together the flour and baking powder. Add the salt, 3 tablespoons of the sugar, and combine.

Add the dried cherries and the cream. Mix with an electric mixer fitted with a paddle attachment on low speed for 30 seconds. Otherwise, hand mix with a fork, then knead on a floured board for about 1 minute.

Form the dough into 2 rounds 6 inches across. Score the tops with a knife into 6 pie-shaped pieces. Brush with butter and sprinkle each round with 1 teaspoon sugar.

Bake on an ungreased baking pan until the tops are golden brown, about 30 minutes. Serve warm with unsalted butter.

Makes 12 scones

Note: The dough can be assembled up to 8 hours in advance, and kept refrigerated. Allow the dough to come to room temperature before baking.

Although Pacific Restaurant No. 1 on Larkin is closer to the Civic Center, the No. 2 branch is worth a special trip. Rarely have I been to any restaurant that cooks with such integrity and care, and we are not talking about an upscale place, but a modest little noodle house that serves mostly noodles in soup (called *pho* and pronounced "faw") in a transitional neighborhood where many Vietnamese families live. *Pho* depends on good beef broth, but at most *pho* houses the broth derives much of its flavor from MSG. At Pacific, the broth is a dream, full of beefy character without a speck of fat. If you order No. 10, a huge bowl of clear soup with paper-thin slices of both well-cooked and rare beef (well cooked being tongue, rare being steaklike cuts) and thin white rice noodles, you will be getting *pho* at its best. With the hot soup comes a plate of bean sprouts, lime wedges, minty Thai basil, and cilantro, which you tear up and push down into the bowl. The Vietnamese friend who took me to Pacific sprinkled bottled red chili sauce into his soup, but I couldn't bear to muddy these pure flavors. This is a soup I could eat every day and never tire of it.

The other kind of dish at Pacific teams the hot and savory with the cold and salady, another example of the genius of Vietnamese cuisine. Try the supremely crisp Vietnamese spring roll called *cha gio*, wrapped in crackling layers of deep-fried rice paper and stuffed with a luscious minced pork and vegetable filling. You place a piece of hot roll in a perfect butter lettuce leaf, add some torn-up cilantro and mint, a tangle of cold rice noodles, add a slice of hot green chili if you like, wrap it up, and dip it into Pacific's clear sweet-and-sour dipping sauce. It's literally sensational. Or for a similar and even more interesting experience try No. 31, a little bowl of thinly sliced

337 Jones Street (between Ellis and Eddy), San Francisco

Tel: 928-4022

Open Wednesday through Monday 10:30 a.m. to 4:30 p.m.

Price: Inexpensive

No credit cards

grilled pork tenderloin, fresh bacon, and tiny meatballs in a clear sauce with a haunting, garlic-enriched aroma. You put pieces of the pork in lettuce leaves with the fresh herbs and cold rice noodles and use the sauce as the moistener—another dish that makes my mouth water as I write about it. This dish comes on a woven bamboo tray, the pork in a glass bowl topped with tissue-thin slices of radish and carrot, the white noodles mounded next to the green herbs and lettuces.

You may have some reservations about the neighborhood, but during the day, the only time that Pacific 2 is open, the streets are full of Vietnamese families (as is the immaculate restaurant), and the sidewalks are clean and unthreatening. This central part of the city has been transformed by the energy and culture of Vietnamese émigrés, as evidenced by this amazing little place. At $3.50 or $4.00 a meal you can start saving for a trip to Saigon, where the same dish costs 40¢.

STARS

150 Redwood Alley (between Van Ness and Polk), San Francisco
Tel: 861-7827
Open for lunch Monday through Friday 11:30 a.m. to 2:30 p.m.; dinner Sunday through Thursday 5:30 p.m. to midnight, Friday and Saturday until 2 a.m.
Price: Expensive
Credit cards: AE, DC, MC, V

After the theater one night I spent two hours at the fascinating bar at Stars. This social crossroads, which some wags have likened to the Moscow train station where the peasants mingle with the bourgeoisie, stretches down one side of the roaring restaurant, requiring at least four lightning-fast bartenders just to service it. We were able to snag two stools at the end of the bar because we knew the people vacating. The place was packed. Both elevated dining areas were completely full, as was a sea of cocktail tables and every stool along the counters. A piano player was holding forth in the din, and the scene was no less lively when we left after midnight.

Stars is the city's premier eating and drinking institution. Chef-owner Jeremiah Tower knows how to throw a *soigné* party every night, and everyone wants an invitation. You can secure one by calling well in advance for a prime-time dinner reservation, or by dropping by and waiting for some seats to materialize. I am now at the point of preferring the bar, because it's more fun. You can order any dish on the tantalizing regular menu plus any dish on the bar menu; the suave bartenders might even honor your presence with an extra splash of Veuve Cliquot, if you spend enough; and it's there you have the best view of the shifting crowd made up of locals, tourists (some wearing white belts), socialites, restaurateurs, Peninsulites celebrating their birthdays, and bon vivants out on the town.

There's a sophisticated European ethos at Stars, though the restaurant is foremost a personal statement of Tower's, an amalgam of New World and Old World style. The look crosses a booming Parisian brasserie with a museum of Jeremiah memorabilia. Tower claims to have invented "California cuisine," and the energy emanating from the bar is fueled by the thousands of American cocktails downed in its environs, but French people and Italians feel at home at Stars. Tower intuitively understands how to satisfy everyone's food fantasies: for the hungry, short ribs, lamb shanks, and steaks teamed with crisp potato gratins, hearty ragouts of vegetables, and long-simmered white beans; for the demure, warm oysters in briny butter sauce, salmon slathered in wild mushrooms, or elegant lobster with two different dressings. Tower makes everything delicious by doubling up on sauce. Almost every dish has a *jus* and a mayonnaise, or a butter sauce and a salsa. But there are always simpler things like deep-fried vegetable threads, house smoked-salmon, ice-cold oysters, caviar, and plates of green salad—from the most lavish to the almost austere, the menu anticipates a world of preferences. Emily Luchetti's desserts strike a clever balance by dressing homey American favorites in Chanel suits. A meal at Stars, after all these years, never feels formulaic. Tower staffs the dining room with such pros (most of whom have been there for years), that they make everyone feel like a star. You end up spending more than you ever expected, seduced by opportunities to buy $25 glasses of wine, rare half bottles of Sauternes, and ancient Armagnacs, but you leave happy because you've had a glittering night out. And we need at least one restaurant in town where you can eat a hamburger at midnight with a bottle of Latour. Jeremiah Tower, one of the world's great restaurateurs, leaves no amenity unexplored.

STARS CAFE

500 Van Ness Avenue
(at McAllister),
San Francisco
Tel: 861-4344
Open Monday through
Friday 11:30 a.m. to 10
p.m.; Saturday and Sunday
brunch 11:30 a.m. to 2 p.m.;
late supper menu Tuesday
through Saturday 10
to 11 p.m.
Price: Moderate
Credit cards: AE, DC,
MC, V

I've never understood why anyone would go to Stars Cafe, the cut-rate Stars, when you could sit at the bar or bar tables in the real thing and eat for the same price. Lunch at the real Stars has always been as reasonable as the cafe anyway, and I never have been completely satisfied by the food at the cafe. But, of course, I'm in the minority. Stars Cafe has been so popular that it moved to serious new quarters on the corner of Van Ness and McAllister (the site of several former Spectrum restaurants), with a full bar that has become the focus of the operation. Now the food is even simpler than before, more like a bar menu, and the clubby room is much larger and more suitable for hanging out. Somehow the hamburgers at Stars taste better than the ones at Stars Cafe, but the desserts are on a par, imaginative and luscious. After eating my way through several predictable lunches, a fresh berry Napoleon assembled to order with crisp squares of warm puff pastry layered with macerated berries and a lovely cream custard made me sit up and take notice. I should have known that crack pastry department of Stars would prevail. In fact, the old Stars Cafe space next to the mother ship has been turned into a retail bakery called Star Bake (see page 90), where you can get Stars desserts for home. As always at Tower's venues, service couldn't be more professional and welcoming.

SUPPENKÜCHE

Small, interesting shops have been opening in the Hayes Valley for a number of years, but especially in the last two after a portion of the earthquake-damaged freeway looming overhead between Gough and Laguna was finally carted away. What was once an alien neighborhood, a bit dicey for potential buyers of arty clothing and off-beat treasures, now basks in the sun of gentrification. These blocks of Hayes Street have become inviting.

Oddly enough, the most exciting culinary development in the area has been a German beer house and restaurant called Suppenküche, a lively, inexpensive place that serves superb German beers and simple German food on unfinished pine tables in a vaulted dining hall. We don't have good German restaurants in San Francisco, and the Western Addition would be the last place you would expect to find one. Yet from the moment it opened, Suppenküche has attracted a young crowd that appreciates beer and substantial, reasonably priced food. The spare, functional decor fits right into a minimally funded urban lifestyle, and sure enough, it has become the rage among a certain set to tuck into a plate of braised cabbage and bratwurst. The food is so good that people are coming from all parts of the city to eat here.

601 Hayes Street (at Laguna), San Francisco
Tel: 252-9289
Open for lunch Tuesday through Saturday 11:30 a.m. to 3 p.m.; dinner Tuesday through Sunday 5 to 10 p.m.
Price: Moderate
Credit cards: AE, MC, V

Thomas Klausmann, a Bavarian home cook, started the restaurant and runs the kitchen along with an experienced staff. The menu sticks to the traditional, though the cooking seems lighter, fresher, and more seasonal than a lot of German restaurant cooking I have tasted. Fresh pea soup comes out peppery and true flavored; the bread basket boasts moist sprouted-wheat bread and a German rye with a crackling crust; sauerkraut with sausages is resonant with bacon and sweet spices, a far cry from the stuff in cans. The oft-appearing mashed potatoes have a fork-mashed texture and a magical balance of butter, nutmeg, and milk. The mustard is hot, grainy, and delicious.

One of the most wonderful daily specials, from a chalked list that enlarges the small core menu, is an oxtail stew served with the tender noodle-dumplings called *Spaetzle*. Others, like huge, soft veal meatballs in a caper cream sauce and a dreamy German-style chicken à la king served on noodles with big chunks of amazingly velvety chicken, represent the highest form of comfort food, especially with steins of cold, crisp, sparkly German lager.

The small place gets noisy as the large tables fill up, often with several different parties, and the beer bar in the middle of the room gets full. The waitresses handle it all with finesse and humor, endlessly describing and recommending dishes for the first-timers. In every way this little soup kitchen knows how to please. It's a marvelous example of grassroots urban redevelopment.

Once again I have to come clean. Vicolo (which is the Italian word for alley) is an operation we set up in a corrugated steel shed behind the Hayes Street Grill to serve the overflow pre-performance crowd. Vicolo does not take reservations and the high-ceilinged room is casual—some might say grungy, when they get a look at the loyal, overworked staff behind the counter. People order at the counter, find their own tables, and eat Italian vegetable salads or house-made soup while they wait for their pizza. The pizzas come by the slice or whole, in black cast-iron pans with torn-off sheets of waxed butcher paper as plates. The crisp cornmeal crust is sturdy enough to act as a shell for substantial fillings made with high-quality ingredients: whole-milk mozzarella, imported Italian cheeses, fresh and dried wild mushrooms, house-made sausage. One interesting property of Vicolo pizza is that it can be successfully finished off at home. The half-baked pies cook in 12 to 15 minutes in a preheated hot (425° F) oven. The half-baked pizzas also freeze well and go right into the oven from the freezer. The crust stays nice and crisp and the rich fillings retain their flavor and texture, whether eaten at home or at the restaurant. Vicolo has been voted best pizzeria in *Focus* magazine and *Bay Guardian* readers' polls year after year.

150 Ivy Alley (between Hayes and Grove), San Francisco
Tel: 863-2382
Open Monday through Thursday 11:30 a.m. to 11 p.m., Friday and Saturday until 11:30 p.m., Sunday noon to 10 p.m.
Price: Inexpensive
Credit cards: MC, V

1658 Market Street

(between Franklin and

Gough), San Francisco

Tel: 552-2522

Open Tuesday through

Saturday for breakfast 7:30

to 11 a.m., lunch 11:30 a.m.

to 6 p.m., dinner 6 p.m. to

midnight; Sunday brunch

11 a.m. to 6 p.m., dinner 6

to 11 p.m.

Price: Moderate

Credit cards: AE, MC, V

Despite its Southwest name (a holdover from its opening concept over fifteen years ago, when every dish was laced with cumin), Zuni Cafe is the most European restaurant/cafe/bar in the city, not just because of the style of the food but because of its function within the community. The place has grown organically over the years into a social crossroads, a meeting spot, a place that has become indispensable if you want a late-night hamburger, an early-morning coffee and roll, a baguette sand wich in the afternoon, or a sophisticated full meal. Zuni works on every level.

The most important development occurred when the restaurant doubled in size by annexing a neighboring triangular space between Market Street and an alley. In this sunny, glass-fronted room, Zuni installed the much-frequented copper-topped bar and indoor and outdoor cafe tables. Upstairs and deeper into the restaurant, a labyrinth of rooms with shelflike built-in banquettes and odd-shaped tables make up the dining areas. In the bar you can get casual food and pizzas from the wood-fired oven, as well as any conceivable drink, be it fresh-lime margaritas or glasses of Condrieu (a rare, flowery, but very dry white Rhône wine).

It was chef Judy Rogers who put Zuni on the national culinary map. She fell into cooking when she lived with the famous Troisgros family in France as an exchange student, and later spent a term at Chez Panisse. She worked with Marion Cunningham to create an American menu at the Union Hotel in Benicia. When she couldn't find the financing to open her own place in Berkeley, she ended up at Zuni as a partner. The match was made in heaven.

Her menus bring together the cooking of southwest France and most of Italy in her own peculiar and winning way. The restaurant's signature dishes come from the brick wood-burning oven in the center of one dining room. Roast chicken for two on a warm bread salad moistened with cooking juices and lightened with arugula has become a San Francisco classic. Her *fritto misto*, a changing array of vegetables, whole little fish, and paper-thin slices of lemon, emerges from the fryer irresistibly crisp. A starter of salt-cured anchovies and thinly sliced celery in olive oil remains my pick if I am not having oysters instead, usually a variety of pristine West Coast mollusks opened to order and presented on a stand holding a tray of crushed ice, with brown bread and butter below. Long-braised meats like *osso buco* or lamb shanks appear regularly, and Rogers is never afraid to offer tripe or salt cod. Another innovation started by Rogers pairs a certain cheese with a fresh or dried fruit, the combination of which becomes a revelation. House-made ice creams and ices and biscotti dependably satisfy the sweet tooth. The menus are always so varied that no matter what the state of your appetite you will find something to eat and drink. So people just drop by, knowing that they will run into someone and that they will get something good. Rogers's genius is that she meets the eclectic needs of San Francisco with such unique personal style.

CAFES

CAFFÈ TRINITY

1145 Market Street
(between Seventh
and Eighth streets),
San Francisco
Tel: 864-3333
Open Monday through
Friday 6 a.m. to 4:30 p.m.
No credit cards

This tiny jewel can be considered a gift to the city from developer Angelo Sangiacomo, whose new office building it graces. No expense was spared in adorning this light-filled room with opulent materials like hand-crafted mahogany woodwork, marble tables and counters, hand-painted panels of native American animals depicted in the style of seventeenth-century European naturalists, and crystal light fixtures. Sitting in this baroque parlor, pondering the street people across the way at United Nation's Plaza makes you feel like a character in a novel by Charles Dickens.

Everything prepared by the young Italian couple who run the cafe is simple and tasty, like a salad of Roma tomatoes, red onions, and capers with tuna, or a cup of minestrone with honest, long-cooked flavor. The proscuitto, mascarpone, and *radicchio* sandwich on focaccia is moist and delicious. Good coffee made from Mr. Espresso beans is a pleasure to be enjoyed slowly while basking in the richness of the surroundings.

MOMI TOBY'S REVOLUTION CAFE

528 Laguna Street (between
Hayes and Fell),
San Francisco
Tel: 626-1508
Open Sunday through
Thursday 7:30 a.m. to 9 p.m.,
Friday and Saturday
8:30 a.m. to 10 p.m.
No credit cards

Noteworthy for its peaceful ambiance, Momi Toby's light-filled corner space has dark wood-framed windows and window seats, weathered wooden floors, and a handsome marble-topped coffee bar with Victorian slatted wood shelving behind it. The whispery, soothing tones of gamelan music engulf you when you walk in the door. The coffee is competent and served in handleless pottery cups. If you are in the neighborhood, this cafe offers a sanctuary for reading or writing.

What a great location this cafe has, kitty-corner from the Veterans Building, across the street from City Hall, and a block away from the Opera House, with huge windows that look out onto Van Ness Boulevard! The room is spacious and very Italian, with black metal chairs and tables, a long marble counter that snakes along the walls, and shelves filled with jars of artichokes, olives, tins of olive oil, and a rainbow of Torani syrups. Noise bounces off all the hard surfaces, including a veneered cement floor, and the sun pours through expansive west-facing windows in hot waves in the afternoon. People order at the counter, and what you don't carry to the table yourself is magically brought to you later. Spuntino offers an unusually full Italian menu for a self-service cafe, and bakes biscotti, breads, and pastry on the premises, but I don't consider this a serious place to eat. The food is competent yet not fully realized, so you end up being tempted without being satisfied. A white bean puree, for example, arrives completely unseasoned, with slices of soft white bread; capellini with fresh tomatoes and basil tastes mostly of the huge hunks of unpeeled, old-tasting tomatoes. The best bets here are the thin-crusted pizzas from the wood-burning oven, crisp and fun to eat, and excellent coffee made with Mr. Espresso beans. I see lots of caffè lattes walk out the door in paper containers. I should add that two ten-year-olds loved Spuntino on my last visit and told me to recommend it as a kids' restaurant. They liked the white bread, which they dipped into the white bean soup, and ate the capellini after pushing aside the tomato hunks. They raved about the pizza. The people who work there couldn't be nicer, and the food comes out pretty fast—a kid's dream.

524 Van Ness Avenue (at Golden Gate), San Francisco

Tel: 861-7772

Open Monday 7 a.m. to 10 p.m., Tuesday through Thursday until 11 p.m., Friday until midnight, Saturday 10 a.m. to midnight, Sunday 10 a.m. to 9 p.m.

Credit cards: AE, DC, MC, V

BARS

MISS PEARL'S JAM HOUSE

601 Eddy Street (at Larkin),
San Francisco
Tel: 775-5267
Open Tuesday through
Thursday 5 to 10 p.m.,
Friday and Saturday until
11 p.m.; Sunday for brunch
11 a.m. to 2:30 p.m., dinner 5
to 9:30 p.m.
Credit cards: AE, CB, DC, D,
MC, V

Connected to a refurbished motel with a swimming pool where the touring counterculture stays, Miss Pearl's provides a lively spot for cocktails and tropical tidbits with a Caribbean motif. The interior suggests a sun-baked island town, with distressed doors in pastel colors for walls and a boat hull suspended over the bar. The music is loud, the drinks creative, the staff laid-back. The tapas-style menu of small, spicy dishes can taste really great after a couple of rounds.

DELICATESSENS/TAKE-OUT

BA LE

511 Jones (between Geary
and O'Farrell), San Francisco
Tel: 474-7270
Open daily 7 a.m. to 7 p.m.
No credit cards

This branch of a wildly successful San Jose Vietnamese delicatessen specializes in ready-to-eat colorful cold and hot foods, packaged to go, or to be eaten at tables on one side of the store. The cold foods, tightly wrapped in clear plastic, tempt with their sparkly combinations of flavor and texture. In one, three large, salady spring rolls filled with rice, whole shrimp, and fresh herbs come with a little cup of piquant brown dipping sauce. Another, my favorite, displays soft fresh rice noodles stuffed with finely minced pork and black mushrooms, next to several slices of Vietnamese mild white pork sausage (like French *boudin blanc*), on a bed of more wide rice noodles, herbs, shredded carrots and lettuce, slices of hot fresh chili, and sweet-and-sour dipping sauce. What a refreshing meal these neatly packed Vietnamese foods make!

For the home cook, Vietnamese white sausage or pâté, still warm from poaching, wrapped in banana leaves or foil, can provide the centerpiece for a meal. The most delicious of them all is the skinny banana leaf-wrapped tube fragrant with garlic. With rice noodles, dipping sauce, salad greens, and fresh herbs (purchased at a nearby Vietnamese grocery), you can put together a fantastic meal.

The hot dishes come off a steam table at the front, though skewers of spicy beef and pork are kept at room temperature during the lunch hour and taste better that way. For dessert, check out the refrigerator at the front filled with a rainbow of puddings and tapiocas. The firm coconut-milk pudding with hunks of banana and beautiful pearls of tapioca, topped with chopped peanuts, is universally appealing. One disappointment was a watery salad of green papaya and carrot threads that was probably defrosted. However, everything else I've eaten has been exceptionally fresh. Ba Le is a hit in the neighborhood and the food turns over fast.

SAIGON SANDWICH CAFE

The immaculate Saigon Sandwich Cafe, which has been turning out delicious Vietnamese sandwiches for ten years, reminds me of snack stalls in the student quarter of Paris, except that the sandwiches are much better. Instead of *saucisson sec*, Saigon fills its French baguettes with five-spice chicken, roast pork, or Vietnamese meatballs, then kisses them with a sweet, hot, and sour dipping sauce, shredded carrots, sprigs of cilantro, and hot green chilies. The result is juicy, savory, exotic sandwiches that soon become addictive. My favorite is the

560 Larkin Street (at Eddy), San Francisco
Tel: 474-5698
Open Monday through Friday 7 a.m. to 4:30 p.m., Saturday and Sunday 8 a.m. to 4 p.m.
No credit cards

warm meatball sandwich, which tastes like a sparkling Sloppy Joe. Long, generously filled sandwiches cost around $2, an amazing buy.

The shop has almost a cult following of Civic Center employees, cab drivers, delivery men, and SoMa types as well as the Vietnamese community that lives nearby. Many drop in for a glass of aromatic Vietnamese iced coffee creamy with sweetened condensed milk. The pleasant people who work behind the counter are efficient and eager to please. When I call ahead for sandwiches for meetings and the like, they are ready exactly at the assigned time, not before and not after. The Saigon Cafe knows the importance of freshness.

BAKERIES/PASTRIES

STAR BAKE

545 Golden Gate Avenue (between Van Ness and Polk), San Francisco
Tel: 861-8521
Open Monday through Friday 7 a.m. to 6 p.m., Saturday 10 a.m. to 4 p.m.
Credit cards: AE, MC, V

Pastry chef Emily Luchetti has been with Jeremiah Tower since he opened Stars, and what with supplying all the Stars cafes and satellites with her marvelous desserts over the years, she has turned the Stars pastry department into a small industry. Now, the old Stars Cafe space has been given to her for a retail bakery and sandwich cafe. As it turns out, she is as talented at baking cheese and apricot Danish as she is at concocting stylish restaurant desserts. In fact, I don't think I have ever tasted better sweet rolls. They look like the typical breakfast pastry, but wait till you take your first bite. They're so buttery, yet light, they practically melt in your mouth, and the fruit toppings aren't jam, but fresh fruit. Her orange-scented almond tea cake has an ideal texture, crumbly, moist, dense without being heavy. You realize that you have never really tasted a great fresh berry muffin until you break into one of Emily's. During the summer they're loaded with fresh raspberries, boysenberries, and blueberries that melt into a delicately sweetened batter.

Of course the glass counters are filled with plenty of desserts such as banana cream pies, fresh fruit napoleons, and miniature chocolate éclairs filled with chocolate mousse instead of pastry cream that I pooh-poohed, but now admire. The shells of these éclairs have a crunchiness to them that I have never encountered in this usually custard-filled pastry, which somehow makes the buttery chocolate-mousse interior work. There are ready-made baguette sandwiches, and savory pastries like quiche. Of course Stars's big, thick, yummy cookies are a hot seller, to be eaten along with coffee at one of the tables that run opposite the pastry cases. Being able to buy a whole Stars' pie or cake for a dinner party is reason enough to throw one, though you can buy most of these tempting desserts by the piece as well.

ICE CREAM/CHOCOLATES

NUTS ABOUT YOU

325 Hayes Street (between
Franklin and Gough),
San Francisco
Tel: 864-6887
Open Monday through
Saturday 10 a.m. to 8 p.m.,
Sunday noon to 5 p.m.
Credit cards: AE, MC, V

When I was a young girl living in Chicago taking ballet lessons, my mother took me to see touring ballet companies at the Opera House. The part of the ritual I liked the best was the stop at a little candy and nut store before the performance to buy a bagful of turtles and chocolate-covered nuts to munch during intermission. (I guess that's why I became a food maven instead of a ballet dancer.) So it was with great delight that I watched the opening of Nuts About You, a tiny shop across the street from Davies Hall, with many glass jars filled with nuts of every sort, candies made with nuts, and chocolates in a sparkling glass counter. Every season owner Bonnie Boren discovers a new sensation, like toasted almonds glazed in the thinnest layer of buttery toffee, or a miniature chocolate truffle that seems to dissolve into pure fragrance. Gift baskets and boxes full of delectable treasures can be assembled and sent, whimsically wrapped and tied. But the real thrill of having this shop right by the Performing Arts Center is stopping there before a performance and choosing your own favorite treats to stimulate your senses during intermission.

ETHNIC MARKETS

NEW CHIU FONG COMPANY

The most complete Vietnamese market in the city, New Chiu Fong has everything from four-inch-thick chopping blocks made out of slices of tree trunk to imported dried Thai snapper. Fresh rice noodles are by the meat counter, and dried noodles of every conceivable kind, from rice threads to Chinese-style egg noodles, fill up their own aisle. Many are used in the Northern Vietnamese soup called *pho*, an amazingly restorative and refreshing soup that combines handfuls of fresh herbs and hot chilies with noodles, beef, and broth. In the meat counter, strips of fat-marbled beef, precut for *pho* and satays, streamline the preparation of these dishes. Every part of the pig, and large fresh stewing chickens, are piled high, while shelves of fish sauce, soy sauce, and hot chili pastes await the home cook. The freezer sections of ethnic markets are always worth a look because they hold useful ingredients like banana leaves for wrapping fresh sausage and rice, or *pandan* leaf, which you rarely see fresh.

But the produce section here is the draw, with its boxes of fresh Vietnamese herbs, some with the most delectable perfumes. Of particular interest for creative cooks is the fresh cumin leaf (*cá nâú chua rau om*), the leaf of the cumin plant, which smells like the seed but is more complex in flavor; the minty, pointy-leafed Thai basil, wonderful in seafood stews with coconut milk; and an herb that looks like flat Italian parsley (*bò xaò cân*) but tastes like a cross between celery and parsnip, and is used for beef cookery in Vietnamese kitchens. There are big, flat, purple-tinted leaves (*rau kinh gioi*)

724 Ellis Street (between Larkin and Polk), San Francisco
Tel: 776-7151
Open daily 8 a.m. to 6:30 p.m.
No credit cards

that have a shiso-like or chrysanthemum flavor, and aromatic elongated greens with pointy edges (*rau ngò gai*) that are used as salad or accompaniment to *pho* or savory grilled meats. And these are but a few. Many of the herbs are raised in Hawaii and flown in, so prices are not cheap, but at New Chiu Fong they arrive in excellent condition, fresh and aromatic. Since the prices and names of the herbs are not posted in English, the best way to find the flavors that interest you is to taste.

PRODUCE

CIVIC CENTER FARMERS' MARKET

**Civic Center Plaza
(Grove Street between Van
Ness and Polk),
San Francisco
Open Wednesday and
Saturday**

This heart-of-the-city farmers' market truly serves the local pedestrian community, especially since parking in the area can be a problem. You can find metered spaces on the other side of Market Street, which limits your shopping to whatever you can carry for several long blocks. As an expression of a market self-molded to serve a specific community, the Civic Center stalls are heavy on fresh and inexpensive Asian vegetables like

long beans, the wonderful purple-leafed Asian spinach called amaranth, Asian mushrooms, bok choys, Vietnamese herbs, lemongrass, and cooking essentials like carrots and onions. As at every vital farmers' market, there will be seasonal surprises, like a stall full of the most fragrant tangerines, thin-skinned Rangpoor limes, or new-crop walnuts. Whenever I want dates to serve with mint tea, I go to the

Civic Center date man. He has barhi and medjool, large and small, sweet and sticky, creamy and juicy, which goes to show that when you need a good date in this town, remember the Civic Center. Just kidding. The beauty of this market is that you can buy fresh food at such cheap prices that a large family can be fed for a week at about half of what it would cost at the supermarket—and the quality will be far superior.

NEW CHIU FONG COMPANY

724 Ellis Street (between Larkin and Polk), San Francisco

Tel: 726-7151

Open daily 8 a.m. to 6:30 p.m.

No credit cards

See listing, page 93

COOKWARE AND BOOKS

A CLEAN WELL-LIGHTED PLACE FOR BOOKS

For other location, see page 579.
The most complete bookstore in San Francisco, A Clean Well-Lighted Place for Books has a well-chosen cookbook section as well as an extensive travel section with much food writing in it. The literature section carries many classic books on food and eating as well. The clerks will help you hunt down anything in the store or out. Authors visit frequently and sign their masterpieces, and if you are a contributor to City Arts and

601 Van Ness Avenue (at Golden Gate), San Francisco

Tel: 441-6670

Open Sunday through Thursday 10 a.m. to 11 p.m., Friday and Saturday until midnight

Credit cards: AE, MC, V

Lectures, a series of talks by authors the profits of which go to Friends of the Public Library, you get a 15 percent discount at the store. Clean Well-Lighted is community spirited and service oriented but, more important, if you want it, they'll probably have it.

RICHARD HILKERT, BOOKSELLER

333 Hayes Street (between Gough and Franklin), San Francisco

Tel: 863-3339

Open weekdays 10 a.m. to 5 p.m., Saturday and most Sundays 11 a.m. to 4 p.m.

Credit cards: AE, MC, V

The one-man bookshop, in which every volume, new or used, reflects the sensibility of the owner, succeeds or fails on taste. Richard Hilkert has a quirky and iconoclastic take on what's interesting, and I am always curious to see which cooking and food books will make it into his long front window. He likes Europe; he likes photographs and high-quality production; he likes local authors; he likes personal expression, but his eccentricity keeps him open to civilization in the broadest sense. He knows a good treasure when he sees one, so it always behooves you to scan the used-book corner. The careful selection of books at Richard's store makes you think about each book on its own merits, a way of looking at books that disappears at supermarket bookstores.

Embarcadero &
Fisherman's Wharf

EMBARCADERO & FISHERMAN'S WHARF

RESTAURANTS

BISTRO ROTI

The one stepchild in the wildly popular Real Restaurant empire (Fog City Diner, Mustards, Buckeye Roadhouse, Bix, Tra Vigne), Bistro Roti has always had a bit of an identity problem, despite its handsome, traditional bistro decor with an open fireplace, an earthquake-liberated view of the bay on the Embarcadero end of the restaurant, and Parisian-style outdoor tables in front of thrown-open French doors. To me, the word *roti* has always meant Indian breads baked in a tandoori oven, and I can't seem to get over the expectation of getting something exotic when I go there. But the menu has been far from it and somewhat inconsistent, taking liberties with classic French dishes that don't always improve them. However, the location and the atmosphere are delightful, and as at all Real Restaurants, you will always find something tasty for a reasonable sum.

155 Steuart Street (between Mission and Howard),
San Francisco
Tel: 495-6500
Open Monday through Thursday 11:30 a.m. to 10 p.m., Friday until 11 p.m., Saturday 5:30 to 11 p.m., Sunday 5:30 to 10 p.m.
Price: Moderate
Credit cards: AE, CB, DC, D, MC, V

BOULEVARD

One Mission Street (at
Steuart), San Francisco
Tel: 543-6084
Open Monday through
Friday for lunch 11:30 a.m.
to 2:00 p.m., bistro menu
2:30 to 5:15 p.m.; dinner
nightly 5:30 to 10:30 p.m.
Price: Expensive
Credit cards: AE, CB, DC, D,
MC, V

This much-heralded collaboration between hometown hero, chef Nancy Oakes, who made her reputation at a tiny dining room connected to a sports bar in the avenues, and superstar restaurant designer Pat Kuleto, has caused such a stir that after twelve months of operation, it still takes three weeks to get a prime-time reservation. Everyone wants one of the 120 seats in this fantasy French bistro in the turn-of-the-century Audiffred building across the Embarcadero from the bay. Oakes's plates are huge, creative, and colorful, with lots of different things going on in them. A mayonnaise-dressed lobster salad might have fried waffle potato chips sticking out of it, a nest of arugula, and a ring of rock shrimp fritters and blood orange segments. Deep-fried nuggets of lamb sweetbreads alternate with shiitake mushroom caps around a giant spinach ravioli in red-wine sauce—and these are just first courses. Main courses might bring a three-inch-thick pork loin chop on a bed of onions with a big square of turnip gratin and a pile of sautéed pea shoots. Oakes has always cooked enthusiastically for vegetarians. One of the most popular dishes at the restaurant is a vegetarian napoleon of crisp potato cakes layered with buttermilk mashed potatoes, flanked by slices of roast butternut squash and shiitakes in a truffle-infused *jus*. Desserts are just as elaborate and multifaceted, my favorite being an espresso-flavored angel food cake with coffee ice cream and a rum sauce.

Boulevard is an upscale, important-night-out kind of dinner house, in the vernacular of California-American culture. The dishes, both as they read on the menu and arrive at the table, are meant to wow diners, not with exquisiteness, but with effusiveness and the chef's drive to please. Oakes is nothing if not generous, and she uses every conceivable combination of ingredients and cooking techniques in her repertoire. At her first tiny place (called L'Avenue), people were won over by the heartiness and ebullience of her cooking, and the amazingly reasonable prices. The tariff has risen considerably at Boulevard, and the informality is gone. The question is whether she can re-create the surprise and delight her patrons once felt at her new restaurant, where major-league brilliance is expected on hundreds of elaborate meals every day.

EAGLE CAFE

This funky, historic workingman's bar and cafe upstairs at Pier 39 is a real piece of old San Francisco, not an amusement park re-creation. The Eagle began serving breakfast and lunch in 1920 across the street from the pier, in what is now a parking lot. When Pier 39 plans were approved, the Eagle was given landmark status and somehow moved unaltered to its current home. It's a bit of a shock walking off the touristy pier into this ancient place with its whitewashed wood-slat ceiling and walls, worn linoleum floors and linoleum tables, a bar tattooed with hundreds of initials and names, and a menu so out of date it seems like a relic, but with a timeless view of the bay framed by the ancient wooden windows.

The best meal at Eagle is breakfast, specifically a crisp, thin circle of finely ground corned beef hash with two perfectly fried eggs. The hash browns are no treat, and the toast, either supermarket whole wheat or foamy white, is saved by a brush with melted butter. The pancakes are airy and good; the meat loaf is the best way to go at lunch. Drinks like Bloody Marys are about half the price of those served at the other pier places, and the ambiance is much more interesting.

Head of Pier 39, Second
Floor, San Francisco
Tel: 433-3689
Open daily 7 a.m. to 3 p.m.
Price: Inexpensive
No credit cards

1300 Battery Street
(at the Embarcadero),
San Francisco
Tel: 982-2000
Open Sunday through
Thursday 11:30 a.m. to
11 p.m., Friday and
Saturday until midnight
Price: Moderate
Credit cards: DC, D,
MC, V

This ground-breaking restaurant (it was the first upscale diner in the country), designed by Pat Kuleto, has achieved a comfortable stability, both in the quality of its updated diner food and the steadiness of its clientele. Fog City tends to get busy later, leaving the earlier dinner hours, until around 7:30, approachable for locals who want to eat on the spur of the moment. The tourists take over later. To my mind, Fog City represents the best Pat Kuleto design of all. He took a wood-framed shack and turned it into a glamorous dining-car-like dining room with luxurious wooden booths, each by a big window, dark wood paneling, a counter with stools, and a long bar that's always crowded. The streamlined metal exterior reminds me of sleek passenger trains with light glowing inside. Whenever you pass it, day or night, you want to stop in because it looks like everyone is having such a good time.

The menu has changed very little over the years, with daily specials adding variety, but to this day, I order the same things: grilled pasilla peppers stuffed with goat cheese and accompanied with a chunky avocado salsa; and a salad of pretty greens tossed with caramelized walnuts, aged goat cheese, and, most recently, peaches. The salads are perfectly dressed, the lettuces of proud California pedigree. At the opposite end of the food chain, Fog City's hamburgers with skinny fries and house-made catsup are always a temptation. The thick onion rings are never greasy though monolithic; you have to like crunchy batter to appreciate them. Sometimes the pot roast with a horseradish-potato pancake isn't cooked quite enough and is tough; and sometimes the tomatoes in the salad with green beans in a Dijon vinaigrette really don't taste like they've just been plucked from the garden, as it says on the menu. For the most part, the food here is peppy, fun, and satisfying. A single order of warm chocolate banana bread pudding with rum caramel sauce will give everyone at the table a sweet send-off at the end of the meal.

GAYLORD OF INDIA

Far and away, this is the best Indian restaurant in San Francisco. In fact, it may be the only restaurant where you can get dependably fresh, lively Indian cooking. All the other places in town seem to lose their chefs or their energy, and end up sending out bland, rewarmed, mediocre food. Not so at the elegant third-floor Gaylord, with its romantic view of the bay, white tablecloths, posh interior, and waiters in uniform. When you walk into the dining room, the luscious smell of spices and roasting foods lets you know you're in for some real eating.

You can begin with roasted *papadums* (spicy lentil wafers) and greaseless, deep-fried vegetable *pakoras* (fritters), always made with an interesting variety of vegetables. The chutneys, green and tamarind, are freshly made. Tandoori-roasted items like lamb chops and chicken are juicy and aromatic, served on hot metal plates with sizzling onions, though the tandoori-roasted chunks of sea bass tend to be a bit dry. The vegetable dishes actually have individual character. You can taste the fresh ginger, cilantro, and freshly ground toasted spices. The spinach with white cheese is still bright green; the cauliflower and potatoes are cooked through but keep their textures and flavor. And the desserts, like hard-to-find *ras malai*, delicate white cheese balls poached in syrup and served in cream, and *kulfi*, real Indian pistachio ice cream made from boiled down milk, are always a delight here.

Ghirardelli Square, 900 Northpoint (at Larkin), San Francisco
Tel: 771-8822
Open daily for lunch noon to 2 p.m., dinner 5 to 11 p.m.
Price: Expensive
Credit cards: AE, CB, DC, D, MC, V

There are two drawbacks, however. Every time I've been to Gaylord the service tends to disintegrate towards the end of the meal. The waiter disappears, just when you want him, even when the restaurant doesn't seem that busy. The other problem is the high price of eating here if you order a la carte. A few vegetable curries and a tandoori item, some *nan* (tandoori-baked bread), *raita* (yogurt and cucumbers), and rice, with a bottle of wine from a serviceable list, always seems to run to $40 a person. If you order the set *thali* plates you get a lot of different dishes, though not necessarily the ones you want, for a lesser price ($16 to $25 a person), and the portions are huge. You either have to go all vegetarian or all tandoori, with only the most popular dishes included. Some of us hold the notion that vegetarian Indian food should be cheap because the ingredients are inexpensive, but to prepare any Indian dish well is labor-intensive. The food at Gaylord is so consistently bright and the appointments so civilized that I always feel a meal here is worth the price.

HAPPY VALLEY

Levi's Plaza, 1255 Battery Street (at Greenwich), San Francisco
Tel: 399-9393
Open Monday through Saturday 11 a.m. to 10 p.m., Sunday 5 to 10 p.m.
Price: Moderate
Credit cards: AE, D, MC, V

This useful restaurant specializes in Mongolian hot pot service, fun when a group is going out to dinner. A pot of boiling broth is set on a burner in the middle of the table and platters of thinly sliced raw ingredients, beautifully arranged, are brought to the table along with spicy and mild dipping sauces, a beaten raw egg, and four kinds of ground dumpling pastes. You use chopsticks and mesh baskets on bamboo handles to cook the beef, crab, scallops, geoduck clam, shrimp, black cod, tofu, Chinese greens, and fresh herbs, and spoons to make little balls of squid, pork, beef, and fish pastes, pulling them out when they float to the top. At the end of the meal you drink the flavorful broth the food was cooked in. All guests at the table get to choose the tidbits they like, cook them as long as they like, and eat as much as they want. This style of dining proves to be light but satisfying, since there's very little fat in either the cooking method or most of the ingredients. Leave it to the twelfth-century Mongolians to invent the ideal modern diet.

HARBOR VILLAGE

This large, bustling branch of a Hong Kong restaurant chain mounts one of the best dim sum services in the city —and there are quite a few now. The variety of dim sum seems never ending and the quality is invariably high. With a view of the bay from the glassed-in room on Halladie Plaza, the tony, well-appointed dining rooms really do feel like Hong Kong. Women in starched white uniforms push carts silently over the carpeting, offering bona fide delicacies. This is one of the few places that makes *shaolin bao*, twisted dumplings filled with shrimp, cabbage, black mushrooms, and an unexpected gush of flavorful stock, which is put into the dumpling as a gelatin but turns to liquid when the dumpling is steamed. Beautiful shrimp pearl balls, coated in opalescent rice, are filled with chopped shrimp barely bound together with a little egg. Elegant slices of cured pork shank rest on a bed of orange soybeans, waiting for a splash of Chinese vinegar from the server. Tender octopus flecked with hot red chilies and served with a mild green wasabi dipping sauce is one of the most delicious items here. Pork dumplings surprise you with the crunch of peanuts, dried shrimp, and Chinese celery. The measure of every teahouse, *har gow* (shrimp dumplings), meet the highest standards of dim sum cookery: The shrimp are naturally sweet and juicy, and the portion in each dumpling is large.

At night the dim sum carts are garaged and a lengthy dinner menu goes into effect. The dishes, many of them inventive in a cross-cultural, Hong Kong style, are

4 Embarcadero Center (at Clay and Drumm), San Francisco

Tel: 781-8833

Open Monday through Friday for lunch 11 a.m. to 2:30 p.m., Saturday and Sunday 10:30 a.m. to 2:30 p.m.; dinner nightly 5:30 to 9:30 p.m.

Price: Moderate

Credit cards: AE, DC, MC, V

refined and attractively presented. I've had lots of intriguing preparations here, including some excellent lobster and whole fish, and a signature chicken salad with fresh fruit that weaves together many different ingredients. Light, flavorful noodle dishes, made here with the thinnest strands of pasta, are a satisfying way to end a meal full of delicacies.

IL FORNAIO

Levi's Plaza, 1265 Battery Street (at Greenwich), San Francisco Tel: 986-0100 Open Monday through Thursday 7 a.m. to 11 p.m., Friday until midnight, Saturday 9 a.m. to midnight, Sunday 9 a.m. to 11 p.m.; weekend brunch 9 a.m. to 1 p.m. Price: Moderate Credit cards: AE, DC, MC, V

I walked down to Il Fornaio the other day for lunch, expecting the usual multiunit, lowest-common-denominator Italian cooking, and ended up with one of the most stunning meals I've had in the City. The Il Fornaio at Levi's Plaza, part of an expanding chain of bakeries (see page 216), cafes, and restaurants that extends up and down the Pacific coast, is the flagship, even if the first Il Fornaio restaurant opened in a shopping center in Marin County. Not only is the cooking at a higher level at the Levi's Il Fornaio, but the space is more lyrical. A large patio filled with tables and umbrellas makes you feel as if you're at an outdoor cafe in Europe, while a high-ceilinged interior, magnificently decorated with marble, hand-painted wall murals, terra-cotta, wrought iron, and majolica, with soaring arched windows that look out to the plaza, could be a trattoria in Milan. As in Italy, elegant materials do not mean formality; they signify the need for endurance because of constant use. People do use this Il Fornaio, nonstop, in all sorts of ways: as a cafe in the morning for coffee, as a take-out *panini* shop, as a bakery and, of course, as a *ristorante*.

My great Il Fornaio meal began with *trippa alla milanese*. Now there aren't many restaurants I trust with tripe, so I looked the waiter straight in the eye and asked if I should order it. He gave me the go-ahead, and I was brought a flat metal bowl of a wonderful, rustic, soup-like stew with red beans, tripe, cabbage, and potatoes that melted together in the most profound way. It was the kind of dish you travel to a small Italian village to eat. After that, anything the kitchen put out would have been fine, and much of it was, including a perfectly grilled piece of fresh Chilean sea bass with rosemary-scented roast potatoes and some buttery spinach, and a lively *penne all'amatriciana*, pasta tubes tossed with tomatoes, pancetta, onions, and pecorino cheese. A molded terrine of eggplant and goat cheese I used to like here has lost its sparkle, arriving as separate piles of ingredients. However, considering the huge size of the menu, which offers everything from pastas and pizzas baked in the wood-burning oven, grilled and rotisserie-cooked foods, pastas, *antipasti*, plus an occasional authentic Italian dish or two like that *trippa*, Il Fornaio does a workmanlike job. With clever ordering you can have an Italian meal found nowhere else. Il Fornaio in San Francisco has the size, staff, and clientele to reach a little higher than the other units, and it gets much praise from omnivorous and adventurous eaters like me when it does.

ONE MARKET RESTAURANT

Chef Brad Ogden, the darling of American cooking, must have wanted a new challenge by taking on such a huge project in the city, when his Lark Creek Inn in Larkspur continues to be a destination restaurant for practically every visitor and resident of the Bay Area. One Market is more urbane and less homey, a sweeping, sleek glass and granite dining room with power booths, a barroom with separate menu, private dining rooms, and a to-go window that allows people to order and sit in the atrium of One Market Plaza. Ogden is a great cook, but in an operation like this you have to delegate, and a number of dishes that made it to the menu have not been his heartfelt best. They aren't bad, but they lack conviction. They

1 Market Street (at Steuart), San Francisco
Tel: 777-5577
Open Monday through Friday for lunch 11:30 a.m. to 2 p.m.; dinner Monday through Thursday 5:30 to 9:30 p.m., Friday until 10 p.m., Saturday 5 to 10 p.m., Sunday 5 to 9 p.m.; Sunday brunch 10 a.m. to 2 p.m.

Price: Expensive

Credit cards: AE, DC,
MC, V

confuse fussiness for character. The very mention of Lark Creek conjures up visions of hearty, luscious plates of food that you want to order again and again. At One Market, the food doesn't get to you in the same way, because too many of the dishes have been fancied up. The meat dishes, however, are still some of the best anywhere, like meltingly tender short ribs; sautéed calf's liver in balsamic onions; braised oxtails; and deeply flavorful pot roasts with root vegetables. The mini-hamburgers in the bar are worth a trip alone. The operation is very professionally run, offering every amenity, anything you want to drink, large dishes, small dishes, and a grown-up, sophisticated ambiance that suits Financial District business needs brilliantly. I guess I'm still looking for the Midwestern boy in the cooking.

SPLENDIDO

Four Embarcadero Center
(between Clay and Drumm),
San Francisco
Tel: 986-3222
Open Monday through
Saturday for lunch 11:30
a.m. to 2:30 p.m.; bar menu
served 2:30 to 5:30 p.m.;
dinner nightly 5:30 to
10:30 p.m.
Price: Moderate
Credit cards: AE, DC,
MC, V

Aptly named, this dramatic restaurant boasts a flamboyant Mediterranean decor sprung from the imagination of designer Pat Kuleto. In typical Kuleto style, different areas of the sprawling room are demarcated by fantasy stage settings, all within a theme. A brick wine cellar entryway turns into a rustic wood-beamed bar-cave, which segues into a canvas-canopied garden area by windows that look out to the Ferry Building. And these are but three of the whimsically decorated areas. A huge and handsome open kitchen with a counter dominates the back portion of the restaurant, and as you walk through the podium level of Embarcadero Four, your eye is caught by a working pastry kitchen, visible through a large window. A full-scale Bill Kimpton production, Splendido's goal is to offer something for everyone, not just in the style of decor, but in food and drink as well, for a good price.

I opt for the pizzas with rich, flaky crusts, my favorite scattered with spicy *merguez*, feta, mozzarella, and threads of fresh mint. Thick house-made ravioli, moistened by rich stock and sprinkled with cubed tomatoes, is typical of many of the dishes here. The kitchen dresses dishes up with reduced brown stock and tomato *concassée*, an odd couple that appears often. A pork chop, slowly cooked in fat in the style of duck *confit*, then crisply sautéed and served on a bed of celery root, presents one of the simplest and best main courses.

As in most of the Kimco restaurants (like the Italian-themed Kuleto's or Postrio), the energy buzz is almost tangible, a commodity. More is better in these restaurant productions, and restraint is not important to the concept.

TOKYO SUKIYAKI

When out-of-town friends come to San Francisco they head straight for Fisherman's Wharf. "We're just like the locals," they tell us with a wink. "We know those barking sea lions by name." As a local who lives a short walk from the wharf, I would shrug and let them go by themselves—until I rediscovered Tokyo Sukiyaki, an elegant Japanese restaurant I first visited twenty years ago. I will never forget the meal I had there. It was my first brush with real Japanese cooking. Little did I know then that I was getting a taste of what would become today's San Francisco, a city that belongs to the Pacific Rim as much as to the United States.

Climbing a flight of handsome stairs (an elevator stands open nearby) to the second-floor restaurant does not prepare you for the change in tone. In a matter of seconds you move from the carny bustle of wax museums and T-shirt shops to the peace of classical Japanese tatami rooms. In fact, Tokyo Sukiyaki has both Western and Japanese seating and English and Japanese menus. Both are accessible to everyone. The Western-style tables and chairs are next to large picture windows that

225 Jefferson Street (at Taylor), San Francisco
Tel: 775-9030
Open nightly 4 to 11 p.m.
Price: Moderate
Credit cards: AE, DC, MC, V

gives diners a bird's-eye view of the wharf, while the tatami rooms, enclosed in rice paper and bamboo screens, are secluded. Beautiful woodwork, a stunning array of pottery, and waitresses in traditional Japanese kimonos give Tokyo Sukiyaki a timeless upscale look. Actually, the simple and classy decor reminds me of restaurants in midtown Manhattan.

The food is not as sophisticated as the look, though the featured dish, beef sukiyaki, is absolutely delicious. An electric burner in a wooden box is brought to the table with a shallow cast-iron pan. The waitress throws a cube of beef suet into the pan, and when it begins to melt, she judiciously throws in petal-thin slices of beef, vegetables, and noodles arranged like a flower on a platter. She moistens the pan with sake and soy sauce, which cook down to form an intense caramelized sauce. You are given a clay bowl with a raw egg, into which you dip the hot foods. The foods are so hot, the egg coats them and cooks instantly, smoothing and enriching the intense flavors, a wonderful culinary transformation that occurs with each bite.

Foods cooked in broth at the table, in a service called *shabu-shabu* (a name that mimics the sound of foods being swished through liquid), represent a very clean way to eat, if not one as tasty as the sukiyaki. From the Japanese menu, which is written in English as well, I have had an excellent whole salt-broiled flounder, filleted and presented on a rectangular ceramic plate. It goes well with a small bowl of cold spinach topped with bonito flakes. Another refreshing starter brings a bowl of cold tofu cubes in a bath of ice and water. You fish out the cubes with a little gold strainer and slip them into a gingery soy sauce, the whole procedure quintessentially Japanese and delightful.

Undistinguished sake is the one surprising lapse at this rather elegant restaurant, but considering all the other civilized amenities here, Tokyo Sukiyaki is a valuable destination in the middle of San Francisco's most popular tourist area.

WU KONG

A large, modern Chinese restaurant in the Rincon Annex, Wu Kong specializes in Shanghai dishes and, in particular, Shanghai-style dim sum. The long menu can seem daunting to the uninitiated, but by seeking out Shanghai dishes, diners can have an exciting regional eating experience.

I especially love Shanghai-style appetizers like vegetable goose, a Taoist monk's dish of fried bean curd wrapped around a savory mushroom stuffing that when sliced actually looks like breast of crispy goose. Drunken squab marinated in rice wine, served cold, is refreshing, boozy, and velvet fleshed. The jellyfish salad is astonishingly crisp-tender in a tasty sesame dressing scented with lacy sprigs of Chinese parsley. Deep-fried eel, crunchy all the way through in a subtle sweet-and-sour sauce, is a must-order—even if you have doubts about eel.

Tea lunch items such as special Shanghai baby dumplings delicately stuffed with ground pork and clear broth, or steamed baby vegetable dumplings filled with Chinese greens and fruity winter melon in season, sparkle. As evidenced by the crispy eel preparation, Wu Kong's kitchen knows how to deep fry. Try yellowfish fritters, speckled with threads of seaweed. They melt in your mouth. If they are available, stir-fried blue crabs are worth the trouble it takes to get at their lovely meat.

One Rincon Center (at Spear and Mission),
San Francisco
Tel: 957-9300
Open for lunch Monday through Friday 11 a.m. to 3 p.m., Saturday and Sunday 10:30 a.m. to 3 p.m.; dinner nightly 5:30 to 10:30 p.m.
Price: Moderate
Credit cards: AE, DC, MC, V

Shanghai-style onion cakes, little balls of flaky pastry dotted with sesame seeds and filled with green onions, are smashing. A bowl of chicken noodle soup, so common, yet so wonderful here, deserves a nod. The broth is the pure essence of chicken, and the little cubes of breast meat stay marvelously tender. Lest you think that the Chinese do not eat dessert, try Wu Kong's deep-fried clouds of beaten egg white with a little red bean paste at the center, deep-fried bean curd pancakes, or pan-fried Seven Treasures Rice. All are something to look forward to at the end of a tea lunch.

I think it is entirely possible to take some wrong turns when ordering a meal here, especially during the busy Financial District lunch hour. You can end up with some uninspired dishes made with canned or frozen ingredients. But weekend tea lunch or a banquet ordered and discussed ahead will offer a rare culinary adventure. The large restaurant is nicely appointed, and service is attentively professional for banquets and efficient at all other times.

EATING ON PIER 39

I had a terrific sandwich the other day from a stand at the beginning of Pier 39, called BBQ Salmon on Sourdough, which pretty much sums up what it serves. For $4.75 you get a nice-sized piece of fresh salmon, grilled to order (ask for it to be pink in the center if you don't want it to be dry and overcooked) and served on a crusty sourdough roll with lettuce, tomato, red onion, tartar sauce laced with fresh dill, and a fresh lemon wedge. When you eat it all together, with a squeeze of lemon, it makes for a very creditable lunch.

Farther down the Pier is the Pier Market and Seafood Restaurant, which also makes grilled salmon sandwiches on a softer bread that has been deep-fried. Better is a fresh, savory salmon burger on a regular bun with tartar sauce and all the trimmings. You can get most of the typical Wharf offerings here, including a cold half lobster with tartar sauce and cocktail sauce for $10.95.

When people ask me for suggestions of restaurants with views, two yacht companies currently offering meal cruises on the bay come up over and over again. Though a bit pricy, the beauty outside their expansive picture windows makes a ride on them worthwhile. Both during the day and at night, as the sun sets, being on the water in these big, comfortable, smooth-riding ships can be very romantic, and you get to see the land from a perspective that makes you appreciate the geographical richness of the Bay Area.

From a food perspective, I like the Sunday brunch cruise on the *San Francisco Spirit*, a Pacific Marine yacht that boards near Pier 39 (tel: 546-2700). The spacious, modern, handsomely appointed boat puts on a generous buffet with miraculously decent poached eggs on English muffins coated in a light, creamy hollandaise, delicious with juicy baked ham sliced to order by a chef on the serving line. The rest of the buffet consists of fruit salad, good, creamy potato salad, wilted spinach and other salads, some quite tasty, and the usual bad commercial bread and pastries. A fine Spanish sparkling wine is liberally poured. While sailing during the day may not be as romantic as at night, you see so much more. Sailboats whiz past your table; pelicans slowly soar by. A protected part of the deck lets you view everything from outside. The price ($40 for adults, $20 for children, tax and tip included) and duration (11:30 a.m. to 1:30 p.m.) feels just about right.

The alternative is a Hornblower dinner cruise (tel: 788-8866, $58 to $73 per person), leaving from Pier 33 at 7 p.m. and returning at 10:30 p.m. The *California Hornblower* is one of the most majestic boats plying the bay. A white wooden structure encircled by rows of large square windows, the *Hornblower* looks a little like a tiered Victorian wedding cake. Inside, the carpeted salons are dimly lit by Art Deco wall sconces and candles, letting the windows frame breathtaking views of sparkling city lights. The service is formal and very friendly. Unfortunately, the food is the least satisfying part of the experience. You can taste all the corners that have been cut in the ingredients, and the execution is of the nondescript hotel variety. But there is dancing to a three-piece combo, and the drinks are not unreasonably priced. You can get a bottle of Kendall-Jackson Chardonnay, for example, for $18, and even if you don't eat very much, you leave the boat enchanted.

A STRATEGY FOR VISITING FISHERMAN'S WHARF

Who can resist going down to a waterfront where monstrous sea lions bark and lounge on the piers, where you can hop on a ferry to Sausalito or Tiburon —or visit a wax museum? That's the problem with the wharf; it has turned into a kitschy tourist attraction with a plethora of T-shirt shops and boardwalk-candy emporia. The working part of the wharf, where San Francisco's fishing boats dock with their hauls of crab and salmon, is getting smaller and smaller as fishing is being regulated to protect diminishing supplies and the real estate gets more and more valuable. There are a number of long-established wharf restaurants that charge a pretty penny for indifferent food; you are paying for location when you eat at them. Then there are the sidewalk seafood bars and crab pots that stretch along the wharf, owned by a variety of different families. These are your best bets for getting a feel of the old workingman's wharf, when people really bought their live crabs and fresh-caught salmon there. Ideally, you can buy a whole live crab and ask that it be cooked to order in one of the huge, steaming, pressurized crab pots. The cooks will crack it for you, and with a glass or two of icy cold California Chardonnay you can have one of the nicest meals in the world. But all too often the crab has been frozen or overcooked, or cooked and then frozen. I've had every kind. You'll never get anything spoiled (the wharf smells only of appetizing fresh seafood), but you never really know what you're getting, unless you see the crabs wiggling in crates. Most of the operations sell identical items: crab-salad sandwiches, shrimp cocktails, cold half lobsters, picked Dungeness crab, and tiny bay shrimp cocktails. If I had to choose one stand over another, I like the looks of Nick's; I like the funky old-wharf feeling of the street-level dining rooms of Sabella and La Torre; and I have actually witnessed the guys at Alioto's stand cook the crabs and crack them to order.

BARS

EMBARKO

My favorite way to use this pleasant restaurant, located at a point in the Embarcadero where it opens up to an unobstructed view of the bay, is to sit at the bar and have one of the well-made special cocktails and some ample appetizers, like skewers of juicy chicken satay served with peanut sauce and a cucumber salad; crisp, oniony potato pancakes; or grilled shrimp slathered with a red spice paste and served with greens. The menu, as you see from the appetizers, is very eclectic, and some things work while others don't. However, you can depend on huge portions, both for main courses and dessert.

100 Brannan Street (at the Embarcadero), San Francisco
Tel: 495-2120
Open Monday through Thursday 11 a.m. to 11 p.m., Friday and Saturday until midnight,
Sunday 5:30 to 10 p.m.
Credit cards: AE, DC, D, MC, V

GORDON BIERSCH BREWING COMPANY

This large, high-tech brew pub may be the most popular bar in town, even though it doesn't serve hard liquor. Every day downtown workers spill out into the street in front of the brewery, unable to get inside the jammed

space. This has become the premier heterosexual meeting spot among those people young enough to prefer hearty beer to any other kind of drink. The place is so noisy and crowded that it's hard to see how anyone could possibly carry on a flirtatious conversation, though the upstairs dining area provides some respite.

2 Harrison Street (at the Embarcadero), San Francisco
Tel: 243-8246
Open Sunday through Thursday 11 a.m. to midnight, Friday and Saturday until 1 a.m.
Credit cards: AE, D, MC, V

HARRY DENTON'S

161 Steuart Street (between Howard and Mission), San Francisco
Tel: 882-1333
Open Monday through Friday 7 a.m. to 2 a.m., Saturday and Sunday 8 a.m. to 2 a.m.
Credit cards: AE, D, MC, V

Ebullient Harry Denton, often on the premises, creates the party at his bar, restaurant, and dance place just south of the Financial District. Everyone flocks here after work for a drink, a bite, and some jazz at the bar. A menu of substantial, stylish pub food is prepared at lunch and dinner. By ten o'clock, the back dining room, with a view of the bay, is cleared of tables and turns into a disco. Denton has the touch. Amidst the madhouse of people drinking, eating, and dancing, everything runs smoothly, professionally, in good spirits. From the moment it opened, Denton's has been wildly popular as a place to go for a good time.

PIER 23 CAFE

Pier 23 (on the Embarcadero between Battery and Broadway), San Francisco
Tel: 362-5125
Open Tuesday through Saturday 11:30 a.m. to 1:30 a.m., Sunday 11 a.m. to 8 p.m.; Sunday brunch 11 a.m. to 2:30 p.m.
Credit cards: MC, V

One of the finest locations in town for a bar, this resonant old longshoreman's shack sits just yards from the bay on the water side of the Embarcadero. Patrons warming stools at the copper bar have a direct view of Treasure Island and sailing vessels just beyond a concrete pier. When the weather is warm, tables go out on the pier so you can eat and drink inches from the water. The place revs into high gear at night when live salsa, R & B, and jazz bands perform. Its excellent weekend brunch has become a San Francisco tradition. The best dish to order on the regular menu is the meat loaf with mashed potatoes in Cajun gravy. Owned by local character Flicka McGurrin, who hangs her expressive oil paintings on the walls between the stuffed marlins and sailfish, Pier 23 offers the best neighborhood ambiance of any bar on the Embarcadero.

The Ramp's location right next to a working shipyard, with towering cranes and dry docks where massive ships are repaired in front of a small boat marina, tests your perspective after a few Bloody Marys or margaritas at the outdoor bar that looks straight into the harbor. Though the food is acceptable, eating it outdoors under an umbrella by all the activity on the water makes it taste much better, especially a breakfast of sunny-side up eggs and spicy Italian sausage. The Ramp is a must-stop for breakfast on the way to Giants' day games if you're coming from the city. You get to the Ramp by turning toward the bay on Mariposa from Third Street. To get to Candlestick, simply continue up Third until you see the Candlestick turnoff sign. (The Third Street route is the fastest and most hassle-free way to go.)

855 China Basin (off Third Street at Mariposa), San Francisco
Tel: 621-2378
Open Monday through Thursday 8 a.m. to 9 p.m., Friday until 1:30 p.m., Saturday and Sunday until 4 p.m.
Credit cards: AE, MC, V

BAKERIES/PASTRIES

BOUDIN SOURDOUGH BAKERY AND CAFE

156 Jefferson Street (between Taylor and Mason), San Francisco
Tel: 928-1849
Open Sunday through Thursday 7:30 a.m. to 8 p.m., Friday and Saturday until 9 p.m.
Credit cards: AE, D, MC, V

When I'm down on the wharf I always stop at this Boudin outlet to buy one of their 1 ½ pound sourdough rounds. This particular kind of San Francisco sourdough has a slightly more tender crust, a soft but dense interior, and is not too sour. The loaves at this original bakery site are always very fresh because of the volume. For $11.50 you can get six loaves in a travel box, ready to check onto airline baggage. You also can buy a small round, walk up to the wharf to buy crab cocktails and a pound of shrimp in the shell, stroll down to a less crowded spot on a pier by the water, and have the quintessential San Francisco wharf picnic.

JUST DESSERTS

3 Embarcadero Center, Lobby Level (at Drumm), San Francisco
Tel: 421-1609
Open weekdays 7 a.m. to 7 p.m., Saturday 9 a.m. to 5 p.m., Sunday noon to 5 p.m.
Credit cards: MC, V

See listing, page 216.

ICE CREAM/CHOCOLATES

SEE'S CANDIES

Three Embarcadero Center (at Drumm), San Francisco

Tel: 391-1622

Open weekdays 10 a.m. to 7 p.m., Saturday until 5 p.m.,

Sunday noon to 5 p.m.

No credit cards

See listing, page 431.

PRODUCE

FERRY PLAZA FARMER'S MARKET

Serious food shoppers are fiercely loyal to their own farmers' market, the one they go to religiously every time it happens, the one where they have their favorite farmers, their favorite tomatoes, their favorite flowers. Well, mine is the Ferry Plaza Farmers' Market, a relatively new market started by organic-produce activist Sibella Krause just a year ago. The Embarcadero market has taken such firm root in the community that after operating only one season it decided to stay open year round. The shoppers wouldn't let it close.

The trip to the market with empty baskets and canvas bags has become a Saturday ritual for thousands of San Franciscans who probably never shopped at a farmers' market before. At first they may have been stunned by

On the Embarcadero in front
of the Ferry Building at
Market Street
Open Saturdays from around
8:30 a.m. to 2 p.m.

the prices, which are high, because most of the produce sold at this market is organic. But once they tasted an organic peach or tomato, picked ripe, carefully packed, and brought to market that morning, they couldn't go back to the flavorless commercial kind. The taste of this organic produce is incomparable, and when you think about the time, effort, and expense of the farmers, paying more for it does not seem out of line. Though supermarket produce may be half the price of the organic produce sold at the market, it's not worth eating if it tastes like cardboard. More and more people, skeptical at first, are being won over. They come regularly to the market, buy more, taste more, learn about the importance of sustainable agriculture, and are feeding themselves and their families much the better for it.

This market is more than a produce depot, though one would be hard-pressed to find a better seasonal gathering of locally grown fruits and vegetables. There is an egg vendor with free-range organic eggs of every size and color, including exquisite-tasting little pullet eggs; a mushroom stand with domestic brown Italian, oyster, Portobello, and shiitake mushrooms, to name just a few; a farmhouse goat cheese producer, Redwood Hill Goat Dairy; an organic cow's milk and butter producer, Straus Family Dairy; a fine producer of sheep's milk cheeses and lamb, Bellweather Farms; Bud Hoffman with his beautiful quail, squab, free-range chickens, rabbit, pheasant, and smoked game birds; Paul Johnson from Monterey Fish with salmon, crabs, mussels, rockfish, yellowfin tuna, and whatever else has come in that day; Postrio's David Gingrass with his unsurpassed salami, pepperoni, and liverwurst; Acme Bread from Berkeley; the Downtown Bakery and Creamery from Healdsburg; Palio d'Asti breads and bread sticks, and Fran Gage with her lovely raisin rolls and croissants; flower vendors,

Anne Haskell, my former partner at Hayes Street Grill and a great French home cook, makes this luscious vegetable stew in spring when English peas and favas come to market. Except for the potatoes, carrots, green beans, peas, and onions, which are crucial, the recipe is quite flexible. Fava beans and leeks are nice additions, as are asparagus, sugar snap peas, and green garlic. In April, May, and June, the vegetables are the most tender and sweet.

In a heavy pot large enough to hold all the cooked vegetables, cook the bacon in the olive oil until crisp. Remove the bacon pieces to a plate.

In the remaining fat, cook and stir the flour until golden, about 5 minutes. Add the chicken broth. Bring to a boil, then lower heat to a simmer. Add the bay leaves, minced garlic, the parsley stems tied with 4 sprigs of thyme, the kosher salt, and 20 turns of a peppermill.

Add the potatoes and cook until they are about half done, 10 to 15 minutes. Add the onions, leeks, and carrots and cook 10 minutes longer. If the potatoes are done at this point (a paring knife pierces them easily), remove them.

Add the green beans and continue to cook until they are crisp-tender. Taste and adjust the seasoning. Return the potatoes, if you removed them. The stew may be cooked several hours ahead at this point.

Shell the fava beans, then remove the skins by blanching the beans in boiling water for 30 seconds and popping out the bright green fava inside the thick gray-green skin.

Ten minutes before serving, bring the *jardinière* to a bare simmer. Add a little water if it looks dry, and add the peas, fava beans, minced thyme, 2 tablespoons of the chopped parsley, and the garlic cloves. Stir gently and cook for 10 minutes.

Stir in the reserved bacon and serve in soup plates with good bread. Sprinkle with fresh parsley.

Serves 4 to 6

---

6 slices good-quality thick-sliced bacon, cut into 1-inch pieces

2 tablespoons olive oil

1/4 cup flour

6 cups chicken broth

2 bay leaves

2 tablespoons minced garlic, plus 2 plump garlic cloves

1 bunch Italian (flat-leaf) parsley, leaves coarsely chopped and stems reserved

2 teaspoons minced fresh thyme (about 6 sprigs), plus 4 whole sprigs

2 teaspoons kosher salt

Freshly ground pepper

15 new potatoes, cut in half or quarters or left whole depending on size

2 onions, cut into quarters

2 bunches small leeks, trimmed to 4 inches

2 bunches small carrots, each about 3 inches long

1 pound green beans (Blue Lakes, Romanos, Kentucky Wonder, or tiny French haricots verts, or a combination), stem ends trimmed

2 pounds fava beans

2 pounds English peas, shelled

Up to 1 cup water as needed

orchid vendors, rose specialists; and the most dedicated, talented array of farmers anywhere. If you just come down once and take a few tastes you'll be hooked. Everyone will think that your cooking has improved, and it will when you start using these flavor-packed ingredients. You'll be inspired to cook more often, to try new things, to taste in a way you never have before.

On top of all the beautiful food, there is an ongoing shop-with-the-chef program, in which local chefs walk around the market assembling a basket of ingredients, demonstrate how they would use them, and then raffle off the basket. Every top chef in the city has made the tour, coming up with some extraordinary menus. For the little ones, there is a nearly free hands-on cooking class every Saturday at 10 a.m., which gives young children a taste of some of the nicest things in the market; and once a month, at the height of tomato season or stone-fruit season or melon season, the Ferry Plaza Farmers' Market sponsors comparative tastings of many different varietals, and local restaurants set up booths where they cook seasonal bites—like grilled corn with spicy chili butter, grilled salmon sandwiches with tomatoes, or grilled asparagus tossed with Parmesan and olive oil.

The feeling here is different from that at any other farmers' market. Although there are few bargains to be found, you can get your hands on the highest-quality produce in the Bay Area for prices under what you would pay at specialty stores, if you could find like quality. That's the big advantage of shopping at a farmers' market: you get the produce in perfect condition, fresh picked, and full of flavor and nutrition. Many of us are unable (or unwilling) to buy the latest consumer luxuries, but why not try a perfect peach? The pleasure it gives ranks as high as practically anything I can think of. For about $1, why not take the plunge?

You can buy superb quail from Bud Hoffman's poultry table at the Ferry Plaza Farmers' Market. He also has rabbit, poussin, pheasant, duck, fabulous chicken, and some smoked birds as well. You can get pancetta, which is unsmoked, cured, and rolled Italian bacon, at any Italian delicatessen mentioned in this book. Serve these quail with polenta, and be sure to use your fingers when you eat them, to get all the meat off the tiny legs. This failsafe recipe came to me from Anne Haskell, adapted from *Marcella's Italian Kitchen* by Marcella Hazan.

6 quail, bone-in

6 thin slices pancetta

17 large sage leaves (about 1 bunch)

1/3 cup plus 2 tablespoons olive oil

2 teaspoons minced garlic

1 tablespoon butter

1 cup dry white wine

Kosher salt and freshly ground pepper to
*   taste*

1/2 cup water

Rinse the quail and pat them dry with paper towels. Stuff 1 slice of pancetta and 2 sage leaves into each cavity.

In a bowl large enough to hold the quail, combine 1/3 cup of the olive oil, the garlic, and the remaining 5 sage leaves. Add the quail, stir them gently in the marinade, cover, and refrigerate for at least 2 and up to 24 hours.

In a skillet just large enough to hold the quail on their sides, melt the butter and 2 tablespoons olive oil over medium-high heat. Brown the quail well on all sides, 4 to 5 minutes. Pour off the fat. Add the white wine, salt, and pepper. Let the wine bubble for 1 minute. Turn the quail and lower the heat until the sauce is just simmering. Cover the skillet with the lid slightly askew and cook, turning the quail every 20 minutes, until cooked through and tender, depending on the size of the birds, about 45 to 60 minutes (insert a knife in the breast at the bone; the flesh should not be pink). Transfer the quail to a warmed dish or serving platter. Turn the heat to high. When the pan juices are boiling, add the water and let the mixture bubble for 30 seconds. The juices will thicken slightly. Pour over the quail and serve.

Serves 3 to 4

COOKWARE AND BOOKS

COST PLUS IMPORTS

2552 Taylor Street,
San Francisco
Tel: 928-6200
Open daily 9 a.m. to 9 p.m.
Credit cards: MC, V

The prices used to be fantastic at this gigantic warehouse of imported goods ranging from foodstuffs to dishes, cotton goods to baskets. I once shopped here for platters and serving bowls, but the prices rose and the pieces weren't as attractive as those I could find at Crate and Barrel for the same price. But there are always bargains, especially in Asian dishware and handwoven baskets. Cost Plus has one of the largest collection of baskets anywhere, and I have discovered, along with every caterer in town, that flat-woven, rimmed baskets in different-sized circles are good for serving foods like cheese, fruit, bread, cookies, and raw vegetables. Baskets are light, unbreakable, and easy to transport. Just by wandering through the aisles at Cost Plus, you'll get some good ideas for presenting food in them.

WILLIAMS-SONOMA

Two Embarcadero Center (between Drumm and Sacramento),
San Francisco
Tel: 421-2033
Open weekdays 10 a.m. to 7 p.m., Saturday until 6,
Sunday noon to 5 p.m.
Credit cards: AE, MC, V

See listing, page 175.

Financial District
& Union Square

FINANCIAL DISTRICT & UNION SQUARE

RESTAURANTS

Southern California chef John Sedlar has taken some knocks in the local press for the wildly mixed ethnicity in his highly conceptual cooking, but some of the dishes he has come up with are knockouts. The name Abiquiu, which comes from a small pueblo north of Santa Fe where his grandparents settled, suggests the Southwest, and we have seen from interpreters like Mark Miller of the seminal Coyote Cafe in Santa Fe that the style can encompass almost any ingredient. But Sedlar takes interpretive southwestern cooking several continents farther, to Southeast Asia by way of France, to create dishes that push the envelope of any cuisine. Even a year ago I might have been too skeptical to give this cooking a chance, but that was before I started doing research for this book and eating warm sweet-corn tamales from the Mission with *queso fresco* and Gujarati green-coconut chutney, an absolutely stunning combination. It turns out that the flavor mix between Asia and New Mexico is not out of the question at all, as evidenced by Sedlar's

Monticello Hotel

129 Ellis Street (between Powell and Mason), San Francisco

Tel: 392-5500

Open for lunch Monday through Saturday 11:30 a.m. to 3 p.m.; dinner nightly 5 to 11 p.m.

Price: Moderate

Credit cards: AE, CB, DC, D, MC, V

Banzai Duck Tamale, a fantastic appetizer of duck-filled tamale slathered in a stir fry of crisp-skinned Peking-style duck, shiitakes, baby bok choy, and a garnish of fresh radish sprouts. His lobster chile makes my mouth water just thinking about it: A half lobster with meat cut into big hunks, tossed with buttery corn bread croutons and put back into the shell for broiling, sits on a bed of flavor-infused pinto beans in a buttery Southwest-seasoned lobster broth, the whole thing topped with crisp fried leek threads. In both dishes, a French style use of butter smooths the way between cultures. Sedlar is onto something here. He needs an editor on some combinations, but a lot of his cooking is sumptuous, crazy, and wonderful.

Each dish comes on a different huge plate, and the way the food is presented plays off the pattern on the plate. Some otherwise disappointing refrigerator-cold miniature tacos arrive carefully arranged on a pop-art comic book plate, while the tamales look demure on a plate decorated with a pastiche of the Virgin Mary. Yes, some of the preparations sacrifice culinary sense to conform to Sedlar's vision, but when the whole thing works, you really get something extraordinary.

The restaurant has another problem in its made-over decor, the now whitewashed dining room that Pat Kuleto originally designed for the Corona Bar and Grill. The toned-down interior does not match the flamboyance of the cooking. The service, however, is enlightened. In a restaurant like this, where the menu doesn't give you a clue about what you'll be getting, some intelligent recommendations from a waiter can make a meal. Every dish our waiter steered us to one night—the lobster, the tamales, and a southwestern banana split for dessert—turned out to be delicious. He had been a waiter in the

Redwood Room of the Four Season's Clift Hotel, and he radiated professionalism and gentle formality. The Four Seasons must have been very sad to lose him.

ANJOU

This cozy, very French bistro around the corner from Campton Place used to be called Janot's, but besides the name, nothing has changed since one partner, chef Pierre Morin, bought out the other, Jacques Janot. This is still a haven for delicious, classic bistro fare such as calf's liver with bacon and onions, and the sweetest, creamiest chicken liver sauté you'll ever run across. A warm spinach salad with bacon topped by a juicy grilled quail, and a house-made seafood sausage on warm cabbage salad in a vinegary butter sauce, are other signature dishes. One of my favorites is a warm duck-leg *confit* surrounded by a wreath of endive and watercress in a tart dressing. Typical of the well-prepared bistro dishes are tender, juicy rib lamb chops on a bed of delicately minted fresh *flageolets*, and a thin steak topped with a rosette of herb-shallot butter and accompanied with good *pommes frites* and French-cut green beans. Who could ask for anything more? The desserts may have fallen down a bit, but if Morin's hazelnut napoleon is available, give it a try. When it's fresh, it's a masterpiece. Prices are still amazingly reasonable, and eating at the tiny pushed-together cafe tables on two levels in this brick-walled dining room, softened by a floral canopy, feels very Parisian.

44 Campton Place
(between Sutter and Post,
Stockton and Grant),
San Francisco
Tel: 392-5373
Open for lunch Tuesday
through Saturday 11:30
a.m. to 2:30 p.m.; dinner
5:30 to 10 p.m.
Price: Moderate
Credit cards: AE, D,
MC, V

252 California Street
(between Battery and
Front), San Francisco
Tel: 956-9662
Open for lunch Monday
through Friday 11:30 a.m.
to 2:30 p.m.; dinner
Monday through Thursday
5:30 to 10:30 p.m., Friday
and Saturday until 11 p.m.
Price: Expensive
Credit cards: AE, DC,
MC, V

George Morrone came to San Francisco via New York where he worked with Alfred Portale at the Gotham Bar and Grill, and via Los Angeles where he was chef at the Bel Aire hotel under Wolfgang Puck. He developed a quixotic, if refined, style of his own, which combines the European formality of New York with the breezy eclecticism of Los Angeles. The result is Aqua, an elegant seafood restaurant inspired in tone by the once great Le Bernardin in New York (though it remains to be seen what will happen there since one of its owners, chef Gilbert Le Coze, recently passed away at forty-nine while working out at the gym). Aqua has garnered a reputation for sophisticated, first-class service. Once you're known there, your treatment becomes personal, completely tailored to your most minute preferences. Even if you're not known, and are throwing an expense account party for business purposes as many do here, the service is so professional and smooth you never have to worry about making the right impression.

The fact is, Aqua is one of the few dining rooms in the city, with the exception of hotels, that offers this degree of comfort and luxury. Conveniently located—right next to Tadich Grill in the Financial District—with big plate-glass windows looking out to California Street and the cable car line, the interior, carpeted and draped in the palest shades of peach and decorated with gargantuan flower arrangements on sculpted pedestals, is indeed a civilized place to dine. While most other rooms in town lean more to the bustling bistro mode, Aqua's heavily linened tables and upholstered armchairs are spaced for comfort. The scale is grander here, yet completely contemporary. People are expected to eat a leisurely full-course meal with wine, and indeed, the complicated plates take some time coming out of the kitchen.

Some dishes are a revelation, like a pairing of rare tuna with foie gras that is absolutely stunning, as odd as the combination sounds. It must have been inspired by the flavor of *toro*, the belly meat of tuna, which does taste like foie gras. I love the balance of refinement and strong flavors when Morrone attacks an ethnic dish, like a delicious seafood couscous full of the most pristine fish, shellfish, and al dente baby vegetables. But some dishes can get very fussy in presentation, which detracts from their purity, especially when first-rate ingredients are being used. A plate full of polka dots of red and green vegetable purees makes the food in the middle an afterthought. At Le Bernardin, which was solidly founded in French technique, you are awed by the beauty of the ingredient first and then by the art of the preparation. Morrone's cooking is jazzier than that, and people eat here for the total experience, as opposed to attending a temple of exquisite foods from the sea.

BURMA'S HOUSE

A Burmese meal can be a roller coaster of hot, sweet, and sour sensations, and Burma's House is a good place to hop on for the ride. Though the large menu looks daunting at first, it can be decoded by referring to small color photographs of selected dishes. The best and most typical plates to order are the Burmese salads, spectacular mélanges of spicy toasted ingredients individually arranged on a plate in little piles and mixed together at the table by the waiter with a squeeze of lime. The ginger salad epitomizes the genre, with tiny threads of fresh young ginger, toasted coconut, lentils and yellow split peas, fried garlic chips, fresh green chilies, and toasted sesame seeds. It's worth a visit to this restaurant just for this, or their mango salad, made of finely julienned strips of green and ripe mangos, cucumber, chilies, and

720 Post Street (between Jones and Leavenworth), San Francisco
Tel: 775-1156
Open daily 11:30 a.m. to 10 p.m.
Price: Inexpensive
Credit cards: MC, V

onion topped with deep-fried onion threads. It really is lovely. There are many Chinese-style stir fries and some strong-flavored stews, my favorite being fork-tender pork, potato, and onions in a classic yellow Burmese curry, served with rice cooked in coconut milk and scattered with fried onion threads. The decor here is nondescript, and the service can run hot or cold depending on your waiter, but when you're in the mood for something very spicy, completely exotic, and like nothing you've ever tasted before, head for Burma's House.

CAFÉ CLAUDE

7 Claude Lane (between Bush and Kearny), San Francisco
Tel: 392-3505
Open Monday through Friday 8 a.m. to 10 p.m., Saturday 10 a.m. to midnight
Price: Inexpensive
Credit cards: AE, D, MC, V

This is one of my favorite lunch places in the city because it so captures the spirit of the cafes I love in Paris. In fact, all the furnishings came from a small bar and *tabac* in the eleventh arrondisement that was about to be torn down. Café Claude's owner saved most of the interior intact and had it shipped to San Francisco, so the small, hidden-away space is full of vintage fifties French cafe chairs, banquettes, and tables, a bona fide zinc bar, and old cinema posters. The food and wines are typical: the delicious, crusty grilled-cheese sandwiches called *croque monsieur*, with a cheesy béchamel broiled on top of the sandwich and smoky Black Forest ham inside; green salad in a simple vinaigrette; *assiettes*, or plates, of charcuterie, or smoked trout with vegetable salads; an authentic *salade niçoise*; and French-style

sandwiches on buttered very fresh baguettes with thin slices of *saucisson sec* or ham inside. To wash all this down, glasses of inexpensive Rhône, Beaujolais, and Mâcon Blanc are sold by the glass, just as in France. The coffee is strong, and the waiters are French, young, and cute.

Before he left to open the Lark Creek Inn (see page 560), Brad Ogden made his reputation as the premier American chef in the country by opening Campton Place in the small, tasteful, luxury hotel of the same name. The hotel changed hands, and likeable Jan Birnbaum took over until he opened his own restaurant in Calistoga called Catahoula (see page 583). A third chef from New York is at the helm now, but frankly, the Ogden years were the best, for the way he elevated American dishes and ingredients to genuine three-star status was ground-breaking.

The restaurant's convenient location a half block from Union Square makes the civilized dining room and bar a good place to repair to during shopping trips, particularly if you're feeling flush and want something tasty and elegant to eat. The service has always been top-notch, and from the moment the uniformed doormen open the doors to the hotel you'll be pampered.

During the holiday season, the restaurant offers a festive caviar service at an affordable price if you order an ounce of the excellent Petrossian ossetra (as opposed to the beluga), which comes with tiny Chinese saucers of capers, crème fraîche, onions, chives, and sieved eggs with baskets of warm toast triangles and sweet butter—perfect down to a tiny silver demitasse spoon for each person. Of course, the best way to eat the caviar is to spoon it generously onto the buttered toast, then eat the condiments after you've finished the caviar, if you're still hungry, in little buttered toast sandwiches. A glass of chilled vodka goes very well with it.

Campton Place's opulent if pricy breakfast service is always fun, offering freshly baked breakfast breads,

340 Stockton Street
(between Post and Sutter),
San Francisco
Tel: 781-5555
Open for breakfast Monday through Friday 7 to 11 a.m., Saturday 8:30 to 11:30 a.m., Sunday brunch 8 a.m. to 2 p.m.; for lunch Monday through Friday 11:30 a.m. to 2 p.m., Saturday noon to 2 p.m.; dinner Sunday through Thursday 5:30 to 10 p.m., Friday and Saturday until 10:30 p.m.
Price: Expensive
Credit cards: AE, DC, D, MC, V

sweet rolls, and corn sticks, and gentle twists on such brunch classics as poached eggs with a delicate butter sauce on house-made English muffins; smoked salmon omelettes; and a breakfast hash made of unexpected ingredients, such as chicken, turkey, or vegetables.

CHINA MOON CAFE

639 Post Street (between Jones
and Taylor), San Francisco
Tel: 775-4789
Open nightly 5:30 to 10 p.m.
Price: Moderate
Credit cards: AE, DC, MC, V

Barbara Tropp originated a cuisine at her small, exquisite China Moon Cafe, a way of cooking that uses the strong, lusty northern Chinese seasonings she adores on both the traditional and nontraditional ingredients that inspire her. Taiwan, where she lived and studied as a graduate student of Chinese poetry, has been an important influence on her cooking, but it is her own modern sensibility, in which she presents New World ingredients in alluring Mandarin dress, that make the meals here so intriguing.

You are surrounded by Tropp's world, and it's a beautifully designed one in which Asian influences are evoked rather than replicated. You don't feel that Asian culture has been lifted, rather that it has been filtered through her imagination and expressed in a myriad of charming details. China Moon is an impressionistic work. Each time you visit you notice something else that makes the experience here unique. On one level you're sitting in an old San Francisco Chinese cafe eating noodles; on another, you're getting a taste of Barbara Tropp's poetry. Whether you've snagged a place at the counter, facing shelves of pottery and glasses, desserts and flowers, arranged simply, but just so, or at one of the lacquered wooden booths with Art Deco chopstick holders on the walls for easy replenishment with each course, you are embraced by Tropp's vision.

Most of the food is cooked in a tiny open kitchen in the front window of China Moon, while the preparation and dessert-making take place downstairs. Tropp's signature dishes include super-crispy egg roll filled with crab or chicken and hot fresh green chilies; and silken, "strange-flavored" eggplant on baguette croutons. Her scallops and clams in hot, garlicky black bean sauce with noodles is one of my favorite dishes in town, as is her sand-pot casserole of tiny pork ribs with black beans served with fragrant rice. Her velvety "tiles" of salmon with watercress salad, and her crispy noodle pillows slathered with juicy stirfries of elegantly cut meat and vegetables, demonstrate the way she uses Western and Asian ingredients together to balance colors and flavors on a plate. Tropp is aware of contrasts, of yin and yang, and her plates are always complete compositions that satisfy all the senses. She sees each dish as a whole, each meal as a whole, and her small, ever-changing menu reflects this aesthetic overview.

Dessert, tea, and wine play a large role in a China Moon meal. The wine list has been chosen with care, and often suggests specific glasses to drink with a dish. It is amazing how a crisp Italian white or an Oregon Pinot Noir can add dimension to dishes full of exotic flavors. Her longtime pastry chef turns out platters of the tiniest, thinnest, butteriest cookies scented with ginger, sprinkled with sesame seeds, textured with ground almonds. There are sparkling fresh-fruit sorbets and the famous ginger sundae, a hot, peppery house-made ginger ice cream draped with hot fudge sauce. Along with fine espresso, which I prefer, there are fruit, herb, green, and black teas to finish a meal or to drink with a meal, iced. Every conceivable choice has been thought out and offered in a form that contributes to the pleasure of a China Moon experience.

CHO-CHO

1020 Kearny Street
(between Pacific and
Broadway), San Francisco
Tel: 397-3066
Open for lunch Monday
through Friday 11:45 a.m.
to 2 p.m.; dinner Monday
through Saturday 5:45 to
10 p.m.
Price: Moderate
Credit cards: AE, MC, V

This fixture on the edge of the Financial District has been serving impeccable tempura from a tempura bar, sukiyaki in the upstairs dining room, and *shabu-shabu* in the downstairs dining room for as long as I can remember. Built to look like a Japanese country inn, the upstairs room has heavy, rough-hewn wooden tables with griddles inset in the middle. The surrounding benches are softened with cushions in Japanese cotton. Blue and white banners and ancient baskets decorate the walls. Groups can spend an evening up here in relative privacy, sizzling their meal on the griddle and chatting away. Downstairs, there are burners instead of griddles for the broth-based *shabu-shabu*. Many people stop in after work for a martini or a jar of sake and some lacy tempura cooked piece by piece by the chef behind the tempura bar, who waits to hear what you want next: an oyster mushroom, a *shiso* leaf, the delicate tail of a small sole, a strip of pasilla pepper. Cho-Cho is one of those places that has not changed a bit since it opened decades ago, and is the better for it.

CYPRESS CLUB

1500 Jackson Street
(between Columbus
and Montgomery),
San Francisco
Tel: 296-8555
Open Sunday through
Thursday 4:30 to 10 p.m.,
Friday and Saturday until
11 p.m.

Stop by this amazing-looking restaurant and bar just to see the opulent decor: a 1930s supper club gone wild. Huge nipple-shaped blown-glass light fixtures hang from a ceiling of enormous blimplike protuberances, glamorously enameled. Gigantic urn-shaped pillars, pounded copper archways, curved inlaid wood-paneled walls, a running wall mural of Northern California scenes that encircles the room, multicolored wooden floors, stone mosaic floors, overstuffed velvet booths and chairs, and a magnificent cast-bronze front door create an almost surrealistic baroque grandeur. Many people, in very chic costume, like to stop by the bar for a drink to check each other out. Others plumb the eclectic menu for a meal. The most interesting dishes feature game, inventively prepared and very good. An important wine list of new and old bottles await pairing with dishes that lend themselves to drinking serious red wine. Intelligent, sophisticated, very professional front-of-the-house man John Cunin is a principal here and has set up a first-class dining room staff that is knowledgeable about wine. However, the bartenders, for whatever reason, don't seem to uphold the same rigorous performance standards. Perhaps the spirits drinkers don't demand it.

Price: Expensive
Credit cards: AE, CB, DC, MC, V

EMPORIO ARMANI EXPRESS RESTAURANT

On warm days, when tables are placed on the sidewalk in front of the monolithic former bank building where the Armani store is, and waiters in white jackets are bringing plates of pasta and antipasti from the cafe upstairs, you have to pinch yourself to remember that you're in San Francisco. The integration of clothing, food, and style that goes on at this Armani store underscores the enlightened way Italians approach life. The fabrics used in the clothing are as beautiful as the raw materials in real Italian cooking. The cut of the clothing is simple and classic; the preparation of the dishes straightforward. At first you think, how can you put food in the middle of all this ridiculously expensive clothing? What if someone spilled? But no one does, and the whole thing works because where else do you want to be when you're Armanied out, looking great, and want someone appreciative to notice?

One Grant Avenue (at O'Farrell), San Francisco
Tel: 677-9010
Open Monday through Saturday 11:30 a.m. to 3 p.m.
Price: Moderate
Credit cards: AE, D, MC, V

You can grab an espresso or a cold bite at the espresso bar downstairs in the middle of the sales floor, or you can go upstairs to the mezzanine for a lively, very Italian meal that leans toward salads and lighter dishes at lunch and some pretty good pastas and risottos at dinner. All told, it's a sophisticated, casual experience, one to look forward to when you're in the neighborhood. Even if you can't afford the Armani jacket you've been eyeing, you can buoy up your spirits by having a little bite from Italy. And who knows what you might find on sale?

ERNIE'S

847 Montgomery Street (between Pacific and Jackson), San Francisco
Tel: 397-5969
Open Monday through Saturday 5:30 to 10 p.m.
Price: Expensive
Credit cards: AE, DC, MC, V

Ernie's reputation as one of the fine dining houses in San Francisco has taken some licks over the last ten years or so. It has lost one good chef after another and been unable to find an identity that bridges the French-Continental opulence of the past with the pared-down cuisine of the present. The prices are so high here that knowledgeable eaters expect something on the cutting edge, but that something has eluded Ernie's. You can get a perfectly decent, dressy meal here, just not an inspired one. However, the famous dining rooms have been tastefully remodeled and provide a luxurious and comfortable setting for that big night out.

Chef Hubert Keller put Fleur de Lys back on the map of important restaurants in the city when he took over this Michael Taylor–designed dining room in partnership with Maurice Rouas. I've had some wonderful meals here, and some pretty pedestrian ones when the kitchen seemed to be on automatic pilot, pumping out the complicated plates composed of many separate little elements without stopping along the way to taste. Keller loves the multifaceted composition, but he sometimes cannot draw them together. He's prolific and inventive, but I've always felt that a little editing would raise his cooking to a sublime level.

I have been treated like a queen in this romantic, softly lit, tented dining room, but also as if I were at the counter of a hash house. On my last visit we were waited on by a fellow so offhanded he would barely answer any questions. We had to pump him for descriptions of the specials and what was on the popular prix-fixe vegetarian dinner that night, whose very existence was only grudgingly acknowledged. This waiter proceeded to slap down bottles of wine and plates of food as if he were serving corned beef sandwiches. I admit that this kind of treatment in a restaurant that costs over $100 a person, and is supposed to be one of the two top French venues in San Francisco, may have colored my opinion of the food, but frankly, the meal that night really tasted like an afterthought.

When Keller is on, you might get foie gras set off stunningly by a compote of endive, Sauternes, and fresh ginger; spinach packages filled with chunks of fresh lobster flanking slices of salmon in saffron-scented butter

777 Sutter Street (between Taylor and Jones), San Francisco

Tel: 673-7779

Open Monday through Thursday 6 to 10 p.m., Friday and Saturday 5:30 to 10:30 p.m.

Price: Expensive

Credit cards: AE, DC, MC, V

sauce; tender veal on a bed of artichokes and wild mushrooms; or the ever-popular corn cakes concealing a thin slice of buttery salmon, the whole thing napped with chive beurre blanc and topped with golden caviar. Keller ought to banish the cardboardy, underripe, peeled cherry tomatoes that often appear as part of a vegetable garnish, and get rid of some of the fussiness on the dessert plates, which have become so elaborate you can't tell which dessert you ordered. And Maurice Rouas should certainly do a better job of weeding out his floor staff.

INDIA HOUSE

New location still to be determined at this writing.
Tel: 392-0744
Open for lunch Monday through Friday 11:30 a.m. to 2 p.m.; dinner Monday through Saturday 5:30 to 10 p.m.
Price: Moderate
Credit cards: AE, CB, DC, MC, V

I have a soft spot for this peculiar place, a holdout of Anglo-Indian decor and cooking. I love the hard-cooked egg curry brightly seasoned with vinegar and hot chilies; the tandoori-roasted kabobs of the highest quality; the juicy tandoori chicken; the rich, creamy chicken *makhanwala*, and some of the brightly seasoned vegetable curries. Start your meal with a cup of spicy *dal*, a traditional Indian legume soup, and be sure to order lots of *nan*, tandoori-baked bread.

The dining rooms of the old location looked like the haunt of a retired British officer once stationed in India, filled with memorabilia of the subcontinent: a Bengal tiger head, a huge leopard skin, intricate tapestries and rugs, a golden Buddha, and old photographs of Indian temples. Patrons sat in theatrically tall chairs and drank a Pimm's cup or a particularly delicious cocktail of brandy, champagne, and Cointreau served in a towering brass goblet. India House is such a relic that it just might catch on again, once it relocates.

Historic Jack's, dating from the turn of the century, epitomized the French-inspired San Francisco grill tradition. I use the past tense, because Jack's has frayed a bit in the sense that it doesn't execute half the dishes on its classic menu, still printed every day, with much conviction. But what is good there is really good, a model of its kind. No one does peeled big, plump asparagus with buttery hollandaise better, or juicy grilled thick mutton chops, or perfectly poached salmon with béarnaise, or deep-fried eggplant fingers that melt in your mouth, or a delicious celery Victor slathered with anchovies and vinaigrette. The dining room looks like it hasn't been touched since the 1950s, when the acoustic ceiling and the graying linoleum floor were installed. Otherwise, the high-ceilinged rooms have a classic pre-Earthquake look, with walls trimmed with gilt floral plasterwork, narrow shoulder-high mirrors, bronze coat hooks and wall sconces at every table, bentwood chairs, small tables covered with white linen, hanging schoolhouse lamps, and a tiny, ancient wood service bar at the front of the room. Curtains of a singular mustard color hang inside the front door to guard against the wind. For a long time women were not particularly welcome at lunch, but now they have been accepted by the older and sometimes hard-of-hearing waiters who have been there for decades. Lunch is the time to go, when the old movers and shakers of the city walk right over to their regular table, never saying a word to anyone, and are brought their martini and crab salad without delay. My one bit of advice is to order what the waiter says are specials. Whatever they are, they will be the best food prepared at Jack's that day.

615 Sacramento Street
(between Kearny
 and Montgomery),
San Francisco
Tel: 986-9854
Open weekdays 11:30 a.m.
to 9:30 p.m., Saturday 5 to
9:30 p.m.
Price: Moderate
Credit cards: AE, DC

453 Bush Street (between
Grant and Kearny),
San Francisco
Tel: 391-2233
Open Monday through
Saturday 11:30 a.m to
10:30 p.m.
Price: Moderate
Credit cards: AE, DC,
MC, V

What the food lacks in brilliance at Le Central, San Francisco's most authentic French brasserie, it makes up for in dependability and the exact replication of a beloved French form. The tiny crowded-together tables covered with butcher paper, the menu written in grease pencil on the mirrors, the celebrity lunchers like Herb Caen, Willie Brown, and pals strategically seated at tables in the front windows all give Le Central its cachet. When you're at the zinc bar sipping a Pernod, you can easily imagine yourself in Paris, and when you're at table, you'll be eating just what you might in the City of Light.

Start with a butterleaf salad with walnuts in a mustardy vinaigrette, tender braised leeks, or celery root rémoulade. Continue with roast chicken with watercress, a grilled tomato half, and *pommes frites*. My favorite dish here is the *boudin noir*, blood sausage from master charcutiers Marcel and Henri. The fat black aromatic sausages are sautéed to the bursting point, with lots of caramelized onions. The restaurant often has poached skate wing with capers in a vinegary butter sauce and prepares it perfectly. The desserts are brought in from Tarts, among others, who do a fine job on their buttery crusts and rich fillings, and the house Chardonnay comes from Chalone, a California winery inspired by the great winemakers of Burgundy. So all a diner's needs are met in a thoroughly French way.

For twenty-three years now MacArthur Park has been slowly smoking the best baby back ribs in town: moist, crisp, tangy, with a nicely balanced sweet-and-sour barbecue sauce served on the side. Half and whole slabs come with piles of skinny french fries and excellent coleslaw in a creamy, horseradish-spiked dressing. Other signature dishes include a tangle of deep-fried onion strings and, to my mind, a rather blandly dressed, if very popular, Cobb salad. Hearty American dishes like pork chops, juicy hamburgers, and sautéed calf's liver with bacon and onions are your best bets. The endless-red-brick building was once a Barbary Coast produce district warehouse. I like the glassed-in front dining room that looks out to the greenery of Jackson Square, away from a long bar that gets lots of noisy play after work.

607 Front Street (at Jackson),
San Francisco
Tel: 398-5700
Open for lunch Monday through Friday 11:30 a.m. to 3:30 p.m.; dinner Monday through Thursday 5 to 10 p.m., Friday and Saturday until 11 p.m., Sunday 4:30 to 10 p.m.
Price: Moderate
Credit cards: AE, CB, DC, MC, V

MASA'S

Julian Serrano's cooking is what I dream about when I want a three-star French meal. He's the only chef in the Bay Area who has taken on the challenge with absolute conviction and unfaltering standards. You have nothing to worry about here. From the moment you walk in the door, the restaurant falls into action, playing its role as dispenser of the highest form of culinary art.

Serrano is a purist. He starts by finding superior raw materials, from *haricots verts* to imported cheeses, from lobster, scallops, and wild ocean fish to game birds, foie gras, and lamb. He bases his dishes around the beautiful ingredients and makes a dish only if he is inspired by what he gets. His suppliers know not to send him anything that is not extraordinary, because price is not an

Hotel Vintage Court
648 Bush Street (between Powell and Stockton),
San Francisco
Tel: 989-7154
Open Tuesday through Saturday at 6 p.m.; last seating at 9:30 p.m.
Price: Expensive
Credit cards: AE, CB, DC, D, MC, V

object. When he conceives a dish, it uses the magic of classical French technique without ever taking a short cut. You can taste the dedication in his cooking. The stocks are fresh and full of flavor, so there never has to be over-reduction, over-salting, or intrusive seasoning. The vegetables, so tiny, yet always ripe and full of sweetness, are handled gently. The birds are marinated in fine wines; the cooking of them is brief but just enough, the outcome brilliant. You don't have to muddle over what to order here because every dish will deliver a little shock of surprise at its deliciousness. Some of my favorites over the years have been a ragout of vegetables, foie gras, and black truffles served in a deep, covered bowl so that when the top is removed at the table, the fragrance of truffles wafts up. It's a glorious dish. Ask for it in the winter. Another dazzling first course brings a napoleon of alternating potato and lobster slices in a sharp, saffron-scented vinaigrette, topped with a beehive of deep-fried leek threads. The whole composition seems to melt together with each bite in a miraculous way. The roast squab, served in its own juice, is rivaled only by Alice Waters's at Chez Panisse. I always have to have it. Lamb is velvety and moist under a coating of herb-scented bread crumbs. Tiny onion tarts, corn custards, and exquisite vegetables are chosen to accompany, but the star of each dish is always the main ingredient.

You can order a la carte, or you can pretty much make up your own prix-fixe meal at two different levels, or you may leave the decisions to the kitchen. No matter which way you go, you should discuss the meal with the sommelier who will match each course with a completely eclectic and fascinating selection of wines, glass by glass if you want, that might range from Sercial Madeira to local small producers to great Sauternes. My feeling is that you should walk into Masa's willing to spend $150 a person, just the way you do in a three-star in France (actually, you would probably spend half again as much in Paris), and put yourself in the hands of the staff, expense be damned—unless you know what you love. I am always tortured by the choice of ordering just two of my favorite dishes with a great bottle of wine, and finishing with the best cheeses in the city, or trying new combinations of food and wine that always prove to be a revelation. Either avenue leads to heaven.

One problem for some people is the way the reservations are booked, either early, between 6 or 6:30, or late, starting at 9, because the kitchen does not want a full dining room of people all ordering at the same time. When you taste the beauty of this cooking, with every single dish started practically from scratch and cooked to order, you'll understand why.

ORIGINAL JOE'S

Once you've tasted one of Original Joe's famous three-quarter-pound hamburger steaks formed from coarsely ground beef, coated in chopped onions, and cooked medium rare on the griddle, you'll brave the neighborhood to eat here. This restaurant has been cranking out quintessential Joe's-type food for over a half century: inexpensive, plentiful, of amazingly high quality. It's a cuisine based on beef (which the kitchen butchers itself from sides); sourdough bread; precooked pasta in meat sauce; fresh, if much-cooked, vegetables; and some daily long-cooked braised dishes. The way the bread is handled, for example—hollowed out, buttered, and grilled for hamburgers; sliced and bakery fresh with lots of pats of cold salted butter for the tables; pressed and griddled for gigantic ham and cheese sandwiches— teaches you something about the practical wisdom of

144 Taylor Street (between Eddy and Turk), San Francisco
Tel: 775-4877
Open daily 10:30 a.m. to 12:30 a.m.
Price: Inexpensive
Credit cards: D, MC, V

San Francisco's culinary past. Once you've made it to the front door (there are attended parking lots directly next door and across the street) on one of the diciest blocks in the Tenderloin, you can sit in one of the commodious ancient booths or grab a seat at the counter in front of the cooking line. Some people like to hide away in the dark, smoky barroom with booths. Original Joe's feeds a lot of older neighborhood residents every day. They order one of the reasonably priced dishes, eat a third of it, and take the rest home to have for dinner and breakfast the next day. To tell you the truth, that's what I do, too. I'm addicted to that cold hamburger steak.

PACIFIC

Pan Pacific Hotel
500 Post Street (at Mason),
San Francisco
Tel: 771-8600
Open for breakfast Monday through Friday 6:30 to 11 a.m., Saturday 7 to 11 a.m., Sunday brunch 10 a.m. to 2 p.m; lunch Monday through Saturday 11:30 a.m. to 2:30 p.m.; dinner nightly 5:30 to 9:30 p.m.
Price: Expensive
Credit cards: AE, CB, DC, MC, V

The airy mezzanine dining room, with a view up to the atrium ceiling and through big windows that look out to Post Street, offers a generous, nicely prepared California menu at both lunch and dinner, noteworthy for its use of good vegetables and other fine local ingredients. Though the menu is about to be revamped by ex-Masa chef Takayoshi Kawai, who had just taken over as of this writing, I have liked the freshly baked breads, crusty miniature crab cakes served with salad, beef tenderloin with truffled mashed potatoes; at lunch, warm duck *confit* salad, and a delicious Boursin omelette with pancetta and a salad on the side. Lunch is very reasonable considering the level of luxury and service, really the same price for lunch as anywhere else in the area. The prix-fixe menu is now served all evening.

The energy behind this alluring modern Italian restaurant comes from Gianni Fassio, whose family owned the original Blue Fox a block away. In a complete break from family tradition, he insists upon serving the dishes he ate in Italy during his years as an international accountant there. This means house-baked Italian breads and bread sticks; a whole range of tasty *antipasti*; pizzas from a wood-fired oven; house-made pastas with rustic, long-cooked game sauces, or delicate ravioli moistened with a little butter and sage; huge grilled veal chops; and braised rabbit. Polenta is preferred over potatoes; a raw, fresh tomato sauce with arugula replaces humdrum cooked tomato sauce; and the desserts are really Italian and quite wonderful, like a whole roasted peach filled with mascarpone and sprinkled with amaretto cookie crumbs. The large restaurant admirably makes practically everything they serve on the premises, including a large variety of breads and focaccias, which they supply to their *paninoteca* (Italian sandwich shop) and cafe around the corner on Montgomery Street.

The theme of the Palio, Siena's fabled bareback horserace that takes place in the central *piazza* two times a year, is manifested in colorful banners hanging from the ceiling. The expansive modern concrete and glass space is broken up by three glassed-in display kitchens, a smart bar that makes for the perfect rendezvous after work, and comfortable upholstered booths and linen-covered tables. You can get all sorts of tasty Italian tidbits at the bar, like a crisp *frittura di mare* of squid, tiny shrimp, smelt, and sardines, or a plate of tomatoes, basil, and real buffalo-milk mozzarella. Palio has adapted itself to the needs of its neighborhood, offering a very

640 Sacramento Street (between Montgomery and Kearny), San Francisco

Tel: 395-9800

Open Monday through Thursday 11:30 a.m. to 9:30 p.m., Friday until 10:30 p.m., Saturday 5 to 10:30 p.m.

Price: Moderate

Credit cards: AE, CB, DC, D, MC, V

reasonable, quickly served lunch and a more interesting and leisurely dinner service. When ridiculously expensive white truffles come to town, or fresh porcini, or very rare, aged, balsamic vinegar, you can depend on Palio to put on a fabulous special meal at terrific prices. Fassio sees his restaurant as an outpost of Italian culture, and everyone benefits.

POSTRIO

545 Post Street (between Taylor and Mason), San Francisco
Tel: 776-7825
Open for breakfast Monday through Friday 7 to 10 a.m., brunch Saturday and Sunday 9 a.m. to 2 p.m.; lunch Monday through Friday 11:30 a.m. to 2 p.m.; dinner Sunday through Wednesday 5:30 to 10 p.m., Thursday through Saturday until 10:30 p.m.; upstairs cafe open 11 a.m. to midnight
Price: Expensive
Credit cards: AE, DC, D, MC, V

Just when I am settling in at Postrio, knowing which dishes to order and basking in the always impeccable, intelligent service, the two great originating chefs, Annie and David Gingrass, are leaving to open their own restaurant in San Francisco. As of this writing they are still at Postrio. Their departure date is unspecified, and a year has been talked about. I'm sure that Wolfgang Puck, the third partner in the "trio" has someone else up his sleeve, but the Gingrasses have made this restaurant their own after what I thought was a somewhat shaky start. San Francisco tastes are different from those in Los Angeles, and the food at Postrio started out too gimmicky, eclectic, and wild. The combinations seemed thrown together for the sake of effect rather than flavor, and when the huge, cavernous restaurant was mobbed almost from the day it opened, the kitchen had trouble executing. Investors were yammering about profits, and the kitchen staff was cut to bad effect. But the Gingrasses hung in there. Gradually they got the situation under control, then they started making the menu theirs, simplifying, taking inspiration from local products, and making their own spectacular ingredients like David's cured salami, smoked liverwurst, and smoked salmon. The dishes took on new focus while still being inventive and Puckish, if you will. Annie came up with a Santa Rosa plum sauce for Sonoma foie gras one spring evening, and it was one of the best things I've ever eaten; the plums had a subtle, haunting perfume. David's charcuterie plates taste like nothing you've ever encountered. Each tissue-thin slice has its own unique character and texture. The delicious squab does not get lost on the plate anymore, but deservedly stars in a dish that supports it. The Gingrasses have discovered the Northern California cult of the ingredient, and their cooking has taken a new direction. Annie, in particular, is a technician, and she is not afraid to take on difficult ingredients like sweetbreads and game, or tricky constructions like a large ravioli wrapped around a quail egg that spills out to enrich the sauce when you cut into it. When she balances this fearlessness with the Gingrasses' solid midwestern taste, the outcome becomes something provocative.

The expansive Pat Kuleto–designed dining room, with a completely open kitchen, practically roars. The restaurant starts at street level with an always-packed bar with its own wood-burning pizza oven and menu, then lowers a level to a mezzanine that is a bit quieter for dining, then cascades down a dramatic staircase into the main dining hall. That staircase has provided an entrance for many a costume, many a celebrity, many an indiscreet pairing. Postrio is fun in that way. It's always full because Prescott Hotel guests get preferential reservations. You have to call way in advance to get a prime-time table, but regulars sneak in. When anyone glamorous comes to town from Los Angeles they always hit the Puck restaurant. For locals, its location near Union Square makes it a natural for a pretheater dinner or a downtown lunch.

RUBICON

558 Sacramento Street
(between Sansome
and Montgomery),
San Francisco
Tel: 434-4100
Open for lunch Monday
through Friday 11:30 a.m. to
2:30 p.m.; dinner Monday
through Thurday 5:30 to
10:30 p.m., Friday and
Saturday until 11 p.m.
Price: Expensive
Credit cards: AE, DC, MC, V

I wonder if Rubicon, the new restaurant from New York's Drew Nieporent, with backing from local celebs like Francis Ford Coppola, will take hold in San Francisco. Nieporent made his reputation on several downtown restaurants in Manhattan—Montrachet and the Tribeca Grill—and physically Rubicon reminds me of the latter, with its location in a converted brick firehouse in the heart of the Financial District. While the downstairs with its small bar and cozy tables evokes some of the spirit of the building, the larger dining room upstairs feels empty and faceless, just a red brick space with earthquake bracing. In New York, Tribeca Grill's free-standing brick warehouse with lots of windows has much more character—and the food is more casual. At Rubicon, young Traci Des Jardins has put together a menu of tasty, if rich, dishes that remind me of Nieporent's more upscale Montrachet. She incorporates all the most interesting vegetables she can find (one spring menu was sprinkled with favas, fresh peas, chanterelles, asparagus, spring onions, leeks, bitter greens, rhubarb, fennel, radishes, Portobello mushrooms, and Jerusalem artichokes) in a list that somehow reads more intriguingly than it tastes. The flavor comes from butter sauces in typical New York/French fashion, but unlike the best examples of this style, the food seems a bit dulled by all the richness instead of opulent. The restaurant is still in its first year, and an operation needs to go through four seasons of business just to figure out what works.

The wine program, under the direction of Larry Stone, is ambitious and pricy. (The restaurant gets its name from Niebaum-Coppola's blended red wine called Rubicon.) I have enjoyed sitting at one end of the small bar, having a glass of good wine and eating some small plates of food, like a lovely presentation of tuna Carpaccio with radish vinaigrette, and some velvety house-cured salmon draped over shaved fennel and onion salad with a crisp potato pancake. Also arresting, and very buttery, has been a goat cheese and leek tart served with a tangy herb salad. My favorite main course has been a loin of lamb with bright flavored Provençal accompaniments. It will be interesting to see how Rubicon develops. There's no lack of talent here, but it needs to be marshaled. Work needs to be done on the physical space upstairs, and the service staff simply needs more training.

SAM'S GRILL

I include historic Sam's because I love the way it looks. The ancient wood-paneled dining room, the private cubicles with buzzers to summon the waiters, the solid-looking facade broken only by a small rectangular window covered with blinds, conjure up the old days in San Francisco when Financial District office buildings emptied every day at lunchtime and people sat down to real noontime meals. Sam's was one of the most popular, masculine, no-nonsense grill rooms, and actually, it still is. Order only local fish like sand dabs, petrale, and salmon. Have a seafood salad or cold asparagus with mustard sauce, and a few slices of sourdough. Have a cocktail or a bottle of wine and there you are. Don't stray much farther than this. The restaurant closes early, and the liveliest time is at lunch.

374 Bush Street (at Kearny),
San Francisco
Tel: 421-0594
Open Monday through
Friday 11 a.m. to 8:30 p.m.
Price: Moderate
Credit cards: AE, DC,
MC, V

704 Sutter Street (at Taylor),
San Francisco
Tel: 771-0803
Open Monday through Friday
11 a.m. to 10 p.m., Saturday
and Sunday 4 to 10 p.m.
Price: High moderate to
expensive
Credit cards: AE, D, MC, V

A new adjunct to an excellent, inexpensive Japanese restaurant that has been open for over sixteen years (called Sanraku), the Four Seasons puts on imaginative and delicious *kaiseki* meals each night in a special dining room next door. The *kaiseki* dinners must be reserved ahead, at which time the menu can be discussed with their young chef, Hiro Hattori. He might suggest a whole fish or crab, an all-seafood menu, or a vegetarian menu, all within the *kaiseki* (or formal Japanese meal) framework. Simply left to his own devices, he will put out one of the most exquisite, lush, varied Japanese repasts you will ever taste. Sanraku Four Seasons is a rare opportunity to taste a new kind of Japanese cooking, some of it gently influenced by the West, in a completely traditional form.

The linen-covered Western-style tables in a peaceful gray and beige dining room are set only with red lacquered place mats and a pair of black wooden chopsticks. A few intriguing brush paintings of geometric shapes and a ceramic pot are the only decorations in the room: The food and its presentation on elegant pottery appropriate to the form of each dish creates the aesthetic. The eight-course dinner always consists of *zensai* (appetizer), *suimono* (soup), *sashimi* (raw fish), *kuchinaoshi* (which translates to "a little break"), *agemono* (fried dish), *yakimono* (broiled dish), rice and pickles with miso soup on a tray, then dessert. Even with this progression, delineated in a typed-out menu, the meal comes as a surprise.

The appetizer arrives in three tiny bowls, each with a sparkling fish or vegetable salad. Next might come a seafood soup in a clay bowl, scented with shiitakes and capped with a delicate egg custard; or clear broth in a tiny teapot with a lilliputian saucer from which to drink it. The *sashimi* course always turns out to be an East-West creation served on a large round plate: slices of raw tuna and halibut perhaps flanked by a salad of red and green seaweeds and tiny Western lettuces in a delicious soy and rice wine vinegar dressing. The "little break" might bring a unique pair of sushi, wrapped in grilled eggplant, or an emerald-green avocado with pieces of sweet eel inside. The fried course brings tempura; one evening the pieces looked as if they were encased in tiny pearls. At this point in the *kaiseki* meal, light eaters might call it quits, but how could they pass up a small piece of butter-tender fillet of beef with *ponzu* sauce? With the meat, a tray of rice bowls, pickles, and steaming miso broth is brought. Somehow, as full as you are, eating these foods cleanses and refreshes the palate for dessert. The last course will be light and cool, perhaps a poached pear in honey syrup or a small dish of green tea ice cream marbleized with a gorgeous dark green tea sauce and served in a turquoise ceramic square. Cold Otokoyama sake served in wineglasses goes wonderfully with the meal.

These *kaiseki* meals offer all the lyricism and art of Japanese cooking along with a certain kind of Western exuberance. Though each course is elegant, they add up to generous, almost hearty meals. Unlike some other *kaiseki* meals I have had at twice the price in a nearby hotel, the focus is on freshness and flavor, not garnish, and the presentations seem organic to the food. Chef Hattori shows a deep understanding of the poetry of his cuisine while still addressing the appetite.

SEARS FINE FOODS

439 Powell Street (between
Post and Sutter),
San Francisco
Tel: 986-1160
Open Wednesday through
Sunday 6:30 a.m. to 3:30 p.m.
Price: Inexpensive
No credit cards

This beloved downtown breakfast and lunch spot remains one of the best places in the city for an old-fashioned American breakfast. Always start with a huge fresh-fruit cup of high-quality fruit marinated in fresh orange juice, a must order here. If you're a one-fruit person, you can get bowls of berries in season, orange slices, juicy melons, papaya, or a large baked Rome Beauty apple served with cream. Then move on to Sears's "famous 18 Swedish pancakes," six baby stacks of airy pancakes the size and thickness of half dollars that have real character; or Sears's crisp dark-brown waffles with tender eggy interiors; or French toast made of well-soaked sourdough bread served with a small cup of Sears' own strawberry preserves, really a barely sweetened compote. The Canadian bacon truly is "the best obtainable anywhere" as the menu boasts, and the smoked country sausage, made especially for Sears and served in crisp patties, is excellent, too. At lunch, after an egg salad sandwich or a BLT, have fresh strawberry shortcake or a fresh-fruit deep-dish pie that comes in a glass cereal bowl filled to the top. If anyone staying around Union Square asks you to meet them for breakfast, do yourself a favor and suggest Sears. It's also a big favorite with kids.

The luxurious dining room in this Financial District hotel is one of the most underrated eating places in the city. The kitchen, under the guidance of young chefs Ken Oringer, Michele Sampson, and Cheryl Pike, with consultation from the ebullient international cooking teacher and chef Ken Hom, puts out some remarkable East-West creations, noteworthy for their sound technique and intriguing combinations. I will never forget a black truffle meal that Silks hosted to honor France's most distinguished truffle broker, Jacques Pebeyre. The chefs came up with truffled egg rolls; beautiful packages of salmon wrapped in Chinese cabbage in a truffled beurre blanc; tomato and lemongrass consommé with truffles; and lobster and truffle ravioli in a green onion butter. From first courses to desserts, the Silks chefs come up with lovely cross-cultural ideas that work on the plate. A number of very successful chefs around town, including Kirk Webber from the singular Cafe Kati, are alumni and have developed their own East-West vernaculars. One rarely thinks about going to a formal hotel dining room in this town full of vibrant, independently owned restaurants, but Silks really merits consideration.

Mandarin Oriental Hotel
222 Sansome Street
(between Pine and
California), San Francisco
Tel: 986-2020
Open for breakfast Monday
through Friday 6 to 10 a.m.;
lunch 11:30 a.m. to 2 p.m.;
dinner nightly 6 to 10 p.m.;
weekend brunch 7 a.m. to
2 p.m.
Price: Expensive
Credit cards: AE, CB, DC, D,
MC, V

475 Sacramento Street
(between Battery and
Sansome), San Francisco
Tel: 296-8696 (info 296-8191)
Open for lunch Monday
through Friday 11:30 a.m. to
2:30 p.m.; dinner nightly 5:30
to 10 p.m.; music Wednesday
through Saturday nights
Price: Moderate
Credit cards: AE, DC, MC, V

The electrifying energy behind this New World tapas restaurant comes from the modern cultural crosscurrents at play in the Bay Area. The decor is unrelentingly austere, a multilevel cement and metal landscape that could be in Milan, Madrid, or Mexico City. The spritely menu of tapas and paellas draws not only from Spain, but from all over Latin America. And the crowd, especially starting about nine at night, is as exotic as you can find in San Francisco. When a hot Latin band plays, the lower dining area is cleared of tables and dancing takes over. Tango, samba, and salsa aficionados of all ages, many of whom have worked out suave routines, perform, fueled by one of the tastiest drinks in the city, Rio-style *caipirinha* made with Brazilian *cachaca*, fresh lime, and sugar. They are dynamite!

Before the dancing begins there is much good eating to do. Some of my favorites on the long tapas menu are the simplest dishes like fried creamy-textured purple potato slices with fiery Spanish-style aïoli, or a plate of exquisite, smoky serrano ham with manchego cheese, a dab of sweet pepper salsa, and some warm flat bread. House-made chorizo sausage comes on a tasty bed of black beans, and crisp cod cakes called *buñuelos de bacalao* are lifted by the delicious house salsa. The gazpacho is excellent, though not served with the traditional Spanish garnishes. Don't forget to order a plate of tiny marinated organic Spanish olives.

Spanish purists may be shocked by the eclecticism of the tapas and the nontraditional presentation of dishes like paella, but the food works on its own terms. This is one place where you can ask your waiter for recommendations. They not only know most of the dishes well, but are eager to send out the kitchen's favorites of the moment. The staff here is first-rate: professional, enthusiastic, polite, and knowledgeable. They contribute to everyone's good time.

SQUARE ONE

One feels invited to eat at Square One, personally invited by Joyce Goldstein, whose presence in the restaurant is felt everywhere. Her cooking is inspired by the home kitchens of the Mediterranean; it is nurturing, full of broad, appealing, bright flavors and comforting textures. A visit to Square One connects you to the traditions behind the cooking of many cultures, and you feel satisfied in a primal way after eating there. Some of the most vibrant dishes are Middle Eastern and North African—the seafood couscous, the Moroccan salads and tajines—though everyone loves Goldstein's Italian cooking, her unique paella, her Brazilian *feijoada*, her grilled lamb and beef with buttery potato gratins, her miraculously tasty low-sodium and low-fat heart-healthy dishes, her lusty vegetarian dishes. The restaurant is driven by her unstoppable desire to feed, teach, satisfy, and embrace, like a brainy Jewish mother who has channeled her deepest instincts into the art of cooking.

The wines are always a major part of the experience; a tremendous amount of effort is put into the wine list and the pairing of different wines with food. A bottle of great wine can be the focus of a meal here; sommelier Peter Granoff is a genius when it comes to finding just the right bottle for a table full of food. No avenue of service has been left unexplored. The smart bar offers its own menu of savory small dishes, like

190 Pacific Avenue (at Front), San Francisco

Tel: 788-1110

Open for lunch Monday through Friday 11:30 a.m. to 2:30 p.m.; dinner Monday through Friday 5:30 to 10 p.m., Friday and Saturday until 10:30 p.m., Sunday 5 to 9:30 p.m.

Price: Expensive

Credit cards: AE, DC, MC, V

Goldstein's incomparable smoked-trout mousse with freshly toasted croutons. A small, charming private dining room with a wonderful view of Jackson Square park has been the site of many a charity dinner as well as private gatherings. Over the years she has personalized the large, airy, modern space, giving it a warmer, more inviting feel like that of her own well-designed home. Square One sprung from a compelling, insightful vision; it's a world-beat restaurant at the most professional, skillful, awe-inspiring level. No culinary visit to San Francisco would be complete without a taste of Goldstein's international, ethnically inspired fare.

TADICH GRILL

240 California Street
(between Front and Battery),
San Francisco
Tel: 391-2373
Open Monday through Friday
11 a.m. to 9 p.m., Saturday
11:30 a.m. to 9 p.m.
Price: Moderate
Credit cards: MC, V

A Yugoslavian family has run this historic fish house since the turn of the century, grilling fresh fish over mesquite charcoal and cranking out a fascinating menu printed daily all these years in offset type. The menus themselves are souvenirs, documents of culinary history, full of dinosaurs such as lobster Newberg, halibut Florentine, and deviled crab. The best way to proceed is to ask your crusty waiter what fish has come in fresh that day and order it simply charcoal-grilled or pan-fried. What a pleasure it is to hang your coat on a brass hook at Tadich's, grab a seat at the long, oval wooden counter, and dig into a fresh seafood salad slathered with an excellent Louie sauce, and a plate of buttery "griddled" sand dabs or rex sole served with Tadich's gigantic fried potatoes. The rex sole, which are small, flavorful local fish, are also delicious charcoal grilled, eaten with mounds of Tadich's unique and addictive tartar sauce thickened with sieved potato. The waiters will quickly fillet them for you, an old-fashioned luxury. Creamed spinach, sautéed spinach, thick clam chowder, and poached salmon with chopped egg sauce are other Tadich favorites. The wine list is simple and cheap—most people still have cocktails here. For dessert, there are huge baked Rome Beauty apples and rice custard pudding, which work perfectly after the straightforward meals.

The wonderful-looking dining room is paneled in ancient dark wood, with compartments that enclose small linen-covered tables and bentwood chairs. The original pressed-plaster ceiling, a white-tiled floor, and a busy wooden counter with wooden chairs that swivel on pedestals set the scene for a timeless experience, especially since most of the uniformed waiters have been here forever. There's always a crowd at the door having a drink at the small bar and waiting for one of the not-so-plentiful tables. However, if you don't want to wait, you can usually get a seat immediately at the counter, where the stools turn over quickly and the regulars are gracious about moving over to accommodate a pair who want to sit together.

YANK SING

Seen through big plate-glass windows, Yank Sing looks like the typical modern, upscale Financial District restaurant, until the carts laden with exotic Chinese delicacies wheel into the picture. Then you know you're looking into a different culinary territory entirely. Yank Sing is one of the best dim sum houses in the city. The variety seems never ending, and every piece is meticulously made from high-quality ingredients: the sweetest-tasting shellfish, the freshest Chinese herbs and vegetables, the cleanest frying oil. The kitchen shows particular strength in everyone's favorite part of the dim sum meal, dumplings. The translucent shrimp-stuffed *har gow* boast pristine shrimp. The liberal use of black mushrooms adds a wild, meaty flavor to vegetarian

427 Battery Street (between Clay and Washington), San Francisco
Tel: 362-1640
Open Monday through Friday 11 a.m. to 3 p.m., Saturday and Sunday 10 a.m. to 4 p.m.
Price: Moderate
Credit cards: AE, CB, DC, MC, V

dumplings seasoned with pickled turnip and to chicken dumplings with bamboo shoots. The pork-filled *sui mai* are savory and toothsome; the dumplings filled with pea shoots and black mushrooms absolutely sublime. In addition to these, you will see at least twenty other tempting little plates or bamboo steamers of food being wheeled by, including extraordinarily crisp, lacy, deep-fried taro balls with creamy taro and pork interiors; deep-fried crab fingers; and rich deep-fried shrimp toasts. Henry Chan, the gracious owner of Yank Sing, has always tried to set his dim sum house apart by experimenting with the form. He started serving individual portions of Peking duck with soft white buns, plum sauce, and green onions; a Japanese-inspired tidbit of deep-fried fresh water chestnut, bacon, and green onion on a toothpick; and stunning little plates of fiery, strongly sauced Chinese eggplant, all firsts for dim sum houses. From a small menu of noodle dishes, try tender noodles with Chinese chives and tiny enoki mushrooms, a taste and texture sensation and a great way to end a dim sum meal. For dessert nab a saucer of flaky-crusted egg custard tarts while they are still warm from the oven. Yank Sing does them better than anyone else.

In addition to the comfortable surroundings and all the lovely food, the staff at Yank Sing shows particular graciousness and efficiency. You are quickly recognized as a regular and guided to special dishes. First-timers are treated patiently and always given a bit of help if they need it. A dim sum specialist—no other meals are served—Yank Sing takes a great interest in teaching about, refining, and expanding the service. Equal numbers of Chinese and Westerners fill the dining rooms, and at Yank Sing, everyone is equally pleased.

CAFES

BRASSERIE SAVOY

This may be the most authentic-looking brasserie on either side of the Atlantic. Parisians do not do it better. The woven chairs, marble tables, marble floors, zinc bar, ceiling fans, banquettes, and waiters in long white aprons come straight out of the sixth arrondissement. The kitchen has had its ups and downs, but as an early-evening cafe and bar, a place to meet for a drink, or to have a bite before the theater, the setting always works its magic.

580 Geary Street (at Jones),
San Francisco
Tel: 474-8686
Open Sunday through
Thursday 5:30 to 10:30 p.m.,
Friday and Saturday until
11:30 p.m.
Credit cards: AE, MC, V

CAFE CAPRICCIO

A tiny but perfect cafe in the Italian tradition, Cafe Capriccio makes the most satisfying coffee from the best beans in the world, Illy Espresso. Intensity of flavor, creaminess, and full-bodied aroma without any bitterness is the hallmark of espresso made with these ultra-expensive coffee beans from Trieste. Whenever a cafe or restaurant chooses them, you know they understand coffee. Not only is the coffee perfect here, the setting transports you to jewellike cafes in Venice, Florence, and Rome, lined in dark wood, furnished with marble tables, and centered around a marble counter. A small, very Italian menu posted on a blackboard includes focaccia sandwiches of ricotta and prosciutto, or salami and tomatoes, fresh little vegetable salads, and a house-made soup, all of which match the surroundings.

701 Market Street (at Third
Street), San Francisco
Tel: 243-8252
Open weekdays 7:30 a.m. to
7 p.m., Saturday 11 a.m.
to 5 p.m.
No credit cards

CAFÉ DE LA PRESSE

352 Grant Avenue
(at Bush), San Francisco
Tel: 398-2680
Open daily 7 a.m. to 11 p.m.
Credit cards: AE, MC, V

Sitting at one of the outdoor tables that hug the building at Grant and Bush across from the entrance to Chinatown makes you part of the international tourist circuit that flows by this very corner. I like to dive in, if even for an hour, at Café de la Presse, which is next to the groovily decorated Triton Hotel (check out the lobby). The cafe not only serves a decent *salade niçoise* and a generous prosciutto and melon plate with a good baguette, but it also houses one of the best international newspaper and magazine stands in the city, so you can buy your *Herald Tribune* and pretend you're an American in Paris, or your *Le Monde* and pretend you're French. Two drawbacks: the waiters are sweet-natured but incompetent, and the Rhône and Beaujolais taste identical, as if they were bought at a French supermarket, a bit of authenticity I could do without.

CAFFÈ MIO

209 O'Farrell Street (at Powell),
San Francisco
Tel: 392-4112
Open Monday through Saturday
6:30 a.m. to 7 p.m., Sunday
7 a.m. to 6 p.m.
No credit cards

I include this minuscule espresso bar because of its consistently excellent Mr. Espresso coffee, rich and aromatic without being bitter, served with steamed low-fat milk that somehow tastes fine with it here. The location of Caffè Mio on the crowded corner of Powell and O'Farrell, with its high-density parade of tourists, shoppers, downtown workers, crazies, and street people, intrigues me. I hold onto my bags when I sit at the one outdoor table next to the shoeshine stand under a canopy, but I covet this table as the best spot to take in the city at its most urban. I find it a refreshing break during a day devoted to buying a skirt.

This espresso bar in the middle of an Armani store could have been transplanted from Milan. The coffee is excellent, and all the supporting *panini*, biscotti, and rolls are just what you expect from an authentic Italian cafe. Rumor has it that Giorgio Armani himself oversaw both the design and the menu, though it is being run by a local operator. Whoever's behind it, the Armani espresso bar is one of my favorite coffee venues downtown.

One Grant Avenue (at O'Farrell), San Francisco
Tel: 677-9010
Open Monday through Saturday 11 a.m. to 7 p.m., Sunday until 6 p.m.
Credit cards: AE, M, V

BARS

BIX

Doug Biederbeck, the genial host-owner (along with Real Restaurants partners) of Bix, has made this *soigné*, intimate restaurant and bar, hidden away in an alley off Jackson Square, into one of the most happening venues in San Francisco. He is a true boulevardier, a man about town who knows what's going on in every spot in the city because he makes the rounds. He throws a sophisticated affair himself every night in his resplendent Art Deco quarters featuring a collagelike mural over the bar, an intimate mezzanine for diners, and a jazz trio holding forth on the main floor. Everyone stops by Bix when they're having a night on the town. It's also a popular Financial District lunch spot, especially when

56 Gold Street (off Montgomery, between Pacific and Jackson), San Francisco
Tel: 433-6300
Open for lunch Monday through Friday 11:30 a.m. to 11 p.m., Friday and Saturday until midnight, Sunday 6 to 10 p.m.
Credit cards: AE, D

the stock market is heading straight up and bottles of champagne are popping. The small menu has its strengths and weaknesses, but I have always liked a crisp chicken hash; an updated Waldorf salad with apples, walnuts, and blue cheese; and some crunchy potato-leek pancakes with smoked salmon. For dessert, the kitchen makes old-fashioned bananas Foster, bananas heated in butter, brown sugar, and rum, served with vanilla ice cream, a dessert that comes as close to being an after-dinner drink as it possibly can.

LIBERTÉ

248 Sutter Street (between Grant and Kearny), San Francisco
Tel: 391-1555
Open for lunch Monday through Friday 11:30 a.m. to 2:30 p.m.; dinner Monday through Thursday 5:30 to 10 p.m. , Friday and Saturday until 11 p.m., Sunday 5 to 9 p.m.
Credit cards: AE, DC, D, MC, V

Both in its former identity as Lascaux, and its current one as Liberté, this resonant cellar dining room has always had the most remarkable decor: warm, exciting, mysterious, comfortable. I have never been in a basement space so welcoming and handsome. Instead of working against the idea of a cellar, the designers of Lascaux celebrated it and no expense was spared. They took inspiration from the famous French cave paintings and used the imagined colors and pictures as a motif, creating one huge rustic room with a handsome open kitchen behind a marble counter, a working fireplace with copper pots hanging over a gas-fueled fire, and a very hip bar with live jazz—the perfect use for a cave. Unfortunately, the kitchen was never able to keep up with such a large dining room, and Lascaux closed. Recently, the place reopened as Liberté. The decor was changed just a bit, with an abstract Statue of Liberty flame taking the place of the etched cave paintings, and chef Elka Gilmore was hired to put together one of her wildly eclectic personal menus.

Since I love this room so much, I drop by the bar for a drink and a dish or two that I like. Though I have tried a number of exotic-sounding creations on the menu, the follow-through has not been rigorous. Sometimes one part of a dish will be exquisite and another will be unappetizing, as if Gilmore can't quite live up to her imagination. I am a fan of her dish called Live Scallops Ossetra Caviar, tissue-thin slices of raw scallop marinated in a shalloty vinaigrette, served with a few tiny leaves of lettuce sprinkled with eggs of caviar, an absolutely divine conception at a reasonable price, I might add. I also like the nuggets of deep-fried sweetbreads on a plate scattered with fava beans and cèpes in a buttery sauce, but the semolina gnocchi that came with them were so redolent of strong cheese that I pushed them aside. So, I order lightly at Liberté. I get excellent service at the bar from bartenders who make perfect drinks in elegant glassware and know how to describe all the wines on the list. Such an evocative space should be enjoyed, and the best way to do it is by using it as a bar.

DELICATESSENS/TAKE-OUT

BLONDIE'S PIZZA

63 Powell Street (at Ellis), San Francisco
Tel: 982-6168
Open Monday through Friday 10:30 a.m. to 9 p.m., Saturday 11 a.m. to 9 p.m., Sunday 11 a.m. to 8 p.m.
No credit cards

See listing, page 524.

Big, thick, floppy slices of pizza, slathered with cheese, tomato sauce, and pepperoni move out the door so fast at this sidewalk pizzeria that the pizza makers can barely keep up. You will always find a hot slice of pizza ready to go, usually two or three different kinds if you don't want to wait for that special slice. Blondie's makes likable fast-food pizza: One slice fills you up, it's not too oily, and the price is right.

MACY'S CELLAR

Union Square (Stockton and O'Farrell), San Francisco
Tel: 397-3333
Open Monday through Saturday 10 a.m. to 8 p.m., Sunday 11 a.m. to 7 p.m.
Credit cards: AE, MC, V

This veritable food hall does a huge business as a quick meal stop. People choose goodies from three tiers of prepared salads of every sort, particularly Asian and Italian noodle salads, cold chicken, piroshkis from House of Piroshki (see page 483), eggplant lasagne, some good-looking premade "wreath sandwiches" sliced off an egg bread circle, and Wolfgang Puck frozen pizzas heated to order in a pizza oven. Concessions include a frozen-yogurt bar, a full Boudin Cafe and bread counter, and a Tom's cookie stand, where the smell of warm cookies draws people like magnets. Many square feet of chocolates fill up one side, ranging from Godiva to Macy's own oversized versions of turtles and honeycombs. A small and pricy California wine department seemingly is there for show, along with cheese and sausage stations that offer nothing out of the ordinary.

The unique draw here is a counter devoted to Petrossian caviar and smoked salmon at lofty prices. (See California Sunshine, page 463, or Polarica, page 462.) When Petrossian had a monopoly on Russian caviar, perhaps these products were worth the extra expense, but now other importers are setting up their own caviar stations and bringing in a fine product. My philosophy is when you eat caviar you want enough to really taste it—I mean an ounce per person at least, which makes Petrossian ridiculously expensive. Of course, if price is no object, just give Neiman a call and they'll send it right out. A small California and European wine department is pricy; the breads come from Bakers of Paris; the cheese is not special, and the pâtés are not particularly vibrant.

150 Stockton Street (at Geary), fifth floor, San Francisco
Tel: 362-3900
Open Monday, Thursday, Friday 10 a.m. to 8 p.m., Tuesday and Wednesday until 6 p.m., Saturday until 7 p.m., Sunday noon to 6 p.m.
Credit cards: AE

What I do love about Neiman's food service is the Rotunda, a dining room just beyond the food department (open Monday through Saturday 11 a.m. to 5 p.m.). Here, two tiers of tables rim a glittering glass dome trimmed in gold, reinstalled in 1981 after being dismantled and restored on the East Coast to its original brilliance. Light pours in through the dome, but diners are nestled in commodious booths around the circumference, sipping cocktails and glasses of champagne, popping the famous hot popovers, devouring amusing lobster club sandwiches, yet saving room for a pecan ball with hot fudge sauce for dessert. A view of Union Square's palm tree fronds, now at eye level, and perusal of fashion models making the rounds add an extra dimension of fun. Of all the department store dining alternatives, Neiman's Rotunda is certainly the most festive.

NOB HILL CHICKEN AND RIBS

447 Stockton Street (between

Sutter and Bush),

San Francisco

Tel: 421-5020

Open Monday through Friday

10 a.m. to 3 p.m.

No credit cards

Across the street from the Sutter-Stockton city parking garage, right next to the Stockton tunnel, is a funny little place that makes one of the most delectable pieces of food in the city: a warm rotisserie chicken sandwich. You order it at a hofbraulike counter, and the counterman takes a half crispy-skinned roast chicken, slides all the meat off of it with a cleaver, and piles it onto two slices of sourdough bread spread with mayonnaise. Wait till you taste this—it's the best chicken sandwich anywhere. You get a choice of salad to go with it, and the marinated-vegetable salad of cauliflower, carrot, broccoli, and zucchini in a juicy, oregano-scented dressing is amazingly tasty. I can't vouch for anything else here, but who wants to get beyond that sandwich?

SPECIALTY'S CAFE AND BAKERY

312 Kearny Street (between

Bush and Pine), San Francisco

Tel: 788-2254 (for daily

specials call 896-2253)

22 Battery Street,

San Francisco

Tel: 398-4691

150 Spear Street (between

Mission and Howard)

Tel: 978-9662

Open Monday through Friday

6 a.m. to 6 p.m.

No credit cards

Americans love sandwiches, but they are particular about what belongs in them and what doesn't. Our sandwiches have more filling than bread, unlike the meager slice of prosciutto or dry sausage that gets buried in an Italian or French baguette. We want nothing of the Danish open-face variety. The English may have invented the sandwich, but their dry, skinny version spread with margarine gives sandwiches a bad name. To Americans, the sandwich is a meal you can hold in your hand. The best ones have to be juicy, rich, texturally varied, a little spicy, and almost impossible to bite through.

Specialty's, a seven-year-old sandwich company with three Financial District locations, understands the American sandwich and is a favorite with the office set. The success of its concept revolves around hot, soft, just-baked breads used in forty different sandwich combinations. Each has a multitude of ingredients, and the effect in the best matchups is symphonic: The whole is greater than the individually undistinguished parts.

One of my favorites is No. 11, the Italian, a conglomeration of paper-thin slices of salami, bologna, mortadella, Swiss, mild peppers, provolone, and the basic set-up of lettuce, tomato, pickles, onions, and black pepper, with mayonnaise and spicy brown mustard on potato–poppy seed bread. All these bland American-style cold cuts add up to a savory submarine-style sandwich with a charm of its own. Another hands-down favorite with everyone is No. 25, the Vegetarian, the classic California combo of avocado, cheese, mushrooms, and ranch dressing. In addition to the sandwiches, a large variety of warm, puffy, gigantic sweet and savory pastries are baked each hour, including huge coiled buns of white bread slathered with great amounts of Cheddar cheese and sliced pickled jalapeño peppers. The outlets are well-staffed counter operations, and the lines that invariably form at 11:30 a.m. move quickly and efficiently. These operations cleverly take the quickly made lunchtime sandwich to a higher level of freshness and appeal.

YANK SING

This great downtown dim sum house (see page 159) has a separate counter next door to the restaurant where you can order boxes of dim sum to go. A large variety of dumplings are kept hot in steamers, ready to be packed up, or you can order dim sum off a large menu, and they are sent from the kitchen as they are cooked. Special sampler boxes posted above the counter are also quickly assembled. If you want to throw a dim sum party, Yank Sing's crack catering department will either deliver the food hot to your door, or set up woks and steamers on site and serve as well. For an amazingly reasonable price, you can impress a group with some of the tastiest and most interesting food this side of Hong Kong.

427 Battery Street (between Clay and Washington), San Francisco

Tel: 362-1640

Open Monday through Friday 11 a.m. to 3 p.m., Saturday and Sunday 10 a.m. to 4 p.m.

Credit cards: AE, CB, DC, MC, V

ICE CREAM/CHOCOLATES

CANDY JAR

210 Grant Avenue (between
Post and Sutter),
San Francisco
Tel: 391-5508
Open Monday through
Saturday 9 a.m. to 6 p.m.
Credit cards: AE, MC, V

The glass counter of this small candy store displays house-made bonbon-sized truffles and imported Godiva chocolates, but everyone I know drops in when they're downtown to refill their own candy jars with hard candies from all over the world, sold by the pound. Jars and jars of them line one wall, allowing you to put together your own mix. The best of them all is a hard, chewy toffee with a whole toasted hazelnut inside—don't be led off the track by the Irish hazelnut toffees that look almost identical, but are not nearly as good. OK, everyone has his or her own favorites, but I know you'll back me up on these toffees, which as of this writing are out of stock. Complain to the manager.

CHOCOLATE ARGONAUT

60 Grant Avenue (between
Market and Geary),
San Francisco
Tel: 834-1060
Open Monday through Friday
7:30 a.m. to 7 p.m., Saturday
10 a.m. to 6 p.m.
No credit cards

Usually, ultra-fancy French pastries are so petrified in butter cream and glazes that they all taste alike. Donna Meadows, the pastry chef at the Chocolate Argonaut, a little cafe and pastry shop with a few outdoor and indoor tables, knows how to make them sparkle. Her many-layered hazelnut torte, covered with rows of whole roasted hazelnuts and full of distinct flavor and textures, is a true triumph in the Viennese mode. Her tall yeasty brioche, and classic croissant buttery with many crisp layers, are worth a special detour, especially if you're downtown. The cookies I've tried have been stale, but the chocolate truffles and larger pyramids have bright flavors infused into their rich ganache fillings. Meadows used to be a partner/pastry chef at the

renowned Flying Saucer in the Mission (see page 229), and, as at that place, she really projects her own ideas about the art of pastry making.

MORROW'S NUT HOUSE

I challenge you to walk by this tiny nut shop without stopping in to buy at least one-quarter pound. The irresistible aroma of roasting (actually deep-fried) nuts wafts out the always-open door and practically pulls you inside. The nuts are of the highest quality: huge, fresh, and whole. The cashews are the size of a child's thumb, and the pecans, an adult toe. Almonds, Brazil nuts, and hazelnuts all look even plumper glistening with nut oil. Morrow's keeps roasting all day, so the nuts are always warm when you get them, but never stale or rancid. A box, even a small bag, of these fresh, fragrant mixed nuts makes just about the best gift I know.

111 Geary Street (between Grant and Stockton), San Francisco
Tel: 362-7969
Open Monday through Saturday
9:45 a.m. to 5:45 p.m.
Credit cards: MC, V

SEE'S CANDIES

542 Market Street (at Sansome), San Francisco

Tel: 362-1593

Monday through Friday 9 a.m. to 6:30 p.m.

846 Market Street (at Powell), San Francisco

Tel: 434-2771

Monday through Saturday 9 a.m. to 7 p.m.,

Sunday 10:30 a.m. to 6 p.m.

No credit cards

See listing, page 431.

TEUSCHER CHOCOLATES OF SWITZERLAND

255 Grant Avenue (at Sutter), San Francisco

Tel: 398-2700

Open Monday through Saturday 10 a.m. to 6 p.m.

Credit cards: AE, MC, V

These ridiculously expensive chocolates are so rich that one—well, maybe two—will satisfy your chocolate craving for a week—well, make that three days. The champagne truffles, little milk chocolate balls of the most buttery, velvety texture with a swatch of champagne cream in the center and a dusting of sugar on the exterior, are what bring most people into this tiny store. I've tried a number of the other chocolates with nuts, marzipan, and different flavors, neatly arranged in formation like tiny soldiers, but those champagne truffles always seem to be worth the expense. You can buy them by the piece or in small gift boxes. Around each holiday, Teuscher makes children's packages, but I would never waste these chocolates on kids. Save them for yourself.

WINES AND SPIRITS

LONDON WINE BAR

Fifteen to twenty California wines and five or so French ones are poured by the glass at this clubby, wood-paneled British-style wine bar and store, in addition to pours from interesting magnums and jereboams of older California wines. Half bottles of white Burgundy, glasses of port and sherry, and a veritable wine cellar of bottles await tasting. What a perfect way to decide what to buy! While the English-pub-like food is serviceable at best, the wine-tasting opportunities are first rate, and owner Gary Locke's picks for the bar and special sales on wines by the case are worth noting. The dual roles of retail store and tasting room work together to help people find the wines they like.

415 Sansome Street (at Sacramento), San Francisco
Tel: 788-4811
Open Monday through Friday 11:30 a.m. to 9 p.m.
Credit cards: AE, D, MC, V

COOKWARE AND BOOKS

CRATE AND BARREL

A good place to find simple, handsome dishware and glasses that will wear well and not cost a fortune, Crate and Barrel prides itself on uncovering these bargains from all over the world. About ten years ago I found some delicate, classic U-shaped hand-blown wineglasses with the thinnest stems and rims, just the right size for white wines and most reds. I bought two dozen and have tried to replace them ever since, but Crate and

125 Grant Avenue (at Geary and Post), San Francisco
Tel: 986-4000
Open Monday through Friday 10 a.m. to 7 p.m., Saturday until 6 p.m., Sunday noon to 5 p.m.
Credit cards: AE, D, MC, V

Barrel discontinued them. So my advice to you is, if you find a plate or a glass that you really like, buy enough of them because you probably won't get a second chance.

MACY'S

Union Square (Stockton and O'Farrell), San Francisco
Tel: 397-3333
Open Monday through Saturday 10 a.m. to 8 p.m., Sunday 11 a.m. to 7 p.m.
Credit cards: AE, MC, V

I always think I can find just the small appliance I need at Macy's, but actually this seemingly large department only stocks one or two brands of items like juicers, toasters, or blenders, often not the one I'm trying to replace. The new model either does more than I want or not quite what I want, but maybe that's the complaint of someone who distrusts gadgets. However, I have found that getting service in this department is no easy matter, so I can't even be persuaded that the model they have in stock is really better.

The extensive pots and pans department at Macy's is another matter. It carries all levels of cooking equipment, from old-fashioned copper-bottomed stainless-steel Revere Ware to the latest generation of space-age, nonstick, nonscratch cooking-surface pans, stopping along the way to pay homage to Le Creuset's heavy enameled cooking pots. To my mind, some pieces from each line serve a cook better than monolithic matching sets. Many people ask my advice on what kind of pans they should buy, but unless I move in with them for a week to see how they cook, an answer is impossible. In my kitchen I couldn't live without a heavy nonstick saucepan with a glass cover, for heating milk for coffee, which I bought at Macy's three years ago for $75. Since I use it every single day it was a terrific investment, amortized over the years. I have a nesting set of copper saucepans, a few cast-iron skillets, a few copper sauté pans, a heavy aluminum restaurant-style skillet, a pressure cooker, a large covered stockpot, a big Le

Creuset covered casserole, and that's about it—except for a wok from Chinatown that I use all the time.

The casual-dishware department harbors some charming painted dishes in five-piece place settings for four (around $100). The glassware selection is weak, but you can find treasures among the French white and painted serving dishes that fill one section. Many of them were on sale the last time I dropped by.

WILLIAMS-SONOMA

For other locations, see pages 124, 498, 580.

The Post Street location has the biggest selection of merchandise of all the stores, from high-quality pots and pans in copper and high-tech materials to cookbooks, kitchen gadgets, and olive oil. If you're looking for the hard-to-find cooking item, like crème brûlée irons, or paella pans along with the rice, this is the place to look first. The prices are not cheap, but the cookware, small appliances, and utensils carried here have the store's backing, which includes the huge mail-order business and all the branches. The buyers do their research; they read *Consumer Reports* and have enough buying power to make a manufacturer improve a product. So the one toaster they carry has been chosen for a reason, winning the competition for quality and price, though quality is the more important factor.

I have always found the clerks to be extremely helpful. If an item is out of stock they will try to find it for you at another store, and they know their own inventories. They'll tell you exactly why Williams-Sonoma carries a specific item, and they're usually so convincing that you buy one. I've never been let down, and that includes the time I impulsively bought a bread machine for my husband who had yearned for one with every Williams-Sonoma catalogue. It really works, if you like soft, airy

150 Post Street (between Grant and Kearny), San Francisco
Tel: 362-6904
Open Monday through Saturday 9:30 a.m. to 7 p.m., Sunday 11 a.m. to 6 p.m.

865 Market Street (at Fifth Street in the San Francisco Centre), San Francisco
Tel: 546-0171
Open Monday through Saturday 9:30 a.m. to 8 p.m., Sunday 11 a.m. to 6 p.m.
Credit cards: AE, MC, V

bread with crisp crusts, and the smell of the warm loaf in the morning is better than an alarm clock. You also can find some handsome dishes and glasses for a moderate sum, and if you are tantalized by catalogues, Williams-Sonoma regularly sends out a thick one full of many items that you didn't know you needed until you saw them there, like nonstick corn-stick molds in the shape of little ears of corn.

RAISED WAFFLES

2 cups milk

1/2 cup (1 stick) butter, cut into chunks

1 teaspoon salt

1 teaspoon sugar

1 package active dry yeast

1/2 cup warm (105° to 115°F) water

2 cups all-purpose flour

2 eggs

1/4 teaspoon baking soda

This classic waffle recipe from an early Fanny Farmer cookbook makes the lightest, crispest, most flavorful waffles I know. I found it in Marion Cunningham's The Breakfast Book, *which I use constantly. If there were ever a reason to buy a waffle iron, this recipe is it. The waffle irons sold today have teflon coatings so that the waffles never stick and always come out golden brown.*

Put the milk, butter, salt, and sugar in a small saucepan. Gently warm over low heat until the butter is almost melted. Remove from heat and let cool to lukewarm.

In a large bowl, dissolve the yeast in the warm water. Add the milk mixture, then whisk in the flour, until the batter is smooth and creamy. Cover with plastic wrap and let stand 6 to 12 hours at room temperature.

The next morning, or just before cooking, whisk the eggs and baking soda. The batter will be thin.

Pour about 1/2 to 3/4 cup of batter into a very hot waffle iron. Bake until the waffles are golden and crisp, about 5 minutes.

Makes about 8 waffles

Lower & Upper Haight, Cole Valley

LOWER & UPPER HAIGHT, COLE VALLEY

RESTAURANTS

CHA CHA CHA

The vibrancy of this popular Haight Street institution has not diminished over the years, even with Cha Cha Cha's expansion to a larger space on the corner. If anything, this Caribbean tapas spot is hotter than ever. With Cuban rhythm bands blaring on the sound system and fetishy folk art leaping off the black brick walls, the place always buzzes. Next door, but connected to the dining room, people both eat and drink at a very hip bar made of marble and pressed sheet metal in Cha Cha Cha's original tiny space.

They come here for tapas, huge plates of tender fried calamari or deep-fried new potatoes, golden and crisp, dressed with a dollop of dried-chili-infused aïoli. From the daily specials board might come a large fillet of trout, spicily breaded Cajun-style and pan-fried, served with grilled asparagus and a capery rémoulade—a surprisingly stylish dish for the venue. Platters of excellent black beans, yellow rice with green olives, and seared flank steak or roast leg of pork make for a dreamy meal if you're hungry. Everything on these Cuban-inspired

1801 Haight Street (at Schrader), San Francisco
Tel: 386-5758 or 386-7670
Open for lunch Monday through Friday 11:30 a.m. to 3 p.m.; dinner Monday through Thursday 5 to 11 p.m., Friday, Saturday, and Sunday until 11:30 p.m.; brunch Saturday and Sunday 10 a.m. to 4 p.m.
Price: Inexpensive
No credit cards

plates is delicious. More tapas, like fried plantains with black beans and sour cream; whole mushroom caps sautéed with sherry, garlic, and olive oil; or a good warm spinach salad with bacon and mushrooms, draw on Spain and Latin America with a bit of California thrown in. The mix works, especially when washed down with pitchers of fruity but not too sweet sangría.

The cooking is eclectic, but not confused or fussy. The unifying theme is spiciness, and each buoyant dish stays true to its ethnic origin. A Cuban dish tastes Cuban; a Cajun dish, Cajun.

This restaurant was made for the Haight; it's an extension of the energy on the street. It projects just enough funk to make neighborhood customers feel comfortable, yet the core of the operation is professional and pretty sophisticated. It has become one of the best neighborhood spots around—so good, in fact, that people come to Cha Cha Cha from all over the city. The loud and colorful dining rooms also happen to be a terrific place to take kids: They can eat a little or a lot (they all get a small empty plate and help themselves) and drink their own version of sangría: exotic fruit juices in ice-filled glasses.

GANGES VEGETARIAN RESTAURANT

775 Frederick Street (at Arguello), San Francisco
Tel: 661-7290
Open Tuesday through Saturday 5 to 10 p.m.
Price: Inexpensive
Credit cards: MC, V

At this modest restaurant in a converted Victorian residence, Malvi Doshi, a cookbook author and cooking teacher, serves aromatic, strikingly different Indian dishes. She runs the place practically singlehandedly, so her menus are small. The fixed-price vegetarian meals always start with *papadums* and little plastic cups of *raita* (yogurt and cucumbers) followed by vegetable *pakoras* (or fritters) and pyramid-shaped *samosas* stuffed with cooked vegetables accompanied with lively tamarind-raisin and bright green chili-and-cilantro chutneys. The main part of the meal brings *dal* (an aromatic, soupy lentil stew) and several curries, perhaps a delicious, classic mixture of bright green spinach and white cheese or an unusual combination of dried beans, sweet potato, and zucchini. These vegetable dishes are cooked to order so they retain their texture and bright color, singing of roasted cumin, cloves, and coriander. One of my favorites is Doshi's baked bananas stuffed with finely chopped fresh coconut, cilantro, and green chilies. Call ahead to make sure it's on the menu. *Chapatis* and saffron rice, hot carrot pickles, and a hot red-chili sauce complete these home-cooked meals.

Dessert is a high point. Ms. Doshi makes her own *kulfi*, a dense Indian ice cream scented with cardamom, and her *ras mali*, a delicate white cheese ball poached in syrup and served in cream, is stellar. Hot mugs of *chai*, Darjeeling tea boiled with milk, pepper, cloves, and honey, is so sweet and spicy it can substitute for dessert, but why not have both? The prices here would make a mendicant happy.

The cozy, almost impromptu dining room offers both Western seating at wooden tables and chairs and low seating on carpets with cushions. A sitar player often perches in the bay window seat. Everyone feels like a dinner guest in Ms. Doshi's home.

HAMA-KO

108B Carl Street (at Cole),
San Francisco
Tel: 753-6808
Open Tuesday through
Sunday 6 to 10 p.m.
Price: Moderate
Credit cards: MC, V

It's a well-kept secret that you can get some of the best sushi in town at this practically invisible little restaurant, especially if you call ahead and order a special meal from sushi-chef and owner Ted Kashiyama. He goes to Pier 33 everyday, specifically to Paul Johnson's Monterey Fish stall, to find scallops, live Dungeness crab, and shrimp. He has his sources for *hamachi* (yellowtail), sea urchin roe, and *mirugai* (giant clam), which is practically still moving when he cuts it. For a modest sum patrons can order a plate of mixed sushi from a small menu, but for a stunning meal Mr. Kashiyama composes a series of hot and cold courses that are simple, exquisite, and unique. He might begin with a few perfect oysters on the half shell and end with a whole Dungeness crab cooked Japanese style, with delicacies like sushi and sashimi of *toro* (tuna belly) and real, fresh *hamachi* along the way. Call ahead to order these meals and reserve a space; otherwise you can walk in and hope to find a seat at the tiny sushi bar or at one of the few tables. Mr. Kashiyama's wife handles the floor with unflagging Japanese graciousness, but if more than two or three parties come in at the same time she does not quicken her methodical pace in bringing drinks, meticulously setting places, and taking orders. Service for her is like a stately dance that will not brook syncopation. Yet when she's with you, you bask in her attention.

INDIAN OVEN

The titillating menu of this California-influenced Indian restaurant promises dishes that you never see on the monolithic Punjabi menus that usually appear in Indian restaurants. Unfortunately, the small open kitchen at this popular lower Haight cafe executes it unevenly. I have had the most maddeningly inconsistent meals here. Some things, like duck and chicken, are precooked and finished off in a tandoori oven to bad effect. Yet some of the vegetable curries, especially one of slightly crisp orange winter squashes in coconut milk, can be delicious, and a mixed-mushroom curry also has been fine. Worth ordering is Indian Oven's version of *pakoras*. Instead of deep-fried vegetable fritters, the dish consists of individually battered and fried spinach leaves and onion rings strewn with slivers of dried apricot, all resting in a pool of chili-spiked yogurt. Vegetarians fare best, though I have liked all the dishes that use chicken thighs, especially Velvet Butter Chicken.

233 Fillmore Street (at Haight), San Francisco
Tel: 626-1628
Open nightly 5:30 to 10 p.m.
Price: Inexpensive to moderate
Credit cards: AE, MC, V

KATE'S KITCHEN

Kate is a little girl, and her mom, Eloise Humphrey Buckner, is an experienced Bay Area chef. The mom decided to open a casual, funky, down-home breakfast and lunch cafe so she could be with her kids. Sure enough, as good karma would have it, Kate's Kitchen has been full ever since it opened. Although I have enjoyed Ms. Buckner's cooking at fancier places (like the now-closed Butler's in Mill Valley), I have never eaten anything better from her hands than buttermilk cornmeal pancakes, the dreamiest pancakes in the city. Light, airy, full of flavor, with a slight grittiness from the cornmeal, they are the only plate-sized pancakes I have ever finished. They come with a big slab of butter and

471 Haight Street (at Fillmore), San Francisco
Tel: 626-3984
Open Tuesday through Friday 8 a.m. to 3 p.m., Saturday and Sunday from 9 a.m. to 4 p.m.
Price: Inexpensive
No credit cards

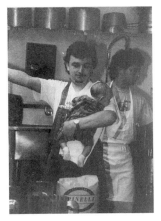

warm maple syrup. All the classic American egg dishes are well prepared and come with scrumptious new-potato hash browns enlivened by grilled onions and green peppers. Red flannel hash is an elaboration on these hash brown potatoes, with chunks of corned beef and root vegetables. It's tasty, but don't expect a crisp pancake. Happily, breakfast is served all day, but around noon a handful of lunch dishes are offered, like a meat loaf with mashed potatoes swirled inside that comes with the best coleslaw in town.

Kate's is always busy, especially on weekends when a yellow pad is hung on the front door and people sign up for a table. Everyone seems to know everybody else in the cafe, particularly if they happen to be under the age of thirty. The owner's sisters and relatives work the dining room, and an all-around good-family spirit pervades. The distressed-looking floors and wooden furniture come by their condition honestly, which only adds to the authenticity of the place. Made-from-scratch food, inexpensive prices, and effcient service set Kate's apart from the many breakfast and lunch cafes that line Haight Street, which are mostly used by neighborhood denizens. For a Kate's breakfast I would enthusiastically travel across town.

TAQUERIA EL BALAZO

1654 Haight Street
(between Clayton and Cole),
San Francisco
Tel: 864-8608
Open daily 10 a.m. to 10 p.m.
Price: Inexpensive
No credit cards

In a leveling transformation typical of the Haight, the arty, slightly upscale Ozone space, which was started by a Star's Cafe alum, has become a very popular taqueria with new owners, where people can eat a lot for cheap. A tasty chicken *mole* goes into burritos and tacos with amazing grace. One wouldn't think that chicken in an aromatic sauce deepened by bitter chocolate would work with guacamole, rice, beans, and salsa in a burrito, but it does. The *carnitas* (pork slowly cooked in its own fat) is fresh, moist, and buttery, delicious in soft tacos sprinkled with extra chopped onions and cilantro, which are set out on the counter. Grateful Dead references (roses, skulls, and dishes named after certain group members) abound in the colorful, folk-art-filled dining room that surrounds the bustling counter. The food here reaches the best Mission District standards: Freshness is key, nothing sits around, and good combinations can be put together with a bit of experimentation. The flavors are authentic, although an awful lot of salt is used in practically everything.

THEP PHANOM

Although Thai restaurants abound in San Francisco, it is not because they are cooking for a Thai community. The ethnic Thai population (as opposed to the Vietnamese or Cambodian, for example) is small in the Bay Area. Thai restaurants cook for Westerners, so the trick is to find a restaurant that will prepare dishes authentically. The excitement of Thai cooking lies in the explosiveness of the seasoning (hot being dominant), and in the sweet, sour, fermented, and aromatic flavors in every dish. The best of the Thai restaurants use fresh ingredients, grind their own pastes for curries, and keep their dishes incendiary. That's why many aficionados consider Thep Phanom one of their favorite Thai restaurants. The kitchen doesn't make concessions. When they warn that a dish is hot, be prepared!

The calamari salad is divine, juxtaposing tender squid with hot chilies, cool lettuces, fresh cilantro, and lime juice. A lot of the appetizers and salads balance similar ingredients, and I love them all whether they are made with minced chicken or duck in the *larb* preparations or

900 Waller (at Fillmore), San Francisco

Tel: 431-2526

Open nightly 5:30 to 10:30 p.m.

Price: Inexpensive

Credit cards: AE, MC, V

with strips of spongy fish cake. The deep-fried dishes here stand out, especially the quail on lettuce with a peanut sauce. Rubbed with dry spices, the plain quail are so flavorful and moist that dipping them is unnecessary. Angel wings—fried chicken wings stuffed with glass noodles—may be the most ordered and delicious dish at the restaurant. If you love chilies, try one of the fiery stir fries from a special section of the menu. Once you get used to the level of hotness you realize how deep the flavors go in these dishes. They are the most characteristically Thai, but you must be able to tolerate hot, hot seasoning. More delicate coconut-milk curries, red or yellow from the particular spice paste used, are well represented on the menu. Deep-fried bananas with coconut ice cream end the meal on a cool note.

Besides the good cooking, Thep Phanom impresses with a pleasant, lowly-lit dining room decorated with elegant Thai artifacts. Lacy gold-trimmed place mats soften the glass-covered tabletops. The waiters and slim, elegant hostesses in Thai dress know how to keep the dining room hopping. The place is always full, but somehow the wait is never long.

CAFES

JAMMIN' JAVA COFFEE HOUSE

For other location, see page 480.

This is one of the most happening units in a small chain of cafes in key hangout neighborhoods. The music (Coltrane, Miles) is particularly well chosen.

701 Cole (at Waller),
San Francisco
Tel: 668-JAVA
Open daily 7 a.m. to 11 p.m.
No credit cards

ONE WORLD CAFE

The One World Cafe is hidden away on a broad, sunny, avenuelike street in a residential section of the Western Addition, a location you would only happen on by accident if you didn't live in the neighborhood. Yet a lot of people know about this cool little spot, another inventive expression of what constitutes a vital cafe. Coltrane plays at just the right level in a room painted in the brightest yellows, turquoises, and oranges. A folk mural behind the counter depicts pastiches of international daily life from India to Mexico. The menu is health-foody, with vegetarian sandwiches and salads based on nice greens. The espresso is worth a detour, and the sunny room gives off universally good vibes.

1799 McAllister (at Baker),
San Francisco
Tel: 776-9358
Open Monday through
Friday 7 a.m. to 6 p.m.,
Saturday and Sunday from
9 a.m. to 6 p.m.
No credit cards

BARS

DELUXE

1511 Haight Street (at
Ashbury), San Francisco
Tel: 552-6949
Open Monday through
Friday 4 p.m. to 2 a.m.,
Saturday and Sunday 3
p.m. to 2 a.m.
No credit cards

When a jazz combo plays on Fridays, Saturdays, and
Sundays, it might cost you $4 or $5 to get in the door. At
other times, the jazz comes from the sound system, and
admission to this suave, retro bar is free. The DeLuxe is
one of my favorite bars in the city, not only for the mix
of people who hang there, some of whom slick back
their hair and make vintage clothing look like Armani,
but because the drinks are so good. Bartenders make
first-rate fresh-lime margaritas with just the right
balance of sweet and sour so that the salt on the rim of
the glass becomes part of the thrill. Ron de Barolito
rum, so rich in flavor it reminds me of butterscotch,
blossoms in a warmed brandy snifter. Dry, ice-cold
martinis come in chilled V-shaped glasses, the very
embodiment of sophistication. The scene is elevated
enough so that people who like to dress feel appreciated.
Yet there's nothing snobby about the DeLuxe. Old and
young, matronly and hip, casual and dressy—everyone
looks good here, and after a perfect drink or two everyone feels pretty good too.

KEZAR BAR & RESTAURANT

900 Cole Street (at Carl)
San Francisco
Tel: 681-7678
Open daily 5 p.m. to 2 a.m.
Credit cards: AE, MC, V

A cozy neighborhood sports bar that was opened by the
people who owned the now defunct Ironwood across
the street, the Kezar offers a comfortable barroom with
two video monitors and an adjoining dining room. The
food here is terrific, just what you want when you belly
up to a bar. There are spicy garlic peanuts and warm,
thick corn chips with delicious tomato salsa. The hamburgers are juicy and full of flavor. More elaborate
dishes turn out to be surprisingly good; Greek-style

spinach salad, pot roast, and seafood chowder have been standouts. Anchor Wheat beer is on tap and drinks are generously poured. Good spirit pervades: Fellow patrons are friendly, the staff accommodating. Kezar fulfills every requirement of a good neighborhood pub.

NOC NOC

Its singular Flintstones-meets-high-tech interior has been lifted by others, but Noc Noc created the original Iron Age–hippie-pad look, augmented by a few glowing video screens without vertical hold, and collaged surfaces embedded with bottle openers. Its patronage has gone through stages: super-counterculture hip and exclusive; then druggie and nodding out in the crannies; and currently, youngish and bohemian from the neighborhood. Beer is the thing—from microbreweries up and down the West Coast to German lagers and ales, all on tap. Tucher lager, a crisp, sweet, scintillating German beer served in a tall pilsener glass with a lemon slice perched on the rim, makes for universally good drinking.

557 Haight Street (between Fillmore and Steiner), San Francisco
Tel: 861-5811
Open daily 5 p.m. to 2 a.m.
No credit cards

TORONADO

This has become a post-college hangout in the lower Haight: a safe place in a dicey neighborhood. The place is mobbed on the weekends by people who arrive in cabs and do not look as if they live anywhere nearby. By the same token, the Toronado is a dead ringer for a collegiate bar, with wood wainscoting and green walls. The list of beers goes on and on—from raspberry wheat to Boont Amber from the Anderson Valley to Guinness Stout, all on tap—and there is enough light in this bar to see the differences in brew color. The bartenders know the brews and describe them well.

547 Haight Street (between Fillmore and Steiner), San Francisco
Tel: 863-2276
Open daily 11:30 a.m. to 2 a.m.
No credit cards

DELICATESSENS/TAKE-OUT

REAL FOOD COMPANY

1023 Stanyan Street (at Carl), San Francisco

Tel: 564-1117

Open weekdays 7:30 a.m. to 8 p.m., weekends 9 a.m. to 8 p.m.

Credit cards: MC, V

See listing, page 399.

BAKERIES/PASTRIES

BAKERS OF PARIS

1605 Haight Street (between Clayton and Belvedere),
San Francisco

Tel: 626-4076

Open daily 7 a.m. to 5:30 p.m.

No credit cards

See listings, pages 271, 483.

JUST DESSERTS

Fulton and Masonic (Plaza Foods), San Francisco

Tel: 441-2207

Open Monday through Saturday 9 a.m. to 8 p.m.,
Sunday from 9:30 a.m. to 7 p.m.

Credit cards: MC, V

See listing, page 216.

1000 Cole Street (at Parnassus), San Francisco

Tel: 664-8947

Open Monday through Saturday 7 a.m. to 11 p.m.,

Sunday 8 a.m. to 11 p.m.

Credit cards: MC, V

See listing, page 216.

ICE CREAM/CHOCOLATES

DOUBLE RAINBOW

1724 Haight Street (at Cole), San Francisco

Tel: 668-6690

Open Sunday through Thursday 11 a.m. to 11 p.m.,

Friday and Saturday until 1 a.m.

No credit cards

See listing, page 273.

GELATO CLASSICO

201 Parnassus Avenue (at Stanyan), San Francisco

Tel: 566-9696

Open Sunday through Thursday 7 a.m. to 10 p.m.,

Friday and Saturday until 11 p.m.

No credit cards

See listing, page 325.

COFFEE

SPINELLI COFFEE COMPANY

**919 Cole Street (at Carl),
San Francisco
Tel: 753-2287
Open Monday through Friday
6:30 a.m. to 9 p.m., Saturday 7
a.m. to 9 p.m., Sunday 7 a.m.
to 7 p.m.
Credit cards: AE, D, MC, V**

One of seven Spinelli coffee stores in the city, this outpost is about to expand next door to become a full-scale cafe with tables and chairs. Very much in the Peet's mold, Spinelli believes in dark roasting, daily delivery of freshly roasted beans, and intense brewing. In fact, the founders of the intentionally small chain were acolytes of Mr. Peet's in Berkeley, and escapees from the corporate-minded Starbucks headquartered in Seattle. Like Peet's, the personnel at each store takes a proprietary interest in the quality of the coffee and the education of its patrons. The Cole Street branch stands out for its pleasant, efficient, enlightened service and consistent brews. In a part of town where counterculture cool outweighs service, earnest Spinelli feels like an oasis of civilization.

MARKETS

ASHBURY MARKET

Wilfred Wong, the ebullient wine writer, California county fair wine judge, and general ubiquitous presence on the wine scene, put the Ashbury Market on the map by gathering together an eccentric but very good selection of California wines and choice wines from France for his family's grocery. Though he no longer works at the Ashbury Market (a bit of a family disagreement), the wine collection still fills a whole back room on closely placed shelves that almost reach the ceiling. A committee of three wine buyers who trained with Wilfred are continuing on, maintaining the Ashbury Market as a neighborhood resource for the likes of Forman Cabernet or Au Bon Climat wines.

It's unusual to find a corner grocery store that carries Acme bread, organic chips, and snacks like the incomparable Newman's Own Pretzels, some organic vegetables, super-high-butterfat Plugra butter (covered in plastic wrap by the store to stay fresh), Straus Family Creamery milk, Hobbs bacon, Gerhard sausages, Rocky free-range chickens, and ground turkey. All of these items are finds a few blocks off Haight Street. Pails of flowers outside the rustic wood-trimmed market signal the upscale goodies within, from cat food to imported pasta. Though the wines are by no means discounted, specials signs can lead the way to some decent buys. The checkout clerks are nice and loquacious, and the wine people in the back will be happy to schmooze about any bottle.

205 Frederick Street (at Ashbury), San Francisco
Tel: 566-3134
Open Monday through Saturday 9 a.m. to 9 p.m., Sunday until 3 p.m.
Credit cards: AE, MC, V

PLAZA FOODS

Corner of Fulton and
Masonic, San Francisco
Open Monday through
Saturday 9 a.m. to 8 p.m.,
Sunday 9:30 a.m. to 7 p.m.

Under one roof at this older, venerable city shopping center, food lovers will find a high-quality grocery store and an excellent meat market, a so-so fish but a good poultry market, and a serviceable delicatessen, liquor store, and outpost of Just Desserts.

FALLETTI'S FINER FOODS

Corner of Fulton and
Masonic (Plaza Foods),
San Francisco
Tel: 567-0976
Open Monday through
Saturday 9 a.m. to 8 p.m.,
Sunday 9:30 a.m. to 7 p.m.
Credit cards: MC, V

Formerly a Petrini's, Falletti's gets high marks for carrying freshly baked breads from Acme, Semifreddi, Grace, and Tassajara among others; Dande's shrimp chips (very tasty if you like this variety of snack); Castle Creamery cream-topped milk and chocolate milk in glass quart bottles; sharp New York Cheddars from the Marin Cheese Company; the superlative Columbus-brand anchovies; and a huge variety of upscale packaged cookies. The snack and chip buyer is discriminating. I found the only "diet" chip I've ever liked here: Michael Season's lightly salted potato chips, with 40 percent less fat (6 grams versus 10 grams of fat per 1 ounce serving). A lively wine section next to a well-chosen fruit juice section that offers lots of tropical fruit nectars strikes me as a smart way to arrange a store: Put all the drinks in one area so you don't forget to buy something for the kids when you're mulling over wine. The produce is commercial but complete, with berries usually featured.

PRODUCE

The Real Food group of natural foods stores made organic produce accessible in San Francisco. Kimball Allen, the owner of the stores, fell into his successful chain by accident. He owned some property that he needed to lease and ended up opening a profitable natural foods chain by letting independent managers run the stores. He prefers being a club owner and jazz impresario (see Kimball's East, page 523).

Produce cognoscenti knew that the Stanyan Street branch of the Real Food Company had the best organic fruits and vegetables in the city. The store managers and produce buyer made personal connections with organic farmers, establishing long-term relationships so the farmers knew they had a market. Granted autonomy in pricing, the Stanyan Street store subsidized organic produce by marking it up the least and balancing the books by charging a bit more for commercial produce. It was a wonderful statement from people who cared about produce and the land. They turned what had been the weakest of the stores into one of the strongest by offering food they believed in.

Unfortunately, the dedicated group at Stanyan Street has left recently. The produce buyer has moved to a farm in Ridley to try growing his own produce, and his sister and brother-in-law, who managed the store, have moved to Santa Fe.

A centralized department now buys for all the Real Food stores and also suggests prices. It remains to be

1023 Stanyon Street
(between Carl and Frederick),
San Francisco
Tel: 564-2800
Open daily 9 a.m. to 8 p.m.
Credit cards: MC, V

seen what effect this move toward corporate organization will have on the individual stores. In some instances, as at the Polk Street location, prices could be better. In the case of Stanyan Street, it may mean changes for the worse in quality and price.

FRESH PEAS

The Real Food Company is one of the few places to find good local English peas during their short season in spring before it gets too hot. Some of the best peas grow in the cooler finger valleys off Half Moon Bay and San Gregorio Beach. When I think about what it takes to bring fresh peas to market, I marvel that it ever happens at all. The peas must be picked at just the right moment before they mature and get starchy, but when they are large enough to make up more than a spoonful after they're shelled. As so often happens, some peas in a batch may be too large and others small and sweet in the same harvest, so picking must be done judiciously with consistency in mind. The picked peas must be cooled immediately and delivered to market quickly so they keep their sugar. (Peas lose up to 40 percent of their sugar in six hours at room temperature.) At the store the same rules apply. The peas must be kept cool and sold fast. Each moment warming on the display shelves and sitting in the coolers in the back detracts from their charm. Too many times I have come away from a market with peas that tasted pretty good when I bought them but changed overnight in the refrigerator. When you take the time to shell fresh peas at home you want them to be worth the effort, and the trip from field to the plate is a long one, fraught with pitfalls. Next to careful buying at a farmer's market, the Stanyan Real Foods produce section has offered the highest probability in town for securing sweet peas.

Melt the butter in a large skillet over medium heat. Add the shallots and cook until soft. Add the peas, salt, pepper, and water. Stir, bring to a boil, then cover and cook over high heat until the peas are tender but not mushy, about 3 to 5 minutes, depending on the size of the peas. If they are still hard after 5 minutes, add a little more water, if neccessary, and cook 2 minutes longer. Most of the liquid should be gone when the peas are ready.

Variation   At the last moment, you may add finely chiffonnaded fresh mint leaves or 1/2 teaspoon minced fresh thyme or chervil. For a wonderful treat, cook peas in this way with chanterelle mushrooms, adding 1 tablespoon olive oil to the butter and continuing on in the same manner with shallots, then chanterelles, then peas, using less water, depending on the moisture in the mushrooms.

Serves 4

2 tablespoons butter

2 large shallots, minced

3 pounds fresh peas
  in the pod, shelled
  (about 2 1/2 cups shelled peas)

1 teaspoon kosher salt

Freshly ground pepper

1/2 cup water

MEAT AND POULTRY

ENRICO'S

Fulton and Masonic (Plaza
Foods), San Francisco
Tel: 346-7934
Open Monday through
Saturday 9 a.m. to 8 p.m.,
Sunday 9:30 a.m. to 7 p.m.
Credit cards: MC, V

This meat counter looks appealing with its neat trays of nicely displayed, freshly cut meat. Showing particular strength in lamb and veal, Enrico's often has veal chops with kidneys still attached; small lamb shanks; meaty racks of lamb trimmed of excessive fat; thick-sliced bacon; hard-to-find fresh country pork ribs; and cured meats used for cooking, like smoked ham hocks. The most attractive cuts of beef here are short ribs, oxtails, tongue, and beef knuckle for stock. Butchers cut and trim to order. Lots of them work behind the counter, so your number comes up quickly. Though there are other Enrico's meat counters in the city, this is one of the best, a fine resource for that fresh, unusual, cut of meat.

UNITED FISH AND POULTRY

Masonic and Fulton (Plaza
Foods), San Francisco
Tel: 567-3855
Open Monday through
Saturday 9 a.m. to 8 p.m.,
Sunday 9:30 a.m. to 7 p.m.
Credit cards: CB, DC, MC, V

I would not buy fish here, but the high-quality chickens come from Fulton Valley at excellent prices and you can get as many of any part that you need: wings, breasts, thighs, legs, or gizzards. Whole chickens abound, and large Rocky free-range roasters are also part of the roster. All cuts of fresh turkey can be found here, including separately ground dark and white turkey meat, breasts, half birds, and small whole birds. Sometimes I have seen fresh rabbit, but use your common sense. If something looks old, don't buy it, or ask for another piece. One would hope that food retailers would groom their cases, but in some instances the line between fresh and what can pass for fresh becomes fuzzy, especially when it's been a slow week.

CHEESE

People like to shop here for large hunks of cheese at wholesale prices, like Reggiano Parmesan at $6.99 per pound—at least a dollar a pound cheaper than most other stores. Extra sharp Cheddars from Vermont and New York, sweet butter in bulk for $1.99 a pound, and huge wedges of Saint-André for $7.99 per pound can make party purchases less expensive. The nuts in bulk could be fresher. The dry goods in bins, like basmati rice for 69¢ a pound, dried beans of all sorts, and popcorn, are the building blocks of dishes that can feed large groups.

415 Divisadero Street
(between Oak and Fell),
San Francisco
Tel: 621-8130
Open Monday through
Saturday 10 a.m. to 6 p.m.
Credit cards: MC, V

SAY CHEESE

One of the better-stocked cheese stores in the city, Say Cheese carries hard-to-find cheeses on a regular basis. Try the Mona Lisa aged Gouda (pronounced "how-da" by the purists), a buttery, nutty semi-hard cheese that merits a trip across town. Say Cheese will have the seasonal Brin d'Amour, an evocative, mild, but complex Corsican sheep's milk cheese rolled in wild herbs that charms cheese-lovers. On the more mundane level, two-year-old Vermont Cheddar is always available, as is English clotted cream (divine on scones if you can get it fresh enough), a large selection of imported English cheeses, and rarities such as a superior brand of bagel chips, Burns & Ricker from Paterson, New Jersey, and buttery madeleines. Good imported and local cured meats and sausages are made into sandwiches on the premises on Semifreddi baguettes or sliced and wrapped

856 Cole Street (between
Frederick and Carl),
San Francisco
Tel: 665-5020
Open Monday through
Friday 10 a.m. to 7 p.m.,
Saturday until 6 p.m.,
Sunday until 5 p.m.
Credit cards: MC, V

to go. Because Say Cheese does carry a large inventory of cheeses, you might want to ask for tastes just to make sure your selection is in good condition.

WINES AND SPIRITS

ASHBURY MARKET

415 Divisadero Street (between Oak and Fell), San Francisco

Tel: 621-8130

Open Monday through Saturday 10 a.m. to 6 p.m.

Credit cards: MC, V

See listing, page 193.

The Marina
& Cow Hollow

THE MARINA & COW HOLLOW

RESTAURANTS

CAFE ADRIANO

This smart Italian restaurant run by the handsome young couple of Adriano and Deborah Paganini is an anomaly in the Marina, whose entrenched residents do not take to change. But once they taste Adriano's chicken and spinach ravioli made with gossamer-thin noodle dough and drizzled with a little fresh sage and melted butter, or his classic risotto slashed with a swath of earthy wild mushroom sauce, they come back for more.

Instead of red-checked tablecloths and Chianti bottles wrapped in straw, patrons get a lyrical, pared-down room, whose color scheme of pale yellow and greenish blue brings to mind Claude Monet's family dining room at Giverny. The menu of five appetizers, five pastas, and five main courses is as reasonably priced as anything in the Marina, and the food is much tastier. The card changes daily, but *osso buco*, rustic Tuscan soups, a delicious antipasto *misto*, and lots of perfectly al dente pastas with light sauces are usually available.

Adriano Paganini learned to cook in Italy and ran a number of San Francisco kitchens, including a short stint at the elegant Donatello. He applies correct Italian

3347 Fillmore Street (at Chestnut), San Francisco

Tel: 474-4180

Open Tuesday through Saturday 5:30 to 11 p.m., Sunday 5 to 10:30 p.m.

Price: Moderate

Credit cards: D, MC, V

technique to seemingly simple dishes, and the resulting quality puts Cafe Adriano well above the myriad pasta houses popping up all over town.

CAFE MARIMBA

2317 Chestnut Street (between Scott and Divisadero), San Francisco

Tel: 776-1506

Open Monday 5:30 to 11 p.m., Tuesday through Thursday 11:30 a.m. to 11 p.m., Friday 11 a.m. to midnight, Saturday 10 a.m. to midnight, Sunday 10 a.m. to 11 p.m.

Price: Moderate

Credit cards: MC, V

Some people confronted by a three-legged stone mortar filled with grilled pork and onions don't know what to do, especially when they are expecting platters of soft, saucy Mexican food finished off under a broiler. At Cafe Marimba, one of the few authentic full-scale Mexican restaurants in the United States, they learn how to tuck the luscious morsels of pork into small, soft corn tortillas, just off the griddle, and spoon on some hot, smoky chipotle salsa. The taste of such regional, made-from-scratch Mexican food is sublime and unexpected, very earthy but punctuated by explosive flavors.

A meal could start with a platter of Cafe Marimba's sparkling snapper ceviche, consisting of big chunks of tomato, onion, and local rockfish in a vibrant lime and chili marinade. Delicious little quesadillas filled with squash blossoms and fresh white cheese; rock shrimp enchiladas in a creamy avocado sauce; or a whole fried snapper, crisp under a blanket of dried red pasilla chilies cut into rings and lime are but some of the dishes inspired by Reed Hearon's travels through regional Mexico.

This passionate chef gets high marks for his culinary purity. He does not so much invent the dishes on his menu as try to reproduce them in a way that works in a city context. He gained experience in the Mexican idiom by cooking for Mark Miller at the Coyote Cafe in Santa Fe. He left to head a *nuevo* Mexican kitchen in San Francisco (the now-closed Corona Bar and Grill) and do some consulting. Finally, all in the same year, he opened three popular San Francisco restaurants: LuLu, LuLu Bis, and Cafe Marimba. Along the way he rethought the form of the restaurant meal. Cafe Marimba's menu is divided into small and large dishes, and

WATERMELON AND
PINEAPPLE-GINGER
AGUAS FRESCAS

The delicious fresh fruit drinks at Cafe Marimba come in many flavors, depending upon the season. Once you've made one, you can easily make any of them. The key is a simple syrup of sugar and water, which can be purchased or made at home. Similar aguas frescas are ladled from huge glass jars on the counters of taquerias all over the Mission. In the Mission you find exotic flavors like jamaica, or red hibiscus flower, pruney tamarind, and almost always a wonderful cantaloupe. Cafe Marimba adds extra ingredients to theirs, such as vanilla bean and lemon to their strawberry aguas frescas, or mint to the mango blend. When the fruit drinks are spiked with dark rum, as they often are at Cafe Marimba, they turn into batidas.

WATERMELON AQUA FRESCA

Cut the watermelon flesh into small chunks. Blend for 10 seconds in a blender or food processor. The mixture should be chunky. Put in a pitcher and stir in the simple syrup and water. Let stand for 1 or 2 hours. Serve over ice. Best drunk the same day.

    Makes about 2 quarts

4 cups watermelon flesh, seeded
(about 2 pounds whole watermelon)
1 cup simple syrup (recipe follows)
2 3/4 cups water

PINEAPPLE-GINGER AGUA FRESCA

Peel the pineapple and remove the eyes. Core and cut into small chunks. Blend in a blender or food processor for about 25 seconds. The mixture will be pulpy. Put the pureed fruit in a pitcher. Add the ginger and simple syrup. Let stand for 1 or 2 hours, stirring occasionally. Add the water and serve on ice.

    Makes about 2 quarts

1 ripe medium pineapple
1 tablespoon grated, peeled ginger
(about one 1 1/2-inch piece)
1 1/4 cups simple syrup (recipe follows)
3 cups water

SIMPLE SYRUP

Mix the ingredients together in a medium saucepan. Boil for 1 minute, cover, and chill thoroughly. Refrigerated syrup keeps indefinitely.

    Makes 1 1/4 cups

1 cup water
1 1/4 cups sugar

most plates are served family style. This makes a meal here both inexpensive and varied, allowing everyone a taste of a lot of different things.

Lest one of the pleasures of eating Mexican be ignored, drinks here get special attention. Fresh fruit juice combos like strawberry-lemonade or pineapple-ginger especially please kids (who love many of the tacos and quesadillas), while fresh-lime margaritas, kept intentionally tart, do fine with the adults. Smooth tequilas from small producers are a revelation—and may cause a few as well.

E'ANGELO

2234 Chestnut Street
(between Pierce and Scott),
San Francisco
Tel: 567-6164
Open Tuesday through
Sunday 5 to 11 p.m.
Price: Moderate
No credit cards

Seated at one of E'Angelo's tiny tables, my nine-year-old and I were horrified to see the host push the table next to us even closer and seat a dad with two young children. This was our grown-up night out, and we did not want two little kids right on top of us. The host thought he was being cute by sticking all the kids and parents together, but that's life at this fifteen-year-old Marina institution. Just be happy you get a seat at all at this popular restaurant, whose dining room is mostly taken up by a partially open kitchen.

In all the years I have been eating here, the menu has not changed, but the traditional house-made pastas are timeless. E'Angelo made them from scratch long before the Italian food frenzy swept the nation. The luscious green lasagne made with the most tender spinach noodles layered with tons of Fontina, mozzarella, and a signature dried porcini and chicken liver meat sauce is both refined and rustic. The kitchen is famous for a delicate eggplant parmigiana that melts in your mouth. The small pizzas with crisp, paper-thin crusts and the simplest of toppings, like tomato sauce, mozzarella, and mushrooms, are among the best in town. Ricotta- and spinach-filled ravioli, and soft, tender gnocchi napped in tomato sauce, are both classics. A crisp, old-fashioned iceberg lettuce salad, briskly dressed in vinegar and oil and topped with a few anchovies, seems retro in this age of arugula, but it always hits the spot. Although in some respects closer to the old school of Italian-American eateries, E'Angelo stays exciting because it knows how to make silken noodle dough and construct a resonant meat sauce.

GREENS

When Deborah Madison, the original chef at this vegetarian restaurant started by the Zen Center, put together her first menus, people could not believe how intriguing and satisfying a meatless meal could be. She developed a whole new style of vegetarian cuisine that looked to France and the Mediterranean for flavors, and local farms and producers for pristine ingredients. Her five-course prix-fixe dinners became legendary for their imagination and elegance—a far cry from the hippie health-food genre that had taken hold in California in the 1960s.

Madison moved to Santa Fe, but her recipes are available to everyone in *The Greens Cookbook* and *The Savory Way* (Bantam). Greens has flourished under the guidance of Annie Somerville, an author in her own right (*Field of Greens*, Bantam), who has kept the standards high and the menus lively. You will find Greens classics like a Bloomsdale spinach salad tossed with creamy feta, croutons, and threads of red onion in a gorgeous dressing fragrant with mint, sherry vinegar, and warmed olive oil; or the best tofu sandwich in the world, made with smoky charcoal-grilled tofu with horseradish

Fort Mason, Building A
(Buchanan at
Marina Boulevard),
San Francisco
Tel: 771-6222
Open for lunch Tuesday
through Thursday 11:30
a.m. to 2 p.m., Friday and
Saturday until 2:30 p.m.;
dinner Monday through
Thursday 5:30 to 9:30 p.m.;
prix fixe dinner Friday and
Saturday from 6 to 9:30
p.m.; Sunday brunch 10
a.m. to 2 p.m.
Price: Moderate
Credit cards: D, MC, V

mayonnaise on Tassajara potato bread. There might be airy vegetable pancakes enriched with ricotta and Gruyère, served with a piquant tomato-sherry sauce and a dab of crème fraîche; or a house-made pasta with chanterelles, leeks, and Parmesan. The range is stunning and the food always tasty. The restaurant uses only the highest-quality ingredients, from olive oil to nuts.

Greatly improved over the years is the service, which used to be performed, more or less, by Zen students. Now the service is brisk and professional. Another big plus, in addition to the lovely view of the Marina and the airy, art-filled dining room, is a list of eight unusual wine specials, offered by the glass or bottle, that go wonderfully with the food. Just inside the front door of the restaurant there is a handy to-go outlet that sells Tassajara breads and pastries along with soups, sandwiches, and pastries made on the premises.

IZZY'S

3345 Steiner Street
(between Lombard and
Chestnut), San Francisco
Tel: 563-0487
Open Monday through
Saturday 5:30 to 11 p.m.,
Sunday 5 to 10 p.m.
Price: Moderate
Credit cards: AE, DC, D,
MC, V

The checks at most steak houses in San Francisco end up in the stratosphere because a la carte ordering adds up fast. Izzy's, a casual neighborhood saloon/chophouse, manages to keep prices down by offering both potatoes and vegetables with the main attraction, like a decent New York, a gigantic baby beef T-bone, or two-inch-thick lamb loin chops. The best of the side dishes are lightly creamed spinach and Izzy's Own Potatoes, which are scalloped and layered with onions, leeks, and Gruyère. The roasted onions with sweet carrot chunks are also a treat. Those who go to steak houses just for the baked potatoes will find them here with all the fixings.

Start with a classic steak-house salad like a halved head of romaine blanketed in crumbled blue cheese, vinegar, and oil; or share the surprisingly well-executed Cajun fried oysters presented on shells dabbed with a salsa of jalapeños and green onions.

The friendly, unpretentious staff at this watering hole for those over thirty keep a party going every night.

PANE E VINO

Claudio Marchesan's contemporary Italian cooking rings with authenticity. Deceptively simple, his dishes depend on a magical balance of first-rate ingredients. The kind of pasta he uses, the acidity and aroma of the olive oil, the age of the Reggiano Parmesan, the cure of the prosciutto and the pancetta, give his cooking, and all true ingredient-based Italian cooking, its character. Pane e Vino defines the almost clichéd preparation of capellini with tomatoes and basil. Now kitchens elsewhere must live up to Pane e Vino's version. The decidedly al dente, barely sauced pastas have such flavor and texture that you never want to eat them swimming in sauce again. Simple dishes like arugula salad; bread and tomato soup; juicy, thick veal chops; a whole striped bass grilled with fennel; lamb stew over soft white polenta; and a sparkling warm salad of cuttlefish, mussels, green beans, and black olives rotate on and off the menu. They are all satisfying.

Two small rustic dining rooms with terra-cotta floors and beamed ceilings are separated by a tiled open kitchen, cordoned off with counters that display attractive *antipasti*. The high noise level counterbalances intimately close tables, so you really can't eavesdrop on the local Pacific Heights politicos, doctors, and lawyers who consider Pane e Vino their club. I always see a lot of restaurateurs there, too, on their nights off, which tells

3011 Steiner Street (at Union), San Francisco
Tel: 346-2111
Open for lunch Monday through Saturday 11:30 a.m. to 2:30 p.m.; dinner nightly 5 to 10 p.m.
Price: Moderate
Credit cards: MC, V

you how good the place is. From the mostly Italian wine list, which draws from the country's best producers, to the insouciant but efficient young Italian waiters, Pane e Vino delivers the real thing.

PLUMPJACK CAFE

3127 Fillmore Street (between Greenwich and Filbert), San Francisco
Tel: 563-4755
Open for lunch Monday through Friday 11:30 a.m. to 2 p.m., dinner Monday through Saturday 5:30 to 10:30 p.m.
Price: Moderate
Credit cards: AE, MC, V

Following in the footsteps of the PlumpJack wine store, which sells popular, predictable, affordable wines, the PlumpJack cafe offers a version of the Mediterranean-California menu currently in vogue at similarly friendly prices. The low-key Pixley Cafe (formerly the Edwardian, for those of you who go way back) has been turned into a small, sophisticated Pacific Heights hangout with a beige, gray, and silver color scheme, irregularly shaped wood and metal chairs, and banquettes upholstered in a material that emits a low metallic glow. An abstract crossed-sword motif vaguely suggests things medieval. Exterior wine racks directly above some of the tables means that the wait staff practically has to climb on top of customers to find bottles. An internal window looks across a walkway to a large Buddha in an Asian antiquities shop, providing a serendipitous bit of decor, while a completely separate and hidden private dining room in the back conjures up visions of society bachelor parties.

I do think that PlumpJack has taken on an important role in the neighborhood as the superior purveyor of hamburgers and Caesar salads. PlumpJack's juicy burgers on soft North Beach focaccia bread smeared with tomato sauce (which alleviates the need for catsup), piled with grilled onions, represents a worthwhile innovation in hamburgerdom. A resonantly dressed Caesar salad, juicy, rich, and made with good romaine, is completely satisfying. The rest of the dishes demonstrate varying degrees of culinary commitment. The menu is small, but foods like sun-dried cherries, fennel, and roasted red peppers appear often. Most every restaurant menu has a format with slots for certain kinds of dishes—pasta, bruschetta, sandwich or meat main course—which are dictated by the physical constraints of the kitchen, but here inspiration runs a bit thin. Some items turn out to be sparkly, like an antipasto one day, while others taste like a collection of unrelated ingredients that happened to be in the larder, pointing to a certain flightiness in the kitchen. Unfortunately, this malaise infects many new restaurants where the pressures to be modern and stylish outweigh a sensibility based on whether something actually tastes good.

What is extraordinary about PlumpJack is its wine prices, which are a few dollars above retail and many dollars below what most restaurants charge. This pricing policy becomes understandable if you consider the restaurant an extension of the wine store. How about Veuve Clicquot (NV) for $7 a glass and Jordan "J" Brut for $5.50? A 1991 Sonoma Cutrer, Russian River is a fantastic bargain at $15, as is "Les Pierres" from the same winery for $24. Le Cigare Volant, 1990, a Rhônelike blend from a Santa Cruz winery called Bonny Doon is a delicious and versatile food wine that can be copiously drunk for all of $17 a bottle. The other terrific thing about PlumpJack is that it is a 100% nonsmoking restaurant, all the better to smell and taste the wines you are buying so reasonably.

CAFES

BUGATTI'S ESPRESSO CAFE

3001 Webster Street (at Filbert), San Francisco

Tel: 922-4888

Open Monday through Saturday 6:45 a.m. to 10 p.m., Friday until 11 p.m,

Sunday 7:15 a.m. to 10 p.m.

No credit cards

Located on a sunny corner on a residential street one block off Fillmore, Bugatti's brings a whiff of authentic North Beach to this preppy part of town. Indeed, the cafe uses Caffè Roma beans to prepare its well-made espresso and cappuccino, though one of the more popular drinks, the Depth Charger, a cup of brewed coffee spiked with a shot of espresso, would never be made in North Beach. (In a properly brewed cup of coffee, espresso would be superfluous.) When Bugatti's was about to open in 1982, the neighborhood put up a fuss, but now it's become a beloved fixture, with full outdoor tables on sunny days and the expansively windowed interior well populated with typical cafe dwellers. The people behind the counter have better dispositions than most cafe workers.

BARS

BALBOA CAFE

The society column reports that a group of bon vivant San Franciscans convene here regularly for lunch. This just goes to show that taste has very little to do with one's social stature. Currently, the hamburgers are merely decent and the Caesar salad just passable, but the Balboa retains its cachet.

As one point of the "Bermuda triangle," a Cow Hollow intersection with active bars at each of three corners, the Balboa attracts crowds of aging fraternity and sorority types, now well into their thirties. The expansive windows let passersby view the party and decide whether they want to join it. During the day, the clubby light-filled interior does make for a pleasant setting for lunch—and that first martini.

3199 Fillmore Street (between Greenwich and Filbert), San Francisco
Tel: 922-4595
Open daily 11 a.m. to 11 p.m.; Sunday brunch 10:30 a.m. to 3:30 p.m.
Credit cards: AE, D, MC, V

BUS STOP

Though the Cow Hollow/Marina area offers a concentration of bars for single heterosexuals of every decade —twenties, thirties, forties and above—the Bus Stop, an endearing neighborhood saloon that has been open continuously since before 1900, knows no limitations. People of all ages hang out here to watch games on readily visible video screens with impeccable reception, shoot pool at two tables, or gaze at the passing parade on Union street. The bar prides itself on its "super well" drinks ($3.50 as of publication), made with such liquors as Dewar's White Label, Bombay Sapphire, Smirnoff Vodka, Cuervo Especial, Ron Bacardi Superior, Jack Daniels, and Seagram's VO. Drinks are generously

1901 Union Street (at Laguna), San Francisco
Tel: 567-6905
Open daily 10 a.m. to 2 a.m.
No credit cards

poured and correctly mixed. The good-natured bartenders happily serve both regulars and drop-ins. On top of all this, you can get your car washed on the corner right outside the bar by a curbside detailer while you watch a game.

THE PARAGON

3251 Scott Street (between
Lombard and Chestnut),
San Francisco
Tel: 922-2456
Open daily 4 p.m. to 2 a.m.;
dinner 5:30 to 10 p.m.
Credit cards: AE, MC, V

The twenty-year-olds migrate here after work and stay late into the night. Opened by a group of young San Franciscans from old families, the Paragon quickly became a place to be seen for the young, straight, and eligible. A clubby muraled back room has been dedicated to dining. While the kitchen has had its ups and downs, the hamburger and grilled tuna sandwich are dependable and go well with beer, the Paragon's most popular drink.

PERRY'S

1944 Union Street (between
Laguna and Buchanan), San
Francisco
Tel: 922-9022
Open daily 9 a.m. to midnight
Credit cards: AE, MC, V

Perry Butler practically started the singles bar movement in the sixties at his eponymously named watering hole. Now many of his patrons, a couple of marriages later, will admit to pushing forty (well, late forties), but the spirit of the place remains convivial and fun. As much a spot for a blue cheese salad and a good hamburger with cottage fries as a bar, Perry's continues to serve classic pub food in congenial surroundings.

DELICATESSENS/TAKE-OUT

Food lovers from all over the city migrate to the well-stocked Lucca delicatessen for two house specialties: superb celery-scented bolognese sauce sold by the pint, and tender hand-rolled spinach-and-ricotta ravioli sold by the box. With either of these items in your shopping bag, you have the foundations for a gorgeous meal.

Opened in 1929 by Mike Bosco, a man with a great recipe, and two partners, Lucca supplied Nob Hill hotels with ravioli. Now his son Eddie and two grown grandchildren Linda and Paul carry on the tradition, thank goodness.

Around lunchtime, a line forms in front of the long counter stocked with always-fresh foods (nothing sits around at Lucca) for made-to-order Italian sandwiches on Italian rolls and wedges of Lucca's famous spinach frittata. Rotisserie chickens; irresistible marinated vegetable salad rife with beans, artichokes, and chunks of avocado; Acme bread; Italian cheeses; an excellent nutty Emmenthal; imported olive oils and pastas; anchovies in salt; and house-made minestrone sold by the pint mean that customers never walk out the door with only one item.

2120 Chestnut Street (between Steiner and Pierce), San Francisco
Tel: 921-7873
Open Monday 10 a.m. to 6:30 p.m., Tuesday through Friday 9 a.m. to 6:30 p.m., Saturday and Sunday until 6 p.m.
No credit cards

IL FORNAIO

**2298 Union Street
(between Steiner and
Fillmore), San Francisco
Tel: 563-0746
Open Monday through
Friday 6:30 a.m. to 7 p.m.,
Saturday 7 a.m. to 7 p.m.,
Sunday 8 a.m. to 6 p.m.
Credit cards: MC, V**

The breads at this first outpost of a northern Italian bakery chain somehow look more tempting than they taste, but I have found this to be true of most breads in Italy as well. The *ciabatta*, which appears as though it were pulled into its flat rectangular shape, has good flavor and a chewy texture if eaten fresh. I personally ranked it highly in the white bread category of a huge blind tasting of local and imported breads put on by *Bay Food* magazine several years ago. The bakery also makes a stunning cookie called a Garibaldi, a sandwich of glazed shortbread filled with raisins. Sweetened mostly by the dried fruit, it has the heft of biscotti, if not the texture, and goes well with strong Italian coffee. Il Fornaio's focaccia rounds work magic as hamburger buns.

JUST DESSERTS

**3735 Buchanan Street (at
Bay), San Francisco
Tel: 922-8675
Open Sunday through
Thursday 7 a.m. to 11 p.m.,
Friday and Saturday 8 a.m.
to midnight
Credit cards: MC, V**

For other locations see pages 118, 190, 272, 485.

Elliot Hoffman started this chain of American-style dessert cafes in 1974 on the strength of a cheesecake recipe. This store, across the street from the mammoth Marina Safeway where relationships blossom among the salad greens, and next door to a popular gym, causes particular anguish to those who work on their bodies. A hefty wedge of Just Dessert's moist devil's food cake with fudge frosting can obliterate the effects of a good workout. And, despite their healthful ring, the classic carrot cake with cream cheese frosting, homey lemon-buttermilk cake, and banana bread made with sour cream and walnuts cannot be considered diet fare. Just Desserts bakes everything from scratch, using whole butter and wholesome products, and delivers to its cafes every morning. Freshness is key here.

In 1992 Just Desserts bought the Tassajara Bread Bakery from the Zen Center and expanded distribution of Tassajara's hearty American breads to supermarkets like Safeway. When the two operations were combined in a large facility in the Bay View/Hunters Point neighborhood, Hoffman was instrumental in giving over an adjacent empty lot to the Garden Project, sponsored by the San Francisco County Sheriff's Department. Now, inmates grow fresh vegetables for soup kitchens all over the city. The bakery also uses some of the produce nurtured next door in the urban garden.

LA NOUVELLE PATISSERIE

The croissant, in all its flaky, buttery glory, brings me regularly to this French pastry shop. I take mine home, but many eat the croissants at small cafe tables in the shop, accompanied with decent café au lait. The cases here are full of colorful fruit tarts and handsome French pastries in generally fresh condition. A favorite item, especially among the French customers, is the bamboo, a crisp puff pastry sandwich filled with raspberry jam. Airy baguettes, just like the ones sold on Paris street corners, are also available.

2184 Union Street (between Webster and Fillmore), San Francisco Tel: 931-7655 Open Monday through Thursday 6:30 a.m. to 8 p.m., Friday and Saturday until 11 p.m., Sunday 8 a.m. to 7 p.m. No credit cards

ICE CREAM/CHOCOLATES

DOUBLE RAINBOW

2133 Chestnut Street (between Pierce and Steiner),
San Francisco
Tel: 922-3920
Open Sunday through Thursday 11 a.m. to 10:30 p.m.,
Friday and Saturday until 11:30 p.m.
No credit cards

See listing, page 273.

COFFEE

PEET'S COFFEE AND TEA

2156 Chestnut Street
(between Pierce and
Steiner), San Francisco
Tel: 931-8302
Open Monday through
Friday 6:30 a.m. to 7 p.m.,
Saturday and Sunday 7:30
a.m. to 6 p.m.
Credit cards: MC, V

For other locations see pages 355, 397, 488, 576.

Widely considered to be the Cadillac of coffee stores, Peet's has set the standard for coffee-bean buying and roasting throughout the country. If you are a true coffee drinker, you will love the intensity and individual character of Peet's carefully roasted beans. Each store, the most famous being the original location at the corner of Walnut and Vine in Berkeley, brews coffee every thirty minutes, throwing out any leftovers. When you buy a pound of beans, you get a free cup—and what a cup it is! You will never taste coffee with as much flavor and depth.

There are many reasons for the heady richness of Peet's brews. Selective buying from known producers all over the world; daily roasting of each type of bean to exact degrees of toastiness; diligent tasting of coffee made with the newly roasted beans; and daily delivery of the beans to the stores all contribute to the coffee's brilliant flavor.

A COFFEE TASTING

Jim Reynolds, the head coffee roaster and buyer for Peet's, invited me to a coffee tasting at the Emeryville headquarters. He set out three flights of short glasses, each with an inch of coarsely ground coffee at the bottom. He poured water that had cooled down a few minutes from the boiling point into each glass and then stirred. We waited to taste until the coffee cooled to warm.

Armed with a brass spittoon and a rounded soup spoon, we began by noisily slurping up, actually drawing in through the teeth, each coffee. We swished each spoonful around our tongues, smelled it in the back of our mouth, chewed it, and spit it into the receptacle. Very distinct characteristics of each coffee became clear.

Coffees from the Americas—Guatemala, Costa Rica, and Panama—define, to my mind, what we dream of in a cup of coffee. They are full-bodied, balanced, unquirky, aromatic, rich. Guatemala is Jim Reynold's favorite of all the coffees. I preferred the slightly fuller cup from Costa Rican beans. Lightest of the three was Panama coffee, with flowery overtones. Peet's House Blend and Blend 101 are made entirely from Latin American coffee beans.

The African coffees—Kenya, Ethiopian, and Arabian Mocha Sanani—have a spiciness and pronounced acidity. The rare Arabian Mocha Sanani, because it is harvested and dried so primitively, has a syrupy, fermented quality to it. We smelled a slight petroleum quality in the Ethiopian, which comes from a treatment to the burlap sacks, a practice that Reynolds is trying to change. Coffees from the Pacific—New Guinea, Sumatra, and Sulawesi—have distinctive herbal and earthy qualities. Given the characteristics of the different coffees, you begin to understand the advantages of blends like Peet's Top Blend, which combines coffees from the Pacific and Latin America, or the famous Major Dickason's, whose regional makeup remains a secret. Each bean has something to say.

Peet's generally roasts darker than most other companies. However, two blends, Italian roast and the really dark French roast, get even longer roastings. Very dark roasting produces a cup with less body, but with an intense flavor and smoky overtone that stand up to milk and sugar, good for morning latte or café au lait. After the coffee tasting, I started enjoying coffee in a new way. What was a generic flavor blossomed with complexity and nuance. Here was a food I have every morning and I had never explored its possibilities. An hour at a Peet's tasting could improve the quality of your daily life significantly.

Although the list of different coffees can seem daunting to the uninitiated, the company has published an extremely helpful booklet describing each one, with recommendations from the head roaster and buyer. It sheds light on the difference in flavor between coffees from different regions of the world, lists the components of Peet's blends, and describes the effects of different degrees of roasting. The booklet is free and available at all Peet's stores. Of course, the only way to understand the differences in flavor is to taste the coffees side by side. Peet's personnel are willing to set up coffee tastings for their customers. Take them up on it and come to your own conclusions.

In addition to coffee beans, Peet's offers a variety of teas, coffee- and tea-brewing equipment from all over the world, and a mail-order service.

MARKETS

MARINA SUPER

2323 Chestnut Street (between Scott and Divisadero), San Francisco
Tel: 346-7470
Open Monday through Saturday 7 a.m. to 8:30 p.m., Sunday 9 a.m. to 6 p.m.
Credit cards: CB, DC, MC, V

With Patricia Wells's cookbook *Trattoria* in hand, I walked into the Marina Super, next door to Cafe Marimba, one day after lunch. This market, along with its independent butcher, Puccini Meats, has been supplying the Italian community of the Marina with all the ingredients needed to cook dishes just like the ones in any classic Italian cookbook. I picked up a free-range chicken, pancetta, and some very lean ground sirloin. Rather nice vine-ripened tomatoes, for mid-October, and beautiful red peppers were piled outside on produce tables. Plump heads of garlic, huge bunches of Italian parsley, fresh thyme, and oregano are regularly available. Though the market does not buy organic produce, they always have the best commercially available representatives of whatever may be in season. You never see bad green beans here when good ones are available. Organic canned tomato products earn their own display shelf. Berkeley Farms dairy products are stocked, although not extra-rich milk for those who prefer it with espresso. Baskets of dried beans, ranging from gigantic borlotti to tiny white beans, call out to be made into a Tuscan soup. A whole rack of fresh breads from Semifreddi completes the family meal. Although very much a neighborhood market, this can be one of the most useful stops in the city for Italian-American shopping.

WINES AND SPIRITS

CALIFORNIA WINE MERCHANT

Hard-to-find California wines line the walls of this tiny eighteen-year-old shop guarded by a huge golden retriever snoring away at the front door. The elegance of a shop that does one thing well cannot be underestimated. Only high-quality California and a few Oregon wines tasted and chosen by the owner, Gregory O'Flynn, get a slot in the floor-to-ceiling wooden racks. Small production wines like Terrace Zinfandel or impossible-to-find Stony Hill Chardonnay or the ele-

3237 Pierce Street (between Lombard and Chestnut), San Francisco

Tel: 567-0646

Open Monday through Saturday 11 a.m. to 7 p.m., Sunday noon to 5 p.m.

Credit cards: MC, V

gant Shafer Merlot can all be found here at fair-market prices. Since the wine selections at this shop have been so carefully edited, shopping here will expand your knowledge of the most exciting California wines. The shop will ship.

COOKWARE AND BOOKS

FREDERICKSEN'S HARDWARE

3029 Fillmore Street
(between Union and Filbert),
San Francisco
Tel: 292-2950
Open Monday through
Saturday 9 a.m. to 6 p.m.,
Sunday 10 a.m. to 5 p.m.
Credit cards: MC, V

Hardware stores don't get better than this. Not only does Fredericksen's stock every conceivable item you might need for your house and kitchen, but the service is so good that you will be steered to exactly the right thing. One third of this packed store is dedicated to kitchen and housewares, and the level of sophistication is high. This is the place to find kitchen timers, food mills, springform pans, juicers, coffee grinders, good basic lines of pots and pans, glass baking dishes, graters: all the building blocks of a practical, old-fashioned kitchen and then some. Fredericksen's will always have the innovation on the traditional item if it is really an improvement, but it does not carry frivolous gadgets. I love the integrity of this store, the dependability, the completeness. I'm willing to pay a bit more here because I know they will have what I need and I won't have to waste time driving around town.

The Mission District, Bernal Heights & the Excelsior

THE MISSION DISTRICT, BERNAL HEIGHTS & THE EXCELSIOR

RESTAURANTS

ANGKOR BOREI

This neighborhood Cambodian restaurant, decorated with handsome Khmer artifacts, turns out intricate dishes with surprising finesse. Though ownership changed recently, the kitchen staff stayed on and continues to perform on the highest level. The dishes here are characterized by a ravishing tapestry of flavors, textures, and colors. Like intricate Khmer carvings, Cambodian food is composed of many tiny, exquisite elements like a mosaic, such as cold white noodles, julienned cucumbers, bean sprouts, basil, red chilies, and carrots, all in separate piles that come together with a fragrant coconut milk dipping sauce; delicate Cambodian spring rolls with moist multi-vegetable fillings; or crisp Cambodian omelettelike crepes folded over a juicy, crunchy filling of vegetables, herbs, and nuts.

I love the curries at Angkor Borei, particularly a fiery green one aromatic with Thai basil and lemongrass served on Japanese eggplant and big chunks of white fish. A milder red curry with many deep layers of flavor

**3471 Mission Street
(between Cortland and
29th Street), San Francisco
Tel: 550-8417
Open daily for lunch 11 a.m.
to 3 p.m., dinner 5 to
10 p.m.
Price: Inexpensive
Credit cards: AE, MC, V**

enhances tender sautéed shrimp on a bed of bright green spinach. The charcoal broiling shows equal skill: Marinated chicken or beef skewers come with delicious vinegared vegetables—the perfect accompaniment. Even the rice, served from a covered silver tureen, has a marvelous, nutty flavor and chewy texture.

Artfully presented and complex, yet immediately delicious, this Cambodian food enchants everyone—even those trying Cambodian cooking for the first time. This so-called neighborhood spot would be a find any-where in the world.

E S P E R P E N T O

3295 22nd Street (between Valencia and Mission), San Francisco Tel: 282-8867 Open daily for lunch 11 a.m. to 3 p.m.; Sunday through Thursday for dinner 5 to 10 p.m., Fridays and Saturdays until 11 p.m. Price: Inexpensive No credit cards

Started by a group of young Spaniards with more crea-tivity than capital, this small, funky tapas-and-paella cafe will appeal to anyone who has eaten in Spain, or in Berkeley in the 1970s, or has dreamed of opening her or his own restaurant. A lot has been done with paint in the airy, high-ceilinged storefront decorated in a vaguely surrealistic, Dalí-esque theme. (Not finding *esperpento* in my Spanish-English dictionary, I learned from a waiter that it means "weird.")

From the moment it opened, Esperpento proved to be a hit in the neighborhood. Good, inexpensive food had a lot to do with it, but people find Esperpento's bohemian authenticity endearing. The rough edges that give Esperpento character also can cause inconsistencies in food and service, but this seems like a fair price for a taste of the real thing.

The tapas really do conjure up memories of Spain. Usually served at room temperature, a *tortilla de pata-tas*, a cake of potatoes and onions held together with eggs, comes out of the kitchen warm and heavenly here.

Garlicky mushrooms are sautéed until all their juices evaporate and their flavors intensify. *Escalivada* is a marvelous mixture of roasted eggplant and peppers seasoned with vinegar. Delicious, creamy chicken croquettes; oven-roasted clams; shrimp drenched in garlic, olive oil, and hot red chilies; and crisp fried squid all can be terrific if you hit Esperpento on the right night. Besides tapas, the main attraction is paella, authentically served in a searing-hot cast-iron pan set right on the table. This luscious rendition, with shellfish, chicken, and pork peeking through a blanket of moist saffron rice, is worth a few scars.

ESCALIVADA

This is a popular Spanish tapa served at Esperpento.

Preheat oven to 350° F. Cut the eggplants in half lengthwise, sprinkle with salt, and lay cut-side down on paper towels for 30 minutes. Dry the eggplant and rub it all over with 1 tablespoon of the oil and 1 tablespoon of the salt, and place cut-side down in a baking pan. Rub the whole red peppers with oil and 1/2 tablespoon salt and add to the baking pan. Bake until tender, about 1 hour.

Remove the cooked vegetables from the oven, place in a bowl, and cover with plastic wrap for 15 minutes.

With your fingers, remove the skin and seeds from the peppers and peel the eggplants. Slice each vegetable lengthwise into 1/2-inch-thick slices. Lay the slices on a platter.

Whisk together the remaining 1/2 teaspoon salt, the vinegar, and garlic. Whisk in the remaining 3 1/2 tablespoons olive oil. Pour the vinaigrette over the vegetables and mix gently. Marinate at room temperature. Serve within a few hours of roasting.

Serves 4 to 6 as a first course

2 medium eggplants, unpeeled

About 2 tablespoons kosher salt

4 1/2 tablespoons extra -virgin olive oil, plus oil for coating pepper

3 red bell peppers

1 3/4 tablespoons red wine vinegar

1 large garlic clove , minced

Spanish wines, like the gratifyingly full, drinkable, yet inexpensive Torres Sangre de Toro or Cornonas, are intrinsic to a meal here, as are glasses of *amontillado* or *fino* sherry. For dessert, *crema Catalana* with a burnt sugar crust or thick rice pudding scented with lemon zest, along with a *cafe cortado*, a demitasse of espresso cut with warm milk, make for a buoyant ending.

FINA ESTAMPA

2374 Mission Street (between 19th and 20th streets), San Francisco
Tel: 824-4437
Open for lunch Tuesday through Thursday 11:30 a.m. to 3:30 p.m., dinner 5 to 9 p.m.; Friday through Sunday 11:30 a.m. to 9 p.m.
Price: Inexpensive
Credit cards: MC, V

Although Gus Shinzato might look more like a sushi chef, one taste of his *parihuela de mariscos* makes it clear that he is a masterful Peruvian cook. A third-generation Peruvian, now living in the United States, he opened Fina Estampa with his wife Tamie Takaesu, a Japanese-born Peruvian who runs the dining room. They serve spectacularly delicious food in a comfortable, if modest, Mission Street storefront, the kind of place that puts glass over the tablecloths.

Before I started eating at Fina Estampa, Peruvian food meant boiled potatoes and skewered beef heart (very tasty, actually). But after several visits here, I discovered that the breadth of the cuisine parallels the spectacular geography of the country. From seaside towns come opulent seafood soups like *parihuela*, a deep bowl full of shrimp, squid, mussels, clams, and rockfish in a tomato broth resonant with dried chilies. Another seafood triumph, *jalea de pescado*, brings a gigantic fish fry served with *salsa criolla* (marinated onions and tomatoes) and a fiery dark green salsa called *ají*. The frying is impeccable. A huge, moist seafood paella has remarkable depth of flavor. Since both San Francisco and Peru share the Pacific coast, the fresh local catch here works particularly well in many of the seafood dishes.

From the mountains come potatoes: orange, yellow, purple, white. Fina Estampa includes them in one of the best ceviches in town, a revelatory combination. Chef Shinzato serves them traditionally, *a la huancaina*, in a pungent cheese sauce as an appetizer, or rubs them with red spice paste and deep-fries them as an accompaniment to skewers of marinated beef heart.

Wonderful, crisp, deep-fried bone-in chunks of chicken called *chicharrón de pollo* come with a bowl of fresh lime juice and chilies and a pile of *salsa criolla*. A luscious dish called *bisteck a la pobre*, a small, tender grilled steak served on a slice of toast that soaks up all the juices, is piled with sautéed onions and tomatoes, a deep-fried banana, and crowned by a fried egg. *Ají panca*, grilled chicken rubbed with a red spice paste, has the texture of velvet. Both Peruvian beer and Chilean and Spanish red wine enhance the food. Don't be put off by the Mission District custom of putting out margarine with soft white bread; the plates to come will be dazzling.

THE FLYING SAUCER

This fanciful, eccentric, extremely personal bistro of chef Albert Tordjman's has doubled in size, and the flamboyant plates coming out of the now glassed-in display kitchen seem to have done the same. What started out as a rough-edged Mission District hideaway has turned into a more comfortable, more controlled dining experience. However, the cooking continues to beam in from outer space—a territory in chef Tordjman's head.

French training sets his eclecticism apart from that of more amateurish endeavors. His mastery of technique adds the gloss of refinement and allows him to incorporate exotic flavors in sauces, vinaigrettes, and marinades

1000 Guerrero Street (at 22nd Street), San Francisco

Tel: 641-9955

Open Tuesday through Saturday 5:30 to 10 p.m.

Price: Moderate

No credit cards

with a high level of sophistication. What differentiates the Flying Saucer from a downtown restaurant like Postrio, also from the California-eclectic school, is its still-small scale and remaining ragged edges, but more significantly, Tordjman's imagination. This chef's creations, whether you like to eat this way or not, have a highly designed look and strong flavors. This is not watered-down cooking. Tordjman is an artist with an uncompromising vision.

The main ingredient of a dish is merely an excuse to fill a plate with vegetables, potatoes, sauces, greens, herbs, noodles—a world of food. The portions are gigantic. A starter could be a slice of an absolutely classic terrine of foie gras with a sharply dressed salad and a buttery slice of grilled brioche; or an exotic seafood *empanada* of soft cornmeal flanked by greens, a jícama-chayote salad, and searingly hot jalapeños stuffed with smoked salmon. Asian flavors are often paired with fish, as in a Japanese-style hunk of salmon served in a flat bowl with soba noodles, shiitake mushrooms, and asparagus. Crisp duck *confit*, with a sprig of thyme growing out of a leg, gets a cylinder of cabbage with red and green layers laced strongly with fennel seed, roasted potatoes, and carrots, all in an aromatic broth. Lots of molded shapes, vegetables fashioned with cookie cutters, and sprigs of fresh herbs are used to architecturally construct the plates. As a fellow food writer noted, all the sous-chefs in town eat here to get ideas.

The Saucer has expanded into the next storefront, thereby adding a bar and six or eight more unlinened tables of different sizes and composition. This means no more waiting outside, although those with later reservations should not expect to be seated immediately. Even though the chefs work nonstop behind their glass wall, the plates are so complicated that it is no surprise that service backs up.

One of the most long-lived (since 1975) and meticulous taquerias in the Mission, La Taqueria earned its reputation through cleanliness, freshness, and efficiency. This family taqueria sports an attractive Mission-style arched façade, adobe walls decorated with a vibrant folk mural, and a dining room full of rustic wooden tables with leather stools. Jars of excellent green and red salsa sit on each immaculate table.

Although a list of typical and well-prepared fillings for burritos and tacos is posted on the wall above the tiled kitchen, La Taqueria's soft, moist, savory, miraculously greaseless *carnitas* (pork slowly cooked in its own fat) deserves special attention. Prepared every day, this rich pork shines brightest in tacos made with two soft, warm corn tortillas and a little salsa. Shredded chicken simmered with tomatoes and chilies, and aromatically spicy chorizo, sausage that has been crumbled and fried, also make for exceptional tacos. This friendly taqueria ranks high on my list of favorites because it fulfills its simple menu perfectly, day after day, year after year.

2889 Mission Street (at 25th Street), San Francisco

Tel: 285-7117

Open Monday through Saturday 11 a.m. to 9 p.m., Sunday 11 a.m. to 8 p.m.

Price: Inexpensive

No credit cards

The chef and owner of this unique French restaurant was inspired by a pixie-eyed French chef and cooking teacher named Josephine Araldo, who brought the secrets and pleasures of the Breton kitchen to a generation of Bay Area cooks, myself included. She died several years ago, but the memories of the dishes she prepared in front of us in her tiny Laurel Heights kitchen live on at Le Trou. Robert Reynolds was her most loyal and loving student, a constant companion to her even after he started his own cooking school, which later turned

1007 Guerrero Street (at 22nd Street), San Francisco

Tel: 550-8169

Tuesday through Thursday 6 to 9 p.m., Friday and Saturday until 10 p.m.

Price: Moderate

Credit cards: AE, D, MC, V

into this little restaurant. He even collected and re-worked Josephine's vegetable recipes in a cookbook called *From a Breton Garden: The Vegetable Cookery of Josephine Araldo.*

The experience of eating at Le Trou transports you to a French country home where *grand-mère* proudly displays her large, heavy silverware, hand-ironed lace-edged napkins, glass salt cellars in the shape of little hens, flower-trimmed china, and dining room walls covered with print fabric. The weekly changing menu consists of four or five first courses, the same number of main courses, and three or four desserts that taste like real home-cooked French food, but of course, only someone with a lot of practical experience and generations of tradition to draw on can cook with as much panache as a provincial French housewife. Reynolds has achieved this exalted culinary persona.

Dinner begins with house-baked bread and a first course that might bring a heavenly little Roquefort custard served with a sliced fresh fig, or a vivid fennel soup seasoned with fresh chervil swirled with browned hazelnut butter. As a main course one evening, Reynolds served an old-fashioned *fricandeau*, here made

with lamb, a light, airy, seemingly hand-chopped patty sautéed in crisp bread crumbs and presented on a bed of braised white beans with creamed zucchini. Moist roast pork loin, stuffed and sauced with pistachios, came with a very Josephine-esque combination of quinces and rutabaga. A rare duck breast was nicely set off by pureed pears, beet greens, and simple boiled potatoes. Desserts are seasonal, homey, and very fresh.

The carefully honed wine list is tiny, but includes just the regional bottles you want to drink in this environment with this food. It adds much to the pleasure of dining here. The perfect ending comes with individual pots of *café filtré*, demitasses, and a tin house of castor sugar, one of the finest coffee services in town.

LOS JARRITOS

While good taquerias abound in the Mission, the sit-down Mexican restaurants are surprisingly similar and uninspired. One of my favorites, Los Jarritos, distinguishes itself by its colorful, folk-art-filled dining room and tasty *chilaquiles*, the current dish of choice in the Mission among those who have partied too hard the night before. *Chilaquiles* are stale tortillas that are fried and then cooked in a sauce, often with other ingredients. At Los Jarritos's, the tortillas are fried with eggs, white cheese, and pickled jalapeños, then braised in a lot of piquant ranchera sauce. A huge portion comes with mashed red beans seasoned with lard and Spanish rice.

Mission families drift in all afternoon for delicious eggs scrambled with cactus and onions, and served with beans, rice, and excellent made-to-order tortillas hot from the *comal*. These tortillas are puffy and lighter in texture than any you have tasted from a package. If you are a tortilla fan, you owe it to yourself to try them. They are especially good with huevos rancheros, two perfectly poached eggs in ranchera sauce topped with melted cheese (ask them to go light on the cheese or the eggs get buried and overcooked).

Jarritos are small clay cups. Strings of them hang all over the immaculate dining room next to shelves of old-fashioned smiling clay piggy banks. A resonant wooden

901 South Van Ness Avenue
(at 20th Street),
San Francisco
Tel: 648-8383
Open Monday through
Saturday 8 a.m. to 10 p.m.
Price: Inexpensive
Credit cards: MC, V

floor and old Formica and aluminum tables with bright blue and red tops add warmth and cheer to this folksy little restaurant.

MOM IS COOKING

1166 Geneva Avenue (at Naples), San Francisco
Tel: 586-7000
Open daily 10 a.m. to 10 p.m.
Price: Inexpensive
No credit cards

When I first heard that Mom Is Cooking had moved a few doors from its original crusty spot, I was worried that this Excelsior District destination for authentic Mexican home cooking might be going upscale. But the best of all possible things happened: Mom moved to larger quarters with more seating and a bigger kitchen, which means no more unbearably long waits either to get a table or to get your food. In the move she acquired a liquor license, which adds good margaritas to the drink possibilities, and chef-mom Abigail Murillo has not changed her cooking or prices at all. The food is as vibrant, earthy, and cheap as ever, the surroundings just as funky. You could be sitting in a neighborhood restaurant in an out-of-the-way district of Mexico City.

For the uninitiated, the menu may seem long and disorganized, handwritten on seven or eight pages enclosed in plastic, but you almost can't go wrong. Take the first item on the menu, *boquitos*, warm tortilla chips individually layered with melted cheese, guacamole, mashed beans, *crema* (Mexican sour cream), and salsa. You can taste each ingredient separately, yet every bite is a complete trip through Mexican cuisine. This same integrity of flavor makes items such as crisp-shelled tacos, soft *flautas*, and airy tamales feel like exciting new dishes.

More unusual preparations, like *huevos con chorizo*, scrambled eggs with delicate, greaseless, house-made sausage crumbled into them, served with beautiful plump red beans; or a *carnitas* plate with buttery, long-cooked pork as a centerpiece to an array of salsas, black beans, Spanish rice, oregano-scented cabbage salad, and chunky guacamole; or a spectacular *quesadilla* filled with whole grilled shrimp and tangy Mexican cheese, expand the horizons of Mexican restaurant cooking. At Mom Is Cooking you can play it safe or explore, and reap equal rewards.

PANCHO VILLA TAQUERIA

When you bite into one of Pancho Villa's monumental burritos, you know why a line always extends past the front door. Though you may have to wait, the endless turnover means that all the components of the various tacos, burritos, and dinner plates have been prepared very recently. This freshness makes the earthy Mexican food sparkle.

3071 16th Street (between Mission and Valencia), San Francisco
Tel: 864-8840
Open daily 11 am to midnight
Price: Inexpensive
No credit cards

The Mission District favorite is the *carne asada* special, a huge flour tortilla lined with melted white cheese and filled with about a pound of Spanish rice, red beans, thinly sliced grilled steak, guacamole, and fresh salsa. All these elements work together in some magical way to make a completely satisfying rolled-up meal. If you eat a Pancho Villa burrito for lunch, don't plan on dinner. *Carnitas*, pork slowly cooked in its own fat, also makes stunning burritos or soft tacos with beans and salsa.

On the lighter side, try a grilled-shrimp burrito with black beans, or a satisfying vegetarian burrito that features firm cubes of tofu in a red ranchera sauce. Besides the tortilla dishes, Pancho Villa puts out some gorgeous-looking platters of butterflied garlic prawns, or hot, spicy prawns griddled with whole dried *chiles de árbol*, all cooked to order. Be sure to get a side order of grilled green onions to go with the shrimp.

Ladled from huge glass jars afloat with strawberries, cantaloupe, or seeded watermelon and ice, Pancho Villa's *aguas frescas* alone merit a visit, especially on a warm afternoon when the kids want something quick to eat and refreshing to drink.

TI COUZ CRÊPERIE

3108 16th Street (between Mission and Valencia), San Francisco
Tel: 252-7373
Open Monday through Friday 11 a.m. to 11 p.m., Saturday 10 a.m. to 11 p.m., Sunday 10 a.m. to 10 p.m.
Price: Inexpensive
Credit cards: MC, V

A real *crêperie* like you might find in Brittany, Ti Couz turns out thin, irresistible pancakes, filled with everything from ratatouille to ice cream and chocolate sauce. As a cheap, satisfying meal, you can't beat them. In fact, so many people were banging on the doors of Ti Couz's tiny dining room that the *crêperie* has doubled in size. Happily, only the seating has expanded; the menu remains the same.

For me, the simplest crepe is the most sublime, and I can barely walk past Ti Couz without sitting down at the counter where the crepes are made for a hot buckwheat crepe spread just with softened butter and sprinkled with sugar. My new favorite, however, has become a crepe spread with almond butter. The Gruyère and cheese crepe topped with an egg is completely satisfying as a main course.

The authenticity of this place comes from owner Sylvie Le Mer, who keeps Ti Couz doing just what it does best. A green salad, sometimes a charcuterie plate, and a soup, are the only other dishes offered. The crepes come off the griddle tender but crisp and buttery on the outside. I hate to order them with too much stuff because the pancakes themselves are the treat.

Mildly alcoholic French cider on tap comes in whole and half carafes, with pottery bowls instead of glasses, a quaint service that only makes the crepes taste that much better. The small wooden tables and chairs, wood floors, French country china cabinets, and blue and white color scheme add to the authenticity of this Mission District *crêperie.*

TIMO'S IN THE ZANZIBAR

Carlos and Theresa Corredor took over the food service at this funky Mission District bar and turned it into a hot spot with their delicious, creative tapas. One fantastic little plate of savory food after another emerges like some kind of miracle from an immaculate kitchen. Crusty roasted new potatoes, the diameter of a quarter, are dabbed with the velvety house-made garlic mayonnaise called *alioli.* Big firm mushrooms, hot off the grill and tossed in finely chopped garlic and parsley, are as delicious as they are simple. Don't pass up a crusty cake of Yukon Gold potatoes, chanterelles, and lobster mushrooms dusted with fresh marjoram aptly named Potato Decadence; or a large, tender ravioli filled with ricotta, spinach, and a just-set egg yolk, drizzled with lots of brown butter and tiny sautéed mushrooms. When you cut into this gossamer ravioli the egg runs out as a delectable sauce. Timo's prepares a superior version of a very typical Spanish dish, salt cod and potato cake, but creatively pairs it with a lively cilantro-mint salsa. The chef takes a detour to neighboring southwest France in his crispy leg of duck *confit* surrounded by tender baby turnips.

The odd, gerrymandered green and purple dining rooms in the Club Zanzibar, hung with a gallery's worth of 1950s artwork, lend a certain cachet to the experience, but only because the food is so unexpectedly wonderful. Timo's ambiance reminds me of Beat coffeehouses, where a coat of paint and collection of photographs of nudes constituted the decor. In fact, moody vintage

842 Valencia Street
(between 19th and 20th
streets), San Francisco
Tel: 647-0558
Open Sunday through
Wednesday 5 to 10:30 p.m.,
Thursday through Saturday
until 11:30 p.m.
Price: Moderate
Credit cards: MC, V

jazz plays in the background, and there are guys sitting at the bar, beer glass stuck in fist, who look as if they have not moved for the last thirty years. Recently, the bar was bought by a fan of Timo's who opened up a back room with a dance floor to diners. This eases the wait and the necessity to sit in the bar, where conditions can be smoky.

VAL 21

995 Valencia Street
(at 21st Street),
San Francisco
Tel: 821-6622
Open for dinner Sunday
through Thursday 5:30 to 9
p.m., Friday and Saturday
until 10 p.m.; Saturday and
Sunday for brunch 10 a.m.
to 2 p.m.
Price: Moderate
Credit Cards: MC, V

More means better for the kitchen at Val 21, a lively and much-loved Mission restaurant that opened originally as a juice bar. The plates created here have more color, more ingredients, more flavors, just plain more going on than most others—though the trend these days in San Francisco's newest uptown restaurants seems to be a similar piling on of stuff. At Val 21, a multicultural representation of seasonings and ingredients throw a powwow in each dish, but meeting together does not mean that all the parties will get along. In Val 21's case, sometimes they do and sometimes they don't.

The mélange of ingredients might transcend their diversity in a wonderful starter of crisp filo pastry stuffed with a savory, aromatic ground chicken filling, served with a fig chutney. They end up losing their identities in a spicy hot ragout of many different wild mushrooms lavished on deep-fried Gorgonzola-polenta fingers. True-flavored passion fruit and coconut sorbets in an elegant tulip-shaped Florentine cookie charm, while a warm, soft chocolate pudding-cake in a berry sauce hits you over the head with obtuse flavors. However, if you are eating out with a vegetarian, Val 21 is a godsend, because it is one of the few restaurants in town that wholeheartedly creates satisfying and stylish non-meat dishes.

The small dining room is filled with original hand-crafted furnishings, round wooden tables with bright green tops, a blond wood floor, and a smart curved bar with matching stools. The service is enthusiastic, and the wine list offers some carefully chosen California bottles like a balanced Ferrari-Carano Fumé Blanc that goes exceptionally well with the wild mix of flavors.

WOODWARD'S GARDEN

This tiny place epitomizes the "let's start our own restaurant" impulse, although the four young partners running it know exactly what they are doing. Far from being a beginner experience, a meal at Woodward's Garden represents the height of civility with the added charm of a hidden location and proudly modest surroundings.

1700 Mission Street (at Duboce), San Francisco

Tel: 621-7122

Open Wednesday through Sunday 6 to 10 p.m.

Price: Moderate

No credit cards

The food, cooked by Dana Tommasino and Margie Conard, veterans of Greens and Postrio respectively, is fresh and seductive, a unique composite of the styles of the two mother-ship restaurants. The minuscule kitchen dictates a small menu, but everything coming from it sparkles. A typical winter menu might include a salad with jewellike segments of blood orange and grapefruit; a deeply flavored vegetable saffron risotto; ravioli stuffed with potato and black truffle; a satiny, tender duck breast on a bed of fava beans, greens, and other winter vegetables in a delicate vinaigrette; and a silken fillet of salmon on a bed of couscous slathered with an assertive tamarind sauce. The meal might end with a simple but gossamer dessert like a Meyer lemon pot de crème with buttery cookies. The completely eccentric and wonderful wine list offers the opportunity to drink such oddities as smooth and spicy Portuguese red wines. For food and wine of this caliber, one would expect to pay twice the price any place else.

This restaurant's diminutive size, minimalist decor, and obscure location only add to its appeal. Nestled near a freeway overpass where Mission and Duboce meet, Woodward's Garden is the only piece left of the entry façade to a famous amusement park and garden that entertained San Franciscans from 1866 to 1892—hence the name of the restaurant. You can barely tell that a restaurant is inside the lace-curtained windows. The small room is about equally divided between tables and open kitchen, with a dark wooden counter and stools demarcating the two functions. Banquettes and white-linen-covered tables, thin, elegant glassware, pretty flowered plates, a very hip, austere room painted white, all help create the cachet of a Paris boîte. Every-thing about this little place is first class and civilized, including the quiet, intelligent service by one of the partners, who unobtrusively makes you feel like a guest at her dinner party.

CAFES

RADIO VALENCIA

Though many funky, if comfy, cafes now dot the Mission, most of them serve burnt coffee and are used more as bohemian hangouts than places for a good cup. Radio Valencia is the exception, probably because it is as much an eating place as a cafe. Though its many neighborhood patrons spend lots of time seated at wooden spool tables in the green-and-yellow-painted corner storefront with loud and eclectic music always playing, they also appreciate its integrity when it comes to food and drink. The emphasis is on house-made pastries and nicely turned-out sandwiches and salads made with healthful ingredients. I particularly like Saturday and Sunday brunch, where perfectly poached eggs Benedict and eggs Florentine arrive bathed in a lovely, creamy hollandaise. You must arrive early on either day to get Eggs Tropical, a layered pile of scrambled eggs, black beans, and melted jack on a thick hand-patted tortilla topped with fresh melon salsa, sour cream, and chipotle hot sauce. The well-balanced café au lait comes in giant cups, and the orange juice is squeezed to order. You might be served fitfully by a typically depressed, disorganized Mission coffeehouse wait staff, but the kitchen is so meticulous it cuts all the fruit to order for its yogurt and granola, and every plate that comes out has been carefully prepared.

1199 Valencia Street
(at 23rd Street),
San Francisco
Tel: 826-1199
Open Monday through
Friday 11:30 a.m. to
midnight, Saturday and
Sunday 10 a.m. to midnight
Credit cards: MC, V
($15 minimum)

525 Valencia Street (at 16th
Street), San Francisco
Tel: 863-8854
Open daily 11 a.m. to
11 p.m.
No credit cards

After a night of carousing in the Mission, stop by Cafe Istanbul for a soothing pot of tea. Sit in the carpeted nook near the front window at low pounded-brass tray tables, or at Western-style tables and chairs under a tented ceiling. Try a mixture of mint and black tea called *damas*, or *chai*, an Indian-style Darjeeling spiced with cinnamon and cardamom, smoothed by milk. Or drink a tiny cup of muddy Turkish coffee. On Wednesdays, at 8:30 and 9:30 p.m., you can catch the belly dancers, exotic Mission District–style performers with tattoos and many pierced body parts. They never fail to draw a crowd inside or, peering through the front window of the cafe, outside.

BARS

DALVA

3121 16th Street (at
Valencia), San Francisco
Tel: 252-7740
Open Monday through
Thursday 5 p.m. to 2 a.m.,
Friday through Sunday
2 p.m. to 2 a.m.
Credit Cards: MC, V

Next door to the Roxie Theater, Dalva offers a tonier atmosphere than most Mission District bars, mostly brought about by its sponged, coral-colored walls. Späten and Bass ale, among others, on tap, sangría, some women bartenders in tight T-shirts, and nightly DJs who seem to specialize in the 1970s keep the action lively. The bar comfortably fills up early and buzzes throughout the night.

Appropriately named, this bar gets so packed with a young crowd that you can barely elbow your way to the bar for a draft beer. Formerly a lesbian bar called Amelia's, the Elbo Room has become the Mission District hot spot for heterosexual singles in their twenties. A $3 cover charge gets you upstairs for dancing orchestrated by a changing lineup of DJs and live bands.

647 Valencia Street
(between 17th and 18th
streets), San Francisco
Tel: 552-7788
Open daily 5 to 2 a.m.
No credit cards

DELICATESSENS/TAKE-OUT

HUNGARIAN SAUSAGE FACTORY

The smell of garlic is so strong it nearly pushes you over when you walk into this tiny deli and restaurant in two connected Victorian storefronts on Bernal Height's main shopping street. In one light-filled, lace-curtained room are cushion-covered wooden benches, handsome varnished tables, and a piano. Jars of fresh flowers sit on all the tables, including a few on the sidewalk basking in the sun. People order at the deli case and then sit down, or take their food to go. The whole system is fairly impromptu, at least during the day when all the ordering is done at the deli counter. Though a very small repertoire of Hungarian specialties is made here, they are all homemade-tasting and delicious, particularly the garlicky Hungarian sausages, which come fresh, smoked or cured, hot, or mild. The hot are barely so and enhanced by long-simmered sauerkraut, a huge pickle, and soft

419 Cortland Avenue (at
Wool), San Francisco
Tel: 648-2847
Open Tuesday through
Thursday 10 a.m. to 9 p.m.,
Friday and Saturday until
10 p.m., Sunday 11 a.m. to
9 p.m.
No credit cards

egg bread on the Sausage Plate. The stuffed cabbage is also soul-satisfying, with as much rice as ground pork in the savory filling. For dessert have a warm crepe (*palacsinta*) with butter and sugar.

The deli augments its own sausages with imported goods from Hungary, including hams, dry sausages, paprika, fruit syrups, and soft, fruity Hungarian red wines that go wonderfully with the food and cost all of $10.50 a bottle. You can drop in for some house-baked Hungarian pastries like a fine, barely sweetened Hungarian cheesecake—two layers of yeast dough with a thick layer of farmer's cheese in between—and some of the best espresso in the city, served in a small glass, just the way I like it.

LA PALMA

2884 24th Street (at Florida), San Francisco
Tel: 647-1500
Open Monday through Saturday 8 a.m. to 6 p.m., Sunday until 5 p.m.
Credit cards: MC, V

Serious lovers of tortillas make regular pilgrimages to La Palma, a "Mexicatessen" and small tortilla factory, where thick tortillas are hand patted Central American style, or thinly pressed Mexican style, or fried into the best thick chips in town. La Palma also sells fresh *masa* dough by the pound for tamales or homemade tortillas. The *masa* has no preservatives in it. Each day a new batch of corn is ground and fresh tortillas are made. A world of difference exists between reheated packaged corn tortillas, even those hot from La Palma's griddle, and ones that are shaped, cooked, and eaten immediately. Just as yeast, flour, and water act a hundred different ways in the hands of bakers, lime-softened ground corn and water can deliver many subtle pleasures depending on how it is handled.

A glimpse into the back of La Palma, where a group of women stand around patting out tortillas from hills of *masa* and slapping them onto a rectangular griddle, will whet your appetite for Mexican food. Hunger can be satisfied on the spot from the counter at the back, which sells tacos and burritos or prepared fillings to go. If you want to cook at home, La Palma is the place to buy your basic ingredients. Bags of freshly ground dried chilies of different varieties (California, New Mexico, pasilla, ancho), fresh *epazote* and other Mexican spices, freshly made *chicharróns*, which are Mexican cracklings, fried-to-order tortillas for tostadas in any size you like, and all sorts of canned and jarred Mexican products fill the immaculate shelves. La Palma renders its own lard, which is ever so much more flavorful than the preserved bricks on supermarket shelves. The lard is sold by the quart from the refrigerator case. If you happen to see little bags of La Palma's potato chips, which are fried in clean vegetable oil, grab them. You will never taste a more satisfying chip. To wash them down, try a glass of *jamaica*, a refreshing red iced tea made from hibiscus flowers. Every time I go to La Palma, I come away with a new Latin American food—either for eating right there or for cooking.

LUCCA RAVIOLI COMPANY

At one time the Mission was home to a large Italian community, and this sixty-year-old Italian delicatessen is one of the last vestiges of it. Lucca still has a huge neighborhood following, because everyone likes their reasonably priced house-made ravioli, tortellini, and sauces. The volume of sales is so large that meat-and-chard-filled ravioli are actually prepared every hour; more perishable cheese-filled ravioli are always frozen, although they cook up well. Chewy house-made spinach tortellini and plain meat-filled tortellini displayed in beautiful wooden boxes in the refrigerator case, along with many different kinds of fresh noodles, offer other

1100 Valencia Street
(at 22nd Street),
San Francisco
Tel: 647-5581
Open Monday through
Saturday 9 a.m. to 6 p.m.
Credit cards: AE, MC, V

mealtime alternatives. A sweet dried-mushroom-infused tomato sauce and an excellent pesto—one of the best I have ever come across—complete the package. The freshness of the pesto, especially in regard to the garlic, makes a world of difference. The fast turnover at Lucca ensures a bright-flavored sauce.

Certain cheeses like the *grana padano* (a less-aged Parmesan-type cheese that Lucca imports itself), aged jack, and house-imported double cream Brie are offered at excellent prices. So are wines. In fact, Lucca Ravioli Company has the best selection of Italian bottles in the $6 to $7 range I have seen in the city. The loquacious ravioli chef, Mike Feno, will steer you to the best bottles, using the huge map of Italy on the ceiling to show you where the wines come from. This store's dedication to good value makes it a shopping destination for olive oils, dried pasta, olives, and all things imported from Italy.

The differences between tamales from different parts of Latin America will take you by surprise. Although all of them are based on corn *masa*, dried corn softened with a lime solution, then stone ground, what happens to the *masa* next creates the contrasts. You can start at Casa Felix at Mission and 24th Street, where three or four kinds of tamales are kept warm in a steamer at the perpetually busy counter. The Mexican tamales wrapped in corn husks have a dense, almost cakey texture with a monochromatic filling of stewed pork or chicken, but the *nacatamales* from Nicaragua are a revelation. Wrapped in foil and thin white paper, the *nacatamales* look like fat baked potatoes. Girdled with a banana leaf, which infuses the tamale with a gentle herbal flavor, the *masa* inside has a soft, light texture from being pre-cooked in broth. The ample filling brings together delicious stewed pork, sliced potatoes, green chilies, tomatoes, *chicharróns* (crisped pork rind), huge capers, hard-cooked egg, and rice. The balance of filling to tasty *masa* is almost one to one, so you feel like you are eating a satisfying casserole.

In Salvadorean tamales, the *masa* has been cooked until it almost turns into a custard, and the generous filling is usually one ingredient, like chicken stewed in a dried-chili sauce with rice. A banana leaf wrapping inside the paper lends this most delicate of tamales its flavor.

La Palma Mexicatessen on 24th Street and Florida also makes an array of tamales to try, and on your walk down 24th Street, the Mission's finest market street, you will encounter a living gallery of folk murals in as many styles as tamales. When you get to Balmy Alley on the south side of 24th between Treat and Harrison, take a right and walk down one side and up the other. The alley must have been named for its microclimate, which is amazingly warm and sunny even within a part of the city that is famous for its tropical temperatures. All the tall wooden fences and garage doors that line the alley have been painted by Latin American artists, some depicting Central American solidarity, others the culture of daily life, all sophisticated and original executions. The tradition of Diego Rivera lives on! Along 24th Street itself, the walls of churches, apartment buildings, and stores provide more canvasses for the buoyant paintings. A map to the murals in the Mission can be purchased for 50¢ at Galeria de la Raza on 24th and Bryant streets. While you're mapping out your route, you can restore yourself with a new set of tamales at La Palma.

BAKERIES/PASTRIES

PANADERIA LA MEXICANA

**2804 24th Street (at York),
San Francisco
Tel: 648-2633
Open Thursday through
Tuesday 6 a.m. to 8 p.m.
Wednesday until 7 p.m.
No credit cards**

At Mexican bakeries scattered up and down 24th Street, you will encounter shelves of largish, bunlike pastries, all pretty much made out of the same dough, but shaped, glazed, or sugared differently. There are crocodiles, conch shells, rocks, ears, turtles, and shoes, all made of the soft, airy, pleasant pastry called *pan dulce*, or Mexican sweet bread. Among aficionados, Emilio Valle, the baker at Panaderia La Mexicana, is considered the reigning master of the *pan dulce*. His shapes are the most whimsical, and I can attest to their freshness and lightness. A cinnamon-and-sugar-dusted *concha* with a cup of Mexican chocolate makes for a morning treat. *Pan dulce* delivers the tactile pleasure of a doughnut but without all the oil, because these pastries are baked.

At a panaderia you do not wait to be served, but grab a tray and tongs from the counter and choose your own pastries, which are then counted and bagged. A dollar will buy you a bagful. Besides the *conchas*, I also pick up sugared sticks of *pan de yema*, which are filled with a layer of sweetened egg yolk; crisp pretzel-shaped cookies sprinkled with rock sugar; and mild spice cookies. Not rich, these cookies boast wonderful texture and gentle flavor.

Along with the typical range of *pan dulce* and soft white Mexican rolls called *bolillos*, this bakery offers something unique: fresh handmade white-flour tortillas, which are a rare find. The bakery usually prepares them on Tuesdays or Thursdays, but not dependably. The only way to be sure to get some is to call ahead. They have no preservatives in them unlike the ubiquitous packaged ones.

3114 24th Street
(at Folsom Street),
San Francisco

Tel: 647-6502

Open daily 7 a.m. to
8:30 p.m.

No credit cards

ICE CREAM/CHOCOLATES

LATIN FREEZE

3338 24th Street
(Mission Street),
San Francisco
Tel: 282-5033
Open daily 10 a.m. to 6 p.m.
No credit cards

From this tiny shop comes a rainbow of fresh fruit *paletas*, or frozen fruit bars, that taste just like the exotic and familiar fruits from which they are made. Any fruit flavor that you have ever dreamed of, and then some, find their way into Latin Freeze paletas. The watermelon bars have chunks of fruit and seeds; the cantaloupe bars have big pieces of pulp. I love the coconut, a red tangy bar called *jamaica* made from dried hibiscus flowers, the pruney tamarind, and the most-strawberry-flavored strawberry. All are made without artificial flavorings. At 55¢ and 85¢ respectively for small and large bars, they constitute yet another reason for spending time in the Mission. The *paletas* are also vended from carts up and down 24th Street on the busiest weekend shopping days.

MITCHELL'S ICE CREAM

688 San Jose Avenue
(at 29th Street),
San Francisco
Tel: 648-2300
Open daily 11 a.m. to
11 p.m.
No credit cards

Although a bulletproof window with sliding panels might seem more appropriate at a bank than an ice cream shop, Mitchell's is a friendly and crowded place —and they do serve ice cream late into the night, which accounts for the safety features. All the ice creams are made on the premises to old-fashioned, light, but creamy specifications, unlike the super-dense ice creams that have become the vogue. This texture allows more delicate, exotic flavors like *buko* (young coconut), avocado, or *ube* (purple yamlike taro) to come through. Personally, I am a big fan of *buko* cones. The tropical Philippine flavors are part of a long and changing list that includes a distinctive Mexican chocolate, a pallid mango, and fresh peach in the summer. The clerks will give you tastes of any flavor before you decide. This ice cream shop also makes ice cream cakes for special occasions, sodas, shakes, and sundaes. Fruit-flavored ice slushes are also popular.

ST. FRANCIS FOUNTAIN AND CANDY STORE

Before the genre dies, you owe it to your kids to take them to the St. Francis for an authentic American fountain and sandwich shop experience. No Disneyland replica this, the St. Francis Fountain was founded in 1918 by the Christakes family, who still make their own ice cream, syrups and fruit toppings, peanut brittle, heavenly hash with house-made marshmallows, and all the other chocolate candies in their counter. They also make their own mayonnaise, which ennobles such sandwich classics as egg salad and tuna salad served open face on slices of sourdough. I adore their grilled ham and cheese prepared just the way I remember: pressed into the grill so the toast ends up thin, crisp, and buttery, the American cheese completely melted, and the thin, thin slices of real baked ham hot. A pile of thin pickle slices makes for the perfect accompaniment. Soup does not come from a can here, but from real stock with real vegetables. A slightly thickened beef barley or minestrone brings back the memory of made-from-scratch American soups. Another reason I love this place is for its old-fashioned strawberry sodas served in tall, thick parfait glasses and made with chunky strawberry syrup, soda water, two large scoops of ice cream, and real whipped cream. What heaven! Unlike chain coffee shops, the food at St. Francis is made from real ingredients. The difference is rewarding.

The shop, which was remodeled after World War II, has wooden booths, a counter with stools, linoleum floors, and Art Deco light fixtures. As much as the food

2801 24th Street (at York), San Francisco

Tel: 826-4200

Open Monday through Friday 11 a.m. to 9 p.m., Saturday and Sunday 11:30 a.m. to 8:30 p.m.

No credit cards

and ambience are preserved in time, so are the prices. The other night two of us had a cup of beef barley soup, a grilled ham and cheese, a strawberry soda, and a small hot fudge sundae and got a check for $11.50. I felt so guilty I had to spend another six dollars on candy and a quart of hand-packed ice cream to take home.

ETHNIC MARKETS

BOMBAY BAZAAR

548 Valencia Street (between 16th and 17th streets), San Francisco
Tel: 621-1717
Open Tuesday through Sunday 10 a.m. to 6 p.m.
No credit cards

The most complete Indian dry goods store in San Francisco, Bombay Bazaar is a large, neatly arranged store with bins of bulk spices, flours, dals—all the myriad ingredients of Indian cuisine. A few fresh items like ginger root, occasionally Kaffir lime leaves, and fresh *kari* leaves, show up. Avoid the sweets. You can find good buys on basmati rice in sacks ranging from five to forty pounds, and Darjeeling tea. I am drawn to the many shelves of shiny stainless-steel *thali* plates and saucers, covered jars and cannisters, both smart and traditional at the same time. They can be adapted to many Western uses. Indian cookware, such as heavy cast-iron woks with sturdy, pounded steel handles (the Chinese wok came from India) and all sorts of stainless-steel skillets and saucepans come at excellent prices. For cooking vessels of similar quality you pay more at Macy's.

See Produce, page 255.

A full range of Mexican ingredients, canned, fresh, dried, and frozen, including cheeses, chorizo, spices, herbs, tons of dried chilies—anything you might need for a Diana Kennedy recipe.

G R E E K   A M E R I C A N   F O O D   I M P O R T S

Anyone who has been to Greece knows that you can throw together one of the best picnics in the world from salty green and black olives, mild and pungent sheep's milk cheeses, cucumbers, tomatoes, radishes, bread, olive oil, and Greek honey. All these ingredients (minus the bread and produce) can be gathered at Greek American Food Imports, a headquarters for important items in the Mediterranean pantry. Solon, a Greek extra-virgin olive oil, this store's best seller, has a buttery olive flavor without being as rich as the super-expensive Italian oils. The beauty of Solon is its mildness and balance. You can use it liberally in vinaigrettes, mayonnaise, and for cooking, without overpowering the dish or your pocketbook. Olympia Extra Virgin has about the same level of pungency but a higher degree of pepperiness. Both are extraordinary buys.

Their imported Greek barrel feta will make you rethink the complexity of this crumbly white cheese, and *manouri*, a Greek cream cheese, has a tantalizing, if subtle, sheepy edge. Fragrant olive-oil soaps for $1.00 a bar sell for $3.50 at other stores. Glorious Greek honey and preserves made from rose petals, grapes, or bitter oranges fill the shelves. The only disappointments in this food shop full of treasures are forgettable Greek pastries imported from Cleveland for some reason.

223 Valencia Street (between 14th Street and Duboce), San Francisco
Tel: 864-0978
Open Tuesday through Friday 9 a.m. to 6 p.m., Saturday until 5 p.m., Sunday 10 a.m. to 1 p.m. (closed on Sunday during the summer)
Credit cards: MC, V

LA PALMA

See Delicatessens/Take-Out, page 244.

The place for *masa*, or ground-corn dough, in all its forms, as well as many prepared items like lard and chips.

SAMIRAMIS IMPORTS

2990 Mission Street
(at 26th Street),
San Francisco
Tel: 824-6555
Open Monday through
Saturday 10 a.m. to 6 p.m.
Credit cards: AE, D, MC, V

A long-established store that caters to Middle Eastern ethnic needs, Samiramis's shelves are piled with everything from videos in Arabic to North African cooking equipment like *couscoussiers*. At least five different kinds of imported couscous are sold in bulk or in packages, along with the Cortas brand of pomegranate molasses, nuts, dried fruits, spices, and olive oils. In the refrigerator section is thick, creamy, deliciously sour Persian-style yogurt, Armenian string cheese, fetas from everywhere, and Mexican *queso fresco*, a mild, crumbly whole-milk cheese that also tastes good sprinkled on Mediterranean dishes. The emphasis, though, is not so much on fresh foods, but on the imported Middle Eastern groceries, spices, and grains necessary to stock a pantry.

PRODUCE

CASA FELIX

The produce is stacked outside on wooden tables underneath an awning, and the small, dark interior is crammed with Latin American products. There's barely a place to wait in front of the three-cash-register counter, where up to six different kinds of tamales are dispensed, along with such delicacies as the best *alfahores* in the Mission. *Alfahores* are elegant sandwich cookies—two thin Mexican butter cookies dusted with powdered sugar and filled with cajeta, a rich buttery caramel made with goat's milk—only the best cookie in town. On the produce shelves you are apt to find unrancid fresh coconuts and other hard-to-find ingredients in good shape. Casa Felix always seems to draw crowds of neighborhood housewives out shopping with their babies.

2840 Mission Street (between
24th and 25th streets),
San Francisco
Tel: 824-4474
Open daily 8 a.m. to 7 p.m.
No credit cards

CASA LUCAS MARKET

The lines can be long at this popular and complete Latin American market with tables of plantains, jícama, and citrus outside its perpetually open doors. There are no carts, so shoppers fill up numerous plastic baskets with young coconuts, tomatillos, fresh and dried chilies in bulk, packets of Latin American herbs, frozen fruit purees for *liquados*, vinegars, capers at good prices, huge purple olives in brine from Peru, cut-up cleaned fresh cactus (*nopal*), *piloncillo* (cakes of moist, molasses-rich brown sugar), three kinds of chorizo, powder mixes for Mexican drinks, and Mexican cheeses. Customers line

2934 24th Street (between
Alabama and Florida),
San Francisco
Tel: 826-4334
Open Monday through
Saturday 7 a.m. to 7:30 p.m.,
Sunday until 7 p.m.
No credit cards

the baskets up on the wooden floor by the check-out counters and push the train forward with their feet. If you cannot find what you need at Casa Lucas, it is probably out of season or unavailable anyplace else.

RAINBOW GROCERY

1899 Mission Street
(at 15th Street),
San Francisco
Tel: 863-0620
Open Monday through
Saturday 9 a.m. to 8:30 p.m.,
Sunday 10 a.m. to 8:30 p.m.
Credit cards: D, MC, V

The Rainbow Grocery is one of the few stores in San Francisco to carry a wide range of organic produce. Everything is housed in a large warren of rooms, where you'll discover Stornetta Farms dairy products, natural yogurt, imported and domestic cheeses, Acme bread, and hundreds of other goods found nowhere else in the Mission. I always have to steel myself when I shop there, however. Rainbow is run by a collective, and the experience of shopping there reminds me of trying to buy something in the former U.S.S.R., where clerks treated all the customers with the greatest indifference and no effort was made to make the merchandise palatable. Either Rainbow feels no competition, or the communal slob ethos is so strong that the workers don't notice the mess. Produce, expensive produce at that, is often stacked so precariously that if one fruit is removed from the pile, eight or ten fall on tomatoes the next level down. Old, wilted vegetables sit forlornly next to crisp, fresh ones. The produce department does deserve credit for labeling all the fruits and vegetables organic or commercial and informing customers from which farms they come. At the checkout line, clerks ring up the items and leave them for customers to bag. People bring their own cloth or used sacks, but lately the store has been providing new paper bags, the only concession to patrons in recent memory.

23RD AND MISSION PRODUCE

This neatly stocked Latin American produce store knows how to entice shoppers. During the winter when people are hungry for fruit, the market stacks up huge piles of sweet, juicy yellow mangoes with blushing red cheeks and sells them for a dollar each when they are at least half again as much anyplace else.

Always in perfect condition, the fruit is either ripe or within several days of ripening. Sometimes flat green organic mangoes from Haiti with deep orange flesh are available, or fifteen perfect mangoes by the case for twelve to thirteen dollars. I happen to be crazy about mangoes, and nothing pleases me more than the thought of having my own case at home to eat as they ripen. The other drawing card of this market are Haas avocados, always in good shape and 25¢ less per piece than anyplace else, and well-priced limes and lemons. The produce buyer for the store knows what he is doing. Most of the produce here turns over quickly and looks fresh and handsome.

2700 Mission Street,
San Francisco
Tel: 285-7955
Open Monday through
Saturday 7:30 a.m. to 6:30
p.m., Sunday until 5 p.m.
No credit cards

LA HACIENDA MARKET

This former branch of Casa Lucas, now under Palestinian ownership, still provides a wide range of Latin American produce and grocery items. From the north part of the city, La Hacienda is the closest outpost for warm packaged tortillas and fresh Mexican cheeses in bulk, kept in a refrigerated case. The excellent *queso fresco* here has a soft, crumbly texture, not gelatinous, and a gentle tang. Stronger *queso cotijo* and smoked and aged Mexican cheeses along with Mexican jack are sold

3100 16th Street (at Valencia),
San Francisco
Tel: 431-8445
Open daily 8 a.m. to 9 p.m.
No credit cards

in large quantities, so they are always fresh. Many markets in the Mission dispense *queso fresco* from an unrefrigerated counter, madness when it comes to such a fresh, delicate cheese. At La Hacienda, and at Casa Lucas on 24th Street, the bulk cheeses are always refrigerated.

AVOCADO QUESADILLAS

1/2 cup (2 ounces) coarsely grated queso chataleño

1/2 cup (2 ounces) coarsely grated queso cotija

1 cup (4 ounces) coarsely grated Monterey jack cheese

1 serrano chili, seeded and minced

1/4 cup minced fresh cilantro

2 green onions, minced

4 teaspoons vegetable oil

4 flour tortillas

2 ripe avocados, peeled, pitted, and diced

1 large tomato, seeded and diced

Kosher salt to taste

La Hacienda Market has the best selection of Mexican cheeses in bulk at their refrigerated front counter, and you can get all the other ingredients for these quesadillas there, too. Of course, everyone has his or her favorite cheese combo— I like to use half sharp cheddar and half mozzarella. When we serve these quesadillas at the Hayes Street Grill, we add a small amount of grilled tuna or shrimp and reduce the amount of avocado, or omit it altogether.

In a small bowl, combine the *queso chataleño, queso cotija,* and Monterey jack cheese. In another small bowl, combine the chili, cilantro, and green onions.

In a 10-inch skillet over medium heat, heat 1 teaspoon of the oil until it spreads over the surface of the pan. Add a flour tortilla. Cook on one side for 30 seconds, then turn over. Reduce heat to medium-low.

Sprinkle over the tortilla one fourth of each of the cheeses and the chili mixture, avocado, and tomato, and add a pinch of kosher salt. Cover the skillet and cook until the cheese is melted and begins to bubble, about 5 minutes. Then, with a spatula, fold the tortilla in half to form a semi-circle and remove it from the skillet to a warmed plate or serving platter. Place in a preheated 250° F oven and repeat with the remaining tortillas. Serve immediately.

Serves 4

MEAT AND POULTRY

LA GALLINITA

You can tell what this tiny, always packed butcher shop specializes in by the aroma of fried pork wafting out the front door and down the street. On a table at the back of this dark little place are two stainless steel pans of crisp, warm *chicharróns*, freshly rendered pork cracklings, which Salvadoreans use in their *pupusas* and on salads, but many people buy them by the bag for snacks. You pick out your own crispy pieces with tongs and put them in a white bag. I know most people don't eat bags of pork fat these days, but one melting bite is not enough. You have to have another. Besides the *chicharróns*, people buy butterflied flank steak for *carne asada* and bags of chicken parts for soup. Fresh blood sausage moves quickly from the counter when it is available, and sometimes super-hot, plump red chilies are sold by the piece. Though the principles of modern marketing have passed this dark hole of a shop by, there are many treasures to be mined.

2989 24th Street (at Harrison), San Francisco

Tel: 826-8880

Open Monday through Friday 7 a.m. to 6 p.m., Saturday until 5 p.m., Sunday until 2 p.m.

Credit cards: MC, V

THE LUCKY PORK STORE

This large and very inexpensive Chinese-run butcher shop housed in a market specializes in pig. Whole heads, snouts, ears, tongues, feet, shins, fat back, ribs, tripe, liver—almost every conceivable part of the animal—are surrealistically piled in the long glass refrigerated counter. More usual cuts like pork butt, loin, and shoulder, good-looking beef short ribs, oxtails, and other cuts of beef that take to long cooking are all abundant, fresh, and low in price. This butcher shop will find you whole suckling pigs and *cabrito* (young goat) for major Mexican barbecues. When you think of more unusual cuts of animals, think Lucky.

2659 Mission Street (between 22nd and 23rd streets), San Francisco

Tel: 285-3611 or 550-9016

Monday through Saturday 8:45 a.m. to 7 p.m., Sunday until 6 p.m.

No credit cards

MISSION MARKET FISH AND POULTRY

2590 Mission Street (at 22nd),
San Francisco
Tel: 282-3331
Open Monday through
Saturday 8:30 a.m. to 6 p.m.
Credit cards: MC, V

What a surprise to find excellent meat, poultry, and fish counters in a multistalled market building off Mission Street. The counters are located at the back of the building, past the gift shop, the taqueria, the sweet shop, and a serviceable produce-grocery shop. Among the treasures to be found in the immaculate refrigerated counters are Harris beef, thick slices of beef shin for stock or succulent stew, beautiful-looking oxtails and short ribs, Rocky free-range chickens, sparkling fresh salmon, freshly ground turkey meat, and fresh, not frozen, turkeys, whole and in parts, fresh chicken gizzards and backs, and rabbits. Strolling by the counters and just seeing what is available makes you want to get cooking. Here are the building blocks you never see for good stocks—poultry and beef—and the cuts you need for the savory stews you crave. Shopping in the Mission on a Saturday comes very close to being in the middle of a sprawling Latin American *mercado*.

MISSION MARKET MEAT DEPARTMENT

Tel: 282-1030
Open Monday through
Saturday 8:30 a.m. to 6:30 p.m.
No credit cards

FISH

MISSION FISH AND POULTRY

See Meat and Poultry, above.

Noe Valley, the Castro, Diamond Heights & Upper Market

NOE VALLEY, THE CASTRO, DIAMOND HEIGHTS & UPPER MARKET

RESTAURANTS

B A C C O

The 24th Street corridor in Noe Valley has been notoriously bereft of good neighborhood restaurants, especially considering that the community has become more sophisticated about food over the years. Tastes in Noe Valley have been moving from hippie health food to European-inspired home cooking. Young professionals, lured by the somewhat-affordable houses in the area, cut their culinary teeth on bistros and trattorias in France and Italy before their kids came along. This group is used to eating out in restaurants, yet they don't want to spend a fortune. So when Bacco, a modern, northern Italian–style trattoria, opened last year on Diamond Street, the bravos echoed throughout the neighborhood. At last there was a place where people could get a plate of well-made pasta, interesting antipasti, and decent Italian wines at a fairly comfortable price.

The brightly lit, cheerful orange dining rooms of this perpetually full restaurant beckon passersby, although a reservation will save you a wait. The small linen- and butcher paper–covered tables turn over at a leisurely

737 Diamond Street (at 24th Street), San Francisco

Tel: 282-4969

Open nightly 5:30 to 10 p.m.

Price: Moderate

Credit Cards: MC, V

pace. The food is similar to that served in a number of small Italian places around town—Alto Adige, Ideale, Milano—fresh, lively, tasty; just what you want to eat on a casual night out.

Start with the terrine of eggplant, peppers, and goat cheese, quite elegantly molded together but rustically flavorful, served with a green salad. Move on to giant ravioli filled with chard and ricotta, drizzled with brown butter and crisp leaves of fried sage. What makes them so lovely is their thin, tender noodle wrappers. For Italian broccoli lovers (those who like the slightly bitter flavor) Bacco makes a wonderful bowl of *orechietti*, ear-shaped pasta, tossed with anchovies, garlic, red chili flakes, and perfectly cooked broccoli rabe, a classic combination.

Simple things like grilled Italian sausages with polenta are dressed up with a tomato and olive puree and accompanied with a favorite Italian vegetable, chard stems. (The green parts, which cook at a different rate, are used in other dishes.) Even desserts, often neglected in small restaurants, get full attention from the kitchen here. One night our meal ended triumphantly with a luscious chocolate pudding cake moistened with hazelnut custard and garnished with strawberries, a real culinary event for 24th Street.

FIREFLY

4288 24th Street (near Douglass), San Francisco
Tel: 821-7652
Open Tuesday through Saturday 5:30 to 10 p.m., Sunday until 9:30 p.m.
Price: Moderate
Credit Cards: AE, MC, V

When a restaurant puts out baskets of costly Acme *levain*, you know it is out to please. Though I had my doubts about Firefly, where the cooking by ex-Embarko chef Brad Levy falls into the California-eclectic school, his good sense keeps the food appealing. One meal might bring dishes from all over the world, but they are unified by Levy's sensibility. In an affordable neighborhood restaurant, the energy and thought behind the creative menu deservedly causes a stir.

A good way to start is with scallop and shrimp pot stickers, densely filled with a chunky mousse of sweet-flavored shellfish nicely set off with black pepper and served with chopsticks, which adds to the pleasure of eating them. A lemony Caesar salad with huge croutons is also popular and good. Items like Thai salmon cakes apply ethnic forms to Western ingredients. Unlike the spongy fish cakes served in Southeast Asia, these were dense and gingery, presented on a bed of room-temperature wilted spinach. They made for a very substantial starter. Firefly presumes that people will be sharing the first courses, so all the wooden tables are already set with blue and white print plates. Main courses are generous as well and span the globe. A moist, perfectly grilled chicken breast crowned a plate of black beans, lemony chayote squash still crisp, and a chunky avocado salsa that was sweet and citrusy. The chef likes to season with both sugar and lemon, but not offensively.

If any sort of fruit shortcake is on the dessert menu, order it. The crisp, sweet, salty, crumbly shortcakes are so tasty they stand on their own.

The neighborhood atmosphere of the Firefly makes it all the more charming. Two small dining rooms, one with a wine bar where people can eat, share the space with a tiny open kitchen. The do-it-yourself decor has home-grown style yet the service is amazingly professional. You can tell that the people behind this restaurant have had experience. The Firefly is not of the "Oh, let's start a restaurant because we cook so well for our friends" ilk. Rather, it reflects a lot of current restaurant-industry trends that have been down-scaled to work in a modestly capitalized operation. The combination is particularly winning—and it's happening all over San Francisco and the East Bay. A food-loving city full of chefs-in-training reaps the benefits of their coming of age.

2337 Market Street
(between Noe and 17th
streets), San Francisco
Tel: 626-2666
Open Monday through
Thursday 4 to 11 p.m.,
Friday and Saturday noon
to midnight, Sunday noon
to 11 p.m.
Price: Inexpensive
No credit cards

Eating styled-out Mexican street food in a gallery of jauntily dressed skeletons and romantically inscribed tombstones may seem an unlikely pastime, but Jesse Acevedo, the creative force behind Pozole, makes it work. Pozole is the most interesting taqueria in the city both for food and surroundings. Unrelentingly casual —you can order at a counter or get table service—and very reasonable in price, the experience nevertheless is upscale: The beautifully presented food comes on carefully chosen pottery, the decoration is more folk art than artifice, and the combinations of flavors will broaden your notion of Mexican cooking. Acevedo draws on a far-reaching market basket of authentic ingredients, and he puts together his burritos and tacos, soups and appetizers with many regional references. Lately he has expanded to include Caribbean and Latin American flavors, the fruits and hot, hot chili sauces of Creole islands, and the fish soups of Peru and Ecuador. Yet the overall style of the food at Pozole mostly reflects Acevedo's personal culinary imagination.

Nearly half of the dishes on the current menu are purposely low in fat, and there are seven vegetarian items. *Pollo sin grassa* (which means "chicken without fat"), for example, is a satisfying pinto bean stew with a skinless chicken breast sparked by chopped onions, cilantro, and tomato, served with white rice and a cooked-to-order corn tortilla. The seafood bisque has tremendous flavor while staying lean. On the vegetarian front are satisfying Cuban quesadillas filled with roasted garlic, roasted peppers, and mushrooms, served with fried bananas, black beans, and rice. Old favorites like fish tacos on handmade tortillas; rich crab quesadillas;

grilled beef burritos; chicken *mole* with apricots, cumin, and grated chocolate; Oaxacan tamales stuffed with bananas and raisins, topped with mango salsa; and burritos filled with pork stewed in an achiote-orange-tequila-spiked broth keep Pozole's customers loyal. The sangría, beers, and Mexican fresh fruit drinks make a meal here even more fun. What all this adds up to is a brilliant, well-run fast-food restaurant that draws on the best of traditional, ethnic, and avant-garde culinary ideas in a highly personal way. Instead of compromising to meet the demands of a fat-conscious vegetarian market, Pozole has simply invented a series of exciting new dishes that stand on their own. People who eat there will not be joining those Day-of-the-Dead skeletons anytime soon.

CAFES

CAFE SANCHEZ

3998 Army Street (at
Sanchez), San Francisco
Tel: 641-5683
Open Tuesday and
Wednesday 7:30 a.m. to 8
p.m., Thursday and Friday
until 9:30 p.m., Saturday
8 a.m. to 9:30 p.m.,
Sunday 8 a.m. to 8 p.m.
No credit cards

The nicest part of this tiny health-foody cafe is its sunny corner location in a residential neighborhood. I give the place high marks for using organic produce, and a lot of it, in the dishes on its small menu, but some demerits for throwing too many dried herbs into everything, a holdover from a certain hippie moment when people discovered them in bulk in health-food stores and figured they had to use them. A potentially good turkey potpie with a buttery herbed crust is made pedestrian by a soggy, over-herbed filling spooned from a soup warmer. The best of the dishes I've sampled is a nut burger, a curry-flavored patty of ground nuts treated like a hamburger with a whole-wheat bun, tomato, lettuce, and onion. It's moist enough to be fun to eat, yet as substantial as meat. A range of coffee, teas, and pastries and some choice outdoor tables for basking in the sun make Cafe Sanchez useful to the neighborhood and to those who still like the earnest health-food cooking of the seventies.

ORBIT ROOM CAFE

1900 Market Street (at
Laguna), San Francisco
Tel: 252-9525
Monday through Thursday
7 a.m. to midnight, Friday
until 2 a.m., Saturday
8 a.m. to 2 a.m., Sunday
8 a.m. to midnight
No credit cards

Years ago this lofty corner spot was an Uncle Gaylord's ice cream parlor. Its current identity as a hip, rather elegantly designed cafe during the day and bar at night does justice to its soaring quarters. Daylight pours in through Art Deco–framed two-story windows onto a pressed-metal ceiling, streaky golden walls, varnished distressed concrete floors, and sculptural cone-shaped tables made out of marbleized plaster. Art Deco–inspired light sconces glow handsomely on wooden pillars. The space draws you in from the street and keeps you there with classical music (during the day), excellent Mr. Espresso coffee from the coffee bar, and the likes of Späten, Sierra Nevada pale ale, Blackthorn cider, and Golden Bear lager on tap at a second bar in the middle of the room. Tables placed outside soak up the sun and provide a choice place to have a coffee while doing your laundry at the handy laundromat next door. The staff here is competent, cool-looking, but friendly; the patrons have that urbane lower-Haight aura. All told, the Orbit Room gives off great vibes.

CAFE FLORE

Call me ridiculous, but the stretch of upperish Market street from Van Ness to Castro reminds me of the boulevard Montparnasse, Paris's broad, traffic-filled thoroughfare lined with historic cafes (La Coupole, Le Dome, Le Select. . .) and movie houses. Our slanting Market Street has two great triangular cafes, Zuni and Cafe Flore, as well as a row of huge, majestic palm trees on the median in the middle of the street. While Cafe Flore does not come close to having the panache of a French cafe, it possesses a certain *je ne sais quoi* that makes it a gathering place. Its outdoor tables on a patio decorated with Cinzano umbrellas and protected from the wind by glass screens are always full, and the red-and-blue-tiled indoor tables turn over constantly. Although the Flore still looks like the gas station it once was, its interior has taken on the patina of age and use. The corrugated-iron roof, the exposed wooden structural bracing, the long Victorian counter where people order their coffees and health-foodish sandwiches and salads (ample and inexpensive), and the wisteria vines

2298 Market (at Noe), San Francisco

Tel: 621-8579

Open daily 7:30 a.m to 11:30 p.m.

No credit cards

all feel organic to the neighborhood. The hundreds of people who come and go at Cafe Flore create the ambiance and energy of the place, just as they do at Parisian cafes. The difference is that even cosmopolitan Paris has never seen the likes of a Market Street crowd at practically any time of day or night. By the way, the counterpeople willingly make excellent Graffeo espresso, which they will pour into a small glass with an equal amount of steamed milk (called an Africano)—the current rage.

BAKERIES/PASTRIES

BAKERS OF PARIS

For other locations see pages 190, 483.

When you break into a Bakers of Paris baguette, lightly crusted and soft inside, you could be starting a meal in Paris. These long, skinny, lightweight breads are exactly what are served in every neighborhood bistro and sold in every corner *boulangerie*. They can be used for sandwiches, for spreading with butter and jam, and for sopping up sauce—all noble purposes. Bakers of Paris baguettes, like Parisian baguettes, are best eaten the same day they are bought. The bakery also makes buttery raisin rolls, and some surprisingly fancy dessert pastries like a hazelnut-espresso daquoise, layers of crisp meringue separated by rich coffee butter cream, that epitomize the French art of infusing butter with flavor. At $2.50 each, they constitute an exceptional buy.

3989 24th Street (at Noe), San Francisco
Tel: 863-8725
Open daily 7 a.m. to 5:30 p.m.
No credit cards

FRAN GAGE PATISSERIE FRANÇAISE

Fran Gage takes a personal and seasonal approach to her baking, and the pretty shop, most charmingly approached by a stairway from Upper Market street, always offers surprises, like a strawberry-rhubarb *confiture* in the spring that sells out almost as fast as it is made; or miniature hand-molded bittersweet chocolates with soft chocolate centers that have become a staple. The bakery is known for a dense, oval-shaped *pain au levain*, a chewy, full-flavored white bread that I like very much, and traditional French morning pastries like crisp raisin rolls, my favorite, and almond toasts made of brioche spread with almond paste. Many of the products can be found around town in specialty shops, but this bakery is

4690 18th Street (at Market), San Francisco
Tel: 864-8428
Open Monday through Saturday 7:30 a.m. to 7 p.m.
No credit cards

by no means a factory. All the items have a hand-crafted quality about them—as if an industrious French housewife had decided to make at home the things she always buys at shops.

JUST DESSERTS

248 Church Street (at Market), San Francisco

Tel: 626-5774

Open Sunday through Thursday 7 a.m. to 11 p.m.,

Friday and Saturday 8 a.m. to midnight

Credit cards: MC, V

See listing, page 216.

SWEET INSPIRATIONS

2239 Market Street (between Sanchez and Noe), San Francisco

Tel: 621-8664

Open Monday through Thursday 7 a.m. to 11:30 p.m., Friday until midnight, Saturday 8 a.m. to 11 p.m., Sunday 8 a.m. to 11:30 p.m.

No credit cards

Old-fashioned whipped-cream cakes made with up-to-the-minute ingredients fill the refrigerated cases of this large dessert cafe/bakery. Albeit with a modern twist, the cakes remind me of the bakery goods my mother used to bring home from the French Swiss Pastry Shop on the north side of Chicago. Our favorite was made of layers of soft yellow cake, sweetened whipped cream, and lots of fresh strawberries. At Sweet Inspirations, airy yellow layers are paved with whipped cream, candied ginger, and thin sheets of chocolate in a jelly-roll configuration—to my mind the nicest of this genre of cakes made here—or whipped cream and shredded coconut between layers of cake soaked with rum. At the rather chilly-feeling cafe you can have a large slice of cake with coffee or a pot of tea, or you can take pastries home. The wholesale bakery sells to Kuleto's, Macy's, and Spinelli coffee stores, among others.

ICE CREAM/CHOCOLATES

DOUBLE RAINBOW

For other locations see pages 191, 218, 395, 487.

Michael Sachar and Steve Fink, two guys from Brooklyn, started this local ice cream company on September 18, 1976, when they saw a double rainbow over San Francisco, an incredibly rare event in that dry time of the year. They took it as a lucky omen—two pots of gold —and started making their rich ice cream with a vengeance, opening their first store at Castro and Market. Currently, they distribute their products through Double Rainbow ice cream shops, many of which have taken on the role of neighborhood cafes, and in cartons at grocery stores. Their sweet eggy vanilla and strawberry, strong-flavored coffee and chocolate, and assorted flavors that come in and out of season have earned them many devoted followers, not the less for Double Rainbow's unceasing contributions to local causes and community celebrations. The vanilla malts and thick shakes have risen to classic status, but Double Rainbow keeps up with the times. Their low-fat strawberry frozen yogurt has such satisfyingly creamy texture and voluptuous flavor you would never guess it has only 5 percent fat. Fresh fruit ices, like an intense and true-flavored raspberry, have become a Double Rainbow signature. The Asian-style ice creams—lychee nut, green tea, and mango—have taken off in San Francisco, perhaps a reflection of Double Rainbow's enormous success in Hong Kong.

Every shop is independently owned and varies in size, menu, and appearance; the Double Rainbow on 24th

407 Castro Street (at Market), San Francisco
Tel: 621-2350
Open Sunday through Thursday 11 a.m. to 10 p.m., Friday and Saturday until 11 p.m.
No credit cards

3933 24th Street (between Sanchez and Noe), San Francisco
Tel: 821-3420
Open daily 11 a.m. to 11 p.m.
No credit cards

Street is one of the most attractive, with large wood-framed front windows that open completely to the street, suggesting the atmosphere of a European cafe.

JOSEPH SCHMIDT

3489 16th Street (between
Church and Sanchez),
San Francisco
Tel: 861-8682
Open Monday through
Saturday 10 a.m.
to 6:30 p.m.
Credit cards: MC, V

For ten years now, Joseph Schmidt has been working his chocolate artistry at this colorful shop filled with seasonal specialties. In the spring, expect lovable Easter bunnies of the richest Belgian chocolate; for Mother's Day, long, thin boxes covered with hydrangeas holding a dozen miniature truffles, Joseph Schmidt's signature confection. Truffles may have catapulted him to fame, but his sculptural talent has kept him there. If Schmidt were not working in chocolate, he might have made a career in stone. His large chocolate bowls and vases with ragged, pointed edges, marbled with white and mint chocolate, serve as Baccarat-like containers for more chocolates or even flowers made out of chocolate. San Franciscans order these dramatic bowls for parties and special events. A new confection, thin round disks of chocolate about two inches in diameter with soft fillings like caramel, coconut cream, or nougat, each disk painted with a colorful and delicate abstract design, now fill one whole case. Rich truffles with flavored fondant interiors fill another. I personally cannot resist the chocolate nut bark and the huge, flat turtles with pecans, buttery caramel, and carapaces of light or dark chocolate, the best of their genre. Schmidt also makes a changing array of small traditional chocolates filled with nuts, creams, and jellies.

While Schmidt chocolates are carried at Neiman-Marcus, Macy's, Confetti, Saks Fifth Avenue, and in special batches at Williams-Sonoma, a trip to the store can net some unique treasures. Schmidt is nothing if not whimsical, and who knows what he might make that day? His wife manages and grooms the shop with passion, for she is a lover of chocolate as well. She runs up and down Telegraph Hill every morning just so she can keep tasting.

COFFEE

SPINELLI COFFEE COMPANY

504 Castro Street (at 18th Street), San Francisco

Tel: 241-9447

Monday through Fri day 6:30 a.m. to 9 p.m., Saturday 7 a.m.

to 10 p.m., Sunday 7 a.m. to 9 p.m.

Credit cards: MC, V

See listing, page 192.

MARKETS

TOWER MARKET

635 Portola Drive
(at O'Shaughnessy),
San Francisco
Tel: 664-1600
Open Monday through
Saturday 8 a.m. to 8 p.m.,
Sunday until 7 p.m.
Credit Cards: AE, D, MC, V

In this part of town, Tower Market looms as the best resource for high-quality ingredients under one roof. A medium-sized store, intelligently stocked, it draws a large patronage from St. Francis Wood and West Portal to Glen Park. The produce department always has seasonal treasures like small, fat stalks of rhubarb in the spring, and year-round organic produce like thick bunches of spinach. The independently owned deli section is a source for prosciutto from Parma as well as German-style cured meats. Viglizzo's Meats has been operating since 1915, and they have kept current with free-range chickens, freshly ground turkey, Harris beef, and butchers who will cut and grind to order. The dairy section is a source for Plugra brand butter, which has twice the butterfat of regular butter and the full, sweet flavor of European butters. Sold in half pounds that cost as much as a full pound of other butter, Plugra turns morning toast into the best dish of the day. Also available in this section are glass quarts of Straus Family Dairy organic milk, a new product from western Marin from cows that are not treated with hormones and only eat organic grains. You have to shake the bottles before you pour to dislodge the cream off the top, and the sweet, delicately grassy flavor of this milk will make you take notice of what you're drinking for the first time (if you're under forty-five).

PRODUCE

HARVEST RANCH MARKET

Really more a spontaneous cafe than a market, this flashy natural foods store has turned into a Market Street hot spot. Day and night customers come in to cruise the salad bar, filling up clear plastic containers with legume and pasta salads, tofu, and the usual salad-bar vegetable assortment with curry dressings. Fast-moving items include giant sushi rolls about the size of a fist, coated with sesame seeds, pinwheeled with sea-weed, and filled with asparagus, cucumber, and surimi: imitation crab. Dipped into soy sauce and wasabi they make for a destination snack or light meal. The sushi, like all the other foods on the salad bar, cost $2.49 per pound and weigh out to about $1.00 a piece. Two will fill you up. Their best trait is their freshness; they move so fast new trays are constantly brought out. People eat outside on impromptu benches made of wood beams and metal crates. For shoppers, the store carries all sorts of bread, including Acme and Grace Baking Company loaves, and a limited selection of organic produce. The usual natural foods store bulk nuts, cheeses, yogurt, chips, and granola are sexily displayed.

2285 Market (at Noe)

Tel: 626-0805

Open Monday through Friday 9 a.m. to 11 p.m. Saturday and Sunday until midnight

Credit cards: AE, D, MC, V

MIKEYTOM

The residents from Mikeytom's outer Noe Valley neighborhood rejoiced when this modern, brightly lit, organic produce and natural foods store opened. While the selection is small, the fruits and vegetables look inviting, nicely set out in baskets. The small heads of lettuce are particularly beautiful here. Breads from the Metropolis bakery in Emeryville and Clover and Straus Family dairy products are good to have in any

1747 Church Street (at Day), San Francisco

Tel: 826-5757

Monday through Sat urday 7 a.m. to 8 p.m. (9 p.m. in summer), Sunday 8 a.m. to 8 p.m.

Credit cards: MC, V

neighborhood market, along with buckets of fresh flowers. Some marble tables have been placed outside for those who want to have a coffee made at the coffee bar inside.

NOE VALLEY COMMUNITY STORE

1599 Sanchez (at 29th Street), San Francisco
Tel: 824-8022
Open Monday through Saturday 8:30 a.m. to 8:30 p.m., Sunday 9 a.m. to 6 p.m.
No credit cards

Part of a small group of cooperatively owned natural foods stores, the Noe Valley branch is particularly well tended. Besides a decent range of organic produce, residents can buy bulk oils, vinegars, grains, herbs, and granola. Clover dairy products, yogurt, and Oliver's Bäcklerei German breads are some of the other items available to make a meal. Above some of the produce are recipes straight from the seventies that recommend tablespoons of dried herbs for small amounts of food. I have no doubt that many of the people who shop here probably appreciate these recipes.

REAL FOOD COMPANY

3939 24th Street (between Noe and Sanchez), San Francisco
Tel: 282-9500
Open daily 9 a.m. to 8 p.m.
Credit cards: MC, V

See listing, page 195.

The highlight of this branch is a refrigerated room for all the items sold in bulk. Turnover is pretty quick at most Real Food stores, but I always worry about the freshness of nuts, flours, grains—anything that loses nutritional value or can change in flavor when stored too long. Keeping these foods cool extends their life.

I learned this recipe for miniature tartlets from my mother when I was a child. They melt in your mouth. All the ingredients can be purchased at any grocery store. The miniature muffin pans can be found at Frederickson's Hardware (page 222), and at cookware stores.

Preheat the oven to 350° F. Butter 2 mini muffin tins (each cup about 1 inch in diameter), carefully coating the bottom and sides.

In a food processor fitted with a steel blade, or by hand, blend together the cream cheese, 1/2 cup butter, and flour to make a smooth uniform dough. Divide into 24 equal pieces. With your thumb, press the dough into the molds, covering bottom and sides.

In a small bowl, blend the egg, brown sugar, remaining 2 tablespoons of butter, and vanilla until smooth.

Layer half the pecans in the dough cups. Using a teaspoon, fill the molds two-thirds full with the brown sugar mixture. Top with the remaining pecans.

Bake until the dough is golden and the nuts toasted, about 30 to 35 minutes. Run a knife around the edges to loosen the tartlets and unmold them. Let cool on a wire rack. These are best eaten the same day.

Makes twenty-four 1-inch tartlets

PECAN TARTLETS

3 ounces cream cheese

1/2 cup (1 stick) butter at room temperature, plus

2 tablespoons butter for filling

1 cup all-purpose flour

1 egg

3/4 cup packed brown sugar

1 teaspoon vanilla extract

2/3 cup pecans, coarsely chopped

MEAT AND POULTRY

VIGLIZZO'S MEAT

See Tower Market listing, page 276.

CHEESE

24TH AVENUE CHEESE SHOP

**3893 24th Street (at
Sanchez), San Francisco**

Tel: 821-6658

**Open Monday through
Friday 10 a.m. to 7 p.m.,
Saturday until 6 p.m.,
Sunday 10 a.m. to 5 p.m.**

Credit cards: MC, V

There are only a handful of noteworthy cheese shops in the Bay Area, and this is one of them. You can taste anything, and the range is extensive. You might find some tangy Pyrenees goat milk cheese set out on the counter, a lusciously runny rice flour-coated teleme (very fresh in flavor, but it must be eaten quickly), a whole table of Cheddars or a *pavé d'affinois*, a small cube of soft cheese encased in rind. Half the price of the *pavé d'affinois* from Paris' Androuët sold at The Cheese Board in Berkeley or at Real Food on Polk Street, 24th Street's brand, unfor-

tunately, does not deliver the same pleasure. When I discussed this with the counterman, he said that Androuët cheeses were simply too expensive for his clientele. This store may be price-conscious, but the staff is meticulous in keeping and cutting the cheeses.

All the merchandise looks appealing and fresh displayed on wooden counters, casks, and shelves. A worn wooden floor only adds atmosphere. A long-time ingredient resource in Noe Valley, this cheese store also carries Mol-inari salami, lots of olives, crackers, Acme bread, bread sticks, and wine—practically anything you might need for an Italian lunch.

WINES AND SPIRITS

CARUSO'S

When you can walk into a wine store and come away with a bag full of surprisingly delicious bottles for under $10.00 each, you know you have struck gold. The owners of Caruso's specialize in reasonably priced imports, and I must say that they have come up with some extraordinary wines for the price. The inventory changes often so you have to depend on their recommendations, but recently they sent me home with a soft, full, remarkably tasty red from Corbières that went smashingly with Indian food, and a Portuguese red of such distinction that it could have sold for twice as much with a different label. If you want to stock up on these kinds of everyday wines, Caruso's is well worth a trip from across town. The store also carries aged rums from Nicaragua, Haiti, and Martinique, single-malt Scotches, and berry wines (not liqueurs) from France. The two owners currently are on the search for a moderately priced Sauterne.

4011 24th Street (at Noe),
San Francisco
Tel: 282-3841
Open daily 10 a.m. to 9 p.m.
Credit cards: AE, MC, V

4121 19th Street (at Castro),
San Francisco
Tel: 864-4411
Monday through Thursday
11 a.m. to 7 p.m., Friday
and Saturday until 8 p.m.,
Sunday noon to 7 p.m.
Credit cards: AE, MC, V

The neatly displayed wines in this eighteen-year-old pioneering shop all come from California. Though the selection is not as deep or interesting as at the California Wine Merchant in the Marina, the gracious clerks will spend as much time as you like trying to fit you with the best bottle for the occasion. This is a spot to find some of the most elegant California Cabernets and French-style blends.

COOKWARE AND BOOKS

CLIFF'S HARDWARE

479 Castro Street
(at 18th Street),
San Francisco
Tel: 431-5365
Open Monday through
Saturday 9:30 a.m. to 8 p.m.
Credit cards: AE, CB, MC, V

Cliff's Hardware has a huge housewares section featuring coffee and espresso makers, Trident knives, peppermills, water filters, old-fashioned wooden ice cream makers, cast-iron skillets in hard-to-find shapes and sizes, as well as a wide range of the ever popular Revere Ware pots and pans (stainless steel with copper bottoms): the bread and butter of outfitting a kitchen. To meet the entertainment needs of its immediate community, Cliff's stocks coolers from small to gigantic, barbecuing equipment including Webers, fire starters, charcoal, wood chips, and many outdoor serving accessories that you never knew you needed until you saw them. Though prices are not cheap, the convenience of shopping in a neighborhood counts for a lot.

This refined new garden and housewares store on a block of 24th Street closer to Mission than Castro gives forth a refreshingly clean esthetic. Sparely stocked with only wonderful things, like huge solid-colored cotton napkins, white hemstitched napkins, bamboo place mats, beeswax candles, and terra-cotta pots in beautiful shapes for plants, each item is displayed so you can understand its merits. Prices are also refreshingly reasonable—a confirmation that taste means more than cost.

3775 24th Street (between Church and Dolores), San Francisco
Tel: 282-3330
Monday through Friday 11 a.m. to 7 p.m.,
Saturday 10 a.m. to 6 p.m.,
Sunday noon to 5 p.m.
Credit cards: AE, MC, V

LEHR'S GERMAN SPECIALTIES

A German cultural-necessities store, Lehr's carries everything from German cleaning supplies to liverwurst. The inventory includes some handsome two-toned horsehair brushes with wooden handles for sweeping up crumbs, and tubes of concentrated traveling detergent for $7.95 each. (I was tempted to buy one for my husband, who does a wash every day on the road, even though he packs a full complement of underwear.) A large assortment of German baking pans ranges from miniature to party

1581 Church Street
(at 28th Street),
San Francisco
Tel: 282-6803
Open Monday through Saturday 10 a.m. to 6 p.m.,
Sunday noon to 6 p.m.
Credit cards: MC, V

size. I was drawn to some patterned springform bundt pans. You can find old-fashioned potato ricers and handy spaetzle makers, which solves the mystery of how these tiny noodle dumplings are made. The gadget is just a large-holed grater with a slide over it that pushes the dough through. Often seeing the right instrument to make a dish inspires me to cook it. Several long aisles are dedicated to candy and chocolates including Lindt and liquor-filled Asbach Uralt, a favorite among those who like a shot of brandy with their sweet. Elaborate beer steins fill the front window. The pretty woman with a sexy German accent behind the counter will be happy to show them to you as she hums along to Aretha Franklin on the radio.

North Beach

NORTH BEACH

RESTAURANTS

ALFRED'S

Alfred's, one of San Francisco's oldest restaurants, reassures us that the old-fashioned steak house, especially a clubby, traditional one with Italian overtones, can live on in a city overtaken by salad and pasta. At Alfred's the cocktails will be forthcoming, the service professional, and the amenities traditional: heavy white linen, booths, big tables, large upholstered chairs. If you want comfort and a luscious piece of dry-aged beef, you can count on this restaurant. It is the same today as when I first ate there fifteen years ago, and probably when it first opened sixty years ago.

Although the menu offers a number of Italian dishes, everyone knows to stick to the steaks. The T-bone and the Alfred's Steak, which is a bone-in New York, are exemplary by today's standards: full of flavor and tender. The Porterhouse is magnificent on both sides of the bone. I have not eaten better beef anywhere in town. Expert grilling over mesquite means that your meat will be cooked to exact specification without acrid burn marks or a cold center. The grillers at Alfred's know how

886 Broadway (at Mason), San Francisco
Tel: 781-7058
Open for lunch Thursday 11:30 a.m. to 2:30 p.m.; dinner Sunday through Thursday 5:30 to 9:30 p.m., Friday and Saturday 5:30 to 10 p.m.
Price: Expensive
Credit cards: AE, DC, MC, V

to control the fire. With these steaks come sweet-fleshed baked Idaho potatoes, properly soft, dry, and light textured, with real, not imitation, fixings.

Everything else on the menu can be hit or miss. The Caesar salad, made at tableside, varies with the mood of the waiter. The house green salad with a ton of blue cheese has a sugary sweet, mayonnaise-based dressing. Believe me, a foray into the Italian section (the antipasto is O.K.) only underscores that Alfred's remains first and foremost an excellent steak house. In this era of chain operations, Alfred's stands out as an individual—crusty, aging, smoky, masculine—and just where you want to go if you're hungry for red meat.

ANTHONY'S

1701 Powell Street (at Union), San Francisco

Tel: 391-4488

Open nightly 5 to 10 p.m.

Price: Moderate

Credit cards: DC, MC, V

This relative newcomer to North Beach has made a niche for itself by offering one-pound lobsters baked in a wood-fired oven on top of ramekins of rich, cheesy rigatoni at down-to-earth prices. While you wait to get in you can watch the live lobsters being cooked through the front window, no sight for sissies. Neither is the garlicky, heavy, buttery food that bears no resemblance to understated Northern Italian fare but follows a broad style of its own. The low-priced lobsters come six different ways, but the dreamiest is the aforementioned lobster rigatoni. The pasta is swathed in a creamy tomato sauce enriched with smoky bits of lobster claw meat. The small lobster tail on top stays juicy, a little chewy, and not overcooked. All the lobsters weigh one pound, though occasionally two- to ten-pound lobsters at $8.95 a pound (a great price) are available. These smaller, less-expensive crustaceans satisfy because they are part of other preparations, like a grilled pizza that is topped with chunks of lobster, fresh tomato, basil, and mozzarella. The pizza has a luscious smokiness to it, but the cheese melts in dabs and the crust stays white, a texture that brings to mind an English muffin. Aromatic garlic popovers, warm from the oven, are another rather strange but successful creation. The small restaurant is bustling and cavelike, with the kitchen getting the front window and the interior a mural of San Francisco. Inexpensive wines, friendly service, and those fresh lobsters at extraordinary prices cause lines to form practically every night.

BUCA GIOVANNI

Giovanni Leoni's *buca*, or "hole," a downstairs dining room made to look like a cozy vaulted wine cellar, has been a San Francisco favorite ever since this chef left Vanessi's to open his own place years fifteen years ago. If one were to describe northern Italian soul food, Leoni's rich game pastas and stews, his use of wild mushrooms and herbs, and the long, deep flavors of his sauces would be the very essence of it. He is the only Italian chef in town who cooks in this way, a revealing contrast to the Italian "lite" that has become so faddish over the last ten years. Mr. Leoni's cooking goes with big, difficult red wines from the Piedmont; with cold San Francisco summer weather; with hunger for substantial food. Everything that comes out of the little open kitchen upstairs (where a few choice tables are also available) possesses such depth of flavor because Leoni knows how to coax the best out of his ingredients. Something as simple as a moist chicken breast slathered in fresh porcini makes you sit up and take notice; so does sweet-fleshed sea bass served with tomatoey pasta and clams. Even the *antipasti* and salads like radicchio with Gorgonzola, or thin, ruby-red slices of *bresaola* (air-dried

800 Greenwich Street (between Columbus and Mason), San Francisco
Tel: 776-7766
Open Tuesday through Saturday 5:30 to 10:30 p.m.
Price: Moderate
Credit cards: AE, DC, D, MC, V

beef) sprinkled with extra-virgin olive oil show character. Exciting pastas like veal-filled ravioli in a white sauce infused with walnuts, called *panzerotti salsa di noci* (from the chef's birthplace); or something as simple as *fagioli alla Toscana*, red beans bursting with the flavors of good stock, garlic, and sage, bring people back time after time. I'm one of those people. I like the friendly professionalism of Buca Giovanni, the casual, neighborhood setting, and eating lush Italian cooking with a pedigree that goes back hundreds of years. To that end, Giovanni is growing fruits and vegetables for Buca on his ranch, knowing, as every great Italian chef does, that the quality comes from the raw materials.

CAFE JACQUELINE

1454 Grant Avenue (between Union and Green), San Francisco
Tel: 981-5565
Open Wednesday through Sunday 5:30 to 11 p.m.
Price: Moderate
Credit cards: AE, CB, D, MC, V

Jacqueline Margulis, the sole owner and chef at this very French neighborhood bistro, is the queen of the soufflé. In fact, that's pretty much all she has been serving for the last twelve years: tall, airy, crusty-topped, aromatic soufflés with sensuous, creamy interiors. The alluring aromas of baking cheese and garlic and the warmth from the ovens enfold you as you walk in the door of this small restaurant, its steamy front windows framed in lace curtains. Each white-linen-covered table sports a fresh rose, heavy silverware, thin wineglasses, and huge napkins. High ceilings, worn wooden floors, original wainscoting, and shaded wall sconces bring back visions of pre-Earthquake San Francisco. Both the cooking and the surroundings at Jacqueline are timeless.

You start with a salad of butter lettuce or watercress dressed in a traditional, mustardy vinaigrette. Baskets of warm, crusty baguettes with sweet butter tide you over until your soufflé finally emerges from the kitchen. In the winter I make a special visit for Jacqueline's magnificent black truffle soufflé made from eggs that have been stored with the truffles (so the truffles' aroma permeates the shells), Gruyère, and lots of slivered fresh truffles. The $50 soufflé, plenty for two and fine for three, becomes affordable when shared, and worth every penny. Her wild mushroom soufflés, textured with roughly chopped morels, boletes, and chanterelles, $30, are also worth a detour. Less lavish, but very savory, are her prosciutto and domestic mushroom, and garlicky broccoli and cheese soufflés, which cost around $20. Whatever you order remember to specify that you want your soufflé runny in the middle. Otherwise, they come baked all the way through and lose their charm. For some reason Jacqueline thinks that Americans want them cooked airy and dry.

If you ever go out for dessert, come here for a spectacular chocolate soufflé. Jacqueline uses tons of dark, rich chocolate, turning the center into a creamy, intense chocolate pudding. It's one of the best chocolate desserts in the city.

ENRICO'S SIDEWALK CAFE

Everyone in the city eventually gravitates to Enrico's, the raffish historic cafe on Broadway with prime outdoor seating. The outdoor tables at the old Enrico's saw action from lunchtime until the wee hours of the morning, but when the scene on Broadway deteriorated in the eighties, Enrico's died a slow, painful death. Former owner Enrico Banducci tried to get it going again with investments from show-biz friends like Bill Cosby, but he couldn't turn it around. The cafe closed and the building stayed boarded up for a couple of years until new owners Rick Hackett, Meredith Melville, and Mark McLeod, formerly of Oliveto, Chez Panisse, and Bay

504 Broadway (at Kearny), San Francisco

Tel: 982-6223

Open Sunday through Thursday noon to 11 p.m., Friday and Saturday until 2 a.m.

Price: Moderate

Credit cards: AE, MC, V

Wolf, took over. They pumped a lot of money into the kitchen and the decor, making the inside as exciting as the outside patio, and they raised the quality of the menu, bar, and wine list. Now Enrico's can stand on its own as a top-notch restaurant as well as a coffeehouse, bar, and live-music venue.

At lunch at a table outside you'll undoubtedly see some of the old crowd of pols, writers, lawyers, and North Beach denizens, conspiring away while they munch on golden-crusted pizzas, Tuscan soups, al dente spaghetti with seafood, and Caesarlike salads. In the afternoon the coffeehouse crowd drops by for excellent espresso and imaginative desserts: ice creams and *sorbetti* made with seasonal fruits; a luscious tiramisù layered in a glass like an Italian trifle; melt-in-your-mouth black satin fudge cake with Grand Marnier crème anglaise; a banana rum crème brûlée with chocolate shortbread.

At dinner chef Hackett comes up with all sorts of lively turns on traditional dishes, like a grilled salmon *pistou* (a soup of all sorts of fresh beans and vegetables topped with salmon, drizzled with a pesto of basil, garlic, and olive oil); a duck breast with sour cherry sauce served over mashed potatoes and wilted spinach; or grilled sea bass with a spicy Mexican tomato sauce with sautéed fresh corn. At all hours people order Enrico's juicy Niman-Schell hamburgers on focaccia with fries and house-made condiments. Some of the best modern music ensembles on the West Coast play here nightly, without a cover charge. Everyone loves the romantic venue and wants to support it. The bar stays open until 2 a.m. every night, and many's the time I've dropped in for an espresso or a glass of cognac on the way home from a night out and wished that I'd spent my whole evening at Enrico's.

The Bay Area boasts so many different ethnic restaurants that it's hard to get excited about one more, but Helmand, a formally appointed Afghani dinner house, rises above exoticism to take its place as one of the best restaurants in San Francisco of any nationality. Afghan cooking draws on Persian, Indian, and Middle Eastern flavors, but the food at Helmand is immediately appealing to Western palates. Start with *aushak*, large, tender ravioli filled with sautéed leeks and topped with a mild, buttery meat sauce, served on a bed of yogurt speckled with fresh mint; or *kaddo borawni*, pumpkin that has been deep-fried, roasted, then sauced with garlic-scented yogurt, achieving a melting texture. Another permutation on pasta, a dish called *mantwo*, fills house-made noodles with braised onions and chopped beef, topping them with a delicious sauce of carrots and slightly al dente yellow split peas. All these appetizers are so yummy you want to make a meal out of them alone—until you taste the soups at Helmand, which are served in huge bowls with just a ladleful at the bottom. Try *aush*, a liquid version of addictive ravioli-like *aushak*. Here thin noodles come in a minted yogurt soup drizzled with the buttery meat sauce. Another warm yogurt soup, *mashawa*, is thick with legumes— mung beans, chickpeas, black-eyed peas—and chunks of beef, a meal in itself.

Several excellent main courses feature lamb in different cuts accompanied with light, airy rice pilaf seasoned with cumin seed and cinnamon. Try *koufta challow*, large soft meatballs in hot cinnamon-scented tomato sauce, or *dwopiaza*, medium-rare lamb kabobs sauced with vinegared onions and yellow split peas on a square of flat bread that soaks up all the juices.

430 Broadway
(between Kearny
and Montgomery),
San Francisco
Tel: 362-0641
Open Sunday through
Thursday 6 to 10 p.m., Friday
and Saturday until 11 p.m.
Price: Inexpensive
Credit cards: AE, DC, MC, V

Desserts may seem the most exotic dishes of all, but a cardamom-scented basmati rice pudding or *burfee*, an ice cream made from reduced milk and served in a sundae glass filled with frozen clotted cream, are well worth trying.

The long, narrow dining room is decorated with polished antique cabinets with glass doors displaying bowls of colorful ground spices and Afghani artifacts. The brick walls, carpeting, soft light, and tablecloths give the room a dressy look belying the amazingly inexpensive prices. The intelligent and attentive service would be welcome in restaurants that charge three times as much.

IL POLLAIO

55 Columbus Avenue (at Union), San Francisco
Tel: 362-7727
Open Monday through Saturday 11:30 a.m. to 9 p.m.
Price: Inexpensive
Credit cards: AE, MC, V

One of my favorite neighborhood hangs, Il Pollaio, does one thing and does it perfectly: chicken. Small chickens with large bones are lightly marinated and grilled over hot rocks, and always come off the fire clean flavored, juicy, and hot. Silver-haired José, the Argentine-Italian owner-griller, never cooks in advance. Served with a mixed salad of crisp, shredded cabbage, carrots, shell beans, and chopped lettuce in a tangy Italian dressing, the half-chicken combo always satisfies. The few other items on the menu, tasty Italian sausage made especially for Il Pollaio; a satiny cold marinated eggplant antipasto; and fortifying house-made lentil, split pea, or minestrone soups, one offered each day, are also impeccable. The pleasant little dining room, always full, looks onto the passing parade on Columbus Avenue, and smiling José knows practically every nontourist who walks in or by the door. Much Italian is spoken at Il Pollaio over many bottles of wine.

You can call ahead for take-out or be buoyed by the cheerful scene in this popular spot while you eat. Everyone in North Beach considers Il Pollaio an essential resource.

LA FELCE

At one time North Beach was considered a mecca for family-style dining in the city, as it was full of restaurants that served copious *antipasti* of sliced meats and canned beans, tureens of good minestrone, pasta in various forms in tomato sauce, then big platters of sliced meat or roast chicken followed by neon green and pink spumone. Though the number—and quality—of restaurants has diminished, La Felce, which opened in 1974, continues on in fine form, pretty much serving this classic fare with interesting variations. The soup might be a full-bodied chicken stock laced with hundreds of white dots of pasta into which you sprinkle grated Parmesan. A meaty baked lasagne might be the pasta of the night, and chicken cacciatore, in a lively sauce made with tomatoes, mushrooms, green peppers, and onions that have cooked down to a puree, the star main course. An a la carte salad Macedonia, a platter of sliced tomatoes layered with transparently thin onion slices, anchovies, and fresh parsley in an excellent vinaigrette, is worth sharing. Though the menu will sound familiar, a broader range of entrees to choose from is offered, and the food is alive, prepared with fresh ingredients and a sure hand. I like the white tablecloths and cheery ambiance of the dining room, a departure from the utilitarian linoleum decor of many North Beach family-style restaurants.

1570 Stockton Street (at Union), San Francisco
Tel: 392-8321
Open for lunch weekdays (except Tuesday) 11:30 a.m. to 2 p.m.; dinner Wednesday through Monday 5 to 10 p.m.
Price: Inexpensive
Credit cards: AE, DC, D, MC, V

LITTLE JOE'S

523 Broadway (between
Columbus and Kearny),
San Francisco
Tel: 433-4343
Open Monday through
Thursday 11 a.m. to 10:30
p.m., Friday and Saturday
until 11 p.m., Sunday noon
to 10 p.m.
Price: Inexpensive
Credit Cards: D, MC, V

About ten years ago Little Joe's moved from its cramped quarters around the corner on Columbus to its current mural-festooned dining hall on Broadway. Despite the fall of several venerable businesses nearby, Little Joe's has been going strong ever since. Little Joe's belongs to the colorful San Francisco genre of eateries characterized by noisy, flame-throwing, open cooking lines cranking out huge plates of North Beach/Italian food for cheap, which has assured this dining hall a place in every guidebook as well as in the hearts of thrifty Bay Area diners. Besides getting a lot to eat for the price, people love Little Joe's raffish spirit and family-style atmosphere. Be prepared to share a long table with other groups.

The regulars know to order chicken livers and onion sauté (be sure to order them pink) in red wine and tomato sauce; calamari sauté finished off with a great deal of garlic, white wine, and tomato sauce; and Little Joe's famous *caciucco*, a fish stew of squid, snapper, clams, and mussels in a broth of red wine, tomatoes, and lots of garlic—well, you get the idea. Garlic, wine, and tomato sauce are the holy trinity here. True aficionados grab a counter seat for platters of beef tongue in a piquant, relishlike green sauce or order the daily special, usually many slices of roast veal in a brown gravy. With your entree you get a huge portion of fresh cauliflower, zucchini, carrots, and chard, or sides of precooked spaghetti in a muddy meat sauce. For a slight surcharge, the accompaniment can be heavy ravioli stuffed with something akin to library paste. Bottles of decent Chianti at excellent prices will greatly enhance the meal if you can somehow catch the eye of a gum-chewing, T-shirted waitress to order some. They like to keep it simple by bringing carafes of dirt-cheap house red and white. (Service is hardly a high point.) However, piles of just-baked and -delivered San Francisco sourdough and butter are liberally supplied. People come here for the refreshing grittiness of the place anyway.

The eponymously named Lo Coco's is one of the few pizza and pasta places in North Beach that serves authentic Sicilian food. The chef-owner, Giovanni Lo Coco, a true Sicilian, is not shy about putting some of his island's most soulful dishes on the menu. This is the place to order the luscious *mezza zita alla Norma*, tubes of hard-durum-wheat pasta imported from Italy tossed with tomatoes, eggplant velvety with olive oil, and lots of garlic: the very essence of Sicily. For those who have acquired the taste, the famous Sicilian *pasta con sarde* is made much the same way it has been for the past thousand years. The combination of saffron-infused curly spaghetti tossed with sardines, anchovies, licoricey fennel tops, pine nuts, currants, and bread crumbs resonates all the way from the Middle Ages. More familiar is Lo Coco's version of spaghetti with meatballs, in this case pasta tubes in a tasty Naples-style tomato sauce with two large, soft, fine-textured meatballs studded with currants and toasted pine nuts.

Demonstrating his versatility, Lo Coco makes two Tuscan pastas with equal finesse: capellini with fresh tomato sauce and lots of nutty arugula; and the classic capellini dressed only with toasted garlic, olive oil, and lots of freshly ground black pepper.

His individual pizzas are distinctive for their rich, almost flaky crusts. The Neapolitan, paved with paper-thin slices of mushroom, is my favorite. The pepperoni

510 Union Street (at Grant),
San Francisco
Tel: 296-9151
Open Tuesday through
Thursday 5 to 10 p.m.,
Friday and Saturday until
11 p.m., Sunday 4 to
10 p.m.
Price: Moderate
Credit Cards: MC, V

pizza comes scattered with green onions, an inspired touch. Whatever topping you order, the thin, yeasty crusts are a main attraction. Starters include a couple of unique salads: *insalata emancipata,* which somehow brings together currants, blue cheese, pecans, olives, romaine and a simple vinaigrette to good effect; and a large platter of arugula, endive, radicchio, and fennel scattered with tiny black olives. The classic presentation of ripe melon and prosciutto is always appealing during melon season. Save room for lovely house-made cannoli filled with ricotta sweetened with bits of the preserved dark cherries called *amarone.* These wonderful imported cherries in liqueur also turn vanilla ice cream into a fantastic Italian sundae. The small Italian wine list is a bit pricy, but the bottles are interesting and include several refreshing wines from Sicily.

Customers can see the small open kitchen from the red brick dining room, which has terra-cotta floors and front windows that slide open completely. On warm North Beach evenings, you feel like you are eating on the Mediterranean, especially since some of the waiters don't speak English.

L'OSTERIA DEL FORNO

519 Columbus Avenue (between Green and Union), San Francisco
Tel: 982-1124
Monday, Wednesday, and Thursday 11:30 a.m. to 10 p.m., Friday and Saturday until 11 p.m., Sunday 1 to 10 p.m.

This little hole in the wall serves authentic and tasty food by keeping its menu tiny and specializing in dishes from the brick-lined oven. The two Italian women who own L'Osteria have attracted a wildly loyal and appreciative following, including my kid Harry, and his parents never complain when he gets his way on this one. We do wrestle over the fingers of crunchy, thin focaccia for which L'Osteria is famous, brought warm from the oven in little baskets during the meal, until Harry moves on to a slice of very thin-crusted pizza, nicely coated with melted mozzarella, good tomato sauce, and tiny balls of

Italian sausage. It's also my favorite thin-crust pizza, and sometimes the boy has to protect it from being nibbled away by you-know-who. We start with a couple of *antipasti*: roasted onions sprinkled with bread crumbs; roasted red peppers in olive oil; tissue-thin *speck* (Italian smoked ham); or *bresaola* with arugula salad and another favorite, canned tuna and white bean salad (see recipe, page 300), a version superior to any I've tasted. I always get a plate of paper-thin sliced roast pork cooked in milk, a traditional method that forms the sublime brown curds that are scattered over the meat. The pork comes with roasted sweet and white potatoes lightly seasoned with herbs—a dish that must be served in heaven. Each day brings one pasta, like house-made green ravioli, tender and light, stuffed with ricotta and sauced in a spritely marinara; or a ramekin of baked rigatoni in a luscious slightly creamy beef and tomato sauce. The women at L'Osteria make one of the best cups of espresso in town—comparable to Caffè Greco's —so I always end with one, then another tiny cup of coffee (very full-flavored, aromatic, almost syrupy, without a hint of bitterness) served with a *biscotto*. A choice of three or four Italian wines, all inexpensive, by the glass or bottle, completes the experience. (I wish there were a few more interesting bottles.) Only eight tables have been squeezed into the tiny storefront, with several stuck into alcoves by the front windows. Every six months or so the women upgrade a bit—paint the walls, improve the lighting, change the color of the tablecloths under the glass-topped tables—but prices stay amazingly low, and everyone understands that any change in scale could ruin the magic.

Price: Inexpensive

No credit cards

INSALATA RUSTICA L'OSTERIA

One 20-ounce can cannellini beans, or
2 cups cooked cannellini beans
One 6-ounce can tuna, packed in water
1/2 cup chopped celery
1/2 teaspoon minced fresh oregano
1/2 cup thinly sliced red onion
2 tablespoons balsamic vinegar
1/2 teaspoon kosher salt
Freshly ground pepper to taste
7 tablespoons olive oil (L'Osteria uses
Fortuna extra-virgin)

This is the best canned tuna salad you'll ever taste. You can get canned cannellini beans at any Italian delicatessen. Fresh shell beans make this preparation superb, and cooked dried cannellini beans are also wonderful, but if you want something fast and really good, use canned. The ratio of beans to tuna is about equal.

Drain the canned cannellini beans, if using. Rinse and drain well. Drain the tuna. In a serving bowl, combine the beans and tuna. Add the celery, oregano, and onion.

In a bowl, mix the balsamic vinegar with the salt and pepper. Whisk in the olive oil. Pour over the beans and tuna and mix gently. Taste for salt.

Serve with Italian bread.

Serves 4 as an appetizer

MO'S

1322 Grant Avenue
(between Vallejo and
Green), San Francisco
Tel: 788-3779
Open Sunday through
Thursday 11:30 a.m. to 10:30
p.m., Friday and Saturday
until 11:30 p.m.
Price: Inexpensive
Credit Cards: MC, V

You can see Mo's grill man scooping up big handfuls of bright red freshly ground beef, gently forming them into patties, and placing them just so on a round revolving grill. All this happens in the front window of this immaculately clean and orderly hamburger joint strategically located within stumbling distance of Grant Avenue's premier saloons. I like Mo's meticulously prepared hamburgers on their unique soft-crusty buns, smeared with mustardy house-made mayonnaise, any time of day. The crisp, skinny fries; thick milk shakes made the old-fashioned way in tall silver containers; and the spicy grilled chicken kabobs tucked into pita bread and seasoned with big spoonfuls of roughly chopped tomatoes, onions, and cilantro make Mo's a destination even if you're not in North Beach. The one drawback is the chilly decor, an attempt at high-tech design. The white tile, chrome, and black Formica under stark lighting give the small room all the warmth of a gym locker room. However, the counter seats with a view of the slim, efficient cook and his grill are just fine.

MOOSE'S

Publican Ed Moose, the former owner of the Washington Square Bar and Grill across the park, has a winner in his new operation, Moose's. The place has everything any self-respecting North Beach schmoozer could want: a lively bar with two video monitors tuned to the latest sporting events, friendly bartenders with impressive memories (once you order a special drink or even ask for something the bar doesn't stock, it will be there the next time you come in), a big, open, grand cafe-style dining room with front windows that open up to the street and the Washington Square Park, Don Asher at the piano in the evenings, and a reasonably priced menu of dishes, which are so delicious and imaginative that Neanderthals like me who care mostly for the food come back time after time. Moose did something brilliant for his new, glittery spot by finding a young and very talented chef, Lance Dean Velasquez, and giving him free rein. The result is a seasonally changing menu that reflects all the marvelous ingredients available in the Bay Area, but still has the earthiness and character that Moose's regulars demand. I couldn't see the city's hard-drinking politicians and journalists tucking into a quail salad in a hauntingly tasty dried-cherry compote with delicate greens and a little dab of truffled mashed potatoes until I had one myself. It was so immediately appealing that the new line in the back rooms of the city became, "Hey, let's go grab a quail."

1652 Stockton Street (between Union and Filbert), San Francisco

Tel: 989-7800

Open Monday through Saturday 11:30 a.m. to midnight, Sunday 10:30 a.m. to midnight; Sunday brunch until 3 p.m.

Price: Moderate

Credit cards: AE, DC, MC, V

Of course there are meatier things, but they get a sophisticated presentation. I personally am addicted to Velasquez's chorizo and roasted pasilla pizza and often order it in the bar with a glass of wine. It has a rich, flaky crust, almost like puff pastry topped with a scattering of spicy Spanish lamb sausage, lots of pasillas, and roasted red and yellow peppers peeled, everything sprinkled with rich *manchego* cheese, a wonderful semi-hard Spanish sheep's milk cheese. Even if you've never ventured beyond pepperoni pizza, I guarantee you'll love this creation. For the less daring, pastas with fresh clams; penne in a peppery tomato sauce; and pappardelle in a rustic meat sauce are very satisfying. A hefty veal chop; perfectly grilled yellowfin tuna, rare and meaty as a fine steak; long-simmered dishes of white beans with duck *confit* and garlic sausage; and sturgeon on a warm salad of celery root in a bacon vinaigrette have shone on the ever-changing menu. Impeccably

fried calamari, artichokes, and oysters in a *fritto misto*, or a stunning salad of shaved fennel, slices of prosciutto, and shards of Parmesan moistened with extra-virgin olive oil and lemon, could have come out of a small trattoria in Florence. Velasquez has announced that he's leaving to open his own restaurant and has been replaced by Mark Valiani, so it remains to be seen if the kitchen can carry on without him. After 2½ years one hopes that the systems will be in place.

The causal wine list—lots of wine by the glass; and California bottles—is ennobled by a few Italian reds at decent prices. I remember a full-bodied but soft-drinking Dolcetto d'Alba, Coppo, 1990 that was made for the food.

Everyone at this restaurant, whether they're part of the regular crowd or not, gets good treatment. The attitude on the floor and at the door couldn't be more genuine, more welcoming, more friendly, a spirit that infects the entire restaurant. People always have gone to Ed Moose's place for a party, but now they go there to eat as well. Moose's throws just the kind of social event that everyone can enjoy.

RISTORANTE IDEALE

I like the Roman vibes in this relatively new North Beach Italian restaurant, very different from the old-fashioned Italian-American joints that line Columbus and your stomach with too much bitter garlic and canned tomato sauce. At Ideale, the regular-menu pastas take a thrilling, al dente, under-sauced stance and come up sparkling. The daily specials, like luscious house-made ravioli filled with ricotta and spinach in a fresh tomato sauce aromatic with basil; or tender fettuccine in a creamy tomato sauce with big chunks of fresh lobster tail, demonstrate a subtler side of noodle cookery. I always order an antipasto of warm grilled vegetables, which includes my favorites, grilled radicchio and endive; and a satisfying classic version of Carpaccio, scattered with shaved Parmesan, capers, arugula, and extra-virgin olive oil and lemon. The *arrosto misto*, a platter of succulent rosemary-perfumed grilled rabbit, a tiny lamb chop, and slices of pork loin with roasted potatoes and vegetables represents the star main course. For dessert, have shaved espresso

1315 Grant Avenue (at Vallejo), San Francisco
Tel: 391-4129
Open Tuesday through Thursday 5:30 to 10:30 p.m., Friday and Saturday until 11 p.m., Sunday 5 to 10 p.m.
Price: Moderate
Credit cards: MC, V

ice with whipped cream, or a coffee ice-cream cake. Ideale knows that to stay ideal the menu has to be small and controllable.

Ideale's location on one of the most picturesque blocks of Grant Street gives it added cachet. The double storefront has red tile floors, high ceilings, walls covered with wine racks, paintings, and mosaics: a spare, modern atmosphere with bohemian overtones. The Italian waiters and maître d' charm the pants off you when things are going well and lose it completely if the restaurant gets too busy.

SAN FRANCISCO ART INSTITUTE CAFE

800 Chestnut Street (at Jones), San Francisco
Tel: 771-7020
Open Monday through Thursday 8 a.m. to 9 p.m., Friday until 4 p.m., Saturday 9 a.m. to 2 p.m. Call ahead, as hours vary during the year.
Price: Inexpensive
No credit cards

Looking for a great $5 lunch with one of the best views in San Francisco? Check out this funky cafe in a cement courtyard inhabited by outré art students, and take advantage of the wholesome cooking of Peter Stanwood, a first-rate cook with experience in well-known restaurants. The cafe offers two hot lunch specials each day, homey baked goods still warm from the oven, nicely dressed fresh salads, and thick made-to-order sandwiches. The portions are so large and prices so cheap that no art students starve around this institute.

The setting of the cafe comes as a spectacular surprise. You enter off Chestnut Street and walk through a tiled courtyard with a fountain. Emotive student art hangs in the arcade surrounding the courtyard and in public galleries to the left. Past these is a large, open plaza with expansive views of the bay and oversized concrete tables and benches. You forget about the utilitarian indoor seating when you gaze through glass walls at the grand vista.

I eat at the cafe often, but I bring my own plate and silverware for perfectly cooked sunny-side-up eggs, bacon, crusty hash browns made from real potatoes, good coffee, and toasted bagels with cream cheese. (I can't eat eggs on paper plates with plastic utensils.) For lunch there may be a big blob of soft polenta covered with a southwestern black bean and vegetable stew or a meatball sandwich on Bread Workshop baguettes overflowing with sautéed red and green peppers, onions, and tomato sauce. Spicy red beans and rice, based on an old New Orleans recipe from photography teacher Pirkle Jones, or tasty Italian meatballs and spaghetti, are perpetual favorites. The cafe makes hearty minestrone and excellent white bean and escarole soup.

The house bakers produce crumbly, plate-sized scones, chewy oatmeal-butterscotch bars, and large chocolate chip–peanut butter cookies that give Mrs. Field a run for her money, and the coffee cakes are most satisfying. Though the operation is casual, almost to the point of sloppiness, all the food tastes really good.

THE HOUSE

A young husband-and-wife team opened this little restaurant to fulfill a dream, and the light, colorful, fresh dishes they turn out show their passion. The particular brand of cooking at The House combines Asian and Western ingredients and techniques, drawing on favorite flavors in a way that an inspired home cook might. With an underlying dedication to freshness—daily shopping in nearby Chinatown for beautiful fish and good-looking produce with some stops at Western produce markets as well—this vision takes on dimension. The food is seriously good. Try the house Caesar salad in a creamy, not too strong dressing that lends itself to the little bits of warm grilled tuna tossed in it, or a Chinese chicken salad of shredded vegetables and juicy hot chicken breast.

1230 Grant Avenue
(near Columbus),
San Francisco
Tel: 986-8612
Lunch Monday through
Friday 11:30 a.m. to 3 p.m.;
Dinner Monday through
Thursday 5:30 to 10 p.m.,
Friday and Saturday until
11 p.m.
Price: Inexpensive
Credit cards: MC, V

The room feels a bit austere in its modernity, especially in contrast to the ancient North Beach spots around it, but the charm and warmth of the young woman who handles the floor and her excitement about her husband's cooking transform the environment. This room begins to feel like home when you return for more and more of the clean, tasty food, good enough and reasonable enough in price to eat every day.

TOMMASO'S

1042 Kearny Street (at Broadway), San Francisco
Tel: 398-9696
Open Tuesday through Saturday 5 to 10:45 p.m., Sunday 4 to 9:45 p.m.
Price: Inexpensive
Credit cards: MC, V

Time stops when you step down into Tommaso's cavelike dining room with partitioned-off tables along the walls and a long communal table stretching down the middle of the dimly lit room. Nothing has changed in this pizzeria for decades, but that's the way the lines of people waiting to get in like it. They're enticed by the luscious smell of pizza baking in a wood-fired oven. Way before everyone else was cooking in wood-burning ovens, Tommaso's was turning out crisp, sweet, chewy-crusted pizzas scented with smoke and layered with copious amounts of whole-milk mozzarella. The aroma of the vegetarian pizza blanketed with green pepper, onions, fresh mushrooms, and olives really gets to me, though my all-time favorite is the super-deluxe pizza with mushrooms, peppers, ham, and Tommaso's allspice-scented Italian sausage. Ask them to hold the anchovies, which are too strong on this pizza (and I'm an anchovy lover). Tommaso's also makes a massive calzone stuffed with ricotta, mozzarella, prosciutto, and a special spice mixture, which all melt together in a happy way inside a crisp folded-over crust. For starters, order plates of peeled peppers, crisp whole green beans, and trees of broccoli all lightly dressed in lemon juice and olive oil. Though most people go for pizza, don't overlook an airy lasagne baked in the wood-fired oven. No matter when you go, expect a wait. Reservations are not taken.

ZAX

A restaurant in a hidden-away location can be both a blessing and a curse. In the case of Zax, a small, handsome dining room lost behind an apartment building construction site on a part of Taylor near the cable car turnaround, the charm of discovery may not outweigh the disadvantages. If more people found the place they would be sitting down to dinner. Zax is one of the nicest new developments in North Beach and, in fact, the city, for diners who like sophisticated, ingredient-inspired dishes of a California-Mediterranean style at prices well below restaurants of similar quality.

2330 Taylor Street
(near Columbus),
San Francisco
Tel: 563-6266
Open Tuesday through
Saturday 5:30 to 10:30 p.m.
Price: Moderate
Credit cards: MC, V

The first courses and salads are absolutely stunning, as evidenced by a plate of romaine leaves scattered with anchovies, lemon, garlic, and romano cheese; a crusty, airy, goat-cheese soufflé with an apple, celery, and fennel salad; and a simple and beautiful pile of tiny field greens with caramelized walnuts. Main courses pair fresh fish like salmon, tuna, or sturgeon with lots of seasonal vegetables, vinaigrettes instead of sauces, and imaginative starches. A free-range chicken breast comes with morels and a potato pancake made of thin potato sticks. A chewy Niman-Schell flatiron steak is dressed up with spicy onion rings and sautéed spring greens. The menu of six starters, six main courses, and a handful of desserts changes monthly, drawing its energy from the fantastic variety of produce in the Bay Area. If you're a vegetable and salad lover you will rejoice at the way they are woven into the cooking at Zax.

The clean-lined, comfortable dining room, with banquettes, a bar where single diners like to sit, and a revolving exhibit of photographs and paintings, makes for a very hip scene. The staff and the two chef-partners who own the restaurant, veterans of a number of excellent San Francisco kitchens, want only to make customers feel at home: well served but relaxed. With such clean and stylish food at moderate prices Zax can be a place for a special night out or a regular spot, and is guaranteed by me to satisfy at either level.

CAFES

Over the years Freddy's has become more of an eating place than a coffeehouse, albeit without a seriously equipped kitchen, but the casual food has a logic of its own dictated by the available cooking methods. The small countertop pizza oven, the kind used in cafes all over North Beach, allows for little pizzas with good prebaked crusts topped with interesting combinations like pancetta, new potatoes, mozzarella, hard-cooked egg slices, and spinach leaves (my favorite). Warm open-face sandwiches made on slices of polenta work nicely too, especially one topped with melted mozzarella, tomatoes, and an aromatic pesto accompanied with a crisp mélange of sliced cucumber and radishes in a red-wine vinaigrette. All the salads and vegetable *antipasti* use fresh seasonal produce and lively vinaigrettes. Well-made coffee, fresh cookies, and pastries brought in daily offer sustenance anytime in two sunny rooms, one filled with roomy booths, the other with small tables and a counter with stools. Oil paintings by David Bruce, the owner, decorate the walls, while the expansive plate-glass windows frame an urban composition of their own: a view of Lombard, Columbus, and crisscrossing cable cars.

901 Columbus Avenue (at Lombard), San Francisco

Tel: 922-0151

Open Monday through Friday 10 a.m. to 10 p.m., Saturday and Sunday 9 a.m. to 10 p.m.

Credit cards: MC, V

CAFFÈ GRECO

423 Columbus Avenue,
San Francisco
Tel: 397-6261
Open Monday through
Thursday 7 a.m. to 11 p.m.,
Friday through Sunday until
midnight
No credit cards

I live on Telegraph Hill because I like the European amenities of North Beach, and the place I walk down to the most is Caffè Greco, owned by Hanna Suleiman, who happens to be Lebanese. His coffee, made from Illy Espresso beans on a machine kept as finely tuned as a concert grand, has the depth, aroma, and body of the best coffee in Italy. Yes, Caffè Greco does offer the option of low-fat milk for its cappuccino and latte, and the portion of espresso does exceed the thimbleful of ambrosia you get in Italy, but Greco's coffee is always delicious. I particularly like a mixture of espresso and hot milk served in a little glass, which has been called at various times the Algerian or the Africano, stronger than a latte and without the tiresome foam of a cappuccino.

The smallish cafe has large sliding windows facing Columbus and a few tables on the street. The floor is so tightly packed with chairs and tables that you have to plot out a path before you make a move—especially with several cups of coffee in hand. You order at one end of a counter that holds baskets of fresh croissants and raisin rolls. A refrigerated glass section displays truffle cakes and tiramisù from the great Pasticeria Rulli (see page 572). Focaccia sandwiches accompanied with pickled Italian vegetables and a variety of *antipasti* are also available, but it is at prime coffee hours that the cafe is the fullest—in the morning, the afternoon, and late evening. The crowd is completely mixed—young, old, local, tourist, Asian, European—everyone who appreciates a great cup of coffee in a clean, well-lighted place.

CAFFÈ ROMA

Though Caffè Roma and the Caffè Roma Coffee Roasting Company are owned by the same family, the coffee at Caffè Roma doesn't hold a candle to the creamy espresso down the street. It's bitter and thin. The service can be flaky, and details like storing the gelato so that it doesn't melt and crystalize tend to be overlooked. On top of this, prices are high, but the sunny Roma space is so appealing I still go there. I love the original hand-painted walls of cherubs, clouds, and blue sky, the high, molded ceilings, the front windows that slide open to Columbus Avenue, and the well-spaced tables that allow for comfortable newspaper reading. I only go there if I have prepared myself beforehand not to get aggravated, or because I crave Roma's puffy-crusted combination pizza laden with mushrooms, olives, fresh tomatoes, mozzarella, pepperoni, salami, Italian sausage, green peppers, and onions—expensive, but tasty.

414 Columbus Avenue (at Vallejo), San Francisco

Tel: 391-8584

Open Monday through Thursday 7:30 a.m. to 11 p.m., Friday and Saturday until 1 a.m., Sunday 7:30 a.m. to 11 p.m.

Credit cards: MC, V

CAFFÈ TRIESTE

I had a delicious, strong, creamy, not-bitter espresso here the other day and it took me by surprise. Consistency has not been a strong point at Trieste, though its scruffy regulars would wrestle me to the ground over this one. There may be new attention to coffee quality—certainly Trieste has stepped up its marketing of house-roasted coffee beans to restaurants and consumers. On the weekend afternoons when live opera singers hold forth, you can't get near the place. During the week, Trieste is the home of vestigial and nouveau beatniks who eye everyone who orders a cup of coffee as a potential soul mate. If you're in the mood, you can talk all afternoon.

601 Vallejo Street (at Grant), San Francisco

Tel: 392-6739

Open Sunday through Thursday 6:30 a.m. to 11:30 p.m., Friday and Saturday until midnight

No credit cards

566 Columbus Avenue (at
Union), San Francisco
Tel: 362-0536
Open Monday through
Saturday 10 a.m. to
midnight, Sunday until
11 p.m.
No credit cards

People gravitate from all over town to little Mario's to eat delicious warm focaccia sandwiches straight from the miniature Baker's Pride pizza oven. They also come to drink coffee expertly made from Graffeo beans, or to drink a cold imported beer or a glass of wine. Seating is so close at this sardine can of a cafe that you cannot help but exchange a few words with the person next to you. I always find Mario's to be an exceptionally friendly, low-key spot. The people who frequent it tend to like eating, which means that attitude does not take precedence over humanity.

Mario's actually was a cigar store at one time, though Mario, Liliana, and son Paul Crismani have been running it for the last fifteen of its seventy years as a coffeehouse with a counter and six or so tables. Windows that look across the street to Washington Square slide open on warm days, letting a breeze into the almost claustrophobic interior lined with photographs of beloved patrons.

Mario's luscious sandwiches are made on soft, olive oil-rich focaccia from nearby Liguria and Danilo bakeries, with rich, savory fillings like tender housemade meatballs in a buttery tomato sauce spiked with thinly sliced onions. Both the chicken and eggplant sandwiches use crisp, breaded cutlets, which are slipped into the focaccia with just the right amount of tomato sauce and melted mozzarella. On the lighter side, try a warm open-face tuna salad sandwich with melted cheese and onions, the best tuna melt in the world. A tumbler of Chianti with them does a world of good for the digestion. These are the kind of sandwiches that stay with you all day.

One of my favorite spots to sip a strong, creamy espresso is on the sunny bench in front of Caffè Roma Coffee Roasting Company, a coffee roastery and cafe run by the Caffè Roma people. Both the beans to take home and the espresso made in the cafe have extraordinary character and richness. Only coffee and a few biscotti are served here, but the coffee is so good that many folks regularly stop by for a quick shot.

526 Columbus Avenue (between Green and Union), San Francisco

Tel: 296-7662

Monday through Friday 8 a.m. to 6 p.m., Saturday and Sunday 9 a.m. to 6 p.m.

Credit cards: MC, V

BARS

GINO AND CARLO'S

548 Green Street (between
Jasper and Grant),
San Francisco
Tel: 421-0896
Open daily 6 a.m. to 2 a.m.
No credit cards

Just a bar with a couple of television sets, Gino and Carlo's belongs to the North Beach old-timers who have staked out a stool and like cheap booze, friendly talk, and no constraints on their habits, like smoking.

SPEC'S

12 Saroyan Alley (on
Columbus between
Broadway and Pacific),
San Francisco
Tel: 421-4112
Open daily 4:30 p.m. to 2 a.m.
No credit cards

Artists, photographers, and merchant marines hang out at this historic seaman's bar with a worn wooden interior that looks like the hold of a ship. On any drinking tour of North Beach, Spec's is a required stop.

THE SALOON

1232 Grant Avenue (at
Fresno near Vallejo),
San Francisco
Tel: 989-7666
Open daily noon to 2 a.m.
No credit cards

Junkies and ex-cons prefer the Saloon during the day; at night when local R & B bands play, passersby and everyone in the neighborhood stop in for a drink and a dance, pulled in by the music and the nostalgic beery, smoky Saloon breath that pours out the front door. Started in 1861, the Saloon's ancient bar and funky walls have seen it all.

The other great outdoor venue in North Beach, along with Enrico's, Savoy Tivoli's patio attracts a young, cruising crowd that congregates on Grant Avenue every night, leaving the Savoy's spacious indoor bar and cafe empty even on the coldest nights. The roar from the patio rivals the noise coming out of the biker bars down the street. People who hang here check out each other, plus everyone else who walks by on the narrow street.

1434 Grant Avenue
(between Green and Union),
San Francisco
Tel: 362-7023
Tuesday through Thursday
5 p.m. to 2 a.m.,
Friday through Sunday
3 p.m. to 2 a.m.
No credit cards

T O S C A

Jeannette Etheredge, proprietor of this beloved, seventy-five-year-old North Beach bar, knows every ballet dancer, movie star, and filmmaker in this town and many others all over the world, and when any of them are in her neighborhood they drop by Tosca. The long bar, vaulted front windows, and antique espresso machine are just half the picture. Beyond lies a large room filled with booths and tables, plus another back room with a pool table where luminaries tend to hang out with their entourages, the setting for hundreds of arty, impromptu parties. Even if you're a nobody, you might enjoy a special house cappuccino served in a glass and composed of hot espresso, steamed milk, sugar, and brandy, guaranteed to warm you up on a cold summer night. A juke box filled with arias competes with the pounding bass from a dance club in the same building.

242 Columbus Avenue
(between Pacific and
Broadway), San Francisco
Tel: 391-1244
Open 5 p.m. to 2 a.m.
No credit cards

VESUVIO

255 Columbus Avenue
(between Pacific and
Broadway), San Francisco
Tel: 362-3370
Open daily 6 a.m. to 2 a.m.
No credit cards

This original beatnik bar next to City Lights bookstore has remained true to its founding spirit year after year. The walls are like a work in progress, full of scribblings, ever-changing photographs, and pieces of art. The upstairs mezzanine overlooking the historic conjunction of Columbus Avenue and Jack Kerouac Alley affords a choice view of North Beach shenanigans, and if you insist, the bartender will flick on a slide show that pays homage to James Joyce.

DELICATESSENS/TAKE-OUT

FLORENCE ITALIAN DELI AND RAVIOLI FACTORY

This deli stocks the essentials of the Italian larder at excellent prices, like three-liter tins of clean, neutral Fortuna Fontana Italian olive oil for cooking (the one with the colorful tiger on the front) and large cans of imported tomatoes. A case of *baccala*—salt cod—and a bin of polenta sit next to each other, suggesting some good winter fare. Beautiful olives, especially the green varieties, the superior oil-packed Columbus anchovies, and a good selection of Italian cheeses are located on the marble counter. Florence carries Reggiano and the even more aged, crumbly Parmesan called *rocca*. Although this deli manufactures veal- and spinach-filled ravioli and sells them to many well-known restaurants around town, the best are made at Lucca on Chestnut.

1412 Stockton Street (at Vallejo), San Francisco

Tel: 421-6170

Open Monday through Saturday 7 a.m. to 6 p.m., Sunday 9 a.m. to 3 p.m.

No credit cards

GOLDEN BOY

They put the big sheet pans of hot, fragrant pizza right at nose level in the open front window, so when you walk by the smell practically grabs you. How can anyone resist eating a slice of pizza that has just come out of the oven? Golden Boy makes its pizzas on soft, olive oil–rich focaccia dough and slathers them with lots of stuff, so that one piled-up square slice makes a satisfying meal. I am partial to the vegetarian, heavily layered with the thinnest slices of zucchini, fresh tomato, olives, onions, and mushrooms, then drizzled with pesto, but if I don't want to wait for a reheat (and Golden Boy slices do reheat well in the countertop oven), I go for the pizza still warm from its first cooking, whatever it may be. I

542 Green Street (between Columbus and Grant), San Francisco

Tel: 982-9738

Open Sunday through Thursday 11:45 a.m. to 11:30 p.m., Friday and Saturday until 1:30 a.m.

No credit cards

usually walk down the street eating the slice, trying not to dribble on my shirt, but for the more civilized, there is a high counter and stools plus a few boothlike tables in the back. Only pizza and beer, wine and espresso are sold here, and that's why the pizza stays so delicious, slice by slice, year after year.

IACOPI'S

1462 Grant Avenue (at Union), San Francisco

Tel: 421-0757

Open Monday through Saturday 9 a.m. to 6 p.m., Sunday until 5 p.m.

Credit cards: MC, V; $15 minimum

Generous Leo Rossi, the oversized man who runs this North Beach nexus of house-cured Italian pork and restaurant gossip, presses brontosaurian-sized tastes of his favorite items on his customers. He always knows who's cooking what in town because he supplies most of them. Leo cures his own prosciutto, which is sometimes available at his store, sometimes not, depending on whether the Feds are after him. (Leo does not have USDA approval for commercial sale of his marvelous prosciutto.) His pancetta, unsmoked bacon rolled with aromatic spices, is the key ingredient in many important dishes around town (see recipe for rabbit). He takes the skin from his pancetta, parboils it, and grinds it into his superb *coteghino*, a huge tied sausage cooked with white beans or as part of *bollito misto*. Leo also makes his own Marsala-scented dried sausages, which are draped over a wood dowel in the side window next to burlap sacks of the largest white beans you'll ever see, grown and dried by a cousin and of limited supply. Grab a pound or two when you see them. His coarsely ground fresh sausages—sweet Sicilian with fennel; hot, red pepper–laced Calabrese; and my favorite, the garlicky Toscano—have an authentically rustic, home-made quality about them. The dried Monterey jack that Leo cures in black pepper, and the oozy, rice flour–coated teleme, two of our oldest and most delightful

STEFANO'S BRAISED RABBIT, ITALIAN STYLE

Leo Rossi, the owner of Iacopi, cures his own pancetta with lots of sweet aromatic spices, such as allspice and cloves. His pancetta really adds character to any dish. You can buy excellent rabbits from Bud Hoffman at the Ferry Plaza Farmers' Market on Saturdays (page 119) or at Polarica, a wholesale-retail operation south of Market (page 462). This recipe comes from a Roman friend who made it for me when he was living in San Francisco. You should cook it a day before you want to serve it; the improvement is miraculous. This rabbit stew is delicious with polenta or flat noodles.

In a bowl large enough to hold the rabbit pieces, combine the marinade ingredients. Add the rabbits, cover, and refrigerate for at least 24 hours.

Drain the rabbit pieces, reserving the marinade, and pat them dry with paper towels.

In a large skillet over medium heat, heat 2 tablespoons olive oil and brown 2 or 3 pieces of rabbit. Discard the oil after browning and repeat with the remaining rabbit until all the pieces have been browned in fresh oil. Put the rabbit pieces in a bowl and reserve the pan juices to add to the sauce.

Put the remaining 2 tablespoons olive oil in a large, heavy pot or Dutch oven and cook the pancetta until it starts to color, about 5 minutes. Add the celery, carrots, and onions and cook over medium heat for 10 minutes. Add the tomatoes, rabbit, and reserved marinade and juices. Cover and simmer on top of the stove for 1 hour. Check the thinner pieces and remove if tender. Continue to cook the legs another 15 minutes, if necessary.

In a colander with a large bowl underneath, drain the rabbit and vege-tables. Place the sauce back in the pot, spoon off the surface fat, bring to a boil, and cook to reduce by one third. Let cool. Add the rabbit and vegetables to the pot. Cover and refrigerate overnight.

Gently reheat and serve the next day, accompanied with pasta or polenta.

Serves 8

Marinade

1/4 cup olive oil

1 bottle decent dry red wine such as Chianti, Zinfandel, or Merlot

10 cloves

10 garlic cloves, minced

30 turns of a pepper grinder

1 cup green olives, pitted and chopped

Stew

2 rabbits cut into 8 pieces

5 to 8 tablespoons olive oil for browning, plus 2 tablespoons

1 cup diced pancetta (about 8 ounces or three 1/4-inch slices)

1 1/2 cups diced celery (about two large stalks)

2 cups diced peeled carrots (about three medium)

2 cups chopped onions (about two medium)

Two 28-ounce cans peeled Italian (plum) tomatoes, drained and roughly chopped

Northern California cheeses, beckon from atop the long meat counter.

You never know what you'll find in or on the long glass counter to eat on the spot. Leo's ex-wife invented a mascarpone torta, terrines of Italian cream cheese layered with pesto, figs, or caviar, and he still moves a lot of them. The little Cariani dry *salametti* hanging from hooks behind the counter can make the centerpiece of a picnic, and you can buy everything else you need right there—either separately or in made-to-order sandwiches.

MOLINARI

373 Columbus Avenue (at Vallejo), San Francisco
Tel: 421-2337
Open Monday through Friday 8 a.m. to 5:30 p.m., Saturday 7:30 a.m. to 5:30 p.m.
No credit cards

The front window of this popular Italian deli is a mosaic made of tightly fitted-together imported tins, jars, and boxes of olive oil, biscotti, anchovies, olives, artichokes, peppers, pasta, polenta, and tomatoes. Just walking by makes my mouth water. Inside, the small, narrow store is similarly packed to the rafters with foodstuffs. Many a great sandwich has been composed around Molinari's spectacular hot, red pepper–flecked salami. Behind the counter, Italian pickled peppers, marinated artichokes, mushrooms, red peppers, olives of every sort—all the stuff you need to construct a dream sandwich—await selection. Fresh mozzarella from Ferrante in Walnut Creek and imported buffalo milk mozzarella sit next to each other not far from handy two-ounce tins of Columbus anchovies. I like the frittata here, a cold cheese, spinach, and bread-crumb cake held together with eggs. The fresh sausages are excellent, vying with Iacopi as the best in North Beach. The sweet Italian with fennel, which cooks up slightly pink in color, is out of this world, and so are the tiny pure pork breakfast links. Any pantry ingredients called for in any Italian recipe, including imported Italian cheeses in good condition, can be found here.

NORTH BEACH PIZZA

I mention the two North Beach Pizza parlors not so much for their sometimes soggy, extremely cheesy, often indifferently put together pizzas, but for the fact that they have an amazingly efficient call-in and delivery system that gets your pizza to your door hot and within forty-five minutes. North Beach pizza is a hundred times better than the chain-style pizzas, and this independent operation has figured out how to beat the chains at their own game.

A lot of people do love this thick, rich pizza and often line up outside the Union and Grant corner door to wait for a booth. (The branch down the block near Green stays full, but isn't as wildly popular.) When made well, the vegetarian pizza has a pleasant balance of savory and fresh vegetables that melt in the oven into pillows of cheese. So much cheese is piled on the pepperoni that it gets lost underneath. However, it takes only a few slices to fill you up, which is just what prompts all those young, hungry, budget-minded kids to cool their heels on the sidewalk.

1499 Grant Avenue (at Union) and 1310 Grant Avenue (at Vallejo), San Francisco
Tel: (both stores) 433-2444
Open Monday through Thursday 11 a.m. to 1 a.m., Friday and Saturday until 3 a.m., Sunday noon to 11 p.m.
Credit cards: AE, DC, D, MC, V

PANELLI BROTHERS

I have gotten such fruity, buttery, nutty, tissue-thin slices of imported prosciutto from Parma at Panelli, I always buy it here. Panelli stocks the usual Italian staples, but shows particular strength as a *salumeria*, a place that sells a wide range of Italian-cured meats like *coppa*, a prosciuttolike cured pork roll; and *soppressata*, a peppery, coarsely ground salami. A large part of their operation is devoted to making sandwiches on soft Italian rolls from the freshly sliced meats, and the friendly deli men behind the counter show no end of patience and cheerfulness while you compose your masterpiece on the spot.

1419 Stockton Street (between Vallejo and Card Alley), San Francisco
Tel: 421-2541
Open Monday through Saturday 7:30 a.m. to 5:30 p.m., Sunday 8:30 a.m. to 2:30 p.m.
Credit cards: MC, V

BAKERIES/PASTRIES

DANILO

516 Green Street (at Bannam), San Francisco

Tel: 989-1806

Open daily 6:30 a.m. to 6:30 p.m.

No credit cards

Bakeries that look just like Danilo are found all over Italy, with shelves full of hard Italian biscotti, hard toast for seafood soups, and crumbly Italian cookies. In back of the cookie counter are wooden shelves of baked breads, the most notable being the yeasted Italian corn bread, so popular that Danilo has started to bake it every day. (It's excellent toasted, buttered, and slathered with caviar.) Rounds of focaccia scattered with coarse salt and rosemary, green onions, or tomato sauce, have a soft, olive-oily texture that appeals to kids. The grandmotherly Italian women behind the counter have a soft spot for children and often hand them a crisp, yard-long bread stick. I have never walked into Danilo without seeing an elderly man or woman peacefully sitting in the chair by the open door, carrying on a running conversation with the counter ladies and anyone else who walks in the door.

LIGURIA

1700 Stockton Street (at Filbert), San Francisco

Tel: 421-3786

Open weekdays 8 a.m. to 4 p.m. (earlier if soldout), Saturday 7 a.m. to 4 p.m., Sunday 7 a.m. until noon

No credit cards

A focaccia store kitty-corner from Washington Square, Liguria sells plain, tomato, or green onion-topped focaccia in big flat sheets, which they cut in half, wrap in waxed paper, and tie with string. If you don't get there before 11 a.m., there's a good chance that your focaccia of choice will be sold out. Not only does everyone in the neighborhood stop by for a square, but Liguria wholesales to lots of cafes who use the focaccia for warm sandwiches. PlumpJack, a new spot off Union Street, came upon the idea of using the tomato focaccia as a bun for hamburgers, thereby internalizing the catsup. Try it. It really works. Early in the morning you can smell the baking dough and see the golden sheets coming out of the huge brick ovens in the back. The singleness of purpose and the perfect consistency of their product make Liguria part of many people's regular North Beach ritual.

STELLA

This tiny bakery specializes in *sacripantina*, an Italian cake made with soft, yellow layers soaked with Marsala, then filled and frosted with airy zabaglione enriched with whipped cream. Twenty years ago these molded cakes, juicy, boozy, and light, with a pleasant sherrylike flavor, used to be served in every Italian restaurant in town. Now, of course, restaurants have their own pastry departments, but they would do well to create a cake as good. I much prefer the original Stella *sacripantina* to some of the flavored ones that have slipped into the repertory since the bakery has taken to preparing single servings in clear plastic cups. Recently, one of these was soaked in orange liqueur, an unexpected and not welcome surprise. Be sure to ask for the original Marsala cake and buy a whole one rather than an individual serving if you want the proportions to be right. The whole cakes, which must be refrigerated, come in several sizes, the smallest quite workable for an intimate dinner party.

446 Columbus Avenue (between Stockton and Vallejo), San Francisco
Tel: 986-2914
Open daily at 7:30 a.m.; closes Monday 6 p.m., Tuesday through Thursday 10 p.m., Friday and Saturday midnight, Sunday 9 p.m.
No credit cards

1362 Stockton Street (at Vallejo), San Francisco
Open daily 7 a.m. to 6 p.m.
Credit cards: MC, V

Each bakery in North Beach has made its reputation on a certain cake. At Victoria, it's the St. Honoré, a festive white-frosted cake rimmed with miniature custard-filled cream puffs. Inside, layers of crunchy Italian "leaf" pastry, custard, and rum-soaked cake make each sweet bite an adventure. Generations of families have celebrated special occasions with the St. Honoré, which can be ordered ahead in many different sizes. The other specialties at Victoria are their molded refrigerator cakes: the *zuccotto*, a bright-red mound soaked in cherry liqueur with custard; my favorite, the Fantasia, a tasty conglomeration of soft cake, mocha cream, and shaved chocolate; and a cheesy tiramisù. All the cakes now come in single-serving sizes so you can try them before you commit to a larger cake. I also like the powdered sugar–dusted cornmeal pound cake, much lighter than a regular pound cake with a hint of grit. Sliced and toasted, buttered and spread with jam, or as a vehicle for macerated berries and whipped cream, the simple cornmeal pound cake is nothing if not versatile. I can see it as a base for your own Italian cake of custard, fruit, and liqueur.

ICE CREAM/CHOCOLATES

For other locations see pages 191, 430.

GELATO CLASSICO

Lots of Italian ice cream shops have opened and closed, but Gelato Classico (with one other location) thrives because it's the best. The ice creams taste natural, and the tricky creamy, thick texture has always been consistently maintained through proper storing and handling. This ice cream is so soft, it gets shoveled into little cups. I cannot pass the shop without stopping in for a *coppa mista*, a lovely mixture of chocolate, pistachio, vanilla, and rum-flavored ice creams all swirled together. The true tropical fruit flavors—coconut, banana, mango—have been the base for a tropical fruit sundae I make at home layered with fresh pineapple, kiwi, papayas, toasted nuts, coconut, and whipped cream. The guys behind the counter at the North Beach store deserve a medal for patience and generosity; they proffer endless tastes and have a particular affection for children.

576 Union Street (at Stockton), San Francisco

Tel: 391-6667

Open Monday through Thursday 11 a.m. to 11 p.m., Friday through Sunday until midnight

No credit cards

MARKETS

THE NATURE STOP

1336 Grant Avenue (between Vallejo and Green), San Francisco

Tel: 398-3810

Open Monday through Friday 9 a.m. to 10 p.m., Saturday and Sunday 10 a.m. to 9 p.m.

Credit cards: AE, D, MC, V

I have watched this roomy Grant Street natural foods store upgrade its inventory over the years so that now it carries a growing variety of organic fruits in season, like white peaches and nectarines, berries, and melons, along with commercial fruits and vegetables. Metropolis and Semifreddi breads are delivered daily, and the full complement of bulk nuts, seeds, and grains from Sun Ridge Farms fills up a portion of the store. A smoothie bar at the entrance takes advantage of the plentiful tropical fruit by offering such delights as fresh mango or papaya yogurt drinks, thinned by fresh orange juice, swirled in the blender to order.

ROSSI MARKET

627 Vallejo Street (at Columbus), San Francisco

Tel: 986-1068

Open Monday through Saturday 8 a.m. to 9 p.m., Sunday 9 a.m. to 7 p.m.

Credit cards: MC, V

One of a dying breed of relatively small neighborhood grocery stores, Rossi's serves a useful role in North Beach as a place to buy Italian vegetables. Rossi's produce section, though commercial, will have broccoli rabe, arugula, bulbs of fennel, large and small artichokes, Italian parsley, chard, cardoons, and other seasonal vegetables in varying condition. Small glass bottles, which are difficult to find, of Italian olive oil of all grades along with large tins, imported dried pasta, lots of pickled Italian peppers, and Berkeley Farms dairy products make Rossi a resource. In the newspaper rack in front of the store, *The South China Morning Post* shares space with *Corriere della Sera*, British, and German newspapers, democratically covering all the bases.

MEAT AND POULTRY

This Italian butcher shop specializes in veal shanks, baby beef liver, veal breast, and other favored Italian cuts. The friendly butchers will order anything they don't have, as well as cut and grind on the spot. Carlo Togni, my Roman friend who lives near Precita Park, travels all the way across town to buy his meat here—and to have an espresso at Greco—because the butchers understand what he needs for his meat sauces and roasts. Excellent fat-marbled boneless chuck roasts are always available, along with fresh pork tenderloin and meaty country-style pork ribs for American cooks. Little City carries Petaluma Poultry Producers chickens, which have excellent flavor and texture.

1400 Stockton Street (at Vallejo), San Francisco

Tel: 986-2601

Open Monday through Friday 8 a.m. to 6 p.m., Saturday until 5:30 p.m.

Credit cards: MC, V

FISH

VALLEJO MARKET

You often can encounter live spot shrimp in tanks at this Chinese-owned fish store and always find live crab, lobsters, and catfish. Whole bright-eyed China cod (with big heads and yellow spots), rockfish, whole and in fillets, clear-eyed sand dabs, and boxes of silvery whitebait sit on metal tables of crushed ice. Less frantic than the fish stores in the heart of Chinatown, but with a reputation for good quality, the Vallejo Market is certainly worth a stop if you hanker fish for dinner. But you must choose intelligently. As in all the Chinatown fish markets, the clerks will cut and clean to order.

712 Vallejo Street (at Stockton), San Francisco

Tel: 391-5423

Open daily 8 a.m. to 6 p.m.

No credit cards

WINES AND SPIRITS

COIT LIQUORS

585 Columbus Avenue (at
Union), San Francisco
Tel: 986-4036
Open daily 9 a.m.
to midnight
Credit cards: MC, V

This vital neighborhood liquor store carries a far-ranging selection of wine carefully chosen for value and quality. When the new Beaujolais arrives in the fall, Coit always has the one from the best producer. If a California wine from a small grower gets some media attention, Coit will get it and mark it up the least. The spirits inventory is complete and sophisticated while still catering to mass tastes. Many locals buy their cigarettes and lottery tickets at Coit, but this independent store aims to please a wider audience with excellent prices on some classy wines, knowledgeable service, and enlightened buying.

COOKWARE AND BOOKS

BIORDI

412 Columbus Avenue (at
Vallejo), San Francisco
Tel: 392-8096
Open Monday through
Saturday 9:30 a.m. to 6 p.m.,
Sunday noon to 5 p.m.
Credit cards: AE, CB, DC,
MC, V

I used to think the hand-painted Italian pottery in the window of Biordi was pretty hokey until I looked deeper into the store. At first I was shocked by the high prices; then I saw a hand-painted pasta bowl in the most elaborate and imaginative geometric design, every inch covered with brilliant color. I could imagine pears in it, spaghetti, or a green salad. I bit the bullet and bought it, as expensive as it was, and haven't regretted the purchase since. I use that flat bowl all the time, and when food isn't in it, I set it in the middle of the dining-room table just to gaze on its peculiar rustic opulence. That piece of ceramic radiates humanity. You can feel the sensibility of the person who painted it. I must say that year after year, washing after washing, it has neither chipped nor faded. Since that time I have bought wedding presents and presents for myself at Biordi in the form of plates, cups, saucers, pitchers, and platters, all with different patterns, but all wonderful together. In this Italian-food-crazed time, a few Biordi pieces will make your Italian favorites look and taste better, I promise.

COLUMBUS CUTLERY

Every cook in town uses Columbus Cutlery. Packed into a tiny space are cooking knives of every size and shape from the foremost makers in the world at the fairest prices, as well as scissors, pocket knives, hunting knives, and any implement used for cutting. The sweet woman behind the counter moves very deliberately, bringing out the samples and carefully looking up the prices. She does one thing at a time, but the shop has such an old world ethos about it, you hesitate to break into the ritual just to drop off your knives for sharpening. I did that the other day when I was parked in a red zone at the corner, sticking my card into my gray canvas knife case and pleading with her to have them sharpened by the following afternoon. I think it was O.K., but I felt that I had breached custom.

The head sharpener is the counterwoman's husband, red of cheek and always with an army-style hat made out of a folded brown paper bag on his head. Over the years, this couple has hired extra sharpeners, so you can get your knives back quickly, crucial if you're a working chef.

358 Columbus Avenue
(between Vallejo and Grant),
San Francisco
Tel: 362-1342
Open weekdays except
Wednesday 9:30 a.m. to 6
p.m., Saturday until 5 p.m.
Credit cards: AE, MC, V

The sharpeners have been trained to take off as little of the metal as possible while still giving the blades a clean, razor-sharp edge; they never butcher your knives. The sharpening charge is reasonable, but one drawback is that the store is closed on Wednesdays. Plan accordingly.

FIGONI HARDWARE

1351 Grant Avenue
(between Vallejo and
Green), San Francisco
Tel: 392-4765
Open daily except
Wednesday and Sunday
8 a.m. to 5 p.m.
Credit cards: MC, V

I love this ancient hardware store with its beautiful worn wooden floors and high wooden shelves. One of Figoni's two storefronts is dedicated completely to Italian cookware, everything from pasta bowls to pasta makers to pasta pots. Pizza stones, ravioli-making equipment, a *mezzaluna* (a double-handled curved chopping tool that you rock back and forth to finely mince herbs and garlic), marble rolling pins, ornate glass bottles with stoppers for putting up flavored liqueurs or vinegars, copper zabaglione pans with wooden handles, painted water pitchers, old-fashioned food mills, knives, simple glassware, cast-iron crepe pans, and a whole rack of Italian vegetable seeds make up but a fraction of the merchandise, all of which takes on a timeless glow in this store. Italian cooking has come full circle. The Italian grandmothers who did it all by hand have been succeeded, not by their children, but by their grandchildren, who want to learn the old ways, rebounding from their mothers who defected to convenience foods. Surprisingly, many of the faces in Figoni are younger and many of them are Asian. More than one culture in the world understands the pleasures of homemade noodles.

Pacific Heights & Japantown

PACIFIC HEIGHTS & JAPANTOWN

RESTAURANTS

CAFE KATI

I resisted going to Cafe Kati for the longest time because I was afraid that chef Kirk Webber's highly stylized "blend of East and West" cuisines would not taste like food to me. But when I finally got there, I had one of the nicest evenings in my memory. The plates did attain new heights of visual whimsy in the tradition of San Francisco's Flying Saucer, and the menu did combine French and Southeast Asian flavors with the crossover aplomb of Wolfgang Puck's Chinois on Main in Venice, California. In fact, the food tasted as spectacular as it looked, though some of the thrill of the presentations waned somewhat when a third or fourth dish arrived with the same window dressing. (I was reminded of my disappointment at seeing Laurie Anderson repeat word for word, inflection for inflection, a performance piece I had seen six months before.) But the flavors of the food did not let down for a second, and the plate decor often worked as part of the dish. I got the feeling that chef Webber, for all the presentation pyrotechnics, really starts with how the food should taste.

1963 Sutter Street (between Fillmore and Webster), San Francisco
Tel: 775-7313
Open Tuesday through Saturday 5:30 to 9:30 p.m., Sunday until 9 p.m.
Price: Moderate
Credit cards: MC, V

Cafe Kati is, above all, a personal statement. This long, narrow storefront with one charming, tiny dining room in the front, an incredibly small kitchen—considering the elaborateness of the food—in the middle, and a somewhat larger back dining room could only support the efforts of a single chef with perhaps a couple of assistants. Webber runs it with his wife Tina and a small, dedicated professional staff who seem as enamored of the restaurant as its fanatically loyal customers are. I can see why it would be a pleasure to work here. Every time a new set of plates reach a table, diners cannot help gasping with delight.

The first dish that came my way won me over forever, a flat bowl of elegantly clear vegetable consommé tasting exactly like tomatoes. A delicious Caesar salad of richly dressed whole romaine leaves bundled together and standing on end had to be deconstructed in order to be eaten. A fabulous salad of whole spot shrimp deep-fried with head and dramatic tendrils attached were bound in crispy noodles, filled with a spicy Thai mousse, and accompanied with little lettuces, nests of beet, carrot, and daikon radish threads, and a lemongrass vinaigrette. Succulent nonfish sushi made with grilled shiitake mushrooms and sheets of toasty seaweed, and mango spring rolls flamboyantly garnished with vegetable threads and carved vegetables bring joy to the hearts of vegetarians. Cafe Kati must be a godsend to those who eat only plants. A wonderful meal could be made out of meatless starters.

For a main course, a clay pot of spot prawns in the most delectable, creamy, aromatic red Thai curry could be the center of my meal, though I would be hard put to pass up a velvety seared fillet of rock cod in a crisp mustard seed crust bathed in pink crayfish hollandaise. Webber does not spare cream and butter in some of his dishes, but the plates are balanced by simple starches like yellow Finn potatoes or jasmine rice and lots of raw and cooked vegetables. Tea-smoked rack of lamb in a natural gravy infused with dried cherries; roasted halibut in a skin of paper-thin potato slices with orange fennel salad; lemon-thyme-seasoned roasted chicken roulade with sweet-potato biscuits that melt in your mouth were all enchanting.

The fantasy does not let up with desserts like butterscotch pudding under a hive of spun sugar, or a plate of warm, gooey chocolate cake splashed with three fruit purees and arranged on the plate like a Sam Francis canvas.

Of course, by the time you read this the whole menu may be different. Webber likes to change his dishes with the seasons. However, the spirit will be the same, and I would be surprised if his patrons will let him take certain items off the menu. Given the choice of Cafe Kati and Flying Saucer, two neighborhood places with global inspiration and strong local followings, I would vote for Cafe Kati. In fact, I think it gives Postrio, Aqua, Cypress Club, Fleur de Lys, Elka, and La Folie (restaurants known for their blending of cuisines and/or dramatic presentations) a run for their money. The drawbacks are that Cafe Kati is small, and the back room isn't as attractive as the front. But the food coming out of that little kitchen dazzles in all sorts of unexpected ways, and the warmth, enthusiasm, and excitement of the chef infects everyone in the restaurant. I have become a real fan.

ELKA

1611 Post Street (at Laguna in the Miyako Hotel), San Francisco
Tel: 922-7788
Dinner Sunday through Thursday 5:30 to 10 p.m., Friday and Saturday until 10:30 p.m.
Price: Moderate
Credit cards: AE, MC, V

Japan and California meet in the menu here with a good deal of cordiality. Of particular note is the *bento* box appetizer holding some delicious tidbits along the line of deep-fried tempura-battered oysters, tuna sashimi, and pretty Japanese salads. Main courses sometimes entertain such radical combinations that I find them hard to like, but more traditional Western fare like truffled mashed potatoes with fresh eastern scallops in butter sauce, a coming together of seasonal delicacies, delivers the satisfactions of the toniest French cooking.

Designer Pat Kuleto attacked a difficult, two-story space in Japantown's Miyako Hotel and came up with a warm, friendly room with lots of visual excitement. The mezzanine bar, where you enter the restaurant, is a sophisticated yet comfortable spot to have a martini or sake and some of Elka's highly conceptual appetizers.

ELLA'S

500 Presidio Avenue (at California), San Francisco
Tel: 441-5669
Open for breakfast Monday through Friday 7 to 11 a.m.; lunch 11:30 to 2:30 p.m., Saturday and Sunday brunch 9 a.m. to 2 p.m.
Price: Inexpensive
Credit cards: AE, MC, V

A sunny, charming corner cafe that puts out a delicious breakfast is a gift to a neighborhood. I know many people who live around the Jewish Community Center and Laurel Heights who could not start their day without stopping at Ella's. The delicious breakfasts are bolstered by excellent home-style baking and first-rate coffee, both American and Italian. Even the white bread is baked from scratch, and what a difference that makes when your poached eggs come on thick slices of yeasty, buttered, gently crisp white toast. Ella's moist banana-nut-cinnamon coffee cake; sticky buns thick with pecans and orange zest; and light, buttery sweet potato-raisin muffins capture the spirit of inventive American home cooking. The orange juice is freshly squeezed; the buttermilk pancakes are airy and flavorful, especially when drizzled with real-maple syrup.

Ella's small lunch menu is also enlivened by home baking: The hamburgers come on buns still warm from the oven; a classic chicken potpie has a meltingly flaky top crust. Salads are prepared with proper conviction and lovely greens and sparkly dressings. The delicious warm spinach salad makes for a fine lunch, leaving room for a tall, judiciously sweetened slice of fresh apple pie.

GARIBALDI ON PRESIDIO

This four-year-old restaurant has taken root in the neighborhood, pleasing the local crowd with a multinational array of dishes that are spicy, hearty, and nicely presented, if lacking in coherent style. The fresh, white-painted dining rooms offer a rare full bar and a bar menu (a first-rate antipasto plate, a yummy whole-wheat quesadilla filled with hot chilies) if you can't get one of the tables covered with linen and butcher paper tucked between big pots of fish-leaf ferns. Garibaldi gives its patrons good value for their money, especially when they order its signature dish, paella, a buoyant mixture of moist saffron rice that has absorbed lots of flavor from the browned chicken, spicy chorizo, shrimp, mussels, and clams piled on top. Also good is a chewy, very tasty grilled skirt steak in a garlic-ginger-coriander marinade. It comes with crisp-fried red-skinned potatoes and a chunky medley of vegetables. Judicious ordering will save you from confused pasta dishes and heavy desserts. The staff couldn't be nicer or more professional.

347 Presidio Avenue (between Sacramento and Clay), San Francisco
Tel: 563-8841
Open for lunch Monday through Friday 11:30 a.m. to 2:30 p.m.; dinner Sunday through Thursday 5:30 to 10 p.m., Friday and Saturday until 10:30 p.m.; Sunday brunch 10 a.m. to 2 p.m.
Price: Moderate
Credit cards: MC, V

3235 Sacramento Street
(between Presidio and
Lyon), San Francisco
Tel: 474-8890
Open Tuesday through
Sunday 5:30 to 10 p.m.
Price: Expensive
Credit cards: AE, DC, MC, V

When the sophisticated Geordy's closed suddenly after barely a year in business, all the serious eaters in town wondered what would happen to its brilliant young chef Charlie Solomon. Happily, he resurfaced at a familiar, and what I think is a perfect, location, the old site of Le Castel, deep in Pacific Heights. Solomon did a small amount of redecorating by painting the three intimate dining rooms white, installing terra-cotta tiles on the floor, and opening up the windows to look out on his new flower and herb garden. The waiters wear black and white vests printed with fruits and vegetables, the same material used for the slipcovers on the chairs, but other than this bit of frippery the rooms present a clean stage for Solomon's dramatic cooking.

The short menu of first and second courses is so mouth watering and interesting that you can't decide what to order. This becomes more difficult when you factor in the six-course Market Menu for $50, which features many varieties of a single vegetable. One late summer evening the potato starred, first in an exquisite salad with scallops, arugula, and truffled vinaigrette; then in a barely warmed-through chowder of tiny shucked oysters, followed by a meltingly luscious medallion of salmon on slices of very creamy textured potato in a saffron butter; then a breast of squab on a puree of potatoes in a sauce scented with lemon thyme from the garden; and ending with the only dish that didn't work, a big scoop of sweet-potato sorbet. It was a masterful display of classic French technique, offbeat inventiveness, and knowledge of the qualities of six different kinds of potatoes. Best of all, the courses were portioned so that you could comfortably eat every last morsel.

Those ordering a la carte will be wowed, too, by creations like crispy-skinned mackerel on a roasted tomato half in a sharp, citrus vinaigrette; a bright green puree of fresh fava beans infused with an intense lobster broth, garnished with huge, tender nuggets of lobster; and sand dabs sautéed, boned, and served on a bed of baby artichokes with a brown butter and caper sauce. The most heavenly warm miniature fresh-fig tart with a buttery ground-nut filling served with house-made vanilla ice cream and caramel sauce disappeared all too soon—but then Solomon sends out tiny cookies and his own hand-dipped chocolate with the coffee, which was perfect, I might add. One rarely sees such appetizing use of the most interesting local ingredients, many of them organic. The a la carte prices—$8 to $10 for a first course even lavished with lobster, $18 to $20 for a second— seem incredibly reasonable for this level of cooking.

The all West Coast wine list is too small to do this cooking justice, but the intelligent, quiet service, so very, very understanding about both the cooking and the art of waiting, is the best you will find anywhere. Solomon joins Alain Rondelli in mounting an exciting, completely personal restaurant of the highest caliber for an amazingly reasonable tariff. As in Paris, some of the most satisfying restaurants are being opened by star chefs in the form of neighborhood bistros that charge relatively moderate sums and keep everyone in their own arrondissement coming in. If you have a restaurant like The Heights around the block, why bother leaving it?

ISUZU

1581 Webster Street (at
Post), San Francisco
Tel: 922-2290
Open for lunch weekdays
(except Tuesday) noon to 2
p.m.; dinner 5 to 9 p.m.,
Friday until 9:30 p.m.,
Saturday noon to 9:30 p.m.,
Sunday noon to 9 p.m.
Price: Inexpensive
to moderate
Credit cards: AE, DC , D,
MC, V

When you are in the mood for a meal of Japanese sea-food served the way Japanese families would eat it, try Isuzu, a large, full-scale Japanese restaurant on the same block as the Kabuki movie theater. People always think of sashimi and sushi as the typical Japanese fish prepa-rations, but the range of Japanese fish cooking is vast and wonderful. At Isuzu, you can sample many differ-ent techniques, and fish, by requesting the Japanese menu and asking your waiter what the specials are.

I cannot eat here without ordering the buttery broiled mackerel, either whole or in fillets, brushed with a teriyaki-type sauce that makes the meaty, oily fish delectable. A whole flounder deep-fried with its bones is another treat: the tiny dorsal bones get so crisp they taste like potato chips. Start with a strong miso soup of the day and an array of vegetables and salads, like a sparkling cucumber and octopus salad; a refreshing, cold cooked spinach salad sprinkled with sesame seeds; and a crisp and vinegary seaweed salad. Whatever you order, don't pass up a salad made of burdock root, that long, skinny carrotlike vegetable you see in Japanese groceries. The Isuzu kitchen shows you how it should taste. All the little dishes go in the middle of the table, and everyone shares. I love the way a table looks filled with pottery in different shapes holding small portions of clean and juicy food, setting up your palate for the rich, hot fish to follow.

Isuzu has a full bar, a sushi bar, and lots of tables in its high-ceilinged dining room. It has become a very popular spot, especially among Japanese, for its reason-able prices, high-quality food and presentation, yet casual setting.

The last time I ate at Jackson Fillmore (about ten years ago) the service and seating policy aggravated me so much that it made me grumpy to be there. The tenor has changed at this ever-popular Pacific Heights trattoria, but reservations still are taken only for parties of three or more, and parties of one and two are assigned on a first-come first-served basis to seats at the counter. The counter seats turn over pretty fast, though, and the people at the door now are cordial and understanding. The casual counter eating suits the tasty, short-order Italian cooking well. This is just the place to drop in for a plate of pasta and a glass of wine, and many, many people do.

The daily menu tempts with first courses like salt cod crostini, which are pleasant if too potatoey (and short on the salt cod), and a tasty, warm asparagus salad with prosciutto, *radicchio*, and toasted bread crumbs. From the regular menu comes the classic Jackson Fillmore dish, *radicchio al forno*, small wedges of radicchio wrapped in pancetta roasted crisp in the oven. Al dente pastas served in flat bowls like *spaghetti all'amatriciana*, in a copious, spicy tomato sauce with pancetta and onions, hit the spot. Three risottos are offered on the regular menu, but getting them out proves tricky for this busy kitchen. A risotto milanese one night—rice stirred with chicken broth, onion, and saffron—almost worked, but in such a simple dish, perfection, especially of texture, is imperative. Lots of veal, chicken, and fish dishes make up the rest of the long menu. For those of you who remember the great counter restaurant, Vanessi's, on Broadway, Jackson Fillmore's menu almost seems like an updated version. The inspiration for much

2506 Fillmore (at Jackson Street), San Francisco

Tel: 346-5288

Open Monday 5:30 to 10 p.m., Tuesday through Thursday until 10:30 p.m., Friday and Saturday until 11 p.m., Sunday 5 to 10 p.m.

Price: Moderate

Credit cards: AE, DC, D, MC, V

of the cooking on Fillmore Street comes from Italy, but the North Beach/Italian influence seems to have flowed right up Broadway to Pacific Heights. Jackson Fillmore, now a professionally run restaurant with many lively, fun-to-eat Italian dishes, has taken on the aura of an old-time San Francisco spot.

MIFUNE

Japan Center, 1737 Post Street (between Webster and Buchanan), San Francisco
Tel: 922-0337
Open daily 11 a.m. to 10 p.m.
Price: Inexpensive
Credit cards: AE, DC , D, MC, V

One of the most beloved small restaurants in Japantown, Mifune has been satisfying San Franciscans' yen for noodles for ten years, its thirty-one or so noodle offerings cast in realistic plastic gracing a glamorously lit front window. First-timers would do well to take a look, because service brooks few explanations. Noodle houses serve quickly; in fact, they really represent a superior version of fast-food outlets.

For under $5 at Mifune, you can get either house-made udon, which are thick white-flour noodles, or soba, thin buckwheat noodles in big bowls of hot, tasty soup topped with the likes of grilled beef and green onions or shrimp and vegetable tempura. True noodle-lovers prefer them cold, as in the Mifune Special, a wooden boat with a cargo of white and brown noodles on deck, sprinkled with seaweed, hot shrimp and vegetable tempura on the prow, and a bowl of cold, gingery dipping sauce with green onions, wasabi, and grated daikon on the stern. You dip the noodles and tempura into your custom-made sauce.

Many of the noodle and rice dishes (there are several *donburis* available) are designed to give you protein in the form of seaweed, egg, or miso without meat, making this a good restaurant for vegetarians. Even if you're carnivorous try No. 3, *wakame udon*, thick white noodles with toasty seaweed, or No. 17, udon with mountain fern. Mifune also appeals to kids who always like noodles and don't want to wait for their food. You can be in and out in half an hour, but are never rushed. You can sit and sip tea all afternoon if you'd rather. I long have treasured Mifune as my haven of noodley comfort in the middle of the city.

ROSMARINO

Hidden away in a courtyard off Sacramento Street, Rosmarino has had to earn its clientele through word of mouth, and it has. In fact, Rosmarino's opening about four years ago anticipated the small, upscale neighborhood-restaurant boom (Zax, Woodward's Garden, and in the East Bay Citron and Rivoli) that has greatly contributed to life in the city. If you live in Pacific Heights and want a sophisticated but simple meal made with fine ingredients, an interesting bottle of Italian wine, and civilized, if casual, service, you do not need to dress up and go downtown. Rosmarino is an outpost of civilization in the neighborhoods. Most recently, I devoured a lovely, pristine antipasto and then a seemingly simple-minded two-ingredient pasta like the ones served everywhere in Italy that taste so wonderful. In this case, hot al dente spaghetti was tossed with tons of freshly ground black pepper and grated imported pecorino cheese until it just melted. I could have eaten bowls of it. The oft-changing menu is mostly Italian, but takes advantage of fresh local ingredients, always adding up to light, clean, satisfying meals. The modern, carpeted, banquette-lined dining room is softly lit and comfortable. On sunny days and those rare warm nights, you can eat outside on wrought-iron tables and chairs in the courtyard. If I lived around upper Sacramento Street, Rosmarino would be my neighborhood hangout.

3665 Sacramento Street (between Locust and Spruce), San Francisco
Tel: 931-7710
Open Tuesday through Saturday for lunch 11:30 a.m. to 2 p.m.; dinner 5:30 to 10 p.m., Sunday brunch 10 a.m. to 2:30 p.m.
Price: Moderate
Credit cards: AE, D, MC, V

SPAGHETTINI WITH PECORINO CHEESE

1 pound dried spaghettini

1/2 cup (1 stick) unsalted butter

1 1/2 cups (6 ounces) grated dried aged pecorino

30 turns of the pepper grinder set to coarse

Kosher salt to taste

When you eat this kind of simple pasta in Italy, you can't believe how good it tastes. When I had a plate of it at Rosmarino, I was hooked forever on this restaurant. The key is to use high-quality butter, either Plugra (see Tower Market, page 276 , or Ashbury Market, page 193), or Straus Family Dairy butter (see Ferry Plaza Farmers' Market, page 119, or Grand Central Market, page 357); pecorino, such as Locatelli brand from Florence Delicatessen (see page 317); and for pasta, Ross Brown of Rosmarino uses De Cecco brand.

Bring a large pot of salted water to a boil and add the spaghettini. Bring the pot back to a boil and cook for 8 minutes. Drain the pasta thoroughly and pour it back into the pot. Add the butter and cheese and toss until the pasta is thoroughly coated. Grind in the pepper. Toss again. Check for salt, add if necessary, toss again, and serve.

Serves 4 to 6

SANPPO

Japan Center, 1702 Post Street (at Buchanan), San Francisco

Tel: 346-3486

Open Tuesday through Saturday 11:45 a.m. to 9:50 p.m., Sunday 3 to 9:50 p.m.

Price: Inexpensive

Credit cards: MC, V

For twenty years I have been going to Sanppo for homey, country-style Japanese dishes served in a cozy, almost communal dining room from a tiny open kitchen. The food is always fresh, the soup stocks well balanced, the tempuras ethereal, the sushi and sashimi honest and clean. I love a dish here called *gyoza nabe*, a cast-iron pot of soup afloat with delicate Japanese pot stickers filled with finely ground pork, glass noodles, Japanese cabbage, and squares of bean curd. A little bowl of gingery soy sauce comes on the side for dipping. Indicative of skillful deep-frying, the always sweet, impeccable oysters have the lightest of batters and the crispiest exteriors. The grilled fillets of fresh-water eel, *unagi*, presented like jewels on a bed of rice in a covered lacquer box, have been of exceptional quality at Sanppo: rich, firm, and not muddy tasting. With lots of small appetizer plates to choose from, such as cold sesame spinach, cucumber, and octopus salad, or an East-West lettuce salad made with sweet-potato noodles, greens, and onions in a creamy dressing, you can share a full Japanese meal or just get one dish. Even if you have to sit with other parties at one of the larger, square wooden tables that look like old ship hatches, this intimate dining room always feels comfortable. Everyone who eats here, Eastern or Western, is united by appreciation of the tasty food.

VIVANDE

Carlo Middione's Italian culinary empire, headquartered at his bustling delicatessen-trattoria on Fillmore, has recently expanded to dinner. Now his patrons can eat both lunch and dinner in his brick-walled kitchen, take home a tempting selection of *antipasti*, Italian baked savories, the best Italian desserts in town, and shop for exquisite Italian ingredients and cookbooks (including Middione's growing opus), or call for catering of any size. Everything that Middione turns out reflects his sense of integrity and the ebullience with which he cooks and creates in his shiny open kitchen.

At the tiny pushed-together tables, which almost seem to be part of the kitchen, regulars return again and again for Middione's creamy pasta carbonara, rich and light at the same time; his barely sauced but delicious fettuccine with vegetables, olive oil, and butter; his impeccable deep-fried oyster sandwiches; a classic spinach salad; and

2125 Fillmore Street
(between Sacramento and
California),
San Francisco
Tel: 346-4430
Open daily 10 a.m.
to 10 p.m.
Price: Moderate
Credit cards: AE, DC , D,
MC, V

deep-fried *arancini*, risotto balls filled with mozzarella. Middione is a Sicilian, so he brings particular passion to dishes like *pasta alla Norma* with creamy slices of eggplant; house-made fennel sausage sautéed with roasted potatoes, peppers, and mushrooms; and rustic dishes like lentils and white beans braised with *coteghino*, a coarse-grained sausage. Save room for dessert. The deceptively simple-looking unfrosted chocolate cakes melt in your mouth in an extraordinary way. Luscious, custardy *zuppa inglese* and tiramisù take on new definition here. Puckery lemon tarts and crisp meringue cakes filled with apricot whipped cream are a dream. To finish off, the espresso is rich and aromatic without being bitter.

If you want to cook an Italian meal at home, Vivande presents a high-level resource. The purest, richest extra-

SPECIALTY RESTAURANTS IN JAPANTOWN
THAT DO A GOOD JOB ON A SINGLE TYPE OF DISH

SAPPORO-YA (West Wing of the Japan Center, Post and Webster streets, tel: 563-7400) is kitty-corner from Tan Tan, the dessert cafe. Sapporo-Ya stays open until midnight. People regularly drop by for a late-night bowl of Chinese-style ramen in broth or wok-fried noodles with meat and vegetables.

Two story IROHA (in the Japan Center mall, tel: 922-0321), owned by the Mifune people, is a good spot for inexpensive Japanese ramen noodles (as opposed to soba and udon) in soup.

AKASAKA (also in the Mall, tel: 921-5360) offers amazing $5.25 lunches that include almost every element of the Japanese meal including soup, pickle, rice, tempura, grilled meat or fish.

In the first building of the Japan

virgin olive oils, rare aged balsamic vinegars, Arborio rice for risotto, dried and house-made fresh pasta, Reggiano Parmesan, a selection of other hard and soft Italian cheeses, prosciutto from Parma, and Middione's *biscotti di Prato* are but a few of the treasures here. You can buy prepared foods, like roasted chickens from the open-flame rotisserie, whole onions slowly baked in balsamic vinegar, crusty walnut breads, and savory Italian tortas to incorporate into your own meals at home. When a group of us were making the trek to the "Big Game" (the annual Stanford–U.C. Berkeley football contest), I ordered box lunches from Vivande, and frankly, the picnic outshone the sporting event. Vivande is there to take care of all your Italian dining needs with great style and consummate deliciousness.

Center on the second floor, KUI SHIN BO, a cozy traditional space handcrafted in wood, puts out fine sushi, sashimi, noodle dishes, and buttery grilled mackerel. But the standout is small, crisp *gyoza,* or Japanese pot stickers, presented in a diagonal line on a square dish.

OSAKAYA (next to Mifune in Japan Center) has earned a reputation around Japantown for its generous take-out *nigiri* sushi at $6 and *bento* boxes (really compartmentalized foil containers) of sushi, salad, and pickles at $6.50.

Everyone loves ISOBUNE (across the walkway from Mifune), for its amusement-park delivery of sushi on wooden boats, which circulate in a waterway around a long oval sushi bar. The sushi makers stand in the middle of the counter, cutting fish and slapping together rice. Diners pluck little plates off the boats as they sail by. At the end of the meal, the number and sizes of saucers at your place determine the check. You can always ask for specially made pieces from the sushi makers, something I like to do because you never know how long some sushi have been traveling.

CAFES

TAN TAN

Japan Center, 1825 Post
Street (between Webster
and Laguna), San Francisco
Tel: 346-6260
Open daily 11 a.m. to 7 p.m.
No credit cards

I highly recommend you visit this tiny Japanese dessert cafe off the skylit second-floor atrium of the Japan Center, right next to the gigantic Kunokuniya bookstore. The room is beautifully crafted, with a bleached wood counter and floors and five small blonde-wood tables. A tall window looks out to Geary Boulevard below. Western-style tarts and cakes are displayed in a refrigerated glass case, but the real treats are the Japanese desserts served on their own square lacquer trays with decorative and culinary accompaniments. A perfect *shiso* leaf holding a little pile of pickled ginger strings comes with a glass bowl of red beans in sugar syrup topped with tiny white rice dumplings that were first poached and then cooled in ice and water. Each Japanese dessert involves a labor-intensive procedure of being cooked and/or cooled, decorated, and assembled, tasks often performed by one young Japanese woman who goes through the motions as if dancing. She looks like she stepped out of a Chanel ad, with her glossy bobbed hair and flawless makeup.

The cold red beans with rice powder dumplings described above are called *shiratama* and are served with a ceramic mug of green tea, which really does complete the range of sensations in the dessert. I also like *tokoroten*, cubes of shimmering agar (crystal-like cubes of gelatin) with bits of strawberry, canned peach, and fruit juice for flavor and dots of red bean for color. It's very refreshing. Yoko Tahara, a resident of the neighborhood long before the Japan Center was built and a patron of Tan Tan, loves a hot red bean dessert called *zenzai*, with super-glutinous *mochi,* or sticky-rice-flour balls, all presented in a lacquer bowl. I found all the red bean desserts wonderfully satisfying after meals at nearby Japanese restaurants (like Kame Sushi, a good eight-seat sushi bar a few yards away run by an eccentric who only opens when he feels like it). The pleasure of Japanese sweets is subtle for the Westerner: You are not assaulted by sugar or butterfat, but really feel as if you have had dessert. For those who insist on something a little more sybaritic, a creamy, beautiful green-tea mousse topped with a dab of red beans and decorated with sliced strawberries offers a compromise between Eastern and occidental tastes.

Many people use Tan Tan as a tea- and coffeehouse for iced coffee, green tea, hot cappuccino, and green tea floats. If the indoor space gets too smoky, you can sit outside in the atrium at cafe tables and thumb through a Japanese or English magazine that you have just purchased at the bookstore next door.

BARS

JACK'S

1601 Fillmore Street (at
Geary), San Francisco
Tel: 567-3227
Open daily 2 p.m. to 2 a.m.
Credit cards: AE

When you ask Information for the telephone number of
Jackson Fillmore the restaurant, you often get the
number for Jack's instead. It might behoove you to stop
by sometime, because Jack's is a blues bar with hot-
looking young women bartenders with low-cut tops,
shorts, and nice legs. The scene is loose and funky. You
can dance to live blues bands on a small floor and work
off some of the pasta you had down the street. Also, if
you're going to a show at the newly revitalized historic
Fillmore Auditorium, your stamped hand will admit
you to Jack's.

DELICATESSENS/TAKE-OUT

BRYAN'S QUALITY MEATS

3473 California Street (between Spruce and Laurel),
San Francisco
Tel: 752-3430
Open Monday through Friday 8 a.m. to 7 p.m.,
Saturday until 6 p.m.
Credit cards: MC, V

See Meat and Poultry, page 362.

On the face of it sushi seems to be the perfect food to go. After all, it's supposed to be served at room temperature (though the fish is kept chilled before it is cut), and unlike salad, it doesn't wilt. But the fact is, held or refrigerated sushi loses its charm. The rice dries out and starts to separate and the delicate flavors of raw fish disappear. I always hesitate to buy prepackaged sushi in groceries because you don't know how long ago it was made. That's why tiny Maruya is such a find. All the delicate sushi is made to order, and only the delicious vegetarian selection, No. 9, which includes two kinds of nonfish sushi, is prepackaged, though usually the woman behind the counter only has one order available at any time. When that one is sold she prepares another. The four large pieces of pickle-and-vegetable-filled *maki* (a fat, seaweed-wrapped roll that is sliced into rounds), and three large balls of sushi rice sweetened just a bit and tossed with threads of seaweed, then wrapped in a thin crepe of egg, add up to a light, delicious, and satisfying meal. You can almost feel each slightly chewy grain on your tongue, yet each finger of rice holds together as if by magic. A pyramid of wasabi, a packet of soy sauce, and a mound of pickled ginger threads nestles into one corner of the package along with green plastic grass and wooden chopsticks. Other types of sushi can be ordered by the piece or off a small menu of combinations. If the order is large or even small, calling ahead is a good idea since everything is made to order. The tiny shop holds a kitchen so miniature that you know that everything is made from scratch each day. Since Maruya is dedicated to take-out, the full attention of the sushi chef can be lavished on your order, with no demanding

1904 Fillmore Street (at Bush), San Francisco
Tel: 921-2929
Open Tuesday through Saturday 10:30 a.m. to 7 p.m.
No credit cards

customers eating at the sushi bar to distract her. When a shop can sustain itself at this level of specialization, you know it makes something people really want.

VIVANDE

2125 Fillmore Street (between Sacramento and California),
San Francisco
Tel: 346-4430
Open daily 10 a.m. to 10 p.m.
Price: Moderate
Credit cards: AE, DC, D, MC, V

See Restaurants, page 345.

BAKERIES/PASTRIES

LE CHANTILLY

2119 Fillmore Street
(between Sacramento
and California),
San Francisco
Tel: 441-1500
Open Monday through
Saturday 9 a.m. to 6 p.m.,
Sunday 11 a.m. to 6 p.m.
Credit cards: AE, MC, V

This French pastry shop looks like a jewelry store, its gleaming glass cases filled with elaborately constructed and decorated cakes and petits fours. The cakes are so architectural that it's hard to believe they're made with eggs, butter, and flour. Are they food? In fact, they are brought in from Le Chantilly's bakery in Novato and their high butterfat content practically preserves them. The best cakes have a chocolate component, like a chocolate-encased pyramid filled with thin layers of chocolate cake and velvety chocolate mousse. The lighter, fruitier petits fours flavored with liqueurs tend to lose their sparkle. I was pulling for a tropical fruit number, but its overwhelming flavor was sugar. The hazelnut daquoise layered with meringue was competent if not thrilling—a description of most of the pastry here. Perhaps that's the price to be paid for such elegant-looking cakes. I do, however, like the small, hand-dipped chocolates very much. They are fresh, lively, and varied in filling and shape, employing nuts and creams as well as ganache. A tony gold box of these would go a long way in wooing someone over to your point of view.

PÂTISSERIE DELANGHE

What wonderful, buttery French sweet rolls come out of the open kitchen of this one-man bakery run by Dominique Delanghe! They are filled with fresh strawberries, plums, or apricots and a bit of custard. His croissants taste like the real thing, flaky, buttery, handmade. Large *palmiers,* palm-leaf-shaped cookies made of crisp, sugar-glazed puff pastry, dissolve on your tongue. Miniature éclairs, chocolate-covered madeleines, and meringue mushrooms make for charming after-dinner desserts with demitasses of coffee. M. Delanghe makes a small version of the classic French wedding pastry called *croquembouche,* a tower of little cream puffs filled with custard and held together with caramel. These towering constructions serve twelve or more, and each serving of the dismantled puffs can be made more festive by drizzling a homemade chocolate sauce over or under them. I can't walk by the shop, especially in the morning when the pastries are still warm from the oven, without stopping in for at least one cheese-filled roll with a cup of good coffee.

1890 Fillmore Street (at Bush), San Francisco
Tel: 923-0711
Open Tuesday through Friday 7 a.m. to 6 p.m., Saturday 8 a.m. to 6 p.m., Sunday 8 a.m. to 2 p.m.
No credit cards

CHOCOLATE SAUCE

4 tablespoons butter

3 ounces unsweetened baking
chocolate

1 cup sugar

1 cup heavy (whipping) cream

This is my recipe for the easiest and most luxurious dark chocolate sauce to ever moisten a cream puff.

In a saucepan over medium heat, melt the butter. Add the chocolate and melt, stirring constantly. Stir in the sugar until completely dissolved. Add the cream. Stir until incorporated and bring to a simmer for 1 minute. Serve hot or warm. This will keep in the refrigerator for a long time if tightly covered, and may be rewarmed or eaten cold like fudge.

Makes about 1 cup

YAMADA SEIKA

1955 Sutter Street (between
Fillmore and Webster),
San Francisco
Tel: 922-3848
Open Tuesday through
Saturday 9 a.m. to 6 p.m.,
Sunday until 5 p.m.
No credit cards

Japanese-baked sweets with red bean fillings may be an acquired taste, but the wonderful aromas at this bakery make you want to try them. While we were sampling the pastel green and pink sweets, a huge Mercedes sedan neatly parallel-parked in front of the shop and out glided a young woman in full kimono, with traditionally piled hair and masklike makeup, holding leather-encased car keys. For a moment it felt like old Japan in the shop with its antique wooden cases. The Japanese woman ever so politely talked to the Japanese baker in his floury garb, who carefully wrapped the selected pastries in paper. Where did she come from? The Japanese consulate? A condominium on top of Nob Hill? Seeing her buy the Japanese sweets in her traditional garments put them in context. I can imagine how satisfying one perfect red bean-filled pastry would taste with frothy green tea. My own preference, completely uneducated and uncultivated, was for *fubiki*, oval sweets wrapped in delicate, barely sweetened white yeast dough with a generous filling of nutty red bean paste. The seasonal pink sweets actually have cherry blossoms in them and a barely detectable flowery taste. For lovers of the chewy and sticky, the *mochi* (glutinous rice–flour squares covered with toasted soybean powder) will deliver a thrill.

COFFEE

PEET'S COFFEE AND TEA

3419 California Street (between Spruce and Laurel),
San Francisco
Tel: 221-8506
Open Monday through Friday 7 a.m. to 7 p.m.,
Saturday 7:30 a.m. to 6 p.m., Sunday 8 a.m. to 5 p.m.,
Credit cards: AE, D, MC, V

See listing, page 218.

SPINELLI COFFEE COMPANY

2455 Fillmore Street (at Jackson),
San Francisco
Tel: 929-8808
Open Monday through Friday 6:30 a.m. to 9 p.m.,
Saturday 7 a.m. to 9 p.m., Sunday 7 a.m. to 7 p.m.
Credit cards: MC, V

See listing, page 192.

MARKETS

CAL-MART

3585 California Street (at
Spruce), San Francisco
Tel: 751-3516
Open Monday through
Saturday 8 a.m. to 7 p.m.,
Sunday 9 a.m. to 6 p.m.
Credit cards: D, MC, V

A fine, versatile neighborhood grocery with a comprehensive produce section, Cal-Mart is further strengthened by Antonelli and Son's meat, fish and poultry counter, which has expanded into the space vacated by Bryan's Quality Meats. While most of the produce is commercial, some organic and/or local specialty items like little Yukon Gold potatoes, small red creamer potatoes, Portobello mushrooms, brown field mushrooms, beautiful Flambeau radishes (pink and white oval shaped), and organic cherry tomatoes from del Cabo farms in Baja, California, represent but a small sample of what's available. Piles of seasonal stone fruit and a myriad of different berries look luscious, but are of varying quality: much better than warehoused, under-ripe supermarket stuff, but not as rewarding as organic produce from farmers' markets. The produce displays are groomed and well cared for, and I have to pat the produce buyer on the back for taking some risks by offering unusual items.

An active deli counter cranks out made-to-order sandwiches, rotisserie chickens, and prepared salads and entrees, while a bakery counter run by Sweet Things from Marin offers time-saving items like pints of fresh lemon curd and raspberry puree along with rich bar cookies and gooey cakes. All the major local bread bakeries deliver here daily, and all the upscale grocery standbys, like a full range of Häagen-Dazs ice cream products (a find at this level of completeness), make Cal-Mart a very useful independent grocery store.

The Cal-Mart produce section features berries, usually commercial ones, but a number of different kinds. This fast, simple recipe, adapted from Jeremiah Tower's New American Classics *(Harper and Row, 1986), turns any kind of berry into an opulent warm compote that tastes heavenly with vanilla ice cream.*

In a large skillet dissolve the sugar in the water by stirring over medium heat. Bring to a boil. Add the lemon juice and berries and cook over medium heat for 2 to 3 minutes. Swirl in the butter until it melts. Remove from heat. Spoon into 4 shallow soup bowls and place scoops of vanilla ice cream in the center.

Serves 4

1/2 cup sugar

1/4 cup water

2 teaspoons fresh lemon juice

1 cup hulled fresh strawberries, halved

1 cup fresh blueberries, halved

1 cup fresh blackberries

4 tablespoons unsalted butter,
  cut into pieces

1 pint vanilla ice cream

GRAND CENTRAL MARKET

This historic market, once the site of Bercut Meat Company (where Bryan Flannery of Bryan's Quality Meats started out), still boasts a long meat counter featuring Superior lamb, Harris beef, and real butchers who will cut and grind to order. Across the aisle is an equally long fish and poultry counter that offers some special items, like turkey and chicken sausages from different makers, including chicken linguiça and spicy or mild Italian sausages made with turkey. Reichardt ducks and Fulton Valley broilers, Petaluma Poultry Company fryers (the same people who raise Rocky free-range chickens) and stewing hens fill the counter. Small hen turkeys and parts come from Ladino. I am not wild about the fish section, but nifty small wooden crates of salt cod at $8.99 per pound, a good price, inspired me to get out the *brandade* recipes.

The produce department is pedestrian, small, and commercial, but the dairy case is stocked with high-

2435 California Street (between Fillmore and Steiner), San Francisco

Tel: 567-4902

Open daily 8 a.m. to 10 p.m.

Credit cards: MC, V

quality Marin Cheese Company packaged cheeses and Pavel's superior yogurt. Breads come from Acme, Grace, and Metropolis. A separately run delicatessen counter offers nothing out of the ordinary. The miniature shopping carts for small children bring great joy, and many a mom and dad shop here just to give their children the pleasure of using one.

ETHNIC MARKETS

MARUWA FOODS COMPANY

1737 Post Street (near Webster), San Francisco
Tel: 563-1901
Open Monday through Saturday 10 a.m. to 7 p.m., Sunday until 6 p.m.
Credit cards: MC, V

Owned by Koreans, Maruwa epitomizes the modern Asian supermarket, which features lots of precooked convenience foods to take out. A quick look at the pickle section confirms the Korean influence. Kimchees of chili-spiked daikon and cabbage share refrigerator space with salted Japanese pickles. Farther along the refrigerated case, simple steamed daikon mixed with other Asian vegetables, wrapped in plastic on Styrofoam boards, stands ready for immediate eating. Like Super Koyama, lots of fresh, pristine-looking fish has been cut and packaged for sashimi or marinated whole (but gutted and scaled of course) in sake lees or miso paste. Fish cakes in all shapes can be bought in bulk. The grocery aisles are stocked with Japanese ready-to-eat products: cereal, soft drinks (cold cans of Calipio Water), snacks, candy, as well as soup bases, rice, noodles, and other ingredients for assisted home cooking. For dessert, cartons of green tea or lichee ice cream beckon.

The cognoscenti in Japantown shop at the relatively new and sparkling Super Koyama grocery, where the fish cut for sashimi, tightly wrapped in clear plastic, look opalescent. A trip to this market inspires you to serve your own Japanese meal at home since you can buy most of the components already prepared: seaweed salad in sesame oil with red chilies; octopus and cucumber salad; jelly fish salad; ready-made sushi; sliced fresh *hamachi* (yellowtail) and *toro* (the rare belly cut of tuna) for sashimi; all sorts of other ready-to-eat sliced raw fish. With Japanese beer of every kind and sake, you have the components of an impressive Japanese spread.

For slightly more ambitious cooks, paper-thin slices of beef for sukiyaki, capellini-thin baby eels, fish cakes, fresh tofu, and fresh roe of all kinds inspire you to get out a Japanese cookbook. All the makings for miso broth and bonito stock are here, along with a healthy-looking produce section, the nicest in Japantown, with fresh burdock root, baby turnips, *shiso* leaves, firm Japanese cucumbers, plump unblemished lotus root, mountain potatoes, and even tiny green plums for pickling. Whole fish, staring out at you with clear, glassy eyes from behind the immaculate sashimi counter, and fillets marinating in sake *kasu* (the lees of sake) or white miso paste stand ready to be broiled. Everything at Super Koyama looks so neat and pristine, from the vegetables to the fish, that you trust that even the marinated fish will be fresh.

1790 Sutter Street (at Buchanan), San Francisco
Tel: 921-6529
Open Monday through Saturday 9 a.m. to 7 p.m., Sunday 10 a.m. to 6 p.m.
Credit cards: MC, V

1656 Post Street (between
Buchanan and Laguna),
San Francisco
Tel: 921-0515
Open Monday through
Saturday 9 a.m. to 6 p.m.
No credit cards

The fish at the ever-busy Uoki Market fish counter is not prepackaged or precut, and often not precleaned. You have to wait for service at this counter, as you do in the Chinatown bustle, to get your allotment of small clams, fresh squid, fat tentacles of octopus, hunks of tuna, and whole salmon. The busy fish clerks will cut small pieces to order, and the quality is generally high. The produce section is not as carefully weeded of old vegetables as at Super Koyama, and there is much less prepackaging of prepared ingredients. Instead, you scoop out your own pickled daikon from vats. Of course Uoki Market has whole aisles of jarred pickles in neon colors to put on rice, tea, soup mix, candy, big sacks of California short-grain rice for the larder, plus up-to-the-minute imports of Japanese breakfast cereal and snacks. By the checkout counter I couldn't resist buying a can of Pocari Sweat Refreshment Water just for its name. It tastes better than it sounds.

MEAT AND POULTRY

ANTONELLI'S MEAT, FISH AND POULTRY IN THE CAL-MART

Antonelli's is the only source in the city for some of my favorite lamb, Bruce and Nancy Campbell's CK lamb from Healdsburg. Their lambs may be a bit larger than the Superior lambs from Dixon sold at many butcher shops in the city, but they have real character without ever being muttony. One evening I roasted CK and Superior racks of lamb next to each other; the CK lamb had a deeper flavor and more personality while being just as tender. The CK racks turned out to be a couple of dollars more expensive because the bones were larger, but this lamb earns its higher price.

The chicken counter features hormone-free though not free-range Fulton Valley chickens, which to my mind are some of the best commercial chickens on the market. They have character without any off flavors and they roast up like a dream. The small, fresh Fulton Valley turkey parts carried here are also delicious and an underused meat alternative. What could be better, or easier to cook, than golden-skinned roast turkey meat for dinner, with leftovers for sandwiches the next day?

Since Antonelli's started out as a fish and poultry seller, you can expect to find some seafood treasures, like jars of tiny Pacific oysters from Johnson's Oyster Company in Point Reyes or fresh whole sand dabs with clear eyes. Antonelli's still cuts halibut and salmon steaks, which actually grill up more evenly than fillets (which are also sold), though you have to contend with a few bones and skin. Antonelli's may not be as complete or

3585 California Street (between Laurel and Spruce), San Francisco
Tel: 752-7413
Open Monday through Saturday 8 a.m. to 7 p.m., Sunday 9 a.m. to 6 p.m.
Credit cards: MC, V

up-to-the-minute as Bryan's down the block, but the strong poultry section and special lamb make it an invaluable resource.

BRYAN'S QUALITY MEATS

3473 California Street
(between Spruce and
Laurel), San Francisco
Tel: 752-3430
Open Monday through
Friday 8 a.m. to 7 p.m.,
Saturday until 6 p.m.
Credit cards: MC, V

Bryan's operated the meat counter at the Cal-Mart next to Antonelli's Fish and Poultry for thirty years, but recently moved to open its own store a few doors away. I consider Bryan's the best all-around butcher in the city. In addition to meat, Bryan's has separate counters for fish, poultry, and prepared foods cooked by Barney Brown, ex-chef from the Mad Hatter and Harry Denton's. Although the fresh corn salad, old-fashioned potato salads, platters of roasted vegetables, and rotisserie-roasted organic chickens entice as you walk in the back door from the Laurel Village parking area, the beauty of the raw ingredients here inspires home cooking.

Bryan's dry-ages its own prime beef for four weeks. You can taste the pedigree in a Prime market steak ($11.95/lb): fat-marbled, tender texture, and tons of flavor. The Choice beef comes from Harris Ranch, which I have come to admire for its consistency and lively western flavor. Bryan's dry-ages its California lamb for two weeks as well, and the racks, completely trimmed of fat and with a plump loin, are marvelously juicy and refined in flavor. Fresh country-style pork ribs and pork roasts and chops make for another dinner alternative. Anyone who has run out of cooking ideas only needs to step into this shop.

All the meat here is beautifully cut, the roasts elegantly tied. The late Bryan Flannery, quoted by Sherry Virbila in her resource book *Cook's Market-place* (101 Productions, 1982), explained, "Well, you see, I learned to cut meat under a Frenchman, Henry Bercut. So did Frank Petrini. Bercut was from Limousin, France. He was the best meat man around. When we were cutting meat, he used to tell us you have to treat it like a rose." Bryan's son, Terry Flannery, now runs the shop, which is full of convenience items that his dad probably never dreamed of carrying, but that meat counter still looks like a French *boucherie* full of promising cuts and roasts.

Of course chicken and fish have become staples in a health-conscious diet, and Bryan's has taken up the banner. It has put together the prettiest fish counter in town. Terry Flannery knows how to buy and who to buy from. I have seen salmon, tuna, striped bass, fresh day-boat scallops, fresh shrimp, delicious northern halibut, swordfish, local rockfish, and seasonal items like soft shell crabs and shad roe in pristine condition. He is not afraid to stock unusual fish like bright red whole bee-liners from the Gulf of Mexico, with eyes so clear they look as if they have just been pulled in from the water. The seafood chowder, sold by the refrigerated pint, is one of the best I have tasted anywhere, and the notion of offering fresh mango salsa at the fish counter is inspired. Moving over to poultry, Bryan's carries a small, young chicken from Frank's Fresh Foods in Napa (among others), which looks like an overgrown poussin, or baby chicken. Pale-skinned and without fat, it cooks up so moist, tender, and full of flavor, you'll drive across town just to get it. Ducks from Grimaud farm, local quail, and excellent, tender squab figuratively fly out the door. The freshest little rabbits I have seen in a market sit between the game birds and the chicken—neither fish nor fowl.

On top of all the choice raw materials, Terry Flannery knows where to get the best restaurant-quality cured and smoked items, like Hobbs's bacon and hams and

Robert Morris's incomparable smoked salmon, trout, and sturgeon. He's got Palio d'Asti breads, among others, and a few crucial produce items like shallots, garlic, onions, lemons, and potatoes. When you buy something of the highest quality, hand cut and perfectly fresh, you do not need a lot of it. Bryan's charges for the quality, but the pleasure of eating fine meat, fish and poultry go a long way.

FISH

ANTONELLI'S MEAT, FISH AND POULTRY IN THE CAL-MART

See Meat, page 361.

BRYAN'S QUALITY MEATS

See Meat, page 362.

MARUWA FOODS COMPANY

See Ethnic Markets, page 358.

SUPER KOYAMA

See Ethnic Markets, page 359.

UOKI MARKET

See Ethnic Markets, page 360.

CHEESE

CALIFORNIA STREET CREAMERY

2413 California Street (at
Fillmore), San Francisco
Tel: 929-8610
Open Monday through
Friday 7 a.m. to 6:45 p.m.,
Saturday 9 a.m. to 6:45 p.m.,
Sunday 9 a.m. to 5:30 p.m.
No credit cards

An interesting if small collection of cheeses can be found at this tiny shop, some of the most alluring right out on the marble counter, like ripe, bulging Chaumes; buttery, crumbly aged Gouda; a strong, creamy Taleggio from Italy; and some high-end triple-cream French imports. An assortment of breads, rolls, and pastries from different bakers are kept in the front window, and the small refrigerated case is stocked with an odd assortment of things like Casa Sanchez tomato salsa and house-made crème fraîche. People in the neighborhood depend on the Creamery for certain favorite specialty items like nonsupermarket cheeses and exotic crackers.

COOKWARE AND BOOKS

BOOKS, INC.

This smallish, but amazingly well-stocked bookstore has a cookbook remainder table, with interesting titles at 50 to 90 percent off retail price. The other day I saw Victoria Wise's classic *American Charcuterie* in a pretty paperback edition marked down to $2.88. Anyone who thumbs through a book like this will find timeless recipes from the woman who brought the French delicatessen to the United States when she ran Pig by the Tail in Berkeley. Next to the remainders, a whole table of new books at full price titillates the seemingly insatiable cookbook buyer. The repetition of subject matter in books stylishly devoted to one ingredient makes me wonder how many recipes anyone needs for potatoes, green salad, or chicken. Books, Inc.'s many shelves of cookbooks do contain an intelligently chosen inventory of classics, like all three of the Greens-inspired cookbooks, for example. For those who associate travel with food, the excellent travel section is stocked with an unusual number of food guides to different countries.

3515 California Street (between Laurel and Spruce), San Francisco
Tel: 221-3666
Open Monday through Friday 9 a.m. to 8 p.m., Saturday 10 a.m. to 6 p.m., Sunday 11 a.m. to 5 p.m.
Credit cards: MC, V

FILLAMENTO

A vibrant housewares store now with three levels of trend-setting merchandise, Fillamento has added extravagant upscale items to its stylish, yet affordable, inventory. Opulent Versace place settings at $500 each are displayed a few steps away from piles of large, serviceable cotton napkins from India that cost $4 apiece. If I were setting up an apartment on a budget I would turn to Fillamento for well-designed silverware, dishes,

2185 Fillmore Street (at Sacramento), San Francisco
Tel: 931-2224
Monday through Friday 10 a.m. to 7 p.m., Saturday and Sunday until 6 p.m.
Credit cards: AE, D, MC, V

glasses, and table linens; and when ready to upgrade my china cabinet, I could return for some finer pieces. Through creative and daring buying Fillamento has kept a step ahead of the big guys like Crate and Barrel and Williams-Sonoma, and now has taken on Gump's. Fillamento may not offer as many choices in every price range as these stores, but what ends up on the floor is both provocative and useful. And since it is a one-unit store, chances are you won't see your dishes and glasses on your next-door neighbor's table.

FORREST JONES

3274 Sacramento Street (between Presidio and Lyon), San Francisco
Tel: 567-2483
Open Monday through Saturday 10 a.m. to 6 p.m., Sunday 11 a.m. to 5 p.m.
Credit cards: AE, MC, V

This cleverly stocked housewares shop often has the very thing you've been looking for all over town, like a plain, heavy glass cake dome (without the plate) or large white rectangular platters at half off the original price, which I found there between Thanksgiving and Christmas one year. Baskets, tote bags, dish towels, Roger and Gallet soaps by the bar, sturdy glassware, and an ever-changing array of goods that households really need make Forrest Jones an invaluable resource, well worth checking out before or after you've shopped elsewhere.

JUDITH ETS-HOKIN'S HOMECHEF

3525 California Street (between Laurel and Spruce), San Francisco
Tel: 668-3191
Open Monday through Saturday 9:30 a.m. to 6 p.m., Sunday noon to 4:30 p.m.
Credit cards: AE, D, MC, V

A complete collection of cooking utensils and some serving and tableware fill the shelves of this densely packed store. It seems to me that the most important tool in any kitchen is a decent knife that is heavy enough to keep an edge, yet many home kitchens overflow with doodads without a decent cutting tool to be found. Homechef does everyone a favor by putting both their special label collection of chefs' knives and a case of first-class imported knives from Solingen, Germany, front and center in the shop. Before people move on to the miniature tart pans and the food processors of every conceivable size, they ought to buy themselves one good knife. Having gotten that off my chest, I must say I was drawn to some brightly enameled charcuterie dishes in cheerful greens and blues. I was happy to see Donvier ice cream makers, an ingenious Japanese invention that only requires a home freezer and a minimum of arm power to quickly turn out fresh fruit ices and ice cream (so wonderful during the summer fruit season). If you're a pots-and-pans fan, the store carries the latest in nonstick technologies. Rolls of hard-to-find untreated cooking twine, wire fish holders for the grill, simple imported crystal wineglasses in classic shapes at $5 a piece, and tons of pure cotton dish towels make for good gifts for your own kitchen or someone else's. Homechef stocks the arcane and the necessary with an eye to finding the best examples in every genre.

KINOKUNIYA BOOKSTORE

This spacious book emporium has racks full of Japanese food and housekeeping magazines written in Japanese, but also a large, interesting collection of Asian cookbooks in English. This is the place to find Chinese, Indian, Thai, Burmese, or Indonesian cookbooks in paper- and hardback, not to mention a superior collection of Japanese cookbooks, including Shizuo Tsuji's *Japanese Cooking: A Simple Art*, the definitive Japanese cookbook in English with a forward by M. F. K. Fisher. Books on Japanese country cooking, on culinary artifacts of Japan illustrated with lively black and white photos, and an international survey of rice cookery are but a few of the gems to be mined. Kinokuniya has the best vegetarian and macrobiotic cookbook section in

Japan Center, 1581 Webster (between Post and Geary), San Francisco
Tel: 567-7625
Open daily 10:30 a.m. to 7 p.m.
Credit cards: AE, MC, V

the city; the titles fill many shelves. The variety of meat-less dishes in Asian cuisines stretches the imagination, and even the most exotic ingredients for many of the recipes can be found nearby. The cookbook aisle segues right into the Asian massage and sexual instruction section, a juxtaposition I find salubrious.

MASHIKO FOLKCRAFT

Japan Center, 1581 Webster
(between Post and Geary),
San Francisco
Tel: 346-0748
Open Wednesday through
Monday 11 a.m. to 6 p.m.
Credit cards: AE, MC, V

The uncased displays in this intimate shop of antique Japanese tableware tempt you to pick things up for close examination, but the eagle-eyed store owner will scold you if he catches you. Nineteenth-century wooden buckets for $7,500 and small antique chests sit next to contemporary bamboo noodle trays. There are lyrical, handmade rice containers carved of cedar; hand-thrown tea mugs at $22; wooden water ladles for the garden fountain; and ladles made of bamboo for the Japanese tea ceremony. The shapes and sizes of the singularly glazed ceramics expand your idea of dinnerware. Many of the prices here have caught up to those at Gump's, but there

A SMALL JAPANTOWN DETOUR

A whole row of original Victorian cottages still stands along one side of a miniature park on Cottage Row, a block-long street across from Yamada Seika (see page 354). These dwellings are the only remnants of the original Japanese neighborhood that was destroyed during the redevelopment of Japantown, according to Yoko Tahara, a personal friend and longtime resident of the neighborhood both before and after her family's deportation to relocation camps during World War II. Take a stroll down the brick pathway to get a closer look at the lovingly maintained cottages and gardens. This is one of the most charming secret streets in San Francisco.

are still bargains to be found. A visit to this small shop of exotic and beautiful things would certainly solve the problem of finding an exquisite house gift or wedding present for people with worldly taste.

R H

It's easy to miss this small, tasteful store around the corner from flashy Fillamento, but there are some beautiful, carefully chosen things here, like leaf-patterned plates in green or white, and simple, colorful Italian crockery. Large, finely woven cotton napkins from India at $7.50, stunning candle holders, and a small but interesting selection of cookbooks, most with photographs, represent some of the seductive merchandise scattered about the small shop. The owner's signature is on every piece, and he does not lead you astray. Though prices are solidly mid-range to expensive, the beauty and simplicity of the objects give them value. RH strikes me as a very hip and civilized spot to shop.

2506 Sacramento Street (at Fillmore), San Francisco
Tel: 346-1460
Open Monday through Saturday 10 a.m. to 6 p.m., Sunday noon to 5 p.m.
Credit cards: AE, MC, V

SANKO COOKING SUPPLY

Looking for an electric rice maker, a rectangular cast-iron skillet for making sweet Japanese omelets, a ginger grater, Japanese knives, ridged Japanese mortars, cast-iron sukiyaki pots, or any shape and size of ceramic dish and lacquered bowl? These and every other utensil or vessel you might need for Asian cooking and serving can be found here at reasonable prices.

1758 Buchanan Street (at Sutter), San Francisco
Tel: 922-8331
Open Monday through Saturday 9:30 a.m. to 6 p.m., Sunday noon to 6 p.m.
Credit cards: AE, MC, V

SOKO HARDWARE CO.

1698 Post Street (at Buchanan), San Francisco

Tel: 931-5510

Open Monday through Saturday 9 a.m. to 5:30 p.m.

Credit cards: MC, V

My husband spotted a most attractive cracked-glaze Japanese vase in the window here six years ago. It looked like something rare, but it cost $70. Now, anytime either of us walk by Soko Hardware, we dash in for a quick look at the ceramics on the main floor. You never know what treasure you might find. Downstairs, everything from child-sized chopsticks with Eggplant Club, Potato Club, and Turnip Club inscribed on them to gorgeous, heavy, $295 cast-iron miso *shiro* kettles with thick wooden tops are filed away someplace in the vast housewares department. I'm a sucker for this store. I love the tiny dishes the size of a half dollar, and the earthy, glazed rectangles of pottery that look as if their edges were torn and bent. I imagine putting together an elegant Japanese table with this pottery and salads, sushi, and sashimi bought at Super Koyama, but laying Super Hero chopsticks at each place. Upstairs, along with the Japanese carpentry tools and larger ceramics, a rack of Japanese seeds for burdock, cucumber, and *shiso* snags you on the way out.

SUE FISHER-KING

3067 Sacramento Street (between Broderick and Baker), San Francisco

Tel: 922-7276

Open Monday to Saturday 10 a.m. to 6 p.m.

Credit cards: AE, MC, V

If you're looking for top-of-the-line imports like Italian tablecloths and napkins, or wonderful, over-sized French silverware with bone or wooden handles at the highest possible prices, Sue Fisher-King has an exclusive, personal selection. Her table of cookbooks is also worth a look for the quirkiness of what's there. I usually find something I didn't know I was looking for.

Polk Street, Nob Hill, Russian Hill & Van Ness Avenue

POLK STREET, NOB HILL, RUSSIAN HILL & VAN NESS AVENUE

RESTAURANTS

ACQUERELLO

Chef Suzette Gresham and maître d'/Italian wine expert Giancarlo Paterlini have formed an inspired partnership at their jewel of a restaurant. They both believe in refinement and civility and insist on the highest quality in performance and ingredients. A meal at Acquerello affords its patrons a moment of pure luxury, not necessarily of the elaborate or showy sort, but of the quiet, deeply satisfying sort—perhaps because the wrapping on the package is Italian rather than French.

The food is a little bit fancy, but held down to earth because of the Italian idiom. Gresham's house-made pastas have the texture of silk, yet her rustic sauces deliver the vitality of the countryside even though they're really quite refined. She uses fresh herbs like a fine oil painter, each small stroke adding dimension. Her *antipasti* are particularly inventive, as evidenced by a warm squab salad with chard sprinkled with extra-virgin olive oil and toasted pine nuts; or tomato slices spread with a paste of anchovies, capers, and cooked egg

1722 Sacramento Street
(between Polk and Van
Ness), San Francisco
Tel: 567-5432
Open Tuesday through
Saturday 5:30 to 10:30 p.m.
Price: Expensive
Credit cards: AE, DC , D,
MC, V

yolk. The main courses bring roasted quail stuffed with pancetta; a classic Florentine preparation of sole rolled around spinach; or beef fillet stuffed with prosciutto, Parmesan, and rosemary. Her cooking imagination is fertile, and she is not timid about trying new dishes, though always with the control of a dedicated professional chef. An ambitious program of special dinners, based around the wines of a certain region or celebrating a single ingredient like tomatoes, pasta, or seafood, is worth following because they represent excellent all-inclusive buys.

Equal to the pleasure of eating such lovely food is the experience of being in Giancarlo's watercolor-filled dining room. To my mind he has always been the best captain in the city. He knows how to make everyone feel like a million bucks—special, cared for, intelligent, sophisticated—by gently offering guidance, helping people get to the best his restaurant has to offer in just the way that will please them. His expertise on Italian wines, and his generosity in cracking open wonderful bottles to pour glasses that fit each course, expands the whole sensual landscape of the meal. The quiet, anticipatory service, the sparkle of the silver and glasses on the table, the unflagging attention to every detail, all speak to Paterlini's highly trained European sensibility, one that understands and appreciates the tradition of service. This unique restaurant maintains a loyal following of people who like to be treated well.

The tiny Cordon Bleu, one of the city's first Vietnamese eateries, reminds me of food stalls in tropical Asia, where cooks set up their steamers and grills right on the sidewalk. I have eaten the best chicken of my life at a card table and folding chair on a Bangkok sidewalk. The Cordon Bleu uncannily replicates this experience. Though there is a front door and ceiling, the painted brick walls suggest food operations set up in a crevice between two buildings with a canopy overhead. Very little light filters into Cordon Bleu during the day; at night a few dim bulbs barely do the job. People squeeze onto stools at a counter in the front of a small stove and grill or sit at two tiny tables at the back. Every time the door opens a blast of cold air sweeps into the room.

This authentic atmosphere only makes the five-spice roast chicken, the house specialty, taste better. For an extremely small tariff you get a half chicken, aromatically marinated, and a pile of crunchy cabbage and carrot salad with a large dollop of rice moistened with a Vietnamese version of bolognese sauce. Only two other dishes are available: crisply deep-fried imperial rolls stuffed with ground shrimp, pork, and vegetables; and beef on skewers, both of which come with the sauced rice and salad. Whatever the combination, all these foods are wonderfully satisfying eaten together. While not as refined or authentic as the top Vietnamese places, the Cordon Bleu has maintained a strong neighborhood following by turning out hearty plates of good chicken year after year.

1574 California Street (near Polk), San Francisco
Tel: 673-5637
Open for lunch Tuesday through Friday 11:30 a.m. to 2:30 p.m.; dinner Tuesday through Sunday 5 to 10 p.m.
Price: Inexpensive
No credit cards

**905 California Street
(between Powell and
Mason), San Francisco
Tel: 989-1910
Open daily for breakfast
and lunch 6:30 a.m. to 3:30
p.m.; dinner 5:30 to
11:30 p.m.
Price: Expensive
Credit cards: AE, DC , D,
MC, V**

The ground-breaking Stanford Court hotel, founded by Jim Nassikas in 1972, has always prided itself on having a restaurant that could compete with any independent. The dining room was designed as a series of rooms cascading down one side of Nob Hill, with views of the cable cars and Financial District. Instead of the usual heavy carpeting and draperies, Mediterranean tile floors, wood-beam ceilings, and hanging strings of chilies became the motif, along with the first wood-burning oven ever to grace the floor of an American dining room. Out of that oven has come delicious, smoky racks of lamb, pork roasts, and sometimes fish. Though the hotel has been bought by the Stouffer chain, the tradition of serving fresh, inventive food is being carried on by a very professional Colorado-born Culinary Institute of America-graduate chef, Ercolino Crugnale, who has a way with vegetables and knows how to present good, rustic flavors in a form refined enough for the hotel crowd.

I will never forget a little first-course dish of his, a plate of whole baby vegetables in a haunting broth with ethereal, garlicky ricotta gnocchi, all sprinkled with truffle oil. He also has a special way with meat, like rack of lamb chops in an intense Pinot Noir and thyme *jus*, with fresh beans and an irresistible Monterey jack potato gratin. Service has always been a bit ragged here, however, as if performed by old tenured hands who punch in and out and don't really have a workable system. Even still, in a city full of excellent restaurants, Fournou's Ovens continues to be a viable choice in the expensive category.

A visit to the comfortable dining room of this first-class Vietnamese restaurant will net you one of the nicest meals in town for the most reasonable price. The small multilevel restaurant is decorated with wall murals hand-carved in wood, and light sconces made of gnarled tree branches. The tables are set with wineglasses and tablecloths. At first you think you've walked into a French restaurant—until the piles of exotic fresh herbs, cold noodles, and lettuces start coming. Many dishes at the Golden Turtle deliver the classic Vietnamese juxtaposition of hot and savory with cold and crisp, like hot, crisp crab-filled spring rolls, which you eat in lettuce leaves with sprigs of fresh mint, cilantro, cold white rice noodles, and a dip into a piquant sauce. Another brilliant combination brings five-spice roast chicken with golden skin and velvety, aromatic flesh, served on a bed of juicy Vietnamese vegetable slaw in a sparkly dressing—a dish I could eat every day. The menu offers one delight after another, like a whole fresh sea bass gently steamed, cleanly sauced, and topped with fresh herbs and ginger threads; or thinly sliced grilled beef marinated in lemongrass and served on a watercress salad. Quail, for which Vietnamese cooks have a special affection, are prepared in several different ways and all are worth ordering. The consistently meticulous preparation and high-quality ingredients insisted on in this kitchen make almost every dish a revelation. The graceful wait staff in long skirts or tunics and pants is well informed and efficient, and they know how to serve the wines on the small, but choice, wine list, which includes some French whites that go superbly with the food. Golden Turtle meals work as either satisfying, everyday fare or as special-occasion food. The beauty is that you can eat so well and so elegantly for a song.

2211 Van Ness Avenue (between Broadway and Vallejo), San Francisco

Tel: 441-4419

Open for lunch Tuesday through Sunday 11:30 a.m. to 3 p.m.; dinner 5 to 11 p.m.

Price: Inexpensive

Credit cards: AE, MC, V

2100 Van Ness Avenue (at
Pacific), San Francisco
Tel: 673-1888
Open Monday through
Friday 6 to 10 p.m.,
Saturday and Sunday 5 to
9:30 p.m.
Price: Expensive
Credit cards: AE, DC , D,
MC, V

When dynamic Anne Harris, who married into the well-known cattle-raising clan, left the fold, she took over a famous, but defunct, city steak house called Grisson's and reopened it as Harris'. Her luxurious restaurant boasts king-sized upholstered booths, tall potted palms, a huge wall mural by Barnaby Conrad, and a clubby bar that serves pour-yourself martinis in miniature glass decanters resting in miniature ice buckets. Her delicious signature sweetbread pâté with fresh toast points makes an inspired accompaniment. The menu is steak-house simple and well executed: juicy grilled Harris Ranch steaks (my favorite is the Harris Steak, a New York with the featherbone left on), baked potatoes with butter, sour cream, and real bacon bits; excellent creamed spinach; and for starters, blue points on the half shell; a tasty Caesar with freshly made croutons; spinach salad with sieved eggs; and decent deep-fried zucchini. Wine drinkers can find a big California red with some age on it on the multipaged wine list. Overall, Anne Harris's place is the most satisfying steak house in the city. It has its role down cold and plays it like a trouper, night after night.

H O U S E   O F   P R I M E   R I B

1906 Van Ness Avenue
(between Jackson and
Washington), San Francisco
Tel: 885-4605
Open Monday through
Thursday 5:30 to 10 p.m.,
Friday 5 to 10 p.m.,

A restaurant that serves slabs of rare roast beef (with a bone if you want, and I do) carved at tableside from huge silver carts should be protected like a national treasure. In this town the House of Prime Rib practically has that designation since it's the last outpost for this kind of eating nearly anywhere. For one all-inclusive price you get a salad dressed at tableside in the famous spinning salad bowl—the waitress spins the bowl on a bed of ice as she pours pink dressing over chopped vegetables and then dishes it up on chilled plates with forks right out of the freezer—followed by roast beef, a baked potato, and Yorkshire pudding. You can decide if you're up to dessert. The old-fashioned windowless dining room, with a large bar that is particularly active preprandially, thick carpeting, booths, and heavy linen, is distinguished on the exterior by an arresting trompe l'oeil mural. Service is professional; the wine list improving; and the experience of dining there totally and wonderfully predictable. People who love prime rib don't want any surprises.

Saturday and Sunday
4 to 10 p.m.
Price: Moderate
Credit cards: AE, DC , MC, V

LA FOLIE

Roland Passot uses this charming, sky-blue dining room as his gallery for artistic plates of very inventive French-California food. He has a passion for decoration, and each plate is conceived for its visual effect, using sauces and purees in a rainbow of colors and a wild array of other ingredients to form his mosaics, architectural constructions, and strata. Passot loves luxurious ingredients —foie gras, lobster, caviar, and the like—and his ability to interweave them into multifaceted plates means that a little of them go a long way, keeping prices under control. The cheerful dining room has always been one of my favorites in the city, with fluffy white clouds painted on the blue ceiling, a copper-framed window that looks into the kitchen, and Roland's wife Jamie and sommelier brother George adding their warmth and generosity to the floor.

2316 Polk Street (between
Union and Green),
San Francisco
Tel: 776-5577
Open Monday through
Saturday 6 to 10:30 p.m.
Price: Expensive
Credit cards: AE, DC , D,
MC, V

LE CLUB

1250 Jones Street (at Clay),
San Francisco
Tel: 771-5400
Open Tuesday through
Sunday 5 to 10 p.m.
Price: Expensive
Credit cards: AE, MC, V

The history of this posh, intimate dining room, hidden away in a classy old apartment building on Nob Hill, goes way back. An attempt was made to revive the place in 1992, but not even excellent, modern Mediterranean cooking from innovative chef Lisa Cannelora, or suave dining room direction from old pro Fritz Frankel could breathe life into it. Now a new group headed by a highly professional French chef, Yves Garnier, has taken over the two clubby, very small dining rooms and bar, hoping that such an urbane, sophisticated venue will always have a built-in clientele.

MAHARANI

1122 Post Street (between
Polk and Van Ness),
San Francisco
Tel: 775-1988
Open for lunch daily 11:30
a.m. to 2:30 p.m.; dinner
Sunday through Thursday
5 to 10 p.m., Friday and
Saturday until 10:30 p.m.
Price: Moderate
Credit cards: AE, DC , D,
MC, V

No one loves Indian food as much as my long-suffering dining-out companion, my husband, but time after time he is disappointed by the repetitive reheated curries and drab deep-fried appetizers that have become the currency on north Indian menus. He does agree with Niloufer Ichaporia, San Francisco's foremost ethnic food expert and street food anthropologist (who happens to be a Parsi from Bombay), who claims that even mediocre Indian food is tastier than most any other, but he hopes for better. We sometimes get it at Maharani, a comfortable, rather pretty Indian restaurant with higher ambitions, though lately the kitchen has been on the downswing.

Understanding the tenor of the times, Maharani makes an effort to prepare some dishes using a reduced amount of oil and salt while still maintaining flavor and texture. Fish, quail, crab, shrimp, and boneless chicken cooked in the tandoori oven, and some vegetarian curries, are marked with a tiny heart on the menu, and I find them to be satisfying. *Nan*, flat-yeasted Indian bread cooked on the side of the tandoori oven, is fabulous here, the restaurant's best dish. I also like the various *dals*, made of lentils or chick-peas. With *raita*, a bowl of yogurt and cucumber, and several fresh chutneys, you can make an inexpensive and delicious vegetarian meal. Tandoori chicken wings are also tasty here. The restaurant features a full complement of Indian desserts, including wonderful milk patties in cream, called *ras malai*; a warm caramelized carrot pudding called *gajjar halwar*; mango ice cream; and pistachio *kulfi*.

Perpendicular to the pink Western-style dining room is a hall of romantic, curtained-off mini-rooms with low tables, cushions, and buzzers to summon the waiter, a setting that stirs up Eastern fantasies. The white-shirted waiters, personable and always professional, strike me as being willing to act out any part.

NOB HILL GRILLE

In a town blissfully short on franchise restaurants and fast-food chains, an independently owned coffee shop like the Nob Hill Grille fills a real need. It offers the inexpensive everyday food beloved by Americans, prepared with integrity and flair. Located across the street from St. Francis Hospital, the Grille is busy all day, cooking platters of eggs, top-notch home-fried potatoes (baked potatoes broken up and crushed against the griddle until they get brown and crusty), sausages, and crisp bacon. The No. 1 club sandwich is thick with real, moist roast turkey, and it comes with a tasty cucumber salad in cumin-scented dressing. Devotees of bacon, lettuce, and tomato sandwiches should make a pilgrimage here—the sandwich comes with a pile of carrot sticks, instead of french fries, and freshly cut coleslaw, a nice touch. Milk

969 Hyde Street (at Pine),
San Francisco
Tel: 474-5985
Open Monday and Tuesday
7 a.m. to 6 p.m., Wednesday
through Friday until 8 p.m.,
Saturday 8 a.m. to 3 p.m.,
Sunday 8:30 a.m. to 3 p.m.
Price: Inexpensive
No credit cards

shakes, malts, and fresh lemonade highlight the drink card. The Nob Hill Grille understands what makes all these seemingly simple things taste so good and unfailingly executes them with high standards.

RITZ-CARLTON DINING ROOM

600 Stockton Street (at California), San Francisco

Tel: 296-7465

Open Monday through Saturday 6 to 10 p.m.

Price: Expensive

Credit cards: AE, DC , D, MC, V

Hotel dining rooms have traditionally earned a bad rap for over-priced luxury and fancy, but soulless institutional cooking, but the Dining Room at the Ritz Carlton is actually one of the best high-end restaurants in the city. Chef Gary Danko has come up with an appealing format: various set-price menus ($36 for two courses, $43 for three, $50 for four, and $57 for a five-course tasting menu, with accompanying wines by the glass an extra $29) that allow diners to order any of the six appetizers, four fish dishes, four meat and poultry dishes, five desserts, and the best cheese service in town for their dinner. If you feel like having two appetizers and a fish course, or a fish course as an appetizer and an appetizer as a main course, or two fish courses and a cheese course and dessert, the kitchen will adjust the portions to make the meal work.

The courses can be mixed and matched because they are stylistically related, even though the inspiration for many of them comes from around the world. Danko is true to the fraternity of California chefs in that he uses beautiful ingredients in unexpected ways, yet his meticulous, classical technique makes the combinations fly. His dishes always taste complete, without rough edges or discordant elements, even when some ingredients seem to come from left field.

Though the menu changes seasonally, look for a grilled quail salad with foie gras croutons and a springtime apricot-ginger chutney. For real foie gras lovers, two huge slices come on a bed of baby spinach set off by a sweet-and-sour rhubarb–blood orange compote. A Thai lobster salad brings the juiciest, sweetest meat flanked by paper-thin slices of avocado and mango in a superb lime-based dressing. Soft-shell crabs, crisp as potato chips, stand on end in a forest of deep-fried parsnips, a light mustard sauce drizzled over all. Grilled sturgeon is napped in a subtle saffron butter sauce, scattered with fresh fava beans, and my very favorite, pan-roasted squab stuffed with leeks and morels, is worth a special trip alone. The desserts bring high flights of color and whimsy, like a gratin of gold and red raspberries surrounding a cardamom-perfumed Bavarian cream; or a peach and blackberry napoleon served with caramel ice cream. The crème brûlée trio really sings.

One reason this high-concept food works so well is that it fits the Ritz-Carlton's high-concept dining room, appointed with soft heavy linens, elegant china, silver, and glassware, heavily draped tall French windows, and lots of polished wood and thick carpeting, with tables placed far enough apart for intimate conversation above the glissandos of a harpist. The dining room staff was trained by rigorous Nick Peyton, who is now the hotel's catering department manager. Every waiter knows what goes into every dish as well as the degree of ripeness of every cheese on the glorious cheese cart, with many opulent French cheeses from Androuet in Paris. The sommelier has put together a tempting wine list, full of lush bottles and glasses in every price range, and will be happy to recommend or discuss any choices. This town's good food reputation does not emanate from our high-end restaurants; in fact, we have very few of real interest. Gary Danko's dining room happens to be one of them.

SWAN OYSTER DEPOT

1517 Polk Street (between Sacramento and California),
San Francisco
Tel: 673-1101
Open Monday through Saturday 8 a.m. to 5:30 p.m.
Price: Moderate
No credit cards

See Fish Markets, page 400.

TAI CHI

2031 Polk Street (between
Broadway and Pacific),
San Francisco
Tel: 441-6758
Open Monday through
Friday 11:30 a.m. to 10 p.m.,
Sunday 4 to 10 p.m.
Price: Inexpensive
Credit cards: AE, MC, V;
$10 minimum

Over the years this modest neighborhood spot, which prepares hot, spicy Hunan and Szechuan dishes, has grown in popularity so that during prime dinner hours you might face a wait. The draw, besides very cheap prices and a Western orientation (which means that the dining room and kitchen are set up to accommodate parties of two instead of large round tables of ten), is the saucy, incendiary northern food. When I get a yen for pot stickers I come here. I could eat a whole plate of these well-seasoned pork dumplings with thick but tender wrappers, dipped into vinegar and red chili oil. Any of the chili-marked hot dishes will be pretty good, like dry-fried long beans with pork, or the indulgent "Hunan-style" preparations in which chunks of boneless chicken or pork are thickly battered, crisply deep-fried, and tossed in a copious amount of garlicky hot sweet-and-sour sauce, divine over rice. Hot-and-sour soup is also O.K., but this is not the place to go to order seafood, or even plates of simple vegetables. Bowls of spicy noodles are the draw, not to mention congenial waiters who are used to dealing with a mostly Western clientele.

VANESSI'S

Those of us who ate out in San Francisco during the seventies and eighties remember what an exciting scene the old Vanessi's on Broadway was. People gravitated there at all hours of the day and night for huge portions of short-order Italian-American cooking. The crowd came from every social strata, every profession, every age group. You had to pay the maître d' just to get into the place, even with a reservation. The tourists stood by and watched the regulars privateered their tables.

As often happens in the restaurant business, things changed quickly. Giovanni Leoni, Vanessi's chef, left to open his own fine place nearby called Buca Giovanni. Broadway became too seedy, and the older clientele stopped coming. The employees went on strike, and gradually, the old Vanessi's lost its energy and closed. So in 1986 owner Bart Shea and his daughter Lorna opened a second Vanessi's on Nob Hill in the Grammercy Tower condominium complex across the street from Grace Cathedral. The new, spacious dining room feels just like the old Vanessi's with the trademark open kitchen, counter seating in front of it, and lots of burgundy vinyl booths, mirrors, and chandeliers. Subsidized parking right in the building brought the old-timers back, many of whom just walk over from their Nob Hill apartments.

As for the menu, it has been edited from its original long version. Some of it survives in all its old glory, while some of it just doesn't work. The Caesar tossed at tableside can be good or terrible depending on who

1177 California Street (at Jones), San Francisco
Tel: 771-2422
Open for lunch Monday through Friday 11:30 a.m. to 4:30 p.m.; dinner Sunday through Thursday 4:30 to 10 p.m., Friday and Saturday until 11 p.m.
Price: Moderate
Credit Cards: AE, DC, MC, V

makes it. However, Vanessi's classic spinach salad with lots of bacon and sliced mushrooms has been consistently good. Also dependable because of a lively house vinaigrette are hearts of romaine salad and tomato slices in season with onions and anchovies. Spaghetti carbonara brings back fond memories of the original Vanessi's al dente pasta in a rich sauce of pancetta, shallots, cream, and egg yolk cooked by the hot noodles. The once beloved white clam sauce now seems thin and flavorless. Chicken sauté Vanessi, pieces of chicken sautéed with peppers, onions, parsley, garlic, and a little white wine, still satisfies. And for dessert, the warm, frothy, made-to-order zabaglione, overflowing its glass dish onto two ladyfingers, remains a lovely constant.

VENTICELLO

1257 Taylor Street
(at Washington),
San Francisco
Tel: 922-2545
Open daily 5:30 to 10 p.m.
Price: Moderate
Credit Cards: AE, MC, V

At Venticello, a chic trattoria hidden away in a valley between Nob Hill and Russian Hill, diners feel as if they are seated in a Tuscan country kitchen complete with enticing aromas emanating from the tiled oven in the middle of the room. Antique china cabinets, polished wooden floors, heavy wooden chairs, and rosy, mottled walls make the room look as if it had been airlifted from some ancient inn in Chianti. The tables, covered with linen and butcher paper, are decorated with little pots of fresh herbs. The windows from the lower dining room afford a glimpse of the Bay Bridge through the apartments across the street. Venticello is the kind of neighborhood secret that savvy tourists consider a trophy.

The meals start with freshly baked loaves of wholewheat bread and a saucer of black olives. Soft red and crisp white Italian wines are poured by the glass for reasonable prices. A lush antipasto brings grilled endive, zucchini, and Japanese eggplant, ripe tomatoes in season, fresh mozzarella, melon wrapped in prosciutto, and fabulous marinated shrimp on a bed of radicchio and Italian parsley. Every item on the plate shines. Grilled shrimp wrapped in pancetta make for another fine starter as do country vegetable soups. The thin-crusted pizzas from the wood-fired oven are delicious, especially the classic pizza Margherita, sublime with only tomato sauce, mozzarella, and basil.

House-made ravioli stuffed with spinach and ricotta, and wide noodles sauced in duck or rabbit ragout, are but some of the satisfying, often rustic pastas. The menu changes daily, but if you find a poussin (a baby chicken) roasted in the wood-fired oven with wild mushrooms, peppers, and garlic, served with mashed potatoes and arugula, order it. For dessert both tiramisù and *panna cotta*, "cooked cream" slathered with fresh berries, are lovely.

ZARZUELA

Finally, the highly visible corner location at Hyde and Union that used to be the Marcel and Henri charcuterie and butcher shop, then La Ferme Beaujolais, has found the perfect new identity: a Spanish restaurant that specializes in tapas and paella. The wine-cellarish back room, used as a cheese-ripening room in its former incarnation, lends itself to a Spanish *cava* motif, while the glass deli counters now showcase a tempting display of tapas. The small front room, with a terra-cotta tile and stone interior and big windows that look out to the cable car line, evokes the Mediterranean. I can't imagine a more suitable match of place and purpose.

The delicious food is as traditional as it can get—if you're eating on Spain's Costa del Sol. Start with, or make a meal of, tapas, little servings of hot and cold

**2000 Hyde Street (at Union),
San Francisco
Tel: 346-0800
Open for lunch Monday
through Saturday 11:30 a.m.
to 3 p.m.; dinner 5:30 to
10:30 p.m.
Price: Moderate
Credit cards: MC, V**

dishes that draw on the entire Spanish pantry. Try a plate of the paper-thin, cold, marinated grilled vegetables called *escalivada*, or a ramekin of hot, miniature, spicy chorizo sausages, served in a gravy that you'll want to sop up with pieces of good rosemary bread (one of the few I've ever cared for) or baguette, brought to the table with a saucer of olives. Or have a typical Spanish tapas plate of bread slathered with a puree of fresh tomatoes and garlic, thin slices of nutty serrano ham and slices of *manchego* cheese (a great all-around cooking and eating cheese that is becoming more and more appreciated in the Bay Area). If you don't make a meal of these excellent small plates, by all means have the paella, an absolutely stunning Spanish rice preparation that comes in an authentic flat cast-iron pan. The pearly, short-grained rice soaks up all the juices from impeccable shrimp, clams, mussels, bits of chicken, and a colorful scattering of fresh peas and red peppers, yet the dish is voluptuously moist and flavorful. Zarzuela makes one of the best versions I have tasted in this country.

You can have glasses of cold *fino* sherry with tapas or a bottle of light, fruity Spanish red wine, a number of which are on the wine list. It's amazing how wonderful these wines are with the food, made more so by their reasonable prices.

The whole experience is so nicely realized, and the tariff so affordable, that I predict people will be lined up in front of the tapas counters crying for little bites of food and sherry while they wait for a table. Currently the service is not organized to accommodate these requests, and that is my only criticism of this terrific new restaurant.

BARS

JOHNNY LOVE'S

This popular bar, favored by the airline industry, rises above being a mating scene during the dinner hour when a hearty, imaginative pub menu of hamburgers, deep-fried calamari, Southwest-accented meat dishes, substantial salads, and the inevitable pasta flow out of the kitchen. It's best to come early, before the room turns into a dance club with live music, so you can talk over dinner.

1500 Broadway (at Polk),
San Francisco
Tel: 931-8021
Open daily 5 p.m. to 2 a.m.
Credit cards: AE, MC, V

NEW ORLEANS ROOM
IN THE FAIRMONT HOTEL

Situated off the Fairmont's grand lobby, the New Orleans Room offers an intimate and civilized venue to take in jazz and veteran rhythm and blues headliners. The bartenders, who happen to be jazz fans, put out well-made drinks and bowls of fancy mixed nuts. There's a moderate cover charge and drinks are a bit pricy, but the room is perfect for a nightcap with some entertainment.

California and Mason
streets, San Francisco
Tel: 772-5259
Open daily 3 p.m. to 2 a.m.;
jazz Wednesday through
Sunday at 8 p.m.
Credit cards: AE, DC , D,
MC, V

DELICATESSENS/TAKE-OUT

PICCADILLY FISH AND CHIPS

1348 Polk Street (at Pine),
San Francisco
Tel: 771-6477
Open daily 11 a.m. to
11 p.m.
No credit cards

When the urge to eat a big pile of fish and chips sprinkled with malt vinegar overtakes you, come to this immaculate little shop that does nothing but fry up fish and potatoes. The cod fillets come from Ireland; they're battered and deep-fried to order, staying moist inside a crunchy golden batter. The thick-cut potatoes are pre-cooked to a creamy consistency, then barely browned in oil a second time. They stay limp and potatoey—just the way true fish-and-chips lovers like them. Though the oil in the gigantic fryer is kept very clean—you can see this—it does have its own special smell, which we neutral-oil fanatics have to get used to. My longtime dining-out companion (otherwise known as "Chicken Bucket" for his love of fried chicken), says that the oil is fine and that Piccadilly is the best fish and chips place this side of the Atlantic.

REAL FOOD DELI

2164 Polk Street (at Vallejo),
San Francisco
Tel: 775-2805
Open daily 8 a.m. to 8 p.m.
Credit cards: D, MC, V

Ever since it opened, the Real Food Deli has increasingly taken on the role of a neighborhood cafe. Its few side-walk tables are almost always full, and people drop by all afternoon for a cup of soup, a salad, or a sandwich. The deli cases are full of an international, natural foods array of dishes—Asian noodles, couscous salads, tofu, grilled vegetables—and house-baked goods. A large kitchen located a store away in the Real Food market supplies the deli with fresh and often inventive preparations, many of which use organic produce. People order at the counter and either take the food to go or find a seat. The deli is also a resource for imported cheeses and breads not carried at the Real Food market—which can be a bit confusing when you have to remember which store has which. Service is minimal; the cheeses are all prewrapped in a refrigerated case. Be sure to look for the date on the cheese labels. I have spotted some very old vintages.

BAKERIES/PASTRIES

AHREN'S

An old-fashioned American-style bakery with a sit-down counter that dispenses thin coffee, white bread toast, well-made eggs, and coffee-shop sandwiches, Ahren's is a hold out for a certain kind of comfort food that is fast disappearing in this town. The doughnuts, especially the crisp holes, are very good, and baked goods like coffee cakes and rolls have a tender, not too rich, easy-to-eat quality about them without the off flavors of artificial ingredients. Ahren's baked goods are the models for the items coming out of supermarket bakeries these days, and frankly it pays to make a special trip for the real thing.

1946 Van Ness Avenue (at Jackson), San Francisco
Tel: 885-5060
Open daily 5:30 a.m. to 7 p.m.
No credit cards

THE BAGELRY

To my mind, the Bagelry makes the best bagels in the Bay Area. They are chewy, not soft and crumbly, and carry some weight. They have a good, deep flavor and toast up fragrantly. Unlike the "lite" bagels being sold everywhere—in supermarkets, natural foods stores, and bagel chains that use bagels for ham sandwiches—the one main purpose of a Bagelry bagel is as a landing for cream cheese and, on flush days, smoked salmon, both

2134 Polk Street (between Vallejo and Broadway), San Francisco
Tel: 441-3003
Open Monday, Tuesday, Thursday through Saturday 7 a.m. to 6 p.m.,

Wednesday until noon,
Sunday until 4 p.m.

No credit cards

of which are sold prewrapped in a small refrigerator at the front of the bakery. The singleness of purpose at this store underscores how important the quality of their product is to them and their customers. In fact, if you don't get there early the egg bagels will be gone (they run out first) and several others, like poppy seed or onion, will be in short supply. The seedy bagel sticks have been attracting a following and will do if the bagels have run out. If you are a true bagel aficionado, the Bagelry merits a trip across town.

BOB'S DONUTS

1621 Polk Street (between
Clay and Sacramento),
San Francisco

Tel: 776-3141

Open daily 5 a.m. to 10 p.m.

No credit cards

There are doughnuts and there are doughnuts, and 90 percent of them are inedible. Bob's, a small doughnut shop that has been open for years, not only makes edible doughnuts, but delicious doughnuts. First of all, they are fresh. They're made in batches and turn over quickly because everyone in the north end of the city makes doughnut pilgrimages there. Secondly, they are perfectly fried in clean, neutral oil. Thirdly, they're made from scratch, just an old-fashioned conjunction of flour, yeast, eggs, and sugar, so they're free of artificial preservatives and off flavors. These doughnuts, crumbly or airy, iced, glazed, or sugared, sprinkled with cinnamon or plain, are never cloying, rancid, sticky, stale, or greasy. Since I am the only one who feels that doughnuts don't taste good with coffee (which makes them taste greasy, except for the milky chickory coffee at Café du Monde in New Orleans, which goes perfectly with their hot beignets), the serve-yourself Colombian coffee station at Bob's gets lots of action. The women behind the counter—efficient, intelligent, not overly friendly—know their regulars and have their doughnuts ready as the familiar faces walk through the door. Once you compare Bob's to other doughnuts, you'll buy them here.

ICE CREAM/CHOCOLATES

DOUBLE RAINBOW

1653 Polk Street (between California and Pine),

San Francisco

Tel: 775-3220

Open Sunday through Thursday 11 a.m. to 11 p.m.,

Friday and Saturday until midnight

No credit cards

See listing, page 273.

PURE T

2238 Polk Street (between

Vallejo and Green),

San Francisco

Tel: 441-7878

Open Monday and Tuesday

noon to 9 p.m., Wednesday

through Sunday until

10 p.m.

No credit cards

I'm not sure yet if tea makes sense as an ice cream flavor, but this whole shop devotes itself to the art of combining the two. Passion fruit tea, jasmine tea, black and green teas, spicy Indian *chai*, and other infusions are the flavoring agents for a rather thin, milky ice cream served in cups with waferlike Japanese tea cakes. I shrugged at first taste, but by the end of a cup of different flavors, some had endeared themselves to me and become quite refreshing. On the face of it, the idea of tea and ice cream seems antithetical: tea is so clean, and its bouquet so delicate that mixing it with thick, rich textures and sugar undermines its best qualities. But there might be meals after which this tea-infused ice cream would work very well, especially paired with certain kinds of fruit or fruit compotes. The shop has a Zen air to it, with a small, well-designed counter and a few tables. It provides the most sympathetic context for tasting the ice creams.

1519 Polk Street (between Sacramento and California),

San Francisco

Tel: 775-7049

Open Monday through Saturday 9:30 a.m. to 6 p.m.

No credit cards

See listing, page 431.

COFFEE

FREED, TELLER & FREED

**1326 Polk Street
(between Bush and Pine),
San Francisco
Tel: 673-0922
Open Monday through
Friday 9 a.m. to 6 p.m.,
Saturday until 5 p.m.
Credit cards: MC, V**

Opened in 1907, Freed, Teller & Freed set the standard for coffee and tea merchandising and still does with its daily-roasted coffee beans from Central America, Africa, and the Pacific, and a wide selection of teas. F, T & F roasts light, which allows you to make a double-strong brew without bitterness. The dark wood shelves are stocked with coffee makers of every conceivable shape and kind, including elegant glass vacuum pots, which run on candle power and can be set up at the dinner table. On the more modern front are a whole shelf of home espresso machines, which the shop services as well as sells. Freed, Teller & Freed has always been a proponent of, and educator about, the culture of coffee and tea drinking, a stance that the new higher end chains have taken as their own. When you walk into this handsome old store with its attractive merchandise displayed like works of art (exquisite demitasses for French roast; old-fashioned coffee makers), you know that this shop has history behind it. The clerks in coffee-colored lab coats know everything about coffee and will be happy to tell you as much as you want to hear.

PEET'S COFFEE AND TEA

2139 Polk Street (between Vallejo and Broadway),
San Francisco
Tel: 474-1871
Mon–Sat 7 a.m. to 7 p.m., Sun 8 a.m. to 6 p.m.
Credit cards: D, MC, V

See listing, page 218.

SPINELLI COFFEE COMPANY

2255 Polk Street (between Vallejo and Green),
San Francisco
Tel: 928-7793
Open Monday through Friday 6:30 a.m. to 9 p.m.,
Saturday 7 a.m. to 9 p.m., Sunday 7 a.m. to 7 p.m.
Credit cards: AE, MC, V

See listing, page 192.

BUTTERMILK BREAD

1 cup buttermilk

3 tablespoons sugar

2 1/2 teaspoons kosher salt

1/3 cup butter, cut into chunks

1 cup warm (105° to 115°F) water

1 package active dry yeast

5 3/4 cups unbleached all-purpose flour

1/4 teaspoon baking soda

The Real Food stores sell organic unbleached flour, stone-ground whole-wheat flour, yeast, wheat germ, oat bran, and every other conceivable flour in bulk for bread baking. This buttermilk bread has a light, firm texture and an amazingly full flavor; it's an old-fashioned white bread, great for toast. I found it in The Margaret Rudkin Pepperidge Farm Cookbook *(Gosset & Dunlap, 1970), which has a number of excellent American bread recipes including a yeasted corn bread and a full-flavored wheat-germ bread. The volume is worth seeking out for these three recipes alone.*

In a small saucepan over low heat, combine the buttermilk, sugar, salt, and butter and warm until the butter is almost melted. Remove from the heat and let cool to warm (105° to 115°F).

Pour the warm water into a large bowl. Sprinkle in the yeast and stir until it dissolves.

Add the warm milk mixture to the yeast mixture. Stir in 3 cups of the flour and the baking soda. Beat with a wooden spoon until smooth. Alternatively, use an electric mixer with the paddle attachment and beat until smooth.

Mix in the remaining 2 3/4 cups flour to make a dough that has a rough, dull appearance and is a bit sticky. Turn the dough out on a lightly floured board and knead until smooth and elastic, about 8 to 10 minutes. Or use the dough hook of the electric mixer and knead for 7 minutes.

Grease a large bowl with butter. Form the dough into a ball and put into the prepared bowl, turning the dough to lightly coat all sides with butter. Cover with a clean, damp cloth and let rise in a warm place free from drafts until doubled in bulk, about 1 hour.

Punch the dough down, turn it out on a lightly floured board, and let rest for 15 minutes.

Divide the dough in half. Shape into loaves and place in 2 buttered 9-by-5-inch bread pans. Cover and let rise in a warm place free from drafts until doubled in bulk, about 1 hour.

Preheat the oven to 375°F. Bake the dough until golden brown, about 35 minutes. When you turn out the loaves onto a rack, knock the bottom with your knuckle. The breads should make a hollow sound.

Makes two 9-by-5-inch loaves

MARKETS

REAL FOOD COMPANY

The Polk Street location is the most active branch of the Real Food Company and has become a full-service market over the years by installing a meat, fish, and poultry counter in the back of the store. As in the produce section, the emphasis is on natural and organic (Bradley Ranch beef, Fulton Valley Farms' chickens) and locally made sausages, many made of chicken, many from Bruce Aidells. A small fish section is useful, if not inspiring. The major draw of Real Food is the wide range of organic produce at exorbitant prices. When it's good, it's very good and worth every penny. When it's disappointing—old perhaps—and you've paid an arm and a leg, you feel like murdering the management, but I go back because it's the only store in the northern part of the city that gives me some choice in buying organically. Early on this Real Food carried Acme bread, but to this day it arrives late and not as fresh as it should be. I may be bitchy about this market because I use it often and want it to be better, but the fact that it has much of what I like—extra-rich Clover Guernsy milk for caffè latte, organic flours, organic fresh nuts and dried fruits in bulk, fruit juices, Vitamin C in every form, hormone-free brown eggs—makes it the only store I use regularly. The problem is that everything seems overpriced.

2140 Polk Street (between Vallejo and Green), San Francisco
Tel: 673-7420
Open daily 9 a.m. to 9 p.m.

1234 Sutter Street (between Van Ness and Polk), San Francisco
Tel: 474-8488
Open weekdays 9 a.m. to 9 p.m., weekends until 8 p.m.
Credit cards: D, MC, V

1023 Stanyan Street (at Carl), San Francisco
Tel: 564-1117
Open weekdays 7

MEAT AND POULTRY

QUILICI'S MEATS
IN THE POLK & VALLEJO MARKET

2150 Polk Street (between
Vallejo and Broadway),
San Francisco
Tel: 885-1134
Weekdays 8:30 a.m. to 7
p.m., Sat until 6 p.m.,
Sun 10 a.m. to 6 p.m.
No credit cards

I go here to buy things like Quilici's unsurpassed house-made pork sausage links, seasoned with a little thyme and absolutely fresh, simple, and satisfying; and free-range chickens at less than Real Food prices. The butchers will cut and bone to your specification, grind pork and veal, and slice whatever cured or smoked meats you need for cooking. They're used to selling small amounts to the Russian Hill apartment dwellers nearby, and have patience for the pickiest requests.

REAL FOOD COMPANY

See listing, page 399.

FISH

SWAN OYSTER DEPOT

1517 Polk Street (between
Sacramento and California),
San Francisco
Tel: 673-1101
Open Monday through
Saturday 8 a.m. to 5:30 p.m.
No credit cards

This little store, half oyster bar with counter and stools, half fish market, has been the premier source for high-quality local fish for decades. I have had the most beautiful salmon from them, elegantly filleted, pristine, full of wild flavor, as well as good specimens of ling-cod, local rockfish, local halibut; the biggest, sweetest Dungeness crabs cooked, cleaned, and cracked per request; as well as some eastern items like scallops and

Swan's standby, blue point oysters. These mollusks are sweeter and milder than Pacific oysters. You can sit at the counter to eat them with an old-fashioned catsup-horseradish cocktail sauce, or take them home, but ask that they not be rinsed in water after they are opened. Regulars sit down at the counter for slabs of velvety smoked salmon on buttered bread and Swan's good, not overly thickened clam chowder. The white tile walls, resonantly worn counter, and pleasant, oceany smell draw people who like their seafood chilled, unadorned, and in large quantity.

CHEESE

LEONARD'S 2001

Leonard Born, the proprietor of this relatively new store, is serious about cheese. He likes to turn his customers on to his favorites from all over the world, and he buys a wide and interesting selection. He seduces you with tastes so you often end up buying two or three more cheeses than you planned. The one problem is that all cheeses are cut and prewrapped so you can't get the size you want, especially under a half pound, a big mistake if Leonard wants his customers to expand their cheese repertoires. You really have to think twice about buying a huge hunk when you know you will only eat a small part of it. However, prices are excellent on popular cheeses like imported Italian Fontina, Parmesan, delicious *manchego* from Spain, and high-quality French cooking cheeses.

2001 Polk Street (at Pacific), San Francisco

Tel: 921-2001

Open Monday through Saturday 9:30 a.m. to 7:30 p.m., Sunday 10 a.m. to 6 p.m.

Credit cards: MC, V

To go with the cheese, Leonard's carries Boudin and soft Bread Workshop baguettes, both excellent and refreshingly different choices, as well as the famous Bread Workshop half-baked pizza dough, a tender, thick round that bakes up crisp and golden when topped with cheese and brushed with olive oil. The large, light-filled corner store stocks grains, dried fruits, spices, and pastas in bulk and in packages, but the cheese is the draw, along with the enthusiastic service.

COOKWARE AND BOOKS

CITY DISCOUNT

2436 Polk Street (at Union), San Francisco
Tel: 771-4649
Monday through Saturday 9:30 a.m. to 6 p.m., Sunday 11 a.m. to 5 p.m.
Credit cards: AE, MC, V

You never know what you might find at this funny little cookware shop. You can depend on kitchen gadgets and utensils, but dishware, pots, pans, and ramekins shift with the tides of restaurant-supply surplus. Large platters with Chinese motifs, heavy white china in an olio of sizes, thick glasses, thin silverware—really all the things you need to set up mismatched housekeeping—can be found here at reasonable prices, especially if you grab something on special.

The Richmond District

THE RICHMOND

RESTAURANTS

ALAIN RONDELLI

French superchef Alain Rondelli is turning out some of the wittiest and most opulent food in America. With glittering French kitchen credentials and his own restaurant in Provence under his belt, he came to California, ending up at Ernie's for a short tenure. Realizing he needed full artistic control, Alain moved into the small quarters of Gerald Hirigoyen's St. Tropez when Gerald left to open Fringale. In typical, no-nonsense French style, he took everything off the walls and started cooking. And what cooking it is! Taking a cue from the seminal JoJo in New York, Rondelli's single-page menu lists the main ingredient of each dish in capital letters with a short, if intriguing, elaboration in lowercase beneath it. In fact, the printed emphasis on a single ingredient sets the parameters of the dish, in which one thing stars and the rest of the preparation serves as its enhancer. Nothing on a Rondelli plate is superfluous or out of step. He has a concept firmly in mind, and when he decides to throw in a seemingly odd flavor, it is always with a purpose and always integrated.

126 Clement Street
(between Second
and Third avenues),
San Francisco
Tel: 387-0408
Open Tuesday through
Sunday 5:30 to 10 p.m.
Price: Expensive
Credit cards: MC, V

Rondelli might offer up foie gras in the form of a sandwich, two thick rounds of sweet, velvety duck-liver terrine separated by a shimmering layer of Madeira aspic; or a stunning preparation of mussels in a soup with orange and saffron. Every night Rondelli prepares a dish to be shared, like a whole roast monkfish tail in a Provençal stew of tiny olives, peppers, tomatoes, and squashes, as well as an elegant vegetarian dish. You might not want to order something as mundane as chicken in a French restaurant, but you may have never experienced Rondelli's two-course treatment of moist breast with a crusty skin braised with bacon and carrots followed by a *confit* of thigh on a salad of romaine ribs dressed in a mint vinaigrette.

Desserts, like a version of warm chocolate cake oozing melted chocolate in the center with pecan praline on the side, or shaved cherry granita with a minted cherry salad next to it, are as creative and stunning as the preceding courses. All the carefully selected French and California wines are offered by the glass, and the honed list has been crafted to fit the menu.

In Paris you would pay $150 per person for this meal; at Rondelli in the avenues, a mere $50 per person. Through sheer work, will, and brilliance, Rondelli is creating one of the most important restaurants in the city.

The owners of China House Bistro, a *soigné*, upscale Shanghai restaurant, took some design cues from the former tenant, a corner grocery store. Joseph and Cecelia Chung ingeniously kept the antique stained-glass transoms advertising meat, poultry, and vegetables, the vintage ceiling fans, and schoolhouse lamps hanging from the high ceilings. Expansive plate-glass windows face the windswept Richmond streets, and passersby looking in can see a room sparsely furnished with bentwood chairs and linen-covered tables set with lacquered chopsticks and tall wineglasses. The stunning wall murals are reproductions of magazine covers that circulated in Shanghai during the 1930s, combining socialist realism with Art Deco style. They add to the sophisticated, international tone of the restaurant. You can imagine men in tuxedos with slicked-back hair and women in long slim dresses sipping champagne and nibbling Shanghai delicacies at this Chinese bistro.

In the muted room, vivacious owner Cecelia Chung, in a bright silk dress, holds court, explaining dishes, reminiscing about Shanghai, discussing the murals. She guides you through the relatively small menu, urging you to order her incomparable vegetarian pot stickers filled with Chinese greens and fresh herbs; or Shanghai-style smoked pomfret, a cold wine-marinated fish. Both go particularly well with warm Shaoxing rice wine, which reminds me of a full-bodied Spanish sherry.

Practically every dish at China House Bistro gets a unique interpretation, even something as commonly prepared as egg foo yung. Here it arrives as a cloud of fluffy scrambled egg whites topped with crisp pink shrimp on a bed of sautéed spinach. An elegant warm,

501 Balboa Street
(at Sixth Avenue),
San Francisco
Tel: 752-2802
Nightly 5:30 to 10:30 p.m.
Price: Moderate
Credit Cards: AE, CB, D,
MC, V

sliced-celery salad is tossed with tiny dry shrimp. Peking spareribs turn out to be shreds of boneless pork glazed with a sweet, hot red chili sauce. The texture of the pork is as dry and chewy as jerky, and the dish gets hotter and hotter, and better and better, as you eat it.

One of my favorite dishes here is a steaming clay pot called Yang-chow lion's head, a meltingly tender pork meatball studded with water chestnuts, resting on a bed of Chinese cabbage in delicious gravy. Platters of spicy, rich Chinese eggplant or garlicky spinach complete a meal with spirit. For dessert try the Yang-chow crepes, crisply fried and filled with red bean paste.

One does not go to China House Bistro with the same expectations as to a neighborhood Chinese restaurant. The prices are higher, in the moderate range, and the food comes out course by course. Be prepared to wait. Even when the restaurant is not full, dishes emerge slowly, giving guests ample time to take advantage of civilized wine service and good conversation.

WARM CELERY SALAD

20 tiny dried shrimp (purchased in bulk at the Chinese market on the corner of Stockton and Vallejo, page XX, or at any Asian grocery)

6 celery stalks cut into 3-inch-long, 1/4-inch-wide sticks

1/2 teaspoon kosher salt

2 tablespoons toasted sesame oil

Try this clean-tasting, delicious warm celery salad as a first course, or as an accompaniment for grilled fish. Adapted from Cecilia Chung's China House Bistro, it's ingenuously simple and so very good.

Soak the shrimp in hot water to cover for 1 to 2 minutes. Drain and set aside.

Add about 2 inches of water to a large skillet and bring to a boil. Blanch the celery sticks in the boiling water for 30 seconds. Drain and place in a bowl. Season with the salt and sesame oil. Add the shrimp and toss. Serve warm.

Serves 4

If you have been raised in a Jewish or Eastern European household, no food speaks to you in the same comforting tone as Russian home cooking. A hot bowl of barley soup or beet borscht with sour cream is at least as good as several visits to the therapist. Cinderella, a long-established bakery and restaurant in newly redecorated quarters, can be there for you—your Russian kitchen. It stays open throughout the day serving breakfast, lunch, and dinner without pause. The bakery shelves are stacked with soft white and dark Russian breads, crescent-shaped sugar cookie sandwiches filled with jam, and crumbly triangles with prune or poppy-seed paste in the center. If the urge for something more substantial hits you, take a seat in the small dining room next door. All the key Russian dishes as well as some American favorites like salami sandwiches are available there.

Start with the house-cured cucumber pickles and shredded pickled cabbage, to be eaten with Cinderella's bread and butter. Vegetable-thick soups, wonton-sized meat dumplings called *pelmeni*, half-moon-shaped dumplings called *vareniki*, filled with a sweetened white cheese and stuffed cabbage in a sweet-and-sour tomato sauce all prove fully satisfying. Cinderella makes its own thick, tender dumpling wrappers, although the potatoes in their various incarnations do taste processed. As in many inexpensive restaurants, you have to eat around the menu to find the gems.

436 Balboa Street (between Fifth and Sixth avenues), San Francisco

Tel: 751-9690

Open Tuesday through Saturday 9 a.m. to 9 p.m., Sunday until 7 p.m.

Price: Inexpensive

No credit cards

FOUNTAIN COURT

354 Clement Street
(at Fifth Avenue),
San Francisco
Tel: 668-1100
Open daily for lunch
11 a.m. to 3 p.m.;
dinner 5 to 10 p.m.
Price: Inexpensive
to moderate
Credit cards: AE, DC , MC, V

This Shanghai-style restaurant has a solid neighborhood following, but it really pulls everyone in for weekend dim sum. People order huge bowls of either gently sweet or lightly salty warm soy milk into which they tear bits of hot, unsweetened Chinese doughnuts. The salty version is particularly delicious, with bits of dry shrimp and pickled radish in it. Crisp, layered green onion pancakes are also eaten with the soy milk soup. With an order of thick Shanghai noodles, stir-fried with vegtables and pork, you can take the whole family out for a luscious tea lunch for well under $5 per person.

This restaurant will also prepare delicacies like braised soft-shell turtle, now available fresh in Chinatown, cooked with bamboo shoots and black mushrooms on an order-ahead basis. For less adventurous eaters, simple mu shu pork sets the standard for other versions.

Fountain Court is relatively small, clean, cheerfully decorated, and comfortable. Lots of light pours in through its large corner window, and you might spot celebrities like Amy Tan there. It's one of her favorite spots.

HONG KONG VILLA

2332 Clement Street
(between 24th and 25th
avenues), San Francisco
Tel: 752-8833
Open daily for lunch
10:30 a.m. to 2:30 p.m.;
dinner 5 to 10 p.m.

One of the newcomers to outer Clement Street, Hong Kong Villa has set itself apart for the sparkling flavor and freshness of its food and the new glow in its two dining rooms, which makes it popular with both Asian and Western diners. Although some of the dishes may not be as adventurous as the creations at some other Cantonese restaurants, Hong Kong Villa's dedication to high quality shines through. I never hesitate to go there for a vibrant seafood and vegetable meal. Currently the restaurant offers live shrimp from the tank for $12 per pound, large meaty crabs for $12 a piece, and lobsters for $20 a piece. These are great prices for pristine seafood.

The restaurant also excels at black cod dishes, velvety textured, dense, full of salubrious fish oil. Salt-baked black cod in chunks, dusted with fresh chilies and garlic or marinated and steamed in sweetened rice wine, are sublime. Whole fish steamed with ginger and green onions; crisp roast chicken; and platters of tender pea shoots stir-fried with egg white and crabmeat make up the building blocks of a stellar meal. I depend on Hong Kong Villa for its simple and beautiful Cantonese dishes and unusually helpful and gracious service. It's a valuable bread-and-butter Chinese dinner house for people who like fresh fish and vegetables.

Price: Moderate
Credit cards: MC, V

JAKARTA

This relatively new Indonesian restaurant has a more extensive menu than we've seen before in the Bay Area as well as a whimsical decor. One room has high ceilings and a tall dracaena, a tree-sized palm with many tufts and aerial roots that uncannily mirrors an Indonesian landscape hung nearby. Another room has a low acoustic ceiling with the silhouettes of Balinese shadow puppets showing through translucent tiles. The airiness of the white walls and gleaming plate glass windows is contrasted by dark burgundy carpeting, chairs, tablecloths, and batik place mats under glass. A gallery's worth of shadow puppets, masks, miniature instruments, and figurines look stunning in the simple surroundings.

Sitting down to a meal here can be a real culinary adventure. Start with *bakwan*, crunchy shrimp cakes studded with corn and bean sprouts laced with hot chilies. They are absolutely irresistible when dipped into

615 Balboa Street
(at Seventh Avenue),
San Francisco
Tel: 387-5225
Open for lunch Tuesday
through Friday 11:30 a.m. to
2:30 p.m.; dinner Tuesday
through Sunday 5 to 10 p.m.
Price: Inexpensive
Credit Cards: AE, D, MC, V

mild, fruity chutney. *Cumi cumi isi*, squid stuffed with a pâtélike mixture of seafood, then deep-fried and cut into wedges, has a hot and haunting flavor, as does *otak otak*, a ground-fish pancake cooked in a banana leaf. *Soto ayam kudus*, a heap of chicken, bean sprouts, and rice noodles in a lightly curried broth, makes for a very substantial starter. The rest of the menu is divided into grills, vegetarian plates, fried dishes, and braised dishes in spicy sauces. A selection from several categories allows you to put together your own impromptu rice table.

Here are my favorites from each menu section, starting with the classic *sate ayam*, juicy chicken satay with two sauces; and grilled rockfish cooked on a banana leaf in a hot, red chili paste. The fish's texture stays moist and velvety. The spicy, saucy dishes are knockouts, like *gulai bantut*, fork-tender oxtails in a thin, aromatic coconut-milk sauce with a background of chili. A braised dish called *gundeg*, from the Javanese city of Jogjakarta, brings chunks of beef, a whole preserved egg, chicken, and jackfruit, which tastes like turnip, in a fruity, fragrant gravy. From the fried section I recommend the spicy-hot fried chicken in chili sauce called *ayam goreng balado*. It's greaseless, batterless, and explosively seasoned. The vegetarian dishes here, like the famous *gado-gado* in peanut sauce, are lifeless and bland, however.

For dessert try *kue dada susudara*, a caramelized mound of chewy coconut on a crepe, an exotic tropical thrill, and finish with thick Indonesian coffee served with the grounds still in it.

Sachio Kojima, the sushi chef/owner of beloved Kabuto, has the demeanor of a marathon athlete, a samurai wielding knives, a cowboy who never leaves the saddle. Yet he presides over his sushi bar like a mother hen who gauges the appetites and yearnings of the brood. He lets new customers order for themselves and then gives them a few things he thinks they'd like. For regulars, Sachio creates.

One evening he started the regulars with a little salad of marinated kelp, followed by a glazed pottery bowl arranged with two slices of monkfish on a pile of pickled onions and a *shiso* leaf. Then came a beautiful composition of sashimi with a gingery dipping sauce. Sushi of *toro*, the rich stomach meat of tuna, arrived, followed by a contrastingly assertive mackerel sushi, then mild yellowtail sushi. From the kitchen emerged a red lacquered bowl with a broiled tofu dumpling, a fried potato dumpling, and a slice of seafood-stuffed squash. Then more sushi appeared, this time of sea urchin roe and of raw shrimp. A tiny pottery teapot of clear bonito stock enriched with bits of fish and vegetables refreshed the palate for a sushi of broiled freshwater eel and a final hand roll stuffed with mountain potato. The meal was a masterpiece, a progression of flavors and textures that made you appreciate every item more fully.

During your service Sachio keeps track of fifteen other diners, all of whom get different things. He makes his patrons feel like they have a private relationship with him. The sushi-bar customers get a bit of theater, just the right amount of food, and special attention. Of course the attraction of sitting in front of Sachio instead of at a table means that you might have to wait for a place. The sushi bar gets more crowded in the late evenings, turning

5116 Geary Boulevard (between 15th and 16th avenues), San Francisco
Tel: 752-5652
Open Tuesday through Saturday 5:30 p.m. to midnight, Sunday 5 to 10 p.m.
Price: Moderate
Credit cards: D, MC, V

into a hot spot around midnight when the scene gets really interesting. You might sit next to chain-smoking Japanese students, aging hippies, or characters that look like they play roles in *yakuza* sagas. What more could anyone want from a restaurant experience?

KYUNG BOK PALACE

6314 Geary Boulevard (at
27th Avenue),
San Francisco
Tel: 221-0685
Open daily for lunch
11 a.m. to 3 p.m.;
dinner 5 to 10 p.m.
Price: Inexpensive
Credit cards: MC, V

You can't complain if your short ribs are undercooked at this Korean phenom because you do the cooking yourself. You not only cook, you also gather your own ingredients from a central refrigerated counter well protected by sneeze guards. The hungry young crowd that lines up at the front door (you write your name on a yellow pad and wait until the next table opens up) pile their plates high with thinly sliced sesame-marinated pork and beef short ribs to take back to long tables outfitted with built-in lava-rock grills. Before the cooking begins, several trips need to be made to the buffet to set up your table with the myriad hot, spicy, garlicky pickles, kimchee, and salads, hot and cold, that make up Korean barbecue service. Nutty rice from a rice warmer and large curly lettuce leaves complete the picture.

Then the fun begins. You flip your meat onto the barbecue with tongs—smoke is drawn up by fans directly over each table—turn it a few times, cut it with a scissors when it's done, and wrap the pieces in the lettuce leaves with rice, pickles, and vegetables. What a divine way to eat! Hot, cold, spicy, juicy, savory, all adjusted just the way you like, a different taste sensation with each combination. The $6.99 lunch and $12.99 dinner price makes for an affordable party, and this way of eating is perfect for groups. Cold Korean beer is the drink of choice, and orange wedges from the buffet serve as the perfect conclusion.

The idea of an all-you-can-eat, do-it-yourself Korean barbecue has taken off. The kind of spicy, pickled foods that accompany it eliminates the main buffet problem, which is tired food. There are two of these barbecues already (the other is in San Jose) and I expect to see more.

LA MARMITE

A *bistro de quartier* in the Parisian sense, this friendly place fulfills all the requirements of a lovable and useful neighborhood restaurant: You can get a satisfying meal with wine for under $25 a person; the congenial owner, Armand, and his assistant will recognize your face after your first visit; and the small storefront dining room is cozy and comfortable.

Chef Guy Ligeon has a way with long-cooked French stews. His dreamy coq au vin has a dark red-wine sauce redolent of bacon, garlic, and thyme—a sauce so mellow you want to drink it with a spoon. The beautiful sauce and the wine-marinated chicken with the velvety texture of *confit* come in an earthenware crock, a *marmite*, topped with a few crescents of puff pastry. *Navarin d'agneau*, also kept hot in its own casserole, boasts the deep flavors of a traditional, slowly cooked, carefully finished French stew. The lamb melts in your mouth, as do ovals of carrots, turnips, and potato. The specials board might offer a superb osso buco, fork-tender veal shanks infused with flavor, served with thick house-made noodles and crisp broccoli.

Hearty main courses like these call for the right starter. La Marmite rises to the occasion with crudités: raw-vegetable salads. One of the best brings crisp julienned carrots and celery root topped with three thin, *merguez*-like beef sausages aromatic with garlic, cumin, and cayenne. Another interesting starter tops a green salad

2415 Clement Street
(at 25th Avenue),
San Francisco
Tel: 666-3781
Open Monday through
Saturday 5:30 to 10 p.m.
Price: Moderate
Credit cards: AE, MC, V

with a large slice of grilled duck sausage. A cup of satiny pureed vegetable soup has a bright, distinctive flavor.

Many of La Marmite's dishes remind me of classic Julia Child fare, which means they have appeared on French menus in America for the last twenty-five years. Most typical is *suprême de volaille*, a chicken breast in a reduced champagne cream sauce with sliced mushrooms, a rich preparation that continues to please. But the great dishes are those stews. Have Armand open one of his specially chosen French bottles from lesser-known regions, like a mildly spicy Côte du Rhône called Château des Adouzes, have a little salad, some coq au vin, and you will leave La Marmite well fed and happy. It is no coincidence that La Marmite celebrates the earthenware casserole in its name and Parisian life in its decor (a charming mural along one whole wall of the restaurant). When you slide into a banquette here, the happiest aspects of French civilization take over.

LAGHI

1801 Clement Street
(at 19th Avenue),
San Francisco
Tel: 386-6266
Open Tuesday through
Sunday 5 to 10 p.m.
Price: Moderate
Credit cards: AE, DC , MC, V

Gino Laghi and his cooks run the Laghi kitchen as if *they* were having the party. The enthusiasm and love of cooking of this chef and his chef/waitress/wife transfer right into the food, which happens to be as good as it can get in San Francisco when you want an authentic Italian meal. Each evening the small typewritten menu changes, offering a handful of intriguing possibilities.

There might be a warm salad of radicchio and endive scattered with crisp bits of Laghi's house-cured pancetta; or a simple green salad in one of the tastiest balsamic vinaigrettes in town; or house-cured prosciutto with sweet, ripe winter pears. A ramekin of baked lasagne features tender homemade noodles, a crumbly meat sauce,

and old-fashioned bécha-mel, all delicately layered. I still dream about a risotto with red wine and fresh black truffles Gino offered one night. At Laghi I want to settle in for a complete Italian meal: an *antipasti*, a pasta, and then a main course like perfectly grilled loin lamb chops dressed with garlic, olive oil, and herbs, served with bread-crumb-topped roasted eggplant and tomato. When the lamb chops or any meat dish comes out of Laghi's kitchen it is consummately Italian.

An imaginative, affordably priced Italian wine list offering almost everything by the glass as well as the bot-tle complements this cohesive dining experience. You eat and drink at Laghi exactly the same way you would at a small trattoria in Italy. The highest-quality raw ingre-dients and traditional, simple preparation give the dishes their beautiful depth and complexity. I love eating this way, and Laghi is one of the handful of restaurants in town that enables you to do so. The rewards for all the integrity and work it takes to keep a small personal place going at this high level must be mostly spiritual. For this good-natured dedication, the Laghis deserve a special kind of culinary sainthood.

6255 Geary Boulevard
(at 27th Avenue),
San Francisco
Tel: 387-8338
Open for lunch Monday
through Friday 11 a.m. to
2:30 p.m., Saturday and
Sunday 10 a.m. to 2:30 p.m.;
dinner nightly 5 to 9:30 p.m.
Price: Inexpensive
to moderate
Credit cards: MC, V;
$20 minimum

The Mayflower, a low-key, one-room family-style Cantonese restaurant, was opened by some ex–San Francisco Flower Lounge employees. It stands out from the pack because of its high standard of food and service. Their earthy clay pot and simple seafood dishes shine. Although parts of the menu read exactly like the one at nearby Flower Lounge, the execution is different. On the more complicated dishes, such as deep-fried sole with deep-fried bones, the kitchen can falter. The successes here come with family fare, like the freshest, crisp-skinned, succulent roast chicken; plates of sparkling fresh vegetables of the day; salt-baked shrimp in their shells or the signature shelled "crystal" shrimp; and the rich double chicken broth that usually comes as soup of the day. Both eggplant with hot sauce in a clay pot and thinly sliced beef short ribs with lots of black pepper explode with flavor. Small 1 ½ pound steamed rockfish are unsurpassed anywhere in the city, and the crabs seem more pristine and sweeter than any others in town.

Of course the place is mobbed and very noisy at 6 p.m., slowing down a bit by 8 p.m. on weeknights, the best time to go. General manager Vincent Chan's effusive personality draws regulars, and helpful service has always been a high point here once you get a seat. The waiters know the menu and make good suggestions, although regulars know to consult the one-page specials menu for such delicacies as salt-baked oysters or velvety textured squab in soy sauce with tender greens.

If you find explosive Asian flavors and exotic tropical ingredients seductive, you must eat at Straits Cafe, a charming Singaporean restaurant operated by chef Chris Yeo. His peculiar Nonya cooking (a cross-ethnic style developed in Singapore) will sweep you off your feet. Yeo keeps the hot, sweet, sour, gingery, garlicky, perfumey, fermented riot of flavors in each preparation under strict control. Working with an intense palette in which balance is everything, he creates a quintessential tropical-crossroads cuisine: a unique mix of Malaysian, Chinese, Indian, and Burmese influences.

You may think you recognize some of the dishes on the menu, but even the most familiar will surprise you. Satays, skewers of juicy beef, are fragrant with layers of flavor from wet and dry *masalas* of spices and herbs. The unique peanut sauce served with them has its own spicing that somehow fits into the larger picture like a jigsaw puzzle. The presentation with chunks of cooling cucumber is simple and beautiful. An appetizer called *murtabak*, an Indian-style flat bread filled with minced beef, comes with a luscious coconut milk–curry dipping sauce and a pile of pickled red onions, a must-order dish. Spring rolls turn out to be a room-temperature crepe stuffed with slivered vegetables and pungent dried shrimp, each section topped with its own dab of plum sauce and a perfect cilantro leaf.

Angel hair noodles get an exquisite, if pungent, treatment in a hot and sour tamarind broth, topped with hard-cooked eggs and tender pink shrimp. Dark green long beans stay crisp, stir-fried with hot chilies, dried shrimp, and minced pork. How good this dish tastes with aromatic jasmine rice! A mild, creamy

3300 Geary Boulevard (at Parker), San Francisco
Tel: 668-1783
Open Monday through Friday 11:30 a.m. to 10 p.m., Saturday and Sunday until 11 p.m.
Price: Moderate
Credit cards: AE, MC, V

coconut milk–based chicken curry, in which the chicken retains its character, will please everyone. Although the desserts sound completely odd, they too are surprisingly delicious. One of my favorites, sago pudding, is a custard of large pearl tapioca in a heavenly palm sugar syrup.

Even the look of the restaurant conjures up tropical romance. The interior resembles a Singaporean street with columns transformed into palms, faux windows with wooden shutters and balconies high up on one wall, an internal sheet-metal roof, and wainscoting, ceiling fans, slatted doors, and vents. Straits Cafe does remind you of the all-night street food stalls of Singapore, but it also offers such Raffles Hotel fillips as Singapore slings and gin and tonics, along with vanilla bean sodas, sweetened iced tea, and coffee, wines, and beer. In every respect, Straits Cafe promises exotic fun and adventure at the foot of San Francisco's avenues.

TAIWAN

445 Clement Street (at Sixth Avenue), San Francisco
Tel: 387-1789
Monday through Thursday 11 a.m. to 10 p.m., Friday until midnight, Saturday 10 a.m. to midnight, Sunday 10 a.m. to 10 p.m.
Price: Inexpensive
Credit cards: AE, MC, V; $15 minimum

This small cafe specializes in superb dumplings and noodles and a wide range of spicy northern Chinese and Shanghai dishes. It's one of my favorite restaurants of any nationality. Once I started eating there I couldn't stop. I had to return every day to taste a few more things. The compact noodle and dumpling kitchen situated right in the front window lets you know how fresh these items are. Behind, a rosy little dining room with a skylight gets constant turnover. People come here for a bite or a full meal all day.

Start with hot-and-sour soup, bright, clean, and bracing. Then choose a *mu shi* dish, a stir fry of julienned vegetables, egg, and sparkling shrimp that you pile onto thin white pancakes. Smear them with bean sauce.

I can't eat at Taiwan without having at least one plate of gingery, pork-filled boiled dumplings (you get ten to an order) or shrimp, leek, and pork boiled dumplings, which have a lovely wild onion edge, or steamed vegetarian dumplings with that slightly grassy herbal flavor lovers of greens adore.

The noodles are also superb. Try the thick, chewy Shanghai noodles tossed with vegetables and slivers of pork; or the stunning mustard green and pork noodles bathed in a smoky broth. In braised beef "ligamen" noodles, gelatinous cuts of brisket add texture and buttery flavor to a beef broth.

Lest you think that you have to stick to noodles, try the luscious crispy chicken, a burnished bird with velvety meat in a rich brown sauce—great with a plate of perfectly cooked young bok choy. Unctuous red-cooked eggplant is sublime over rice, as are the addictively tasty dry-braised Chinese long beans.

Thirty years ago the island of Taiwan inherited uprooted northern chefs from Shanghai, Beijing, Hunan, Sichuan, and Shandong provinces, while many of the Cantonese master chefs immigrated to Hong Kong. Reflecting the northern influence on Taiwanese cooking, a special menu offers soulful cold-weather dishes with lots of tripe, pickled greens, and fish paste for the adventurous.

On top of all the exciting cooking, the obliging waiters will pace your meal so you don't get all your dishes at once. What's hard to believe is that these sensuous, spicy, well-served meals cost under $10 a person.

3148 Geary Boulevard (at
Spruce), San Francisco
Tel: 752-4440
Open daily 11 a.m. to 10 p.m.
Price: Inexpensive
Credit cards: MC, V

This Ton Kiang in the Inner Richmond serves as an all-day Chinese cafe frequented by a wide spectrum of San Franciscans ranging from cab drivers to nearby Pacific Heights families. Everyone comes to this friendly place for Hakka specialties like skinless salt-baked chicken served with two fabulous dipping sauces and flavorful clear chicken broth with Hakka-style beef or fish balls and emerald leaves of spinach.

The Hakka people immigrated to Canton province several hundred years ago from northern China, retaining their own dialect, costume, and cuisine. Hence the chefs at Ton Kiang cook not only Hakka dishes but Cantonese and some northern Chinese dishes as well. The most characteristic are dark and dusky stews of pork or beef, full of dried and fermented ingredients—the soul food of China. Order one of these rich dishes to share, perhaps Hakka home-style braised pork cooked in a clay pot with tofu and lily stems; or bacon with dried mustard greens, big slabs of soft, fresh bacon in a slightly sweet gravy. Another of my favorites is tofu stuffed with ground pork braised in Hakka wine sauce with julienned vegetables. These items can be found on the one-page list of Hakka specialties on the front cover of the huge menu.

The restaurant is divided into two brightly lit dining rooms. At lunch the Formica tables are uncovered; at dinner Ton Kiang pulls out the tablecloths. The classic meal at either lunch or dinner includes the aforementioned salt-baked chicken, one rich Hakka clay pot dish, either fish ball or a terrific wonton soup made with the restaurant's signature broth, and a plate of very simple, always sparkling fresh vegetables like baby bok choy, young spinach, or Chinese broccoli. Steamed with a little stock, garlic, and oil, the vegetables are always refreshing and beautiful, a high point of the meal.

TON KIANG

This new, two-story branch of Ton Kiang excels at dim sum, the freshest in town. At the bigger houses you never know how many rounds the dumplings have made before the carts pull up to your table. At small Ton Kiang, the dim sum arrive hot from the kitchen and the variety is astounding. You cannot eat fast enough to keep up with the stream of new temptations.

What surprises me is the quality of it all. Clean, lean, bright, fresh, Ton Kiang's dim sum taste homemade. Different delicate noodle-wrapped dumplings are filled with a stunning combination of scallops and shrimp or shrimp and pork or just very fresh, sweet shrimp, a sign of well-made dim sum. Look for deep-fried taro croquettes, the outside coated with crackling shredded taro threads, the inside filled with soft, creamy, mashed taro. The Shanghai-style dumplings, filled with pork and Chinese chives, are wrapped in thinly rolled raw bread dough. They are fried on one side and then steamed to create a taste sensation. The miniature egg custards have shimmering fillings and warm, flaky crusts. For a change, try a plate of miniature doughnuts, soft and chewy with a rich egg-custard filling.

The first-floor dining room has more amenities than the incredibly low prices of its food would warrant. Painted pale rose with Chinese landscapes on the walls and patterned carpeting, the room comfortably seats parties of four at blond-wood booths and larger groups in the center of the room at round tables. This branch of Ton Kiang is going for a more upscale Hong Kong crowd than the bustling cafe on Spruce.

5821 Geary Boulevard (at 22nd Avenue), San Francisco
Tel: 387-8273
Open Monday through Thursday 10:30 a.m. to 10 p.m., Friday until 10:30 p.m., Saturday, Sunday, and holidays 10 a.m. to 10:30 p.m.
Price: Inexpensive
Credit cards: MC, V

CAFES

LITTLE RUSSIA

5217 Geary Boulevard
(between 16th and 17th
avenues), San Francisco
Tel: 751-9661
Open daily 11 a.m. to 11
p.m.; live music 6 p.m.
Credit cards: MC, V

A wonderful Russian deli called Acropolis used to be at this address, so I was disappointed to find the deli case gone and the strangely austere dining room of Little Russia instead. I was so hungry for *pelmeni* that I sat right down in the new place anyway. Glass-covered tables with pink tablecloths rimmed an expanse of linoleum floor probably used for dancing, if the microphone in the corner was any indication. A steady flow of customers, some older in babushkas, some young, male, and hungry, filtered in and out all afternoon. This place, barren looking though it was, reminded me of the little cooperative restaurants I had visited in Russia: lots of tea drinking, smoking, and sipping of Stolichnaya, with the food, of course.

Though the *pelmeni* may very well have been wrapped in wonton skins, the fact is that Little Russia's plump, pork-filled dumplings served with rich sour cream and snipped dill were tasty. So were the half-moon-shaped *vareniki*, the wonton skins filled with cheese, sautéed, and topped with caramelized onions and mushrooms. A plate of house-cured pickles, cabbage, and red peppers (which were fermented on one occasion) or a bowl of cabbage borscht in a tomatoey broth loaded with vegetables, sour cream, and fresh snipped dill serves as a classic starter.

The young Russian waitresses are many times nicer than their counterparts in Russia. One inexcusable lapse is in the bread basket, however, which is full of presliced air bread, both white and dark. Even during the bleakest of times, good, heavy brown bread has been a highlight of Russian cuisine. Luckily, you can buy some good rye across the street at House of Bagels and smuggle it in.

SAM AND HENRY'S COOL BEANS

Painted blue like the summer sky, this miniscule coffeehouse has but four or five stools and a counter, with a tiny table and a bench outside next to a metal newspaper rack with the local sheets and the daily *New York Times.* The two owners, Sam and Henry, make absolutely exquisite coffee: intense, rich, aromatic without any bitterness, on a par with what you get in Italy. One major problem is that the cafe uses paper unless you beg, the way I did, for an espresso in a ceramic cup. Sam gave it to me in one with a twist of lemon. I will never forget the flavor of that coffee. From then on I brought my own glass or cup, well worth the trouble when the coffee is so good.

4342A California Street (at Sixth Avenue),
San Francisco
Tel: 750-1955
Open daily 7 a.m. to 7 p.m.
No credit cards

The Cool Beans guys know practically everyone who hangs out in their shop, and most of the patrons seem to know each other. Laid-back reggae seems to be the sound of choice, a background for talk and reading. People also buy their coffee beans here and pluck cookies from jars to munch. A funny assortment of photographs and jars of wrapped candy constitutes the decor along with the whimsical paint job. Everyone who steps into Sam and Henry's knows that something special is happening here. If you love coffee, get over there and see for yourself.

BARS

PAT O'SHEA'S MAD HATTER

3848 Geary Boulevard (at Third Avenue), San Francisco
Tel: 752-3148
Open Monday through Friday 11 a.m. to 2 a.m., weekends 10 a.m. to 2 a.m.
Credit cards: D, MC, V

This rollicking neighborhood sports bar was catapulted to culinary fame when Nancy Oakes started cooking lunch here. No self-respecting, beer-guzzling football fan could believe he was eating and loving the likes of stuffed quail, grilled veal sweetbreads, and roasted monkfish with mussels, but Oakes put it out for the price of barroom hamburgers. Later on she opened L'Avenue in a tiny and charming spot next door. Most recently she launched the multimillion-dollar Boulevard with super-designer Pat Kuleto, and Pat O'Shea's food service floundered. Now, an apprentice of Oakes's has taken over the bar's kitchen and the food is back to being its imaginative best. And it's still a great bar, with many easily visible televisions mounted on the walls, new pool tables, and pints of draft beer for low prices.

DELICATESSENS/TAKE-OUT

One of the few Jewish delis in the city, Shenson's does much more take-out business than serving on the premises, perhaps because this well-established operation used to be across the street in smaller quarters. Shenson's does a good job preparing many Jewish specialties, like relatively light, well-seasoned gefilte fish; dense, sweet-flavored chopped liver; and house-pickled green tomatoes. The fat garlic sausages are absolutely delicious, better than the pedestrian skinny hot dogs. Items like satiny smoked sablefish and pickled herring are fresh and tasty. The corned beef and pastrami are as good as you can get in the city. Some patrons eat at one of the eight or so tables in front of the counter in a carpeted dining area decorated with shelves of matzoh and other packaged products, but no crusty waitresses take your order. You pick up the food yourself at the counter. While this is no Carnegie Deli, Shenson's does take care of the needs of San Franciscans who crave a nice piece of smoked fish.

5120 Geary Boulevard (at 15th Avenue), San Francisco
Tel: 751-4699
Open daily 8 a.m. to 5:45 p.m.
Credit cards: MC, V

TIP TOE INN

This funny, whimsically decorated Russian delicatessen looks like a fairytale castle from the outside and, true to form, has a dour woman in a uniform behind the counter. A range of Russian specialties is available, some of the best being house-cured pickles, pork-and-rice-stuffed cabbage rolls in a buttery tomato sauce, and thin blintzes coated in bread crumbs with a sweet cheese stuffing, which reheat in the oven quite well. Russian

5423 Geary Boulevard (between 18th and 19th avenues), San Francisco
Tel: 221-6422
Open Monday through Saturday 9 a.m. to 7 p.m.
No credit cards

savory pastries take up a large section of the counter, particularly sheet pans of baked *pirog*, two layers of yeasty egg dough filled with meat, cabbage, or potato, cut into squares, and sold by the pound.

BAKERIES/PASTRIES

CINDERELLA

See Restaurants, page 409.

HOUSE OF BAGELS

5030 Geary Boulevard (between 14th and 15th avenues), San Francisco
Tel: 752-6000
Open daily 6 a.m. to 5:30 p.m.
No credit cards

Bagel lovers from all over the city converge on this Jewish bakery for authentic, chewy, substantial bagels. I love them. The onion bagels are not coated with burned bits but rather a scattering of sweetly caramelized onion. The sesame bagel is judiciously sprinkled with the perfume of the Middle East. When you buy the bagels at the bakery they are always fresh, which allows a texturally correct bagel to be chewable. The difference between a House of Bagels bagel and Noah's bagels, which seem to be taking over the city, is one of style. Noah's bagels are soft, crumbly, and easy to chew: the Wonder Bread of bagels. They do make for easy-to-eat bagel sandwiches, but bagel sandwiches are preparations with no basis in tradition (as are croissant sandwiches). Anyone even a little bit Jewish knows that you eat bagels open-face, spread with cream cheese and perhaps lox. If you covered the cream cheese with another half bagel you really couldn't bite through it.

House of Bagels also makes an old-fashioned rye bread, a bit soft but full of flavor. The rye with seeds is laced with too many assertive caraway seeds; the plain rye is better. Other Jewish baked goods are available, like corn rye and sweet rolls, but the bagel reigns supreme at this house.

SCHUBERT'S

Among the mousse-cake set, Schubert's has been a hangout since 1911, but I like the old-fashioned coffee cakes, particularly a walnut–sour cream ring that tastes gloriously of sour cream. It is lighter and less sweet than most others of its ilk but full of honest flavor, just like the simple sugar cookies. The bakery also carries luxurious Joseph Schmidt truffles (see Upper Market Street listings).

521 Clement Street (between Sixth and Seventh avenues), San Francisco
Tel: 752-1580
Open Monday through Friday 7 a.m. to 6 p.m., Saturday until 5:30 p.m.
No credit cards

ICE CREAM/CHOCOLATES

GELATO CLASSICO

750 Clement Street (at Ninth Avenue),

San Francisco

Tel: 751-1522

Open Monday through Friday 11 a.m. to 9 p.m.,

Saturday 10 a.m. to 11 p.m., Sunday 10 a.m. to 10 p.m.

No credit cards

See listing, page 325.

JOE'S ICE CREAM

5351 Geary Boulevard
(at 18th Avenue),
San Francisco
Tel: 751-1950
Open Sunday through
Thursday 11 a.m. to 10 p.m.,
Friday and Saturday until
11 p.m.
No credit cards

The home of the It's It, a chocolate-encased ice cream sandwich made with two oatmeal cookies, Joe's charms by staying so old-fashioned. All the ice cream is made on the premises and scooped to order. The wonderful milk shakes are constructed with a lot of ice cream, and blended with enough milk to make them drinkable. The young counterpeople couldn't be sweeter or more meticulous, and the place looks timeless and well used. There is a small sit-down counter with stools where you can get grilled sandwiches and fountain items, and a ledge with short stools in the window provides just the place to sip a shake and watch the activity at the Alexandria Theater across the street. Joe's also sells frozen chocolate-covered bananas, another old-fashioned classic. The only concession to modern trends comes in the form of Bud's frozen yogurt.

For other locations see pages 119, 172, 396.

Everyone in San Francisco knows about See's peerless peanut brittle: crunchy, buttery, and liberally studded with fresh peanuts. You find yourself nibbling one piece after another until you're a quarter pound into a box. The brittle is as beloved and symbolic of San Francisco as Dungeness crab and sourdough bread, and it travels a lot better. Hence the convenient stands at the San Francisco airport. The company was started by the See family in Los Angeles in 1921, and expanded to San Francisco in 1934.

Many treats present themselves in long glass cases in See's immaculate, white-tiled candy shops. The thrill of putting together a box of your favorites piece by piece— dark- and light-chocolate-covered nuts, turtles, the fabulous milk chocolate–covered English toffee rolled in chopped almonds (you can tell I'm a nuts and chews gal)—ranks with a walk across the Golden Gate Bridge on a sunny day. See's makes solid, middle-of-the-road, moderately priced, American-style chocolates of the highest order. Their candy is always fresh, and with every purchase, large or small, the buxom ladies in their white uniforms hand you a free chocolate.

754 Clement Street (at Eighth Avenue), San Francisco Tel: 752-0953 Open Monday through Friday 10 a.m. to 6 p.m., Saturday until 5 p.m. No credit cards

MARKETS

BANGKOK GROCERY

3236 Geary Boulevard
(at Parker), San Francisco
Tel: 221-5863
Open Monday through
Saturday 10 a.m. to 5 p.m.
No credit cards

This small grocery dedicated to Thai ingredients has ten-pound sacks of nutty, aromatic jasmine rice for $6 and small covered baskets for serving Thai sticky rice. At the counter are freshly made, albeit packaged, Thai snacks like chewy sago balls stuffed with savory sweet pork on a bed of lettuce leaves, whole chilies, and cilantro. They make a fine lunch to eat on the run.

HAIG'S DELICACIES

642 Clement Street
(between Seventh and
Eighth avenues),
San Francisco
Tel: 752-6283
Open Monday through
Friday 9:30 a.m. to 6:30 p.m.,
Saturday 9 a.m. to 6 p.m.
Credit cards: MC, V

One of the oldest international food shops in the city, Haig's shelves are packed with jars and cans of exotic products from all over the globe. Patak brand Indian curry pastes, Indonesian ingredients, Middle Eastern and Armenian prepared foods, coffees, teas, Louisiana hot sauces, candy, spices—any sort of packaged food necessary to prepare a mind-boggling variety of ethnic dishes can be found here. The problem for Haig's is that many of these items now appear in stores either dedicated to one cuisine, like Indian markets, or in large Asian supermarkets. The ethnic population has caught up with Haig's and opened their own specialized shops. It's wonderful to have a Haig's in the neighborhood, but serious shoppers need produce and other fresh ingredients. If the *kecap manis* (Indonesian soy sauce) is on the shelves of their vegetable market, they will buy it there.

Not nearly as exciting or large as the May Wah on Irving Street in the Sunset, this branch still covers most Asian cooking needs. Some meat, fish, and poultry has been frozen and sits defrosting in the refrigerated cases—a common sight on Clement Street—but much is fresh. You have to be observant. Such delicacies as live soft-shell turtles and live frogs are sold here. You can find fine produce like big bunches of very fresh watercress, plump mangoes, and young ginger, while other produce will be wilted. For Clement Street, New May Wah is as large and complete as any Asian grocery.

547 Clement Street
(between Sixth and
Seventh avenues),
San Francisco
Tel: 668-2583
Open daily 7 a.m. to 8 p.m.
Credit Cards: MC, V

PRODUCE

CLEMENT PRODUCE

This long, narrow, bustling produce store does not carry unusual produce, but the prices are cheap. Sometimes there are piles of desirable things like blood oranges or Fuji apples that are especially inexpensive. Clement Produce is but one of many serviceable produce stores within five blocks or so on lower Clement. Each one might display one or two special items—mangoes, some good-looking pea shoots—at an excellent price to tempt people into the store, so on a serious shopping trip you might want to give them all a quick visit to grab the best things.

645 Clement Street
(between Seventh and
Eighth avenues),
San Francisco
Tel: 221-4104
Open daily 7 a.m. to 8 p.m.
No credit cards

VILLAGE MARKET

4555 California Street
(at Eighth Avenue),
San Francisco
Tel: 221-0445
Open daily 9 a.m. to
7:30 p.m.
Credit cards: MC, V

This market deserves a trip across town. It has one of the prettiest, most inviting organic produce sections in the city. In front under an awning, wooden shelves of fruit and buckets of the most luscious flowers—in April, daffodils, tulips, and ranunculuses at excellent prices—make you want to fill your arms with them. Indoors, the old wooden floors are stacked with casually arranged displays of organic strawberries, white asparagus, organic bananas, spring greens, and del Cabo tomatoes (organically grown tomatoes from Baja California to get you through most of the winter). Other items of interest include organic jarred baby food, the excellent and hard-to-find sharp New York Cheddar from the Marin Cheese Company, Semifreddi breads, and all sorts of organic dried beans in burlap sacks. Only a couple of years old, the Village Market combines a commitment to healthful and organic foods with an aesthetic that makes you want to join up. Two wooden benches with cast-iron legs have

been placed outside the store between large wooden flower boxes, and you are tempted to plop down and admire the beauty and color of nature's gifts, so appealingly offered. Not overly arranged or boutiquey, the Village Market helps you discover what you really want to eat.

MEAT AND POULTRY

NEW ON SANG
AND SAN FRANCISCO CHICKEN

One address, but two operations in this Richmond District headquarters for chicken. In the New On Sang side you can get Chinese-style butchered chickens with head and feet, and partridges, pheasants, and ducks with all appendages attached. Nothing enriches a chicken stock more than gelatinous chicken feet. Duck wings and feet by the pound are also available. You find this impeccable poultry past the Chinese deli counter with hanging roast ducks and premade dishes kept warm on steam tables. A branch of the bustling On Sang Poultry Company on Stockton Street in Chinatown, New On Sang's raw birds can induce real culinary excitement if you're a cook.

Across the aisle from New On Sang, an Italian-style wood-fired rotisserie slowly turns behind a counter that demarcates the San Francisco Chicken shop. The chickens on the rotisserie have been marinated in lemon juice and rosemary, and though a bit over-cooked, especially if they have been kept warm in a heated drawer, they do stay moist and boast a flavorful golden skin. They make for wholesome take-home meals.

**617 Clement Street
(at Seventh Avenue),
San Francisco
Tel: 752-4100
Market open daily 9 a.m. to
6:30 p.m.; rotisserie open
daily 11 a.m. to 9 p.m.
No credit cards**

FISH

SEAFOOD CENTER

**831 Clement Street
(between Ninth and
Tenth avenues),
San Francisco
Tel: 752-3496
Open Monday through
Saturday 9 a.m. to 6 p.m.,
Sunday until 5:30 p.m.
No credit cards**

This fresh-smelling Chinese fish store features fillets of local snapper and petrale, whole sand dabs, rockfish, and pomfret, a small silvery fish that bakes and barbecues well. I have spotted skate wing, live sea bass, carp, catfish, crab, and lobsters. The beauty of whole flatfish, like sand dabs or rex sole, is that they cook quickly in the oven. Here's how. Preheat the oven to 400°F. Sprinkle the whole fish with chopped shallots, salt, pepper, a little white wine, and some olive oil or butter. Cook for about 5 minutes, depending on the thickness of the fish. You can test for doneness by sticking a knife in to the bone. If the fish is ready, the delicate meat will easily lift off, and you will have a delicious main course in no time at all.

CHEESE

SIXTH AVENUE CHEESE SHOP

A tiny shop filled with cheese, charcuterie, cold imported beer and ale, bottles of wine, and a small selection of necessary groceries like Sasso extra-virgin olive oil, French brown-sugar cubes, and fresh Semifreddi baguettes is always a welcome addition to a neighborhood. Being able to taste the cheese and get the size you want cut to order remains a civilized amenity. A few tiny tables covered in cheerful yellow-print oilcloth beckon those who want to eat their bread and cheese or a made-to-order sandwich on the spot with a bottle of wine plucked off the shelves.

311 Sixth Avenue (between Geary and Clement), San Francisco
Tel: 387-1436
Open Monday through Friday 10 a.m. to 6:30 p.m., Saturday until 5 p.m., Sunday 11 a.m. to 5 p.m.
Credit cards: MC, V

COOKWARE AND BOOKS

GREEN APPLE BOOKS

In the heart of the best food shopping section of Clement Street, Green Apple Books holds down the food literature front with one of the largest collections of new and used cookbooks in the city. Shelves and shelves of practically new volumes marked down to half price, plus many rarities (like Doris Muscatine's guide to San Francisco restaurants with recipes, published thirty years ago, a book many of us cut our culinary teeth on), make it difficult to leave the store without an armful of books. By thumbing through some of the treasures, such as a

506 Clement Street (at Sixth Avenue), San Francisco
Tel: 387-2272
Open Sunday through Thursday 10 a.m. to 10 p.m., Friday and Saturday until midnight
Credit cards: MC, V

yellowing volume called *Southern Cooking* by Mrs. S. R. Dull, a 1928 edition for $10, you might find a recipe for orange juice ("cut oranges in half . . .") or Foolish Pie. More-current works by the best food writers, including Betty Fussel's evocatively photographed *I Hear America Cooking* ($12) and Paul Prudhomme's volumes (which always stay current if you like rich, spicy food), are well represented, which indicates that the store's cookbook buyers know what they're doing.

KAMEI HOUSEHOLD WARES

606 Clement Street
(at Seventh Avenue),
San Francisco
Tel: 666-3688
Open daily 9 a.m. to 7 p.m.
Credit cards: MC, V

Some stunning china for both serving and setting the table can be purchased for a song at the many Asian cookware stores in the city. At Kamei, Clement Street's entry, one finds Japanese bowls with intricate, speckled glazes, Chinese bowls in gorgeous shades of jade green, and all sorts of plates and platters in useful shapes and sizes. Heavy stone mortars and pestles at a fraction of the cost at tony houseware stores, and hard-to-find coconut graters, in both stool and portable configurations (the latter for all of $1.50), can be gleaned from the piled-high shelves. There might be seven-gallon calibrated plastic food containers with covers for home pickling, woks large and small, bamboo steamers, and a whole section of hanging car deodorizers, which lends Kamei the authentic aroma of Hong Kong.

South of Market
& Third Street

SOUTH OF MARKET & THIRD STREET

RESTAURANTS

BISTRO M, IN THE HOTEL MILANO

Los Angeles chef Michel Richard, of Citrus fame, is the creative force behind this major 180-seat restaurant adjacent to a stylish new hotel in a pioneering location on Fifth Street, near Mission (next door to Nordstrom). This is a serious, upscale effort. No expense has been spared on decorating the large, modern space with beautiful Kandinsky-esque light fixtures, heavy wooden Limn-style chairs, and a gigantic wall mural that runs along the windowed front depicting scenes of San Francisco. The room is more comfortable and luxurious than Stars and Postrio, and you really feel you are having a "restaurant experience" when you eat here, albeit a stylish, modern, Southern California one, yet Bistro M's prices are nonetheless lower.

Though much hoopla was made about the food being casual and bistroish, in fact it falls into the more elegant if iconoclastic side of classic French cooking. Richard started out as a pastry chef, and his dishes all have a finished and rather elaborate presentation, whether they call for it or not. A classic French salad of tiny *haricots*

55 Fifth Street (between
Mission and Market),
San Francisco
Tel: 543-5554
Open daily for lunch noon to
2:30 p.m.; dinner 5:30 to
9:45 p.m.
Price: Expensive
Credit cards: AE, D, MC, V

verts in mustardy vinaigrette was absolutely complete and wonderful by itself, without being tented with many slabs of cold smoked duck breast. While a *rillette* of sardines tasted too much of the can, a bowl of thumbnail-sized ravioli filled with cheese in a vinegary tomato *jus* was fun to eat, whimsical, and inventive. A delicious thin slice of New York steak in a deeply flavored red wine sauce served with an irresistible potato gratin rang a classic note. I'd come back to eat that dish any day. And I was much taken by a savory oxtail ragout somehow stuck in the middle of a slice of molded macaroni, surrounded by a wreath of baby vegetables. What a delicious plate! How did he get that macaroni and oxtail stew to form a terrine? Richard is nothing if not a technician.

The desserts are lovely and original, like one described as a *vacherin*, which turned out to be a mound of intense raspberry sorbet completely covered with piped whipped cream into which was stuck sticks of meringue, porcupine fashion. The cookies are thin and buttery; the passion fruit sorbet captures the very essence of the tropical fruit. The one disappointment was the cheese from Chantal Plasse, who imports from Androuet and other exclusive French cheese stores. These weren't ripe enough and the selection was unbalanced, but I'm returning to give them another try. A restaurant gets special credit for mounting a cheese service!

A pricy, if complete, wine list, with several fine wines and champagnes poured by the glass, thoroughly professional service, and Richard's creative cooking grounded in classic French technique make Bistro M the latest competitor with our busiest upscale dinner houses.

This small, terrific bistro boasts an unusually creative menu of Mediterranean-inspired dishes and a smart, resonant decor. The chef, Loretta Keller, a Stars veteran, and her husband Joseph Graham have put together a model restaurant and bar for the nineties: small, manageable, visually uncluttered, culinarily sophisticated, yet moderate in price. Bizou works because it is a unified statement, a completely realized vision, anchored in a European tradition but free enough to draw on the New World eclecticism of California.

The menu derives its energy from a wood-burning oven in which all sorts of surprising things are cooked, like sand dabs, our wonderful local flatfish served on the bone, or a ramekin of rich rigatoni baked with pancetta, ricotta, and tomato. Addictive thin-crusted pizzas emerge from the oven, topped perhaps with bitter broccoli rabe, smoky wood-roasted onions, and thin slices of pancetta. My favorite dishes here mine the French country repertoire, but imbue them with current style. *Chou farci* comes as a wedge of a round cake made of layers of Savoy cabbage, thinly sliced ham, and sliced apples in a sauce of crème fraîche enriched with the cooking juices. Keller's ethereal *brandade* of salt cod is one of the best versions to be found anywhere. The pastas tend to be untraditional, like chewy fresh pappardelle moistened with a hot, spicy tomato broth, onions cooked in the wood-fired oven, eggplant, and assertive feta. They work because the kitchen understands how to balance a dish of disparate ingredients, making a reason for them to come together.

True to form, the concise one-page wine list is culled from many small importers and introduces interesting

598 Fourth Street (at Brannan), San Francisco
Tel: 543-2222
Open for lunch Monday through Friday 11:30 a.m. to 2:30 p.m.; dinner Monday through Thursday 5:30 to 10 p.m., Friday and Saturday until 10:30 p.m.
Price: Moderate
Credit cards: AE, MC, V

bottles from lesser-known wine-growing regions of France and Italy. Cocktails are also available, and it is fun to have them at a small, handsome bar at the front of the restaurant with a signature Bizou flat bread, crisp and paper-thin, studded with olives, onions, and cheese.

Small white-linen-covered tables are pushed very close together, and the noise level can be high despite carpeting. The walls of the restaurant are painted a particularly delicious color of mustard yellow. Lots of light pours in through oversized square windows during the day, and soft light from hanging glass lamps adds a glow to the dining room at night. A lyrical flower arrangement on a buffet represents the only nonfunctional object in the room. I find the economy of space, of scale, of decor, as refreshing as the food.

FLY TRAP RESTAURANT

606 Folsom Street (at Second Street), San Francisco
Tel: 243-0589
Open Monday through Friday 11:30 a.m. to 10 p.m., Saturday 5:30 to 10 p.m.
Price: Inexpensive
Credit cards: AE, DC, MC, V

The Fly Trap re-creates a famous San Francisco restaurant that operated from the turn of the century until 1963 in various locations. Indeed, a glance at the Fly Trap's daily printed menu conjures up meals taken at Jack's, Sam's, Tadich, and the Old Poodle Dog; the bentwood chairs, wooden floors, butcher-paper-covered tables, shaded wall sconces, and a tailored wooden bar all seem familiar and appealing.

The decor suits the menu, which offers lots of old-fashioned salads, chops, steaks, pastas, and grilled fish with a la carte accompaniments, a number of them very good. A spectacular celery Victor brings a gigantic half head of gently braised chilled celery, generously garnished with niçoise olives, anchovies, and slices of hard-cooked egg, all moistened with a mild French dressing. Perfection. The classic Caesar is enhanced with high-quality anchovies and big house-made croutons. One of my favorites, white salad, brings together hearts of palm, endive, and mushrooms in a sour-cream dressing topped with a round of goat cheese. A big plate of vinegary pickled herring served with mounds of sour cream and pickled red onion really makes old-timers happy, and me, too.

For a main course, two chicken dishes stand out: a wonderful old creation called chicken Raphael Weill, napped in sour cream with lots of mushrooms and big pieces of braised celery (ask for it if it's not on the menu); and coq au vin, chicken in a rich red-wine sauce full of bacon and mushrooms. The kitchen can come up with some lovely hand-formed tortellini stuffed with minced ham and sauced in cream and wild mushrooms; and perfect plates of steamed asparagus and broccoli in hollandaise. For dessert, have a chocolate sundae.

True to old San Francisco grill form, not all the dishes on the long menu are worth ordering, but the Fly Trap does evoke a beloved native restaurant style that is as much fun today as it was eighty years ago. Given the choice between a trendy SoMa statement and the updated Fly Trap, I'd buzz into the Trap any day.

FRINGALE

J'ai la fringale means "I'm starving" in colloquial French; it's what you utter when you're overtaken by a sudden hunger. If this condition should hit you, Gerald Hirigoyen's smart, casual little bistro, Fringale, provides the antidote. This French-Basque chef turns out an inventive repertoire of dishes that will satisfy deep hunger without taxing a shallow pocketbook.

Start right in with a frisée salad with bacon, croutons, and a poached egg, tossed in a warm vinaigrette; or if you're really hungry, have the Fringale classic mashed-potato cake studded with shredded duck *confit* and walnuts, and sauced with a mild, savory vinaigrette.

570 Fourth Street (between
Brannan and Bryant),
San Francisco
Tel: 543-0573
Lunch Monday through
Friday 11:30 a.m. to 3 p.m.;
dinner Monday through
Saturday 5:30 to 10:30 p.m.
Price: Moderate
Credit cards: AE, MC, V

Tricky presentations that draw on classic French technique, such as a chilled terrine of lentils with a rosette of pink lamb tenderloin in the center, sauced in a shalloty mustardy rémoulade, are as delicious as they are stunning.

Hirigoyen has a fine touch with fish. His poached halibut drizzled with nutty brown butter served with a psychedelic puree of beets, a mound of buttery spinach, and a pile of green beans is dreamy. If monkfish is on the menu, swathed in a lively bordelaise sauce of shallots and red wine, don't pass it up. Of course a tasty steak *frites*, with a shalloty red wine butter and thin fries, is always a welcome sight at a good price, but so is a tender roast rack of lamb with the most luscious potato gratin and green beans tossed with fresh herbs, a plate made in heaven, for only a few dollars more.

Since Hirigoyen started his cooking career as a pastry chef, better save room for a crisp, warm apple tart with a puff pastry crust; or a Biarritz *rocher* of chocolate mousse on a crisp meringue surrounded with crème anglaise; or a palate-cleansing iced Armagnac and coffee parfait.

The cheerful interior has been done in beiges and shades of white with blond wood trim and an elegantly  curved bar. Very small tables covered with linen and white paper are pushed close together in front of banquettes. The ambiance is 100 percent French bistro. The waiters are mostly French and completely professional; the wine list reasonably priced and full of good little imported wines; the noise level high. From the moment Hirigoyen opened his bistro, it has been packed with discriminating diners who recognize a great bargain, trying to edge out the customers who are there for a great time. Be sure to call ahead, particularly for dinner.

The design-showroom district, perpetually in need of good eating places, has a treasure in Kiss, a gift from chef Morgan Song, a man possessed of a romantic soul and lots of French technique. His salads look like flower gardens; his desserts, like abstract sculpture. If there is a way to add color or whimsy to a dish, Song will find it. Such a bent toward the decorative often means that flavor comes second, but not in this chef's hands. The lush flavors and classic balance of his dishes reveal an innate sense of taste.

At lunch, a marinated shrimp salad with mango is piled high with baby lettuces and rimmed with juicy warm shrimp, cubes of mango, orange segments, carrot flowers, diced red and green peppers, and tiny tomatoes: a rainbow of colors and flavors all dressed in a perfect,

680 Eighth Street (at Brannan), San Francisco
Tel: 552-8757
Open for lunch Monday through Saturday 11 a.m. to 4 p.m.; dinner 5:30 to 10 p.m.
Price: Inexpensive
Credit cards: AE, MC, V

Try these chicken burgers at home for your kids. Everyone likes them. Ground chicken can be found at most of the meat and poultry counters discussed in this book. This recipe is adapted from Morgon Song, of Kiss.

In a large bowl, combine all the ingredients, except for the oil. Cover and chill the mixture for about 30 minutes. Divide the mixture into 4 patties. Warm the oil in a large skillet over medium heat. Sauté the patties on each side until done, about 5 minutes per side; they will be firm when pressed with your finger. Serve on hamburger rolls with hamburger fixings, or eat separately with a salad.

Serves 4

CHICKEN-VEGETABLE BURGER

1 pound ground chicken, preferably dark meat

1/4 medium red onion, finely diced

1/4 medium carrot, peeled, finely diced

1/4 zucchini, finely diced

3 fresh basil leaves, minced

1 teaspoon minced fresh garlic

2 tablespoons dried bread crumbs

1 teaspoon Worcestershire sauce

1/2 teaspoon kosher salt

10 turns of the pepper grinder

2 tablespoons vegetable oil

fruity vinaigrette. Song also makes wonderful salads of duck breast and pheasant or grilled chicken breast dressed with walnut vinaigrette. His grilled sandwiches are luscious, such as a moist, rare tuna on crisp, buttery sourdough. Another triumph is a chicken and vegetable burger (see recipe sidebar) served on a soft Kaiser roll with fries and a hamburger setup. This is the only non-beef burger I know that tastes better than most hamburgers, with less fat. At dinner, however, the dishes can get a bit rich and a little too fancy.

Kiss's gaily painted walls look like children's book illustrations; the polished concrete floor resembles old stone, but the gauzy material that billows from the ceiling softens the room. Hostess Unni Song remembers everyone who walks through the door, and her cadre of waiters could not be more pleasant or efficient. You feel like planting a kiss on her after a beautiful, light lunch at this cafe.

KYO-YA AT THE SHERATON PALACE HOTEL

2 New Montgomery Street (at Market), San Francisco
Tel: 392-8600
Open for lunch Monday through Friday 11:30 a.m. to 2 p.m.; dinner 6 to 10 p.m.
Prices: Sushi bar, expensive; restaurant, moderate
Credit cards: AE, DC, D, MC, V

A branch of a Japanese restaurant chain, Kyo-ya brings a higher level of ingredients and Japanese cooking technique to San Francisco. Far and away, it's the best sushi bar in town. To eat here, have at least $50 in your pocket, then don't worry about the cost of each pair. You'll get some of the most exquisite sushi you have ever tasted, along with a couple of martinis or jars of sake. Some of the most fabulous sushi at Kyo-ya are made with raw scallops flown in live in the shell from Boston, scooped out, and sliced to order, and fresh *hamachi*, or yellowtail, which tastes completely different from the frozen served everywhere else. Also spectacular are the *toro* (at

$16 a pair), tuna-belly meat not even available most places, which reminds me of a slab of butter; sea urchin roe that has a creaminess and nuttiness I've only experienced when I've pried them off the rocks myself; and delicacies like clean-flavored and refreshing Japanese red snapper. There are no fire-works, no inventions, nothing to distract the diner from the perfection of nature. The fish is framed by fingers of rice, each grain huge, fragrant, and chewy, barely adhering to the mass, seasoned with the most judicious application of hot wasabi. If you want to experience sushi at its best, a meal here is worth every penny.

The food is much less expensive in a series of small, luxurious, simply appointed dining rooms in the restaurant. In fact, many of the authentic dishes served here are tasty, unusual, and a terrific buy. A selection of sushi served at table will be much less expensive than at the sushi bar, but of a more mundane quality. Instead, try a whole crab, stir-fried with matsutake, enoki, and shiitake mushrooms enriched with egg, which all melts together into a fantastic sauce that you spoon over a bowl of chewy Japanese rice; or a butter-tender steak, sliced into thick pieces and brought sizzling to the table in a covered ceramic dish with two dipping sauces. In addition to these hearty dishes, a whole range of vibrant Japanese salads and small dishes, soups and rice porridges, are artfully presented and carefully made. Service by waitresses in kimonos brings traditional graciousness to the dining room floor, where you hear as much Japanese spoken as English. This Tokyo-based restaurant, set up to accommodate Japanese visitors to San Francisco, is an emissary of the best of Japanese culture for those of us who live here.

LULU

816 Folsom Street (between Fourth and Fifth streets), San Francisco
Tel: 495-5775
Open Monday through Thursday 11:30 a.m. to 11 p.m., Friday and Saturday until midnight, Sunday 5:30 to 11 p.m.
Price: Moderate
Credit cards: AE, MC, V

Flames leap high in a huge wood-burning rotisserie and fireplace at center stage in the cavernous dining room of LuLu, letting you know where their priorities lie. This relatively new restaurant near the Moscone Convention Center has put together one of the most alluring menus in town. The food is as simple and as delicious as it can get. LuLu starts out with first-rate raw materials and puts 90 percent of its effort into manipulating them over one open fire or another. Delicious thin-crusted pizzas and iron pans of mussels in the shell come out of the wood-burning oven. Juicy rotisserie chickens and pork loin are licked with smoke as they slowly turn in front of a roaring wood fire. They come on large platters for sharing, accompanied with mashed potatoes enriched with olive oil or roasted potatoes with arugula. From the grill, sweet-fleshed Alaskan spot prawns with roe, shell, and head should not be passed up when they are available; nor grilled asparagus dusted with shaved Parmesan. Except for the pastas, which somehow don't have the focus of the other dishes, the one-page daily printed menu is full of delicious-sounding choices, large and small. I'm not the only one who thinks so, because the large, barnlike dining room has been packed from the moment it opened. The noise level is deafening. The fact that both the bar and most of the kitchen are in one room, along with a sea of small wooden tables packed close together, does not help matters. No one really cares, because the place has become a scene, attended as much for the action as the terrific, reasonably priced food. If you're an eater, the best time to arrive is for late lunch, when the dining room has emptied and the cooks have a moment to take a deep breath. You can order a bottle of an interesting French or Italian wine and linger over the rustic French desserts, which always include a warm, caramelized upside-down tart and house-made ice cream, and have a good cup of espresso.

LULU BIS AND LULU CAFE

On either side of big LuLu are satellite food operations. A cafe specializing in coffee, morning pastries, and sandwiches takes care of the impromptu needs that the big LuLu does not cover, and LuLu Bis, a separate operation with its own wood-burning rotisserie and grill, puts out fixed-price family-style meals and serves them at long communal refectory tables in a narrow candle-lit room hung with large, dramatic canvases. Reed Hearon, the chef behind all this good Provençal/Italian/California food, has absorbed the lessons of Chez Panisse. The concept here owes much to the original set menus at the downstairs restaurant there, though at LuLu Bis, the emphasis is a bit more Italian. A meal might start with an antipasto of shellfish and grilled vegetables, move on to Tuscan bean soup, give diners a choice of whole roasted sea bass with *rouille* or spit-roasted duck with crusty potatoes, and finish with a fresh fruit country tart, all for $27. A three-course meal can be ordered for $21.

816 Folsom Street (between Fourth and Fifth streets), San Francisco

Tel: 495-5775

Open Tuesday through Saturday 5:45 to 10:30 p.m.;

LuLu Cafe open Monday through Thursday 7 a.m. to 11 p.m., Friday until midnight, Saturday 8 a.m. to midnight, Sunday 5:30 to 11 p.m.

Price: LuLu Bis, moderate; LuLu Cafe, inexpensive

Credit cards: AE, MC, V

RISTORANTE ECCO

101 South Park (between
Second and Third,
Bryant and Brannan),
San Francisco
Tel: 495-3291
Open for lunch Monday
through Friday 11:30 a.m.
to 2:30 p.m.; dinner
Monday through Saturday
5:30 to 10 p.m.
Price: Moderate
Credit cards: AE, DC , MC, V

A second venture in the neighborhood by the South Park Cafe people (see following entry), Ristorante Ecco embodies breezy, sophisticated urbanity. Taking advantage of its location in the hidden enclave of South Park, one modern dining room looks out to the greenery through tall, clean-lined wood-framed windows. An airy, high-ceilinged barroom and cafe, hung with lithographed maps of Rome and clever, small black Italian light fixtures, draw a steady crowd of people who just want a bite or a drink. The food here is ample and lively, though the one-page Italian menu does not break any new ground. Its most noteworthy aspect is the price column. If you are watching your pocketbook and still want a stylish evening out, you can do well at Ecco. The colorful *antipasti* plates are generous enough to split, my favorite being one with grilled tuna, eggs, olives, white bean salad, and pickled baby beets. The individual pizzas are puffy and golden; the skewers of grilled scallops and shrimp served with new potatoes, sautéed greens, and Ecco's addictive garlic mayonnaise make up one of the best lunch specials around. At dinner, braised short ribs simmered in red wine and topped with *salsa verde* on a bed of white beans has been my favorite dish. The unfocused pastas have not. The wine list is as smart as the surroundings, with a handful of interesting American wines and a large, enticing selection of Italian bottles at excellent prices.

From the moment this charming, very French cafe and restaurant opened ten years ago, I wanted to be there. The design of the narrow room, with front windows that open completely onto the sidewalk, a copper bar, and painted wooden banquettes that stretch the length of the restaurant, is so simple, yet so perfectly done, that I felt I was sitting in a Left Bank bistro in Paris. The food here has had its ups and downs with partnership and chef changes, starting off terrific, faltering a bit, but now at its best ever under the direction of chef Ward Little. I have sat at the bar in the evening and eaten crispy *brandade* and potato cakes, savory quail salad, and juicy slices of roast pork loin with luxurious potato puree. At lunch you can have a perfect roast chicken with skinny *pommes frites*, or aromatic *boudin noir* sautéed with apples and surrounded by watercress, served by a French-speaking wait person. The wine list, augmented by many interesting, inexpensive glasses listed on a blackboard, only waits to be mined. The prices are gratifyingly moderate, and the casual bistro atmosphere allows you to order as much or as little as you like. The place gets very full during lunch with nearby designers and architects who vie for the few choice outdoor tables on the sidewalk, but the light is so good in this cafe that it doesn't matter where you sit. You'll be bathed in the warm glow of an authentic bistro.

108 South Park (between Second and Third, Bryant and Brannan), San Francisco
Tel: 495-7275
Open Monday through Friday 7:30 a.m. to 10 p.m., Saturday 6 to 10 p.m.
Price: Moderate
Credit cards: AE, MC, V

UNIVERSAL CAFE

2814 19th Street (between Florida and Bryant), San Francisco

Tel: 821-4608

Open Monday 7:30 a.m. to 4 p.m., Tuesday through Thursday until 9:30 p.m., Friday until 10 p.m., Saturday 8:30 a.m. to 10 p.m.

Price: Inexpensive

Credit cards: AE, MC, V

My heavy-equipment-mover friend Roger, who hangs out in funky bars with house bands, bowled me over the other day when he told me I had to have lunch at the Universal Cafe, "because it felt so cool to be there." A fabricator of objects for his own Potrero Hill fixer-upper, he appreciates the craftsmanship that has gone into converting a small wooden warehouse on an unexpectedly charming, semi-industrial south-of-Market block into a very hip cafe. Cement, cast aluminum, and maple veneer plywood have been used in witty ways. A bank of floor-to-ceiling windows with hefty-looking aluminum hardware opens entirely onto a quiet block dotted with trees. Smart aluminum and wood chairs and marble-topped tables from the workshop of South Park fabricators, run by Jeff and Larissa Sand, somehow combine modernity with cafe tradition. Half the room is taken up by a long benchlike banquette with tables, the other by an open kitchen and counter dominated by a coffee roaster. All the excellent coffee served here, at Ristorante Ecco, and the South Park Cafe, has been roasted in it.

The connection between these stylish SoMa cafes comes as no surprise. They all share a common partner, Bob Voorhees. However, the menu at Universal is based on pizza dough and focaccia. The individual pizzas are particularly stunning, with light yet chewy crusts. One topped with caramelized onions, prosciutto, ricotta, and Fontina is a brilliant invention—though not one Italian purists would be likely to order. Don't miss it. The focaccia sandwich filled with roasted chicken and aïoli is another triumph. In a town where every second restaurant offers individual pizzas and focaccia sandwiches, the Universal has actually made its own mark with them. The sandwiches come with a pretty green salad, larger versions of which can be ordered with Gorgonzola and glazed walnuts or strips of moist grilled duck breast with mango. The Italian wines by the glass will not strain your pocketbook, and you should be sure to end with a creamy-topped espresso. All the details of the Universal Cafe please so much that I have to agree with Roger's unusual enthusiasm for a cafe that serves designer pizzas.

CAFES

BRAIN WASH

1122 Folsom Street
(between Seventh
and Eighth streets),
San Francisco
Tel: 861-3663
Daily 7:30 a.m. to 11 p.m.
No credit cards

This cafe-laundromat kills two birds with one stone. One part of this eye-catching two-story glass building contains thirty-two state-of-the-art, heavy-duty computer-operated washers, twenty-four dryers, a wash-and-fold service, and a dry cleaner. Separated from the machinery by a diagonal glass wall is a self-service cafe with cement floors, clever metal chairs covered with epoxied collage, and a loud jukebox, giving it a Cafe Flore feel. Though most of the food is mediocre, with the exception of a tasty Chinese chicken salad in a light soy and walnut-oil dressing, you can fill yourself up with the likes of thick focaccia pizzas or baked apples. The scene is so weird and happening that it makes washing your dirty clothes an important social experience.

CAFFÈ CENTRO

102 South Park (between
Second and Third, Bryant
and Brannan), San Francisco
Tel: 882-1500
Open Monday through
Friday 7:30 a.m. to 7:30 p.m.,
Saturday 9 a.m. to 5:30 p.m.
No credit cards

Caffè Centro's South Park location gives it its cachet. Outdoor tables on the sidewalk around the perimeter of the cafe bask in the ample sun in this protected good-weather belt in the middle of the city. Light floods in through usually open windows and seems to make the creamy-colored walls glow. Details in the design of the cafe, like a poured and painted floor that looks like a mosaic, bottle-glass light fixtures, tiny round metal tables that tend to wobble, and metal chairs, set the backdrop for lots of arty, expressively dressed young patrons. Caffè Centro offers the inexpensive alternative to Ristorante Ecco and South Park Cafe in the same neighborhood.

Warm sandwiches, like a delicious open-faced sandwich of roasted red peppers with melted Gruyère on toasted bread, star on the menu. Frittatas layered with all sorts of vegetables held together with garlic-scented custard are also good, as are the house-made soups. Unfortunate in a cafe, the coffee consistently has a bitter edge.

BARS

CARIBBEAN ZONE

55 Natoma Street (between
First and Second, Howard
and Mission), San Francisco
Tel: 541-9465
Open Monday through
Thursday 11:30 a.m. to 10
p.m., Friday until 11 p.m.,
Saturday 5 p.m. to 2 a.m.,
Sunday 5 to 10 p.m.
Credit cards: D, MC, V

Trader Vic may have invented the tropical drink and island decor, but Caribbean Zone takes it to new, campy heights. This sheet-metal beach shack in an alley between parking lots is a jungle of plastic tropical plants and trees, complete with a waterfall tumbling over artificial rocks and a real airplane cabin as a cocktail lounge. Nothing is more fun than repairing down the aisle to an uphol-stered seat, with videos of passing clouds lighting up the windows, a large and expensive ($6.50) tropical drink in hand. Sex in the Jungle, a rum-spiked slush of guayabana pulp with plenty of nutmeg, or my favorite, Goomba Boomba, fresh bananas, lime, and rum blended with ice, will get you flying relatively fast. As you can imagine, the Caribbean Zone is a place where life can be zany and laid-back, but not necessarily the site for great eating. If you need something to counteract the effects of tropical drinks, order the conch fritters or jerk chicken, rubbed in a lively spice mixture and grilled. They'll ground you enough for a second takeoff.

CAVA 555

555 Second Street
(between Bryant and
Brannan), San Francisco
Tel: 543-2282
Lunch Tuesday through
Friday 11:30 a.m. to 2 p.m.,

In a narrow black-painted room with a galvanized-sheet-metal bar, vinyl booths, and odd-shaped high-tech tables, bottles of great and not so great champagne are poured by the glass and sold by the bottle, accompanied with small dishes of tasty food. Cava 555 was conceived for people who like the combination of champagne, classical jazz, and casual, if stylish, eating-in-a-bar ambi-ance. The best thing about this place is the wealth of elegant bottles of champagne on the wine list for a reasonable price, which, of course, is a relative concept. I can tell you that Krug Grand Cuvée and Bollinger R.D., two of my favorite champagnes, hover around $130 and $100 respectively, and that you can drink Louis Roederer Cristal and Dom Perignon if you're feeling flush. Twenty or so tasty French champagnes are priced under $45, along with a considered selection of California, Italian, and Spanish sparkling wines. The menu, under the guidance of a new chef, Stephen Brendlinger, offers hearty portions, at appetizer prices, of rare roast sirloin with grilled radicchio and herb aïoli; lightly grilled romaine, which sounds weird but actually works very nicely in a Caesarlike dressing; and perfectly grilled salmon on mashed potatoes with a tomato-caper vinaigrette. While the preparations are tasty, they don't necessarily pair with champagne, although I have found that champagne tastes amazingly good with practically anything (except smoked salmon and caviar, with which it's most often served). Cava 555 is one of the few spots that stay open late, and is frequented by staff from other restau-rants when they get off duty.

Monday and Saturday
5:30 p.m. to 2 a.m.
Credit cards: AE, MC, V

ELEVEN

This lyrical, high-ceilinged space across the street from Slim's has had a number of different identities since it opened. All of them have been appealing, but the fickle nature of the South of Market crowd dictates a short life span for anything more ambitious than a watering hole or club. Such is the case with Eleven. Its handsome, dark wood bar and SoMa location are now the draws, though the new, inexpensive Italian menu is certainly service-able. Its predecessor, Undici (Italian for eleven), had the

374 11th Street (between Harrison and Folsom), San Francisco
Tel: 431-3337
Monday through Thursday 6 to 11 p.m., Fri day and Saturday until midnight; bar open until 2 a.m.
Credit cards: AE, DC , MC, V

same owner, a different chef, an interesting southern Italian menu, higher prices, and a witty faux piazza decor that supported dining. Now the bar and casual bar food command the center of attention.

Paper-thin-crusted pizzas come out of the kitchen quickly, a relief for starving drinkers, and the appetizers really make up the best part of the menu. Seared rare *ahi* tuna with a fruity little sauce—the dish of the nineties—has been blessedly fresh and attractive. Deep-fried zucchini sticks are tender and not greasy. The salads use fresh greens and are lightly dressed.

The pastas, like penne tossed with a ragout of lamb and peppers, satisfy at best. Tiramisù, biscotti, and espresso provide a civilized conclusion—something you hope for after a night of amusement south of Market.

HAMBURGER MARY'S

1582 Folsom Street
(at 12th Street),
San Francisco
Tel: 626-1985
Open Tuesday through
Thursday 11:30 a.m. to 1
a.m., Friday until 2 a.m.,
Saturday 10 a.m. to 2 a.m.,
Sunday 10 a.m. to 1 a.m.
Credit cards: AE, D, MC, V

Everybody who hangs out at Hamburger Mary's looks like they're dressed up for a party, though most of the time the party is in their own head. A scene can't get much weirder or wackier, but even blatantly straight customers can feel at home here because some people come in that costume. The hamburgers have a health-food overlay. They come on soft whole wheat bread with sprouts, all the better to go with a bourbon and a smoke. The bizarre energy of the place has made it a famous and beloved South of Market landmark, which continually attracts new generations of weirdnesses.

HOUSE OF SHIELDS

This historic bar, now under new, energetic management, serves hearty blue-collar fare to white-collar workers: stockbrokers and lawyers, South of Market small businesspeople and their employees. A piano plays in the ancient dark wood barroom with white tile floors and brass rails. It's noisy and smoky, especially after work. The drinks are nothing special, but just what you'd expect at a resonant old San Francisco watering hole. A nice-looking young bartender, who has been there for ages, takes care of everyone with friendly conviction.

39 New Montgomery Street (between Market and Mission), San Francisco
Tel: 392-7732
Open Monday through Friday 10 a.m. to 9 p.m.
Credit cards: AE, DC , MC, V

JULIE'S SUPPER CLUB

Still a happening spot after a decade, Julie's serves updated American diner food with a spicy twist, amid the din of a bar that attracts a young crowd. There's always a wait for a table during prime meal hours, and everyone seems to like it that way. Large groups tend to come here to celebrate special occasions.

1123 Folsom Street (between Seventh and Eighth streets), San Francisco
Tel: 861-0707
Monday through Friday 4 p.m. to 2 a.m., Saturday 5 p.m. to 2 a.m.
Credit cards: AE, DC , MC, V

**1151 Folsom Street
(between Seventh
and Eighth streets),
San Francisco
Tel: 626-2388
Open Monday through
Saturday 8 p.m. to 2 a.m.
Credit cards: AE, MC, V**

Partially owned by model Christy Turlington, who hangs out here when she isn't on a shoot, the Up and Down Club is the bar of choice for local photographers, art students, budding designers, and people interested in style who like to be seen. Amenities include live music, dancing, and a fairly ambitious menu of vegetable-sensitive bar food. Even the bartenders, male and female, are cute.

MEAT AND POULTRY

POLARICA

**3107 Quint Street (near
Third Street and Army),
San Francisco
Tel: 647-1300
Open Monday through
Friday 9 a.m. to 5 p.m.,
Saturday 11 a.m. to 4 p.m.
Credit cards: AE, MC, V**

Polarica imports game, meats, and specialty products from all over the world and sells them both wholesale and retail, delivered and on site, for the same price. Home cooks can visit the attractively facaded storefront warehouse or call ahead to order something specific. This is the place where many cooks go for one of my favorite birds, the rich-flavored, dark-fleshed guinea fowl (roast or grill the breasts, braise the legs, and serve with long-cooked cabbage), as well as fresh pheasant. The fresh California-grown rabbits have no off flavors, and the vacuum-packed fresh lamb from Australia in all cuts is some of the best available. Fresh venison from New Zealand and duck, whole and in parts, from the Grimaud duck farm are always in stock. Both Hudson Valley foie gras and our local Sonoma foie gras, and smoked salmon from Norway and Scotland at half the price you find them in delicatessens (Polarica will sell the salmon in small quantities if you wish), are but a few of the items available and listed on a detailed product list that will be mailed to you if you call. Polarica is also a source for fresh black truffles and all sorts of fresh wild mushrooms. Russian and American caviars are also sold at competitive prices. Finally, if the urge to eat emu or eland overtakes you, Polarica has them. This outfit, with offices both in Manhattan and San Francisco, prides itself on finding sources for every conceivable kind of domestically raised game, worldwide. In fact, if you're looking for any rare or exotic ingredient you might want to check here first.

FISH

CALIFORNIA SUNSHINE

Mats and Dafne Engstrom have ascended the throne as the king and queen of American, eastern Russian, and Chinese caviars, having been in business now for twenty-one years. Their seven-ounce tins of Tsar Nicoulai (their trademark) ossetra, the medium-sized caviar with a nutty flavor that I like the most, offers the best price for the quality I have encountered. California Sunshine set up their own caviar-making operation in Russia once the market opened, and both quality and freshness are monitored. Buying caviar, of course, is a crapshoot, because every fish produces eggs of different quality. The ideal is to get it as fresh as possible, which is why buying new-crop caviar in the spring will net you

144 King Street (between Second and Third streets), San Francisco
Tel: 543-3007
Open Monday through Friday 8 a.m. to 5 p.m.
Credit cards: AE, MC, V

the best flavor. Of course, most Americans want caviar around the winter holiday season, but once you've tasted the fresher eggs, you'll be tempted to have it earlier in the year. When I was in Soviet Georgia, just months before it blew up, we ate, with a spoon, small plates thickly paved with the most delectable, nutty, barely salted sturgeon eggs and washed it down with icy vodka. Now I serve caviar this way here, in California; the prices at California Sunshine are so reasonable you can do it for a special occasion. On a smaller budget, you can make a rather pretty and not too expensive presentation of caviar toasts using California Sunshine's crunchy, bright golden whitefish caviar, orange salmon roe, and black Russian sevruga. Though the wholesale outlet does not have a retail salesroom per se, people are welcome to drop in if they are planning to buy.

WINES AND SPIRITS

WINE HOUSE LIMITED

535 Bryant Street (between Third and Fourth streets), San Francisco

Tel: 495-8486

Open Monday through Friday 10 a.m. to 6 p.m., Saturday until 4 p.m.

Credit cards: MC, V

The yeasty smell of wooden wine crates greets you when you walk into this red brick room with exposed beams and a cement floor. Stacks of these boxes full of Cru Bordeaux at decent prices—a 15 percent discount on two cases—call out to be examined. Many Bordeaux are available in hard-to-find half bottles. The Wine House also brings in the Robert Kacher selection of Burgundies, a favorite label of wine guru Robert Parker. The Wine House sells no liquor, and 90 percent of the fifteen-year-old wine store's bottles are imported, making the Wine

House a real bottle shop, not just a room filled with very good wines. The people who work here care about wine and want to help you find great bottles. This is one of the few places of its kind left in the city, and is well worth a trip if only to visit a wine operation with old-style values.

K & L WINES

A parking lot makes it easy to shop at this small but fully stocked wine shop with most bottles displayed in wooden racks. An excellent Bordeaux selection at some surprising prices draws collectors here. In fact, on a recent visit I saw several elegant Bordeaux, like 1988 Domaine de Chevalier Blanc, on sale below cost. An eclectic selection of imported wines from Chile, Spain, and Australia entices cost-conscious buyers. K & L also sells fine spirits like grappa and double-malt scotch. Nestled onto its shelves you will find at least one of the Gourmel cognacs, a cognac whose smoothness, delicacy, and finesse make the inevitable headache you get the next morning, when one taste has led to another, worth the pain.

768 Harrison Street
(between Third and Fourth streets), San Francisco
Tel: 896-1734
Open Monday through Friday 9 a.m. to 7 p.m.,
Saturday until 6 p.m.,
Sunday 11 a.m. to 5 p.m.
Credit cards: AE, MC, V

WINE CLUB

Small high-quality wine merchants hate the Wine Club, the way independent bookstores hate Crown Books. I, myself, never shop at large bookstore chains because I passionately support booksellers who know their inventories and will find me the odd books I need. I feel the same way about wine stores. The Wine Club gives huge discounts on some wines, which they offer up as loss leaders at 10 or 12 percent above cost, but service and knowledge about wine is not part of the equation.

953 Harrison Street
(between Fifth and Sixth),
San Francisco
Tel: 512-9086
Open Monday through Saturday 9 a.m. to 7 p.m.,
Sunday 11 a.m. to 6 p.m.
Credit cards: MC, V

On a recent visit, for example, 1990 Chalone Pinot Noir was marked down from $30 to $22.49, about 10 percent over cost. If you know exactly what you want you can pick up a good deal, but beware. Because some prices are discounted so heavily, the store does not buy from the most rigorous shippers and wholesalers. You might get a bottle of Bordeaux that has sweltered during a long passage in an unrefrigerated container. Interspersed among the buys are cases and cases of wines that are no bargain at all, because they are from off vintages. Still, people load up their shopping carts with inexpensive California wines in this cinder-block wine warehouse, and I suppose if price is your main consideration, the Wine Club is the way to go.

COOKWARE AND BOOKS

ECONOMY RESTAURANT SUPPLY

1375 Howard Street (at Tenth Street), San Francisco
Tel: 626-5611
Open Monday through Friday 8 a.m. to 5:30 p.m.
Credit cards: AE, D, MC, V

All the restaurant people come here to buy supplies. There are rows and rows of restaurant-style aluminum skillets and pots, all sorts of large cooking utensils, cutting boards, knives, metal bowls: all the essentials for a production kitchen. I have outfitted many a home kitchen here as well, with basic, useful equipment. All the marked prices are 10 to 15 percent higher than the actual price, so remember to ask for a discount. Just tell them you're opening a restaurant, and thank your lucky stars that you really aren't.

The Sunset District

THE SUNSET DISTRICT

RESTAURANTS

HANA

Hana started out as a closet-sized restaurant, but its tasty, hearty Japanese cooking, cheap prices, and residential location only a few blocks from the University of California Medical Center caused overflow business. The demand for something decent to eat in the neighborhood far exceeded the number of seats available, especially since people were coming from other parts of the city to eat at this little place. Happily, Hana expanded, making conditions much more comfortable. The enlarged dining room looks like an old Japanese inn, with weathered wooden booths, thick wooden tables, and a beautiful deep blue and red paint job. The prices are still reasonable, and the Japanese mainstays on the menu just as delicious.

Although sushi is available at both a sushi bar and in the dining room, I prefer the cooked dishes. The kitchen has a way with chicken, like a breast with wing attached, basted in the lightest of teriyaki sauces and sprinkled with sesame seeds. The meat stays miraculously tender and juicy. The same extraordinary texture makes chicken *tonkatsu*, a battered and fried chicken cutlet, a

408 Irving Street (between Fifth and Sixth avenues), San Francisco
Tel: 665-3952
Open Monday through Saturday for lunch 11:30 a.m. to 2 p.m., dinner 5 to 9:30 p.m.
Price: Inexpensive
Credit Cards: MC, V

standout. Frying is always nicely done at Hana. The fried oysters are barely coated in a crumbly batter and cooked in very hot oil until they are just firm. They melt in your mouth. *Gyoza*, Japanese pot stickers with spicy pork filling in a crimped noodle wrapper, have an intense gingery flavor and a light texture. Hana is also famous for its *yosenabe*, a perfectly cooked stew of clams, shrimp, oysters, and vegetables in a ginger-scented broth. Portions are geared to Western appetites, and dinners include little plates of pickled cabbage, miso soup, and a lettuce salad, albeit with cellophane noodles and a delicate sweet-and-sour dressing. Service by a group of Japanese women in kimonos could not be friendlier or more efficient. They know most of their customers and will quickly get to know you.

JEONG HYUN CHARCOAL BARBECUE HOUSE

2123 Irving Street (between 22nd and 23rd avenues), San Francisco
Tel: 665-0966
Open daily 11 a.m. to 2 a.m.; except Monday afternoon from 2:30 to 5 p.m.
Price: Inexpensive
Credit Cards: MC, V

Of all the Asian cuisines one can sample in San Francisco, Korean barbecue is the most familiar and the most exotic at the same time. Charcoal-grilled beef is the heart of the meal. These thin slices of short rib appeal to beef-loving Americans. But the rest of the meal, a table full of little bowls of hot, spicy, garlicky pickles and salads, some fermented and some fresh, tastes like nothing you would find in an American pantry. The combination of these assertive, juicy cold vegetables with savory hot meat makes for exciting eating, especially when they are wrapped up together in a lettuce leaf so you get the flavors and textures of all of them in each bite.

Jeong Hyun does the whole service so well it has become a Sunset District destination with a broad cross-cultural clientele. There are two rows of roomy wooden booths. Each booth easily seats six people and has its own ventilation system, a hood and a fan descending from the high ceiling. If you elect to barbecue at the table, which is what everyone does, the waitress comes out with a large hibachi full of white-hot coals. The tables are big enough so you don't feel threatened by the fire and the fans are so strong—and loud—that they pull off all the heat and smoke. Then, platters of sesame oil–marinated beef and at least fifteen little bowls of vegetables, *kimchee*, tofu, and glass noodles, along with rice and curly leaf lettuce, are brought out. The meat, cut very thinly, cooks so fast you simply can't go wrong. A few flips with the tongs and it's ready.

Actually, the cooking done in the kitchen of the restaurant is worth a trip across the city. On being seated, fabulous toasted-rice tea and deep-fried mung bean pancakes appear; crisp, laced with green onions, and with a delightfully creamy texture, they remind me of the best potato pancakes. The famous Korean steak tartar is done beautifully here, a mound of hand-shredded beef tossed with sesame oil, garlicky hot cabbage pickle, and minced onion, topped with a raw egg yolk and garnished with vinegared pears. For a less-beefy meal, try *jap chae*, a luscious stir fry of bean-thread noodles, bits of beef, peppers, mushrooms, and ribbons of egg in a delicately sweet, rich brown gravy. Nutty Korean rice stars in a preparation that comes in a hot stone pot, topped with spinach, seaweed, onions, shredded beef, and a raw egg yolk, which quickly cooks as you stir it into the rice. The crusty rice at the bottom is the prize. Boneless barbecued chicken, which arrives on a sizzling hot cast-iron plate, has a velvet texture.

Of course the central culinary experience of a tableful of tastes with grill-it-yourself beef is that each meal here feels like a feast. Yet, as is the genius of Asian style, you leave without feeling overfed.

JUST WON TON

1241 Vicente Street
(between 23rd and 24th
avenues), San Francisco
Tel: 681-2999
Open Tuesday through
Sunday 11 a.m.
to 10 p.m.
Price: Very inexpensive
No credit cards

This tiny place in a converted house in the Sunset devotes itself entirely to making wontons. The skins are gossamer thin, tender, and flavorful, the filling simple and sublime: roughly chopped sweet, impeccably fresh shrimp bound with just a little ground pork. The wontons come in soup with noodles, soup without noodles, with fish balls, roast duck, barbecued pork, spicy chicken, different cuts of beef, innards, and pigs' feet. For a small pittance you can get wonton soup with any of the above and extra wontons.

Also good are thick, white *chow fun* noodles made with rice flour, tossed with bright green bok choy and bits of velvetized beef. Although this is primarily a noodle house, it is also known for two appetizers: vegetarian duck, made with ribbons of tofu skin wrapped around a filling of savory mushrooms, and something called a Chinese tamale, a gigantic mound of sticky rice with a center of braised Chinese sausage and taro paste. The beauty of a visit here is that you can take the wontons to go and serve them in your own rich chicken broth, a meal that pleases a lot of kids I know.

RISTORANTE MARCELLO

2100 Taraval (at 31st
Avenue), San Francisco
Tel: 665-1430
Open Tuesday through
Saturday 5 to 10:30 p.m.,
Sunday 4 to 10 p.m.
Price: Moderate
Credit Cards: MC, V

The food, the customers, the look and feel of Ristorante Marcello, take you back to another era, when arugula, grilled radicchio, and balsamic vinegar hadn't entered the common culinary vocabulary and spaghetti with meat sauce held sway. To tell you the truth, this was not a bad time, and at Ristorante Marcello its best qualities have been preserved. This restaurant reminds me of the old Vanessi's on Broadway: It has the same raffish spirit and the same broad cooking style.

Furnished with red vinyl banquettes, padded wooden chairs, linen-covered tables pushed close together, and a long, active bar where people also eat, the room has that classic Italian dinner-house style. The waiters, in tuxes, know the menu and have a sense of humor. They don't coddle their customers but they serve efficiently.

This is the place to get a classic Caesar salad or hearts of romaine in a fabulous shalloty, mustardy, relishy, rémouladelike vinaigrette. The spaghettini comes bathed in a celery-scented bolognese sauce with an authentically gravelly texture from finely chopped beef, chicken livers, and prosciutto. The house-made ravioli, moistened with a little bit of this sauce, are plump with well-seasoned ricotta. The tender green *panzotti*, large ravioli also filled with ricotta and spinach, are sauced with a clean-flavored tomato puree. Don't pass up the old-fashioned *cannelloni della casa*, made with hand-rolled dough and stuffed with finely chopped veal, spinach, and pro-sciutto, covered with a creamy tomato sauce. The spicy *spaghetti alla matriciana* juggles bacon, tomatoes, and onions masterfully.

People come to this restaurant for two main courses: *pollo ai ferri*, a flattened-on-the-grill half chicken with a superb satiny texture, and a gigantic veal chop, very tender but pink enough to have flavor. Try the rest of the menu at your own risk. The wine list is woefully short on good Italian or California red wines, but most people who eat here prefer their martinis and Manhat-tans anyway. When the place is packed on the weekends you can almost feel the specter of crusty old San Francisco North Beach hovering overhead.

RIVER SIDE SEAFOOD RESTAURANT

1201 Vicente Street
(at 23rd Avenue),
San Francisco
Tel: 759-8828
Open daily for lunch
11 a.m. to 3 p.m.; dinner 5
to 10 p.m.
Price: Inexpensive
Credit Cards: MC, V

A chef and a manager from the well-regarded Fook Yuen on the Peninsula opened this neighborhood restaurant within the last year. The room is clean, comfortably appointed, and miraculously quiet, due, perhaps, to low acoustic ceilings, and large groups of eight or ten can eat well here for a very reasonable sum. Value is much prized in the Sunset, and River Side aims to please.

Saucers of barely pickled cucumbers tide you over while you order your dinner off the handwritten list of specials clipped to the cover of an otherwise long menu. The list simplifies the entire process. Start with soup of the day, a magnificently rich and restorative chicken broth. Have Peking duck: Tuck the crackling skin into tender white buns smeared with plum sauce and green onions. Then eat the meat of the duck as a separate course, minced with crisp white rice noodles, which you eat rolled in lettuce leaves. The spicy pork ribs are hot, sweet, vinegary, and chewy, just the way they should be. The oxtails in wine sauce with carrots could have come out of a French kitchen. They are delicious over rice. The sake-marinated black cod, a large, thick hunk, defines the sensation of velvety and rich. The service is pleasant, the experience civilized. You pay more here than at bargain-driven places like Szechuan Taste, but the price is less than at many Richmond District restaurants for equally high quality.

This modern, light-filled neighborhood cafe run by two generations of Macedonians has become famous for its savory and sweet Greek pastries made by the elder Stoyanof. His borek, a hot turnover of the lightest, flakiest filo pastry imaginable stuffed with a combination of Greek cheeses, is a masterpiece. So are the spinach-, lamb-, and feta-filled pastries. The many layers of filo in nut-filled *baklava* disappear on your tongue like snowflakes. A beautiful raspberry cake roll with homemade cream custard over a thin layer of sponge cake will tempt anyone to eat dessert. Seventy-one-year-old Georgi Stoyanof also makes luscious *baba au rhum*, a crumbly rum-syrup-soaked brioche, and he offers gigantic slices of fresh apple strudel.

The emphasis here is on high-quality ingredients and simple preparation. Angel Stoyanof, Georgi's son, gets his seafood from Paul Johnson's Monterey Fish, which means that the swordfish brochettes strung with bay leaves and thin slices of lemon taste like butter. Sweet fresh shrimp get a classic Macedonian treatment with tomatoes, feta and oregano. The *moussaka* served in a ramekin has a crusty cheese and béchamel topping blanketing layers of velvety eggplant and spicy ground beef instead of lamb. Georgi says his patrons prefer beef. They also love an appetizer called *saganak*i, a rectangle of tangy kasseri cheese dipped in egg and homemade bread crumbs and sautéed.

The uncovered tables are placed close together cafe style in a gaily painted, spacious high-ceilinged room. Most of the kitchen is in the middle of the dining room. At lunch, it serves as a cafeteria counter; at night, waiters take over. The beauty of Stoyanof is that it elegantly meets the needs of the neighborhood by putting out fresh, honest, tasty food and keeping prices low.

1240 Ninth Avenue (between Irving and Lincoln), San Francisco
Tel: 664-3664
Open Tuesday through Sunday for lunch 10 a.m. to 4:30 p.m.; dinner 5 to 9:30 p.m.
Price: Inexpensive
Credit cards: (dinner only) AE, MC, V

SZECHUAN TASTE

917 Taraval Street
(at 19th Avenue),
San Francisco
Tel: 681-8383
Open daily 11 a.m. to
9:30 p.m.
Price: Inexpensive
Credit cards: MC, V

You can eat a large, pretty tasty multi-course meal at this smallish Hakka and Szechuan bistro for $10 a person, and everyone in the Sunset seems to know this. Szechuan Taste has become *the* inexpensive Chinese family spot in the Sunset, so expect a loud and crowded dining room, some food that comes out of the kitchen prepared in advance in anticipation of quick turnover, and clearers who throw a tableful of dishes and teacups into bus tubs with only speed in mind. People flock here for crisp roasted chicken and salt-baked chicken, plates of simple bok choy, Chinese broccoli or mustard greens, addictive, vinegary house-special spareribs, bargain Peking duck with thick buns, and braised squab. This is not the place to order seafood.

The dining room has the resonance of some of the old Chinatown restaurants, with dark wood trim, a bright red wooden internal roof-canopy, carpeting, and a mob waiting on the sidewalk outside the door. It's fun, it's a scene, and it's better to go on weeknights when it isn't so frenetic.

WIN'S

3040 Taraval Street
(between 40th and 41st
avenues), San Francisco
Tel: 759-1818
Open Tuesday through
Sunday 11 a.m. to 10 p.m.
Price: Inexpensive
Credit cards: MC, V

People come here to eat Chinese-style roast duck, especially at lunch when it is still hot and juicy from the ovens. The burnished skin crackles; the velvety brown flesh is infused with the perfume of the Chinese spices that have been rubbed into the meat before roasting. You can get these ducks and other good barbecued items like hunks of pork belly and Chinese spareribs to go, or you can eat them there over rice accompanied with steamed iceberg lettuce leaves, a luscious combination. Although many of the dishes on the amazingly long menu are not worth trying, there are some standouts: excellent, rustic pot stickers; crisp-skinned soy sauce chicken; stir-fried Chinese broccoli; and crisp, pan-fried Hong Kong–style chow mein noodles topped with lots of bok choy, Chinese broccoli, and chicken.

YAYA CUISINE

Chef Yahya Salih grew up near the ruins of Nineveh in northern Iraq. In his wittily decorated restaurant next to Golden Gate Park, he celebrates ancient flavors in dishes that generations of Iraqis ate in their mothers' kitchens. He applies modern cooking techniques to them, and the result is completely original and surprising food that looks quite beautiful.

Cardamom, cumin, pomegranate syrup, pickled mango, dried lime, sumac, tamarind, allspice, cinnamon, mint, cilantro, and basil weave their way throughout a meal, fragrant and assertive, yet always in balance. The layers of flavor remind me of Indian cooking, but the large portions, particularly of protein, seem lavishly Western. The abundant use of vegetables cooked lightly to keep their color and texture demonstrates the salubrious influence of California.

Golden roast baby chicken is stuffed with rice, raisins, and cashews surrounded by a wreath of brilliant vegetables and tender dried apricots. The vegetarian dolmas molded into a Cubist mosaic turn out to be whole vegetables stuffed with delectably moist bulgur spiked with chilies and surrounded by a yogurt-mint sauce. It's the best vegetarian dish in town. A dreamy *biriani* brings velvety chunks of lamb, basmati rice, and potatoes aromatic with onions, garlic, cumin, cinnamon, and sundried lime, heaped on a plate rimmed with creamy lemon sauce. Another lamb stew might be composed of

1220 Ninth Avenue (at Lincoln), San Francisco
Tel: 566-6966
Open Tuesday through Friday for lunch 11:30 a.m. to 2 p.m., dinner 5:30 to 10 p.m.
Price: Moderate
Credit cards: AE, MC, V

thick slices of Japanese eggplant and squashes in a dark red sweet-and-sour pomegranate sauce that explodes with flavor.

The eclectic wines on the small list have been chosen carefully to work with this food. The Italian whites and soft, spicy California Zinfandels do the job admirably. Two dense little desserts also hit the spot after a meal of powerful flavors: pistachio baklava topped with shredded coconut, and a honey cake. Both are voluptuously surrounded by Iraqi-style clotted cream drizzled with date syrup.

The interior of this small restaurant somehow evokes the shapes, colors, and history of Mesopotamia, the ancient land between the Tigris and Euphrates rivers. In the middle of a detailed, sandy-hued mural of the walled city of Babylon, which decorates one full side of the dining room, is a tiny blue arch, the gateway into the city. When you walk into the restaurant a series of ceiling-high blue arches echo the painting. Dramatic blue-rimmed front windows and a tiled open kitchen frame a sand-colored dining room furnished with ziggurat-patterned banquettes and small linen-covered tables.

The service is accommodating and enthusiastic. Chef Yahya himself comes out of the kitchen frequently to talk with customers. His energy sets the tone for this modern crossroads of civilization south of Golden Gate Park.

CAFES

This indoor-outdoor cafe boasts one of the most charming garden settings in the Bay Area. Nestled in a protected courtyard basking in sunlight, the outdoor seating area is furnished with wrought-iron tables shaded with umbrellas around a small pool. The surrounding garden is particularly wonderful in the spring when the rhododendrons are in bloom. A Victorian arbor, landscaped and dotted with sculpture, serves as one enchanting wall.

M.H. de Young Museum in Golden Gate Park, San Francisco
Tel: 752-0116
Open Wednesday through Sunday 11 a.m. to 3:30 p.m.
Credit cards: MC, V

The cafe is run by Rick O'Connell, a well-known chef and caterer in San Francisco. Her menu emphasizes fresh, colorful seasonal produce best shown off in excellent salads prepared at the moment behind a cafeteria counter where you order. Items like warm goat cheese *crostini*, showered with a luscious tomato, cucumber, and red onion salad in a sparkly balsamic vinaigrette, are delivered to the table when they're ready. All the sandwiches are made to order and exceptionally tasty. A children's menu offers half sandwiches with cups of house-made soup. O'Connell understands quality and simplicity, and her dishes always make good culinary sense.

One drawback to using the de Young Cafe as a drop-in destination is the $5 admission charge you pay at the museum gate to get there. However, admission to the de Young is free from 10 a.m. to noon every Saturday and all day the first Wednesday of the month. And if you are a museum member, you can use this first-rate cafe in the park whenever you want without a surcharge.

JAMMIN' JAVA COFFEE HOUSE

1398 Judah Street (at 9th Avenue), San Francisco

Tel: 566-JAVA

Open Monday through Friday 6 a.m. to midnight, Saturday and Sunday 6:30 a.m. to midnight

No credit cards

Typical of so many coffeehouses in the city outside of North Beach, where coffeehouses take their mission seriously, this popular corner cafe exudes grunge. From the uncleared tables to the overflowing lattes, Jammin' Java couldn't be more relaxed. This environment attracts a steady flow of young and middle-aged patrons from the neighborhood as well as students from the nearby University of California San Francisco. The drawing card for food-lovers is the steamed-milk drinks. The coffee-makers ascribe to the more is better philosophy, so an espresso comes as a brimming-full demitasse of strong, rich coffee without the intensity or creaminess of the best espresso. However, this copious kind of espresso makes for a good latte. Eclectic and loud music, revolving art shows, and friendly, efficient counterpeople keep the scene hopping.

JAVA BEACH CAFE

1396 La Playa Boulevard (at Judah), San Francisco

Tel: 665-5282

Open daily 6 a.m. to 11 p.m.

No credit cards

A civilized little cafe at the end of the N-Judah streetcar line, Java Beach is a hangout for surfers, cyclists, and that peculiar kind of person who would live no place other than the edge of the ocean. The smell of the sea, the moist soft air, the beach stretching for miles just over an embankment, make a good cup of coffee taste even better. The juxtaposition of a cafe that turns out full-flavored, unbitter espresso—and offers ten or so blends of brewed coffee (kept warm in Thermoses on the counter)—with laid-back beach life gives Java Beach its cachet. A brisk walk could be planned with a payoff at this welcoming cafe.

DELICATESSENS

JUST LIKE HOME

A dining room with vinyl booths looms in the back of Just Like Home, but I rarely have seen anyone eat there. Most people take home the Middle Eastern standbys displayed in the refrigerated counter at the front of the store. I particularly like Just Like Home's garlicky *baba ganoush* (smoky eggplant puree) and a tasty, saffron-tinted potato salad. The green and black olives are both nice. Try some hot sauce made with roasted red sweet and hot peppers; it adds sparkle to everything. Although the pastries made on the premises look tempting (filo-topped custard squares and honey cake), they have been rancid on occasion. Augment your meal with cucumbers and Persian yogurt bought at the Twenty-Second and Irving Market.

1924 Irving Street (between 20th and 21st avenues), San Francisco
Tel: 681-3337
Open daily 10 a.m. to 9 p.m.
No credit cards

NEW HAI KY

Although many people eat noodles and plates of Chinese roast duck over rice here, the main draw of this place for me is Chinese barbecue to go. Hai Ky makes several different kinds of roast and barbecue duck and pork, which stay moist and fresh from generally quick turnover. For a change, try the Roast Duck Chinese Guitar, in which the bird is splayed out (in a vaguely guitarlike shape) to take on extra-strong curing and deeper roasting. The guitar duck's skin and flesh is saltier, sweeter, and more aromatic of Chinese five spices than the regular roast duck, and the meat has an even more velvety texture.

2191 Irving Street (at 23rd Avenue), San Francisco
Tel: 731-9948
Daily 9 a.m. to 9 p.m.
No credit cards

SUNRISE DELI

2115 Irving Street
(at 22nd Avenue),
San Francisco
Tel: 664-8210
Open Monday through
Saturday 9 a.m. to 8 p.m.,
Sunday 9:30 a.m. to 6 p.m.
No credit cards

A small, homey Middle Eastern deli, Sunrise stocks a variety of Middle Eastern cooking supplies, like fruity Lebanese extra-virgin olive oil, flat breads in several sizes, and huge sheets of whole-wheat flat bread. The pistachio Turkish delight, a very sweet jellylike dessert, is fresh here. Rich whole-milk Persian yogurt takes up a section of the deli case along with tabbouleh, hummus, *baba ganoush*, grape leaves—all the usual. The felafel are better eaten hot on the premises. People sit at a few round tables in the store while they nibble pita bread sandwiches constructed to order.

YAYA'S DELI

1224 Ninth Avenue (at
Lincoln), San Francisco
Tel: 661-4442
Open daily 11 a.m. to 7 p.m.
Credit cards: AE, MC, V

Next door to the restaurant, with a similar brightly painted facade, YaYa's deli will supply the Middle Eastern cook with a full pantry of spices, grains, pickles, as well as prepared food to take home or eat there. Some of the more interesting dry goods include tiny round balls of couscous, dried Ormani lemons good for lemonade or tea, fresh pistachios, whole bunches of fragrant dried Greek oregano, and macaroni in the shape of rice grains. Everything in the deli counter is made on the premises, including an excellent tabbouleh, which is composed mostly of chopped parsley so that it tastes like a tart, pungent salad; hummus; smoky *baba ganoush* (pureed eggplant); grape leaves that were mushily overcooked the time I tried them; and some interesting fritters called *kebbe*. They look like small footballs, and the best are vegetarian, filled with mushrooms and encased in rice flour. The pita sandwiches, generously stuffed with two large lamb kabobs, hummus, yogurt, and tomatoes, are very tasty, especially with a side order of saffron rice pilaf. Yahya Saleh has big plans for the deli. He wants to bring in a wide variety of Middle Eastern products not found anywhere else, and to that end, the deli is already putting up jars of its own pickles, colorfully stacked up in the back.

BAKERIES/PASTRIES

BAKERS OF PARIS

1101 Taraval Street (at 21st Avenue), San Francisco

Tel: 863-8726

Open daily 7 a.m. to 6 p.m.

No credit cards

See listings, pages 190, 271.

HOUSE OF PIROSHKI

When I walked into House of Piroshki, the Russian man at the cash register was speaking Spanish to a cook. "You speak Spanish?" I asked. "Yes," he said. "I speak a little Spanish and Russian. And not too much English." But his English was just fine. And so were his piroshki, even though Spanish was being spoken in the kitchen. These large, oval, doughnutlike pastries get savory stuffings, the most delicious being crumbled ground beef or spinach and cheese. One of these piroshki makes for a very substantial snack. Two comprise a meal that will

1231 Ninth Avenue (between Judah and Lincoln), San Francisco

Tel: 661-1696

Open Tuesday through Saturday 10:30 a.m. to 5 p.m.

No credit cards

FILO-WRAPPED APPLE TART

4 tablespoons Calvados or dark rum

1/3 cup raisins

6 tart apples, peeled, cored, and cut into 1/8-inch slices

2 tablespoons plus 1/2 cup sugar

Juice of 1/2 lemon

12 sheets fresh or thawed frozen filo

1 cup (2 sticks) unsalted butter, melted

The fresh filo dough from Sheharazad Bakery is soft, luxurious, moist, and easy to use. It will keep in the refrigerator for 5 days. This is a luscious and dramatic-looking dessert, inspired by the Medieval Apple Tart from The Silver Palate Cookbook, *but it should be served immediately to stay crisp. My friend John Chalik cooked it for me one evening, and I have been playing around with the recipe ever since.*

Preheat the oven to 400°F.

Warm 2 tablespoons of the Calvados or rum in a small saucepan. Remove from heat and add the raisins.

In a mixing bowl, toss the apples with 2 tablespoons of the sugar and the lemon juice.

Unwrap the filo dough and cover it with a damp cloth. Using a pastry brush, lightly butter a 14-inch pizza pan or baking sheet. Lay 1 sheet of filo in the center of the pan, brush it with melted butter, and sprinkle it with 2 teaspoons of the sugar and 1/2 teaspoon of the rum or Calvados. Repeat this process with 5 more sheets of filo, laying each new sheet a one-quarter turn from the previous one to create a circle effect.

Combine the apples and raisins. Mound them onto the center of the dough in a pile about 6 inches in diameter. Brush the top with butter and sprinkle with 1 tablespoon of the sugar.

Cover the apple-raisin mixture with another sheet of filo, brush it with butter, sprinkle with 2 teaspoons of the sugar and 1/2 teaspoon of the Calvados or rum, and repeat the process with 5 more sheets of filo, placing each sheet a one-quarter turn from the previous one. Brush the topmost layer of the filo with butter but do not sugar or sprinkle it.

Gently turn the edges of the dough up to seal it. Brush any dry edges with butter.

Bake in the middle of the oven until golden brown, about 30 to 40 minutes. Serve immediately.

Makes one 9- to 10-inch tart, serves 4 to 6

stay with you for a long time. The dough is the best in the city, light, airy, and yeasty, if soak-through-the-bag oily on the golden exterior from being deep-fried. Eaten warm as you walk down the street (ask for extra napkins) or at a Formica table in the ancient shop, these piroshki certainly could be a reward for a strenuous walk in Golden Gate Park.

JUST DESSERTS

836 Irving Street (between Ninth and Tenth avenues),

San Francisco

Tel: 681-1277

Open Monday through Thursday 7:30 a.m. to 11 p.m.,

Friday 8 a.m. to midnight, Saturday 7:30 a.m. to midnight,

Sunday 8 a.m. to 11 p.m.

Credit cards: MC, V

See listing, page 216.

SHAHARAZAD BAKERY AND FILO SPECIALISTS

Filo dough has many uses, especially for those of us who have trouble working with dough. You can buy a pound of tissue-thin filo sheets at Shaharazad and make a fresh fruit dessert wrapped in crisp pastry that will impress anyone. The freshly made filo at Shaharazad can be used like puff pastry, though you actually form the layers yourself by using multiple sheets of filo brushed with butter. Shaharazad also carries premade Greek and Middle Eastern desserts and turnovers, including sour cherry and apple turnovers made with filo, and heavenly finger baklava, called *burma*, which can be exceptionally

1586 Noriega Street (between 22nd and 23rd avenues), San Francisco

Tel: 661-1155

Open Monday through Saturday 9 a.m. to 6 p.m.

No credit cards

crisp and light if you catch them at the right time. This is the only place in the city that makes its own filo dough and sells it fresh.

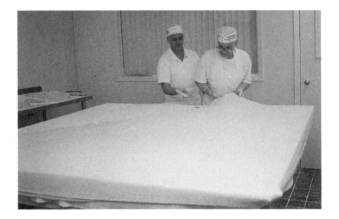

ICE CREAM/CHOCOLATES

2116 Irving Street (at 22nd Avenue), San Francisco

Tel: 665-3090

Open Monday through Thursday 8 a.m. to 10 p.m., Friday and

Saturday until 11 p.m., Sunday 9 a.m. to 10 p.m.

No credit cards

See listing, page 273.

68 West Portal Avenue (between Ulloa and Vicente),

San Francisco

Tel: 564-9412

Open Monday through Thursday 11 a.m. to 11 p.m.,

Friday and Saturday 11 a.m. to midnight,

Sunday noon to 10 p.m.

No credit cards

See listing, page 273.

Stonestown Galleria, 19th Avenue (at Winston), San Francisco

Tel: 731-1784

Open Monday through Saturday 10 a.m. to 9 p.m.,

Sunday 11 a.m. to 6 p.m.

No credit cards

See listing, page 273.

COFFEE

PEET'S COFFEE AND TEA

54 West Portal Avenue (between Ulloa and Vicente),
San Francisco
Tel: 731-0375
Open Monday through Friday 7 a.m. to 7 p.m.,
Saturday and Sunday 8 a.m. to 6 p.m.
Credit cards: AE, MC, V

See listing, page 218.

SPINELLI COFFEE COMPANY

Lakeshore Plaza, 1509 Sloat Boulevard, San Francisco
Tel: 665-9055
Open Monday through Friday 6:30 a.m. to 10 p.m.,
Saturday 7 a.m. to 10 p.m., Sunday 7 a.m. to 9 p.m.
Credit cards: MC, V

See listing, page 192.

MARKETS

Andronico's, an independently owned chain of grocery stores with four branches in Berkeley, just opened a huge, clean supermarket in the Sunset with a large prepared-food section, an "international" hofbrau with cafe seating, and a full-service meat counter. Some of the best features of the market are amenities like an olive bar, with eight different kinds of olives that customers scoop into containers and bring to the check-out line. In

1200 Irving Street (between
14th Avenue and Funston),
San Francisco
Tel: 661-3220
Open daily 7 a.m. to 11 p.m.
Credit Cards: D, MC, V

NILOUFER'S TURKEY KABOBS

My Parsi friend Niloufer Ichaporia King makes these turkey kabobs all the time, and now I do too. I serve them with basmati rice, Persian yogurt purchased at the Twenty-Second and Irving Produce Market, cucumbers, and mango sliced and marinated in lime, salt, and red chili flakes. You can serve these kabobs with almost anything and they will disappear.

Soak the bread crumbs in the half-and-half. In a large bowl, combine all the rest of the ingredients, except the oil, with the soaked bread crumbs.

Heat a little oil in a large skillet and cook 1 teaspoon of the turkey mixture. Taste for salt and correct the seasoning if necessary.

Form the turkey mixture into patties about 2 inches in diameter and 1 inch thick.

Heat 1 to 2 tablespoons vegetable oil in the skillet. Sauté the kebabs until they are crisp and brown on one side. Then turn and cook until firm to the touch, about 5 minutes. These kabobs are almost as good cold as they are hot.

Makes about 8 kabobs, serves 4

1/2 cup fresh bread crumbs
1/4 cup half-and-half or milk
1 pound ground turkey, preferably
    dark meat
1 1/2 inches ginger, peeled and
    minced
1 teaspoon kosher salt
3 garlic cloves, minced
3 serrano chilies, seeded and minced
1/2 bunch cilantro, seeded and minced
1 egg
Vegetable oil for frying

the long deli case, salads and prepared foods (like four different kinds of lasagne to take home and warm up) cater to the family that does not have time to cook. You'll also find delicacies, like four kinds of smoked salmon sliced to order. In front of the deli case are breads from the best local small bakers: Acme, Metropolis, and Semifreddi to name but a few. The meat department will cut to suit and has hard-to-find items like freshly ground turkey and chicken. Andronico's has brought Western grocery shopping to a new level in this part of town.

ETHNIC MARKETS

IRVING SEAFOOD MARKET

See Fish Markets, page 494.

MAY WAH

This is a terrific, all-around Asian market specializing in Chinese, Vietnamese, and Thai ingredients. Produce, fish, meat, dry goods, prepared foods—practically anything imaginable needed to cook these cuisines is available at May Wah. At the meat and fish counters you can get pork ground to order or any sort of cut, slices of Smithfield ham (dry, salted ham akin to Yunan ham), chickens, bones, chicken parts, and fresh shellfish, much of it still alive in tanks. Gorgeous silvery pomfrets, a small, tasty fish much used in Asia and convenient for home cooking, sell quickly here, as do local whole flatfish like rex sole and sand dabs. In the produce department you often find a multicultural mix of Asian items like beautiful fresh *shiso* leaves, lotus root, boxes of pickled Chinese greens, young ginger, and piles of lemongrass. There are whole aisles of Asian candies and cookies from all over the world that happen to appeal to the Asian palate. Sacks of rice—black, pink, white—are stacked into tall piles. At the front of the store near the cash registers are elegant taro leaf bundles bound with stems, filled with sticky rice

2201 Irving (at 27th Avenue), San Francisco

Tel: 665-4755

Open daily 8 a.m. to 7 p.m.

Credit Cards: MC, V; $10 minimum

to take home and steam. What lovely packaging for an age-old convenience food! Bins of cashews and macadamias share the same display with bins of tiny dried shrimp and fish. The abundance of things to buy, to try, to find out about, dazzles; under-scoring how lucky San Franciscans are to have so many vital ethnic communities to support markets like this.

TWENTY-SECOND AND IRVING MARKET

22nd Avenue and Irving,
San Francisco
Tel: 681-5212
Open Monday through
Saturday 8 a.m. to 6 p.m.,
Sunday 8:30 a.m.
to 5 p.m.
No credit cards

Only in the Sunset can a market with so many eddying cross-cultural currents thrive. The outer Sunset (19th Avenue toward the ocean) has become the place where immigrants from Russia, the Middle East, Eastern Europe, and Asia converge, and this store caters to everyone. In one small area of the refrigerator case for example, I sighted tofu, *queso fresco*, Armenian string cheese, Persian yogurt, Greek feta, and Danish cream cheese in glass jars. On the grocery shelves bottles of Cortas pomegranate syrup, Bulgarian jam, Calamata olives, Polish cookies, and pitted sour cherries sit next to each other in mind-boggling proximity. You think that you're in the Adriatic or Mediterranean section, until you notice the boxes of Japanese soup base. Such variety, such turnover. No dust gathers on the jars.

The other great draw of the Twenty-Second and Irving Market is the produce section, full of fresh nut meats and seeds along with hard-to-find seasonal items like olives to cure at home, green almonds, pickling cucumbers, and other products most often found at farmers' markets. Maybe because rents are cheaper out in the Sunset the markets can be large and variously stocked, and prices can be low, which encourages a large volume of shoppers. Fuji apples, a loss leader at practically every other store, cost 39¢ a pound here ($1.29 for extra-large ones at Andronico's, 29¢ for blemished ones in the Richmond). The Twenty-Second and Irving Market is one more reason to award the three or so blocks on Irving between 21st and 24th the best-food-shopping award.

YAYA'S DELI

See listing, page 482.

PRODUCE

INNER SUNSET
COMMUNITY FOOD STORE

Ecological considerations aside, organic produce usually tastes better. But you can pat yourself on the back for seeking it out. Since it's grown without pesticides, synthetic fertilizers, and herbicides, buying organic supports sustainable agriculture and the life of the planet. For eighteen years the Inner Sunset Community Food Store has devoted its shelves to mostly organic produce and organic products, from coffee beans to pasta. The produce section is relatively small but pretty, featuring only fresh, attractive, and seasonal fruits and vegetables. In early April, bins of citrus—blood oranges, Rangpoor limes, Meyer lemons, mandarins, Seville oranges, navel oranges—share the shelves with baby leeks, braising greens, and the usual bread-and-butter produce.

1319 20th Avenue,

San Francisco

Tel: 664-5363

Open daily 9:30 a.m.

to 8:30 p.m.

No credit cards

Inner Sunset is part of a small group of natural foods stores that began in the 1970s as produce collectives and later became stores. They are worker owned and run as communes with varying degrees of pleasantness. Unlike some, the Inner Sunset store is neat as a pin and civilly run.

TWENTY-SECOND AND IRVING MARKET

See Ethnic Markets, page 492.

FISH

IRVING SEAFOOD MARKET

2130 Irving (between 22nd and 23rd avenues), San Francisco

Tel: 681-5000

Open daily 8:30 a.m. to 7:00 p.m.

No credit cards

Smaller and less frenetic than the large May Wah across the street, this tidy market displays a wide variety of fresh fish and shellfish, pork and beef, and some good-looking produce as well as Asian groceries in a connecting storefront next door. Whole sparkly-eyed sand dabs, carp, tiny smelt, large and small trout, and rex sole glisten on tables of crushed ice. Tanks full of live crabs and lobster stand ready to be mined. Different varieties of shrimp are arranged like jewels behind a glass case. You don't have to be assertive to be waited on at the Irving Seafood Market. This smaller store is eager to serve, out to compete with the big guys across the street.

In addition to pristine fish, this market puts out some choice produce at the front of the store, which recently

included (in April) tiny pea shoots, (delicious sautéed like spinach with garlic and ginger), exceptionally fresh lotus root, durian, whole winter melon sold by the hunk, Fuji apples, real green papayas (as opposed to underripe papayas), and ripe, flesh-heavy navel oranges. In the grocery section next door, look for bags of the spectacular, explosive, true-flavored ginger drops called Jae Jae Ginger Drops. Each clear amber candy gets its own wrapper, so you can carry them around to refresh your mouth any time.

YUM YUM

Western shoppers like Yum Yum, a branch of Nikko Fish on Third Street, for its neat refrigerated counter full of easy-to-handle filleted fish. However, the selection at nearby May Wah or Irving Street Seafood surpasses the one here. At Yum Yum you can buy local snapper fillets and other filleted fish without being growled at. If you need a salmon steak or two, Yum Yum has them. A sushi-to-go bar prepares sushi to order, a nice amenity at a fish store.

2181 Irving Street (between 22nd and 23rd avenues), San Francisco

Tel: 566-6433

Open daily 9:30 a.m. to 6:30 p.m.

No credit cards

WINES AND SPIRITS

MR. LIQUOR

250 Taraval

Tel: 731-6222

Open Monday through
Saturday 10 a.m. to 5 p.m.,
Sunday 8:30 a.m.
to 6:30 p.m.

Credit cards: MC, V

A friendly, sophisticated wine shop in the outer reaches of Parkside? Yes. Though Mr. Liquor also carries beer and liquor, this nineteen-year-old operation knows how to put together a tasty selection of California, French, and a few Italian wines from the best importers (Kermit Lynch, Chambers and Chambers). Beautiful champagnes and elegant Burgundies share the limited shelf space with handpicked wines in the $6 to $15 range, some of which you can taste at a serve-yourself wine bar for 50¢ a pour. I recommend that you do so. Some of the least expensive wines may not be worth the savings. The knowledgeable clerks are eager to guide you. They hold special vertical tastings every Saturday as part of their education program, and Mr. Liquor's monthly newsletter is both informative and literate. If you are a serious collector or just a drinker, Mr. Liquor is well worth a trip. The store also stocks hard-to-find single-malt Scotches and specialty bourbons, *grappas*, and imported stouts and ales.

COOKWARE AND BOOKS

EASY MONEY DISCOUNT OUTLET

When I walked into Easy Money in search of a note-book, the jumble of cheap merchandise made me dis-count this discount store. Then my eagle-eyed shopping expert spotted some large white oval and rectangular gratin dishes for about $3.99 each that cost six times as much anywhere else. The glaze on these had a few imperfections, but I had to put on my reading glasses to find them. I bought them all, debating over some fluted crème brûlée cups at three for a dollar, identical to some three times more expensive. Then the owner took me to the back to show me some rather elegant champagne glasses he had, unfortunately stamped with a logo. No go. But who knows what other treasures might show up at Easy Money. If you're in the neighborhood, you should stop by.

2312 Irving,
San Francisco
Tel: 731-3538
Open Monday through
Saturday 8:30 a.m. to 7:30
p.m., Sunday 10 a.m. to
6 p.m.
Credit cards: MC, V

KITCHEN FRIEND

Chinese and Japanese cookware and china fill the shelves of this well-organized store. A careful perusal will turn up treasures like a pair of deep Japanese bowls in an exquisite dark green, almost black, glaze, or a heavy red clay charcoal brazier wrapped in aluminum with a carrying handle for somewhat-portable cooking (the brazier must weigh about thirty pounds). Rice cookers in all sizes fill up a long shelf, as do a variety of huge stainless steel steamers at excellent prices. A wall of kitchen gadgets and shelves of Western implements like wooden rolling pins and covered saucepans of different grades can be a boon to any budget-minded cook looking for the right tool.

2200 Irving,
San Francisco
Tel: 564-3385
Open daily 9 a.m. to 7 p.m.
Credit cards: MC, V

SUNSET BOOKSTORE

2161 Irving Street,
San Francisco
Tel: 664-3644
Open Monday through
Saturday 9 a.m. to 9 p.m.,
Sunday 10 a.m. to 9 p.m.
Credit cards: MC, V

Right in the thick of the best food-shopping district in the Sunset, a large section of used cookbooks waits to be mined. My shopping routine includes a stop at the Sunset Bookstore. On a recent visit I spotted the superb Paula Wolfert's *World of Food* (perfect for the neighborhood), a Diana Kennedy *Art of Mexican Cooking* (better for the Mission) and *The Pepperidge Farm Cookbook*, all in hardback and in almost pristine condition for about half the original price.

WILLIAMS-SONOMA

Stonestown Galleria, 19th Avenue (at Winston), San Francisco
Tel: 681-5525
Open Monday through Saturday 10 a.m. to 9 p.m.,
Sunday 11 a.m. to 7 p.m.
Credit cards: AE, MC, V

See listing, page 175.

OUT OF TOWN

THE EAST BAY

The East Bay

RESTAURANTS

BAY WOLF

Michael Wild, the intellectual, twinkly-eyed chef-partner of Bay Wolf, has been putting out a different seasonal menu every two weeks for eighteen years. This East Bay institution is ensconced in a graciously converted house with a wide front porch for outdoor dining, two wood-paneled dining rooms with good modern art on the walls, and a pleasant little bar. The food has gotten better and better over the years, simpler rather than fussier, as it draws on a marketplace offering ever more naturally delicious ingredients and focuses more directly on Provençal- and Italian-inspired preparations. Bay Wolf has always had a style of its own: generous, homey, good on meats, great on wines, with a few mannerisms. Over the years the kitchen has been influenced by a number of its different chefs, but francophile Wild has been a steadying constant, insisting on luscious dishes like roast chicken with chickpea flour crepes and grilled leeks; juicy leg of lamb with garlic custard; grilled northern halibut with roasted rosemary

3853 Piedmont Avenue, Oakland
Tel: 510-655-6004
Open for lunch Monday through Friday 11:30 a.m. to 2 p.m.; dinner Monday through Friday 6 to 9 p.m., Saturday and Sunday 5:30 to 9 p.m.
Price: Moderate
Credit cards: MC, V

potatoes; and of course a duck dish with a fruit sauce, a Bay Wolf specialty. The starters might be a chilled shrimp salad in mustard vinaigrette with greens, or a yellow pepper stuffed with goat cheese. An apple *galette* with lavender honey, or a chocolate-ginger pot de crème might be dessert.

I went to a book party for a mutual friend of Michael's and mine, put on at Bay Wolf, and I don't think I have ever been served such nice food for a large group. After all these years, Bay Wolf still has conviction, energy, and integrity. So many people eat there regularly that they feel part of the extended Bay Wolf family, with much exchanging of books, talk about wine, and discussion of art. In many ways, Bay Wolf is the quintessential East Bay restaurant, and many of the neighborhood new-comers, like Citron, have been inspired by it.

BOMBAY CUISINE

2006 Ninth Street, Berkeley
Tel: 510-843-9601
Open for lunch Tuesday through Sunday 11:30 a.m. to 3 p.m.; dinner Tuesday through Sunday 5 to 9 p.m.
Price: Inexpensive
Credit cards: AE, MC, V

On a good day, a diner at this little Indian cafe might be served a brightly seasoned vegetarian *thali* plate, or all sorts of South Indian snacks like *vadas, dosas, idli* and *uttapam*, as well as vegetable curries and wonderful *chapatis* and *parathas*, Indian breads cooked on a griddle. Bombay Cuisine does not have a tandoori oven, which means it is liberated from the omnipresent Punjabi lamb-centered menus. The hard-to-find Indian snacks can be a real treat, like *dahi vada*, small, tender, fried balls of *dal* flour sauced in yogurt and served with pruney tamarind chutney; or *bataka vada*, deep-fried potato fritters served with cilantro-mint chutney. A fried chickpea *vada* flattened into a patty and laced with onion is particularly crisp and savory, a favorite of mine, especially with a white chutney made from dried coconut and chilies. *Dhokla,* airy steamed squares of chickpea flour, tastes like nutty, fragrant risen bread. The *raita,* yogurt mixed with onions and cucumber, is great on everything. Don't pass up the puffy bread called *puri,* worth ordering just for the warm wheaty breath they expel when you tear into them. Use the pieces to scoop up a vegetable curry. For dessert, *gulab jamun,* Indian doughnuts soaked in rose water–scented syrup, maintain their fluffy texture.

The small dining room is clean and pleasantly decorated. Service may not be a high point here, but when the food finally gets to the table it tastes freshly made and homey. You get the feeling that the cooks themselves get true satisfaction feeding an expatriate Indian community real tastes of home.

BRENNAN'S RESTAURANT, INC.

This beloved Berkeley hofbrau and bar has undergone a face-lift after thirty-three years, but the pensioners and students who depend on its first-rate cafeteria food for basic sustenance don't have to worry that the place is going upscale. A coat of bright Egyptian-green paint has been rolled over the old, amazingly drab institutional shade, and customers are dazzled by such modern turns as clear glass windows, perimeter lighting, wooden partitions with coat hooks, and two large new televisions for sporting events. Though Brennan's has taken on a publike cachet—well, kind of—prices have stayed the same. The blown-up photos of Mr. Brennan posing in front of prize steers at 4-H auctions still gaze down at customers tucking into their chewy roast beef sandwiches, French

720 University Avenue,
Berkeley
Tel: 510-841-0960
Open everyday 11 a.m. to
9 p.m.; bar open
weeknights until 1 a.m.,
weekends until 2 a.m.
Price: Inexpensive
No credit cards

dipped, of course. And the same cast of characters—artists, sailors from the nearby marina, metalworkers, people off the dinner shift from restaurants around Berkeley—still stops by for late-night drinks. The food on the cafeteria line still includes gigantic roast turkeys, whole briskets of corned beef, and massive top rounds of roast beef, thickly sliced to order and generously stacked onto French rolls, rye bread, or white. Excellent coleslaw in a creamy dressing and incendiary horseradish on the tables enhance all the sandwiches. Turkey plates with nicely seasoned bread stuffing, mashed potatoes, canned or frozen vegetable of choice, and gravy mean that hundreds can celebrate Thanksgiving every day. Some people make a point of going to Brennan's on Wednesdays for the smoked tongue plate with boiled potatoes and cabbage; others always get there early enough to grab the almost giraffe-size turkey necks while they last. One truly new development is the chicken rotisserie, the source for a juicy half-chicken plate, which has become the most popular to-go item. For dessert, the pies, with flaky crusts made with lard, especially the rhubarb, have fillings that aren't too sweet. For cheap, substantial eats and a friendly bar, Brennan's is still the best.

BRIDGES

44 Church Street, Danville
Tel: 510-820-7200
Nightly 5:30 to 9:30 p.m.;
lunch served Fridays 11:30
a.m. to 2 p.m.
Price: Moderate
Credit cards: AE, MC, V

This stunning modern restaurant in the center of a bucolic suburban village provided the setting for some of the most hilarious scenes in Robin Williams's movie *Mrs. Doubtfire*, but beyond its big-screen stardom, Bridges has earned a reputation for an eclectic, well-executed East-West menu. The inspiration comes from the far corners of the world, with special attention focused on Japan, south Asia, and the Mediterranean. In fact, the dishes are so far flung you have to think about how to compose a palatable meal, matching up geographically compatible appetizers and main courses like a puzzle. You could start with a mildly spicy Thai beef salad with julienned vegetables and cellophane noodles and follow it with a ravishingly delicious Thai seafood stew in coconut-milk broth with shrimp toasts. Or, you might pair a Caesar salad with an orange- and star anise–scented smoked pork loin on top of wild rice and almonds. The desserts are Western and rich. The superb wine list draws together unusual wines from all over Europe and California, making it possible to find both bottles and half bottles to go with so many disparate flavors. Thoroughly professional service adds to the sophisticated attractions of this restaurant. Several generations of chefs have run the kit-chen, but the overall tone and quality of the cooking stays high, always with a special nod toward vegetarian diners.

CAFE AT CHEZ PANISSE

Some happy developments have occurred at the moderately priced cafe upstairs at Chez Panisse. Reservations are taken, so you don't have to wait for hours anymore while the regulars are seated before you, and there's a three-course fixed-price meal for $19.50, which brings you the best of the daily menu for an affordable sum, especially when you consider the unsurpassed quality of everything that is served at this temple of beautiful ingredients. Still anchoring the menu are crusty pizzas, aromatic from the wood-fired brick oven, and the definitive green salad of the tastiest, tiniest lettuces with

1517 Shattuck Avenue, Berkeley
Tel: 510-548-5525
Lunch Monday through Thursday 11:30 a.m. to 3 p.m., Friday and Saturday until 4 p.m.; Dinner Monday through Thursday 5 to 10:30 p.m., Friday and Saturday until 11:30 p.m.

Price: Moderate
Credit cards: AE, DC , D,
MC, V

garlic croutons and a perfect vinaigrette. The rest of the menu changes with the seasons, but you can always count on something sublime and ingenuous, like toasts covered with wild mushrooms drizzled in fragrant olive oil and baked in the wood-fired oven; or LuLu Peyraud's Provençal-style grilled steak served in thin, juicy, rare slices, topped with anchovy butter, a few bitter greens, and some roasted potatoes that taste better than any others. That's the thing about *Chez Panisse*. You get food here that you think you have tasted before— roasted peppers, tomatoes, melon, lamb chops, scallops —that take you by surprise: You never realized that they could taste like this. The key to serving such naturally delicious food goes way, way back to the growing, the picking, the collecting. Alan Tangren, who used to be a chef at Chez Panisse, now works full-time as a forager, discovering and commissioning ingredients, gathering, searching, encouraging farmers to raise certain species, and teaching everyone through the lusciousness of the stuff he finds about the importance of ecologically sound growing practices. Of course, the cooking itself certainly plays a large part, but letting the ingredients, when they're at their peak, dictate the menu has been the Chez Panisse breakthrough. I marvel at the presentations, so simple, yet so beautiful. Nothing is crowded onto the plates or fussy; the arrangements are naturally full of color and life. Eating here is always a pleasure. You feel nourished, refreshed, delighted, meal after meal, year after year. Not enough can be said about the influence of Alice Waters's vision and the enormous impact she has had on cooking and eating in America. If you're a believer, you might as well be nourished at the source.

I have a soft spot in my heart for this old-fashioned steak, prime rib, and fried-chicken house in Orinda, with a long western bar, wonderfully warm service, and practically everything made from scratch. John Goyak, the second generation of his family to run this sixty-five-year-old roadhouse with a racy past, called on some chef friends from Chez Panisse to help him update the menu. But he could only change a little of it without disappointing his regulars, thank goodness. No customer would tolerate giving up the hot cream biscuits with honey that go with Casa Orinda's southern-fried chicken. Casa Orinda actually uses the original Kentucky fried chicken cooking equipment and formulas, which they bought when the Colonel was selling his process door to door. The way the chicken comes out at Casa Orinda makes the greasy fast-food version seem pale. People buy tons of prime rib and steak and a delicious chicken cutlet breaded in fresh Acme bread crumbs and fried in clarified butter. The pastry department makes all sorts of fresh fruit pies and cobblers, and even old customers love a sparkling fresh lemon tart taught to the kitchen by Patty Curtan from Chez Panisse. There aren't many old-fashioned American restaurants left, and very few that are owned by individuals with integrity. Casa Orinda is one of them, and you can tell the moment you walk in the door: People are happy to work here, the dining rooms are immaculate, and the food is comforting and tasty.

20 Bryant Way,
Orinda
Tel: 510-254-2981
Nightly 4 to 10 p.m.
Price: Moderate
Credit cards: AE, MC, V

1517 Shattuck Avenue,
Berkeley
Tel: 510-548-5525
Monday–seatings at 6, 6:30,
8:30 and 9 p.m.;
Tuesday through Saturday
seatings at 6, 6:30, 8:30
and 9:15 p.m.
Price: Expensive
Credit cards: AE, DC , D,
MC, V

The famous prix-fixe dinner that has been served for over two decades is now in the hands of two chefs: Catherine Brandel in the first part of the week and Jean-Pierre Moullé in the latter. Catherine comes up with spectacular, rustic three-course meals on Mondays for $35; one recently included Catalán tapas, a risotto with fish and shellfish from Valencia, and lemon-cinnamon ice milk with shaved coffee ice for dessert; on Tuesdays and Wednesdays for $45, a typical Chez Panisse downstairs meal might include a vegetable antipasto, a white-corn soup with a spicy shellfish relish, an exquisite chicken breast with a warm salad and chicken liver *crostini*, followed by an incomparable buttery, flaky apple and currant tart. Jean-Pierre Moullé's weekend menus at $65 begin with an aperitif, an elixir of white wine scented with fruit or herbs. The stunning meal I ate the other night continued with salads of Chino Ranch vegetables, shrimp beignets with fried leeks, the most succulent tiny lamb chops and loin in a fresh shell bean and chanterelle ragout, and for dessert a fresh berry soup with vanilla ice cream.

None of these descriptions does justice to what actually comes to the table. Once you eat at Chez Panisse you'll know how magically everything fits together; how superb the individual dishes are; how every detail from flowers to lighting to bread to wine service flows out of a single vision. I've praised this restaurant to the skies so many times that now all I want to say is that it continues on at the highest level; that no other restaurant in the world possesses its purity, simplicity, and charm; that a meal here is worth every penny—even though they can really mount up what with tax and 15 percent service added right onto the bottom of the check—and that I'd rather eat here than anywhere else in the world.

Chef Craig Thomas's ode to the neighborhood bistro has charmed the picky East Bay crowd in a way that I haven't seen since Chez Panisse opened its cafe years ago. Romantic yet low key, the small dining room glows with warmth. Someone got all the details down just right: the wicker chairs and banquettes, the little bar, the soft lighting, the tile floors, the casual large arrangements of flowers. The menu is small, interesting, nicely executed, and always delivers a couple of clever new twists on classic dishes. Generous portions and simple presentation complete the picture.

The first courses sound heavier than they are; they're really green salads accompanied with a tiny puff pastry filled with goat cheese, or a few shreds of duck *confit*. These light starters work well with the substantial main courses: a smoky coq au vin served with polenta, flanked by sweet little turnips; a seafood couscous with *harissa* on the side. Real bistro fare featuring pork loin, duck breast, or thick fillets of fish on lentils is the order of the day. Desserts follow suit with a more American bent, like fresh fruit crisp with ice cream or crème brûlée (which has become an American dessert based on how often it appears on local dessert menus).

An elegant but reasonably priced international wine list plays a large role in the pleasure of meals taken here. Each bottle on the small list has won its place for versatility and character. Citron reminds me of one of my favorite new restaurants in San Francisco, Woodward's Garden, in that it is very small, personal, yet professional, and delivers outsized satisfaction for its scope.

5484 College Avenue, Oakland

Tel: 510-653-5484

Open nightly 5:30 to 9:30 p.m.

Price: Moderate

Credit cards: MC, V

1820 Fourth Street,
Berkeley
Tel: 510-644-0444
Open Monday through
Thursday 11:30 a.m. to 9:30
p.m., Friday and Saturday
until 11 p.m.; Sunday
brunch 10:30 a.m. to 2:30
p.m., dinner until 9:30 p.m.
Price: Inexpensive to
moderate
Credit cards: AE, DC , MC, V

Bruce Cost, whose pricy but wonderful Monsoon couldn't gain a foothold in San Francisco, has hit on a winning formula at his new place, Ginger Island. Drawing from all over Asia, he is turning out inexpensive, colorful, fun-to-eat dishes in a tropical cafe setting that was once the Fourth Street Grill. The space is perfect for his East-West concept, especially during warm days when people can sit outside on the patio or in the dining room with its retracting glass roof. Customers gravitate to these sunny tables all day for large and small plates of clean, spicy, brightly flavored food, such as a cool noodle salad with shredded chicken breast and cucumber sticks in a fruity peanut sauce, or bowls of tender wontons, filled either with savory pork or green vegetables in a spectacular hot, vinegary, gingery gravy. The little skewers of juicy chicken satay with a spicy red peanut sauce are universally loved by kids, while adults can't get enough of the tiny spareribs in black bean sauce. The velvety red-cooked pork shoulder with mustard greens and soft chunks of daikon radish is a destination dish that you can actually make at home (see recipe, page 513). Stir-fried dishes have never come out better. Try a combination of shrimp, jícama, red peppers, and green onions in a hot sweet-and-sour sauce, or stir-fried chicken with oyster mushrooms and snap peas with a haunting smokiness from being cooked in a super-hot wok. How about Thai yellow curry noodles with flank steak, or a grilled half duck in a ginger glaze beautifully carved into slices, accompanied with salad greens and steamed rice? Ginger Island offers so many appealing dishes in such an enticing, breezy way that I cannot walk by without stopping in for at least a little something.

Cost has plans to open a second Ginger Island in the Stanford Shopping Center in Palo Alto. Knowing Bruce's meticulousness and organization, this expansion will only make the Palo Altoans happy without diminishing the quality of the Berkeley restaurant. If all goes well, people may be eating Ginger Island noodles up and down the state.

RED-BRAISED WHOLE PORK SHOULDER

This opulent braised pork has been a favorite dish of mine since Bruce cooked it for my birthday once, surrounding the meat with baby bok choy. The recipe, from Bruce Cost's Asian Ingredients (William Morrow, 1988), is not difficult to make, and the pork fills the kitchen with the most exotic aromas. You can buy all the dry ingredients you need at any of the Chinese markets listed in the book and the pork at any of the Chinese meat counters.

3 to 4 quarts water

One 5- to 7-pound pork shoulder, with bone and rind

3/4 cup Shaoxing wine (Chinese rice wine)

6 star anise pods

One 3-inch cinnamon stick

8 garlic cloves, smashed

Fresh ginger cut into 10 thin slices

2 or 3 pieces dried tangerine peel

2 dried red chilies

1 whole green onion

1 1/3 cups soy sauce

6 Chinese rock sugar crystals, each about 1-inch square

1 tablespoon kosher salt

In a large pot, bring the water to a boil and add the pork. When it comes to a boil again, skim off any foam and reduce heat to medium. Add the wine and cook, partially covered, for 20 minutes.

Add the star anise, cinnamon stick, garlic, ginger, tangerine peel, chilies, and green onion and cook for another 20 minutes.

Add the soy sauce, sugar crystals, and salt, and continue to cook, turning the meat occasionally, for another 2 to 3 hours. The rind and fat should be very soft when the pork is done.

Remove the pork from the liquid and keep warm. Strain the sauce into a large skillet and, over high heat, reduce to a syrup. This may take 15 minutes or longer.

When the sauce is the consistency of thin syrup, put the pork in the center of a large platter and pour the sauce over the meat. Eat with lots of rice and a green vegetable.

Serves 10 to 12

HONG KONG EAST OCEAN

3199 Powell Street,
Emeryville
Tel: 510- 655-3388
Open for lunch Monday
through Friday 11 a.m. to
2:30 p.m., Saturday and
Sunday 10 a.m. to 2:30 p.m.;
dinner nightly 5 to
9:30 p.m.
Price: Moderate
Credit cards: AE, DC , D,
MC, V

I have had sparkling Cantonese dishes at this large, modern restaurant perched at water's edge with a sweeping view of the Bay Bridge and the city. The food has been delicious, inventive, and impeccably fresh both at dim sum lunch and full-scale dinner. That it is served in a comfortably appointed dining room on several levels, all looking out to an expanse of water, only makes the experience more fun, especially after a cocktail or glass of champagne in the sunset-lit barroom. You should not eat dinner here without ordering a thick fillet of velvety black cod, smoked and marinated in sake lees, which slightly beats out a salt-baked version sprinkled with fried minced chilies. If there are enough people at the table, order one of each. Marinated calamari with spicy sesame oil are crisply deep-fried and completely addictive; scallops, shrimp, and water chestnuts finely chopped and served in an iceberg lettuce–leaf cup makes for another amusing starter. Seafood, as in all the best Cantonese restaurants, is subtly handled. One of my favorite dishes here is a clay pot of pristine shellfish, glass noodles, and lots of Napa cabbage in a clean but luscious broth. Tea lunch brings many Cantonese classics as well as Shanghai-style dumplings, pan-fried and stuffed with a juicy pork filling. *Yee mien*, soft, wide, very fresh noodles, are barely sauced so their remarkable texture can be appreciated. I have attended several banquets for groups of ten, planned ahead with the manager, with stunning food and first-rate service. When people ask where they can eat seafood with a view of the bay, I send them to Hong Kong East Ocean.

This highly regarded Cambodian restaurant specializes in fish and seafood dishes. The most delicious is the Mekong fish chowder, my dream fish soup, prepared with clean, sweet-smelling broth; gently cooked fresh squid, clams, rockfish, and shrimp; rice stirred into the soup porridge-style for texture; and bright aromatic seasoning from ginger and mint. It's a dish that's so satisfying, yet light, I could eat it every day. The other great catch here is the fisherman's stew, a spicy, fragrant coconut milk–enriched broth full of catfish, scallops, shrimp, and crab with big chunks of pumpkin, straw mushrooms, zucchini, and spinach. Eaten with nutty, slightly sticky Cambodian rice, the dish is sublime. For starters have the shrimp and green papaya salad, tart and crunchy with mint-infused dressing. A seafood crepe has a tasty stuffing of bean sprouts, onions, and shellfish, served with a sweet-and-sour dipping sauce. And everyone loves tiny, crisp spring rolls filled with ground pork. The Mermaid is one of the few Southeast Asian restaurants that prepares *amok*, a firm, velvety-textured fish mousse steamed in a banana leaf and seasoned with red curry, a lovely creation. With banana fritters and chunky coconut ice cream and a slow-dripping Vietnamese coffee for dessert, you can put together an exquisite meal at the Mermaid for unrarified prices.

824 University Avenue, Berkeley

Tel: 510- 843-1189

Open for lunch daily 11:30 a.m. to 3 p.m.; dinner nightly 5 to 10 p.m.

Price: Inexpensive

Credit cards: AE, MC, V

O CHAMÉ

1830 Fourth Street,
Berkeley
Tel: 510-841-8783
Open for lunch Monday
through Saturday 11:30
a.m. to 3 p.m.; dinner
Monday through Thursday
5:30 to 9 p.m., Friday and
Saturday until 9:30 p.m.
Price: Moderate
Credit cards: AE, DC , MC, V

David Vardy, the chef-owner of this unique teahouse and restaurant, arrived at his culinary calling by studying t'ai chi in a monastery in Taiwan with a Taoist master. He sailed to Japan for further study, but became interested in *kaiseki* cooking and the tea ceremony instead. He returned to California with a Tokyo-born wife and opened the Daruma Tea Shop, where he baked tea cakes in such perfect traditional style that teahouses in Japan started importing them. Several years ago he closed Daruma and opened O Chamé, a charming, peaceful tearoom with hand-crafted wooden furniture and a menu of noodles, soup, *bento* box lunches, and seasonal Japanese dishes. Many lunches are packaged to go and dispensed from an outdoor kiosk that also sells Pure T ice creams (see page 395).

Indoors, people order surprisingly hearty and tasty Japanese vegetarian stews of wheat gluten and root vegetables like burdock. I'm not kidding; they're really delicious and satisfying. At dinner you can make a meal of all sorts of little dishes served on a striking assortment of Japanese pottery. Start with a smoky miso broth with big cubes of kabocha squash, rings of leek, and shiitakes. Sashimi usually brings two kind of pristine raw fish such as halibut and sea urchin roe with *shiso* leaves. If you like your fish cooked, try simmered white-fish dumplings in a clear broth with pale green winter melon, orange squash, and shiitakes; or grilled sea scallops split and filled with a slice of kiwi. One of my favorite dishes is a rich stew of tea-flavored hard-cooked eggs, velvety chicken livers, and diced tomatoes. Cold dishes bring a salad of fine organic greens in a rice wine vinegar dressing, and a traditional octopus and cucumber salad.

Then, of course, there are many teahouse amenities to be savored after a meal or in the afternoon. Japanese teas are individually brewed in tiny brass pots. I find that the slightly bitter but nutty green teas finish off a Japanese meal like a cup of coffee, though fragrant jasmine tea, or a full-bodied Daruma blend served with milk, works well too. Hard, crunchy tea cakes full of peanuts go brilliantly with the teas, though O Chamé's chilled custard studded with pears poached in Zinfandel, or little dumplings made of mashed potatoes topped with plum sauce, also are fun. You never know what will turn up on Vardy's menus.

One of the meanings of O Chamé is "precious little girl." At the opening of the restaurant, Vardy's then one-year-old daughter, half Californian, half Japanese, charmed the room with her laughter. Though it was her mother who designed the lovely space, the little girl seemed to be the very incarnation of O Chamé's spirit.

OLIVETO

Paul Bertolli, a former downstairs chef at Chez Panisse, has taken the helm here as executive chef, and the difference in the cooking is quite amazing. The food here was always good because the kitchen has always been committed to using fine ingredients, but now the cooking reflects Bertolli's unique style, which is traditionally Italian, intensely flavorful, but wonderfully light. The menus, though small, are dreamy. There are always two or three dishes that you can't decide between and simply no disappointments. Instead of raising prices, Oliveto has lowered them to cafe levels, and the result is a full house every night. It certainly has become my top choice in this part of the East Bay.

5655 College Avenue, Oakland

Tel: 510-547-5356

Open for lunch Monday through Friday 11:30 a.m. to 2 p.m.; dinner Monday through Saturday 6:30 to 10 p.m., Sunday 5:30 to 8:30 p.m.

Price: Moderate

Credit cards: AE, DC , MC, V

Some of the beautiful dishes I've had come as a result of Bertolli's intuitive ability to offer what people want to eat at the moment. One summer evening I had a pasta of tender homemade noodles bathed in tiny, crisp chanterelles, tons of fresh peas, and a little cream. It couldn't have been better. Shrimp poached in an aromatic court bouillon came on a salad dressed with Bertolli's signature cucumber vinaigrette, the very taste of summer. Even though it was a warm evening, a grilled quail salad in a warm pancetta vinaigrette couldn't have been more welcome. Sweet, juicy slices of leg of lamb came with an irresistible potato pancake; crisp-skinned chicken cooked under a brick was accompanied with a squash gratin and grilled tomatoes; juicy pan-fried skate wings in brown butter came nestled next to spinach and new potatoes. These compositions profoundly satisfied.

The airy upstairs dining room, painted in warm Mediterranean sienna, with the partially open kitchen in the middle of the room, has always been a welcoming environment. All the important details—good bread and olives to start, an imaginative wine list, knowledgable service, graciousness—have always been in place. With Bertolli and a new, first-rate crew in the kitchen (from Stars and Campton Place) to execute from day to day, Oliveto is finally living up to its potential. It's almost as if a new restaurant had opened, though paradoxically, the changes have been relatively small.

Jim Maiser, the manager of Cafe Fanny, and Alice Waters's brother-in-law, bought this straight-ahead flatlands taqueria last year and has gradually introduced a new set of dishes and standards. Maiser draws on his own eating experiences in Mexico, where he spent quite a bit of time traveling, eating, and taking classes from Diana Kennedy. When he opened Picante Taqueria, he consulted with Rick Bayless, the chef of the peerless Frontera Grill and Topolobambo in Chicago. Picante is now making tortillas to order from fresh *masa*; serving whole black beans slowly simmered with *epazote* and other Mexican herbs; and offering delicate little soft tacos laid flat on a plate and piled with beautiful fillings including house-made chorizo and potatoes with an avocado-tomatillo sauce; *rajas* (roasted-pepper strips) topped with *queso fresco*; and moist, long-cooked pork carnitas topped with fresh tomato salsa, among other things. The house-made tamales are light and tender, filled with zucchini, corn, poblano chilies, and *epazote*, or pork braised in ancho-chili sauce. The fresh tortillas and Picante's carefully made fillings give new vitality to the traditional taqueria menu. With lots of tasty vegetarian alternatives, house-baked rolls for Mexican sandwiches, avocado-rich guacamole, fried-to-order chips, and many other carefully rethought components of the basic menu, Picante takes the genre to new, interesting heights. A liquor license is in the works, though now good margaritas are made with agave wine and fresh lime. Two long bars, two large, gaily painted dining rooms, lots of room for families at booths and large tables, and inexpensive prices for high-quality food make Picante a true destination taqueria.

1328 Sixth Street,
Berkeley
Tel: 510-525-3121
Open Sunday through
Thursday 11 a.m. to 10 p.m.,
Friday and Saturday until
11 p.m.
Price: Inexpensive
Credit cards: MC, V

CAFES

CAFE 817

817 Washington Street,
Oakland
Tel: 510-271-7965
Open Monday through
Friday 7:30 a.m. to 5 p.m.,
Saturday 10 a.m. to 4 p.m
No credit cards

In a narrow high-ceilinged storefront that adjoins G.B. Ratto, Oakland's great international foods store (see page 536), Sandro Rossi, a former electrical engineer from Northern Italy, and Teresa Sevilla, a Peruvian architect-designer, have created a resonant, art-filled, modern cafe that serves great coffee and miraculously inexpensive but authentic Italian cafe food. I was originally hooked by a small caffè latte made from Illy Espresso beans and served in a short tumbler, my idea of heaven. The coffee, aromatic and deep in flavor without bitterness, was smoothed with just the right amount of velvety steamed milk. Acme baguettes, *levain*, and focaccia are used for delicious sandwiches: combinations of ham, Fontina, and marinated artichokes; or warm grilled prosciutto, mozzarella, and tapanade, crisp and buttery, accompanied with a little green salad. The few hot dishes come straight from Rossi's home village and Northern Italian soul. You practically can taste the land in a Tuscan bean soup thick with cabbage and chard, and topped with grated real Parmesan. A bowl of soft, cheesy polenta is striped with mushroom ragout, sausage, and cherry tomatoes. Only Chiantis and Vernaccias are poured, and these light Italian wines taste terrific with the grilled sand-wiches and soups. Medium-sized bottles of cold San Pellegrino come with just the right little glasses. In fact, all the carefully chosen plates, glassware, and cups, and the exquisitely designed room, make the food and drinks taste even better, one more proof that a great cafe can turn the act of drinking a cup of coffee into a religious experience.

This is the third star in the triumvirate that sparkles in the Chez Panisse food universe. It's a charming little stand-up cafe in the tradition of French *tabacs* and Italian espresso bars, but the open-faced sandwiches, pizzas with bright Provençal toppings, house-baked pastries, and oven-fresh Acme breads are a cut above anything else of their kind. You get salads made of the tiniest lettuces topped with baked goat cheese; or a farm-egg-salad sandwich moistened with house-made mayon-naise, topped with Italian sun-dried tomatoes and anchovies. The café au lait comes in bowls. The house-made granola has become so popular it has been packaged for customers to take home. You have to get to the cafe early to snag the lacy buckwheat crepes with fresh fruit conserves. They always run out. The crunchy millet muffins are some of the best I've ever tasted—a recipe I tried to get for this book, but manager Jim Maiser wouldn't let me have it. Even the orange juice is extraordinary, usually mixed with tangerine or blood orange juice and always freshly squeezed. Though there is only a stand-up bar, an indoor bench, and some outdoor tables that are always full during nice weather, the satisfaction you get from a quick, informal meal here lasts all day. Cafe Fanny's location between two other Chez Panisse–inspired businesses, the Acme bread bakery and Kermit-Lynch wine store, make a visit here all the more compelling.

1603 San Pablo Avenue, Berkeley

Tel: 510-524-5447

Open Monday through Friday 7 a.m. to 3 p.m., Saturday 8 a.m. to 4 p.m., Sunday 9 a.m. to 3 p.m

No credit cards

CAFE AT OLIVETO

5655 College Avenue,
Oakland
Tel: 510-547-4382
Open Monday through
Wednesday 7 a.m. to 10
p.m., Thursday until 11
p.m., Friday and Saturday
until midnight, Sunday
until 9 p.m.
Credit cards: AE, MC, V

One reason this partially outdoor cafe is a popular spot is that people can get quick, savory little bites for under $3, like a plate of braised fresh shell beans topped with shaved Parmesan, or croutons with roasted yellow peppers in anchovy vinaigrette with black olives. For a dollar more, warm toasts piled with marinated tomatoes look very appealing, as do pretty green salads. Pizzas and focaccia sandwiches provide more substantial sustenance, and of course there's coffee, wine, and Oliveto desserts. You order at the high marble counter in front of a tidy open kitchen framed in stone. The food comes on handsome gray-green pottery plates. People sit at the bar or at tables by the open French doors, and on very crowded days they bring their food upstairs to the naked Oliveto tables.

CAFFÈ STRADA

2300 College Avenue,
Berkeley
Tel: 510-843-5282
Open Monday through
Saturday 6:30 a.m. to
midnight, Sunday 7 a.m. to
midnight
No credit cards

In a choice location across the street from Boalt Hall, the architecture building, and the anthropology museum, Caffè Strada rises to the challenge of supplying thousands of students in this part of the U.C. campus with first-rate coffee, especially their fortifying *cappuccino doppio*, and surprisingly fine croissants baked on the premises. The croissants are buttery, flaky, and crisp, though I can't recommend any other baked goods here. With more outdoor seating than indoor, even on the coolest days the outdoor tables stay full. The large, constant flow of customers, morning, noon, and night, gives Caffè Strada the vitality of the great urban cafes in Europe.

BARS

BRENNAN'S RESTAURANT, INC

See Restaurants, page 505.

KIMBALL'S EAST

The supper club is alive and well at this spacious, comfortable, full-service venue owned by Kimball Allen, the man who started the San Francisco Real Food Company in some rental properties he owned. But his real passion is jazz, and Kimball's East provides a welcoming home for it by offering a small, decently priced menu of California-Caribbean dishes, a full wine list, a full bar, freshly squeezed fruit juices and espresso, and a well-trained, accommodating staff. The tiers of booths allow for an easy view of the stage no matter where you sit. By the time you've finished dinner, the lights dim and the music begins. The advantage of eating at the club is that you get the best seats, and besides, it's fun. You feel very grown up (even if you're pushing fifty), dining and drinking and then sitting back for the show. My parents used to go out for nights like this at the Chez Paree in Chicago in the fifties and early sixties, Mom in a cocktail dress, Dad with a cigarette between his fingers, always with a large group seated around a swanky table. The scene is more casual at Kimball's East—no tablecloths, no waiters in tuxes—but some of that grand old supper club spirit lives on. I've seen performances ranging in style from the Kronos Quartet to Wayne Shorter here, and attending this club never feels like an ordeal. It's the one venue that is set up for the comfort of both the artists and the audience, and believe me, the civilized surroundings don't diminish the music one bit.

5800 Shellmound Street, Emeryville
Tel: 510-658-2555
Open Tuesday 11 a.m. to 6 p.m., dinner Wednesday through Sunday 10 a.m. to 10 p.m.
Credit cards: MC, V

DOUG'S BAR-B-Q

3600 San Pablo Avenue,
Emeryville
Tel: 510-655-9048
Open Monday through
Thursday 11 a.m. to 9 p.m.,
Friday and Saturday until
midnight, Sunday noon to
9 p.m.
Credit cards: MC, V

I like Doug's. I'm not that much of a barbecue fan, but I like Doug's. I love the fresh green beans cooked with ham and sausage; the smoky baked beans that are whole, firm, but creamy; the potato salad in a pleasant, sweet-relish-studded mayonnaise with potatoes that still have texture. When it comes to the barbecue, the pork ribs are meaty and tender; the barbecue sauce balances hot, sweet, and sour with precision in all three degrees of hotness. I actually like the gigantic beef ribs, moist and meaty, better than the pork ribs, but I'm the exception. Doug's does not stick to the usual; they barbecue goat and turkey and deep-fry turkey as well, which gives the meat a bit of an aftertaste although it stays juicier than the smoked. Both turkeys are immersed in sauce. Doug's calls itself a Texas-style barbecue and under-scores the point by displaying several pairs of longhorns above the counter. The people working under them could not be nicer at this twenty-some-year-old smoke-house, and when I get the urge for barbecue I seriously consider coming all the way here.

BLONDIE'S PIZZA

2340 Telegraph Avenue,
Berkeley
Tel: 510-548-1129
Monday through Thursday
10 a.m. to 1 a.m., Friday
and Saturday 10:30 a.m.
to 2 a.m., Sunday 11 a.m.
to 2 a.m.
No credit cards

For other location, see page 166.

This original Blondie's location must sell more slices of hot, cheesy, saucy, bready pizza than any other place in the world. The line never stops, and the army of pizza makers barely keeps up with the demand. A fresh hot slice of this not-too-oily pizza is dirt cheap and fills you up for most of the day.

Silvana La Rocca does an excellent job gathering all the necessities of the upscale East Bay pantry at her multi-faceted food store. In addition to good olives in bulk, serrano ham from Spain, prosciutto from Parma, anchovies in salt, buffalo-milk mozzarella, high-quality Rustichella dried pasta, and house-made fresh pasta, La Rocca makes three types of Italian sausages; lots of bean, rice, and pasta salads; pesto sauce; and chicken stock for soups. During the season, Made to Order carries both black and white truffles and brings in a range of extra-virgin olive oils and balsamic vinegars, among other rarities. The store has everything from inexpensive wines to ceramic dishes, practically anything you might need to put together a good meal, either from scratch or with the help of some prepared foods. The staff is friendly and knowledgeable, the displays attractively arranged and the deli counter freshly stocked, making it one of the few vigorous, independent, full-scale delicatessens left in the world.

1576 Hopkins Street, Berkeley

Tel: 510-524-7552

Open Monday through Saturday 9:30 a.m. to 6 p.m.

Credit cards: MC, V

MARKET HALL PASTA SHOP

5655 College Avenue,
Oakland
Tel: 510-547-4005
Open Monday through
Friday 10 a.m. to 8 p.m.,
Saturday 10 a.m. to 7 p.m.,
Sunday 10 a.m. to 6 p.m.
Credit cards: MC, V

The busiest spot in a busy market hall by the College Avenue BART station in Rockridge, the Pasta Shop offers a huge variety of prepared and imported foods. Though it made its reputation on excellent fresh egg pasta, used by many restaurants in the Bay Area, its ravioli and pasta sauces are a bit of a disappointment, and the filled pastas really need some editing. I like the idea of being able to buy house-made mayonnaise for $2.95 a pound, which gives you a generous cup for $1.25. Olives in bulk from Liguria, Provence, Peru, California, and Morocco, among others; prosciutto, salami, Hobbs' pancetta, and a good-sized cheese department with lots of Italian cheeses and French goat cheeses just begin to scratch the surface of the large inventory here. A gigantic refrigerated counter with salads, highly seasoned house-made sausages, lasagne, meat loaf, grilled marinated half chickens, marinated artichokes, and whole roasted vegetables always has a crowd in front of it. Among the dry goods on shelves are Rustichella d'Abruzzo dried pastas, rare imported extra-virgin olive oils and vinegars, as well as more affordable ones, and small tins of my favorite Columbus anchovies packed in oil. Service is fast and efficient, and your number comes up quickly. If you don't need anything from the deli counter you can pay without a number at the cheese counter, a humane system.

What's not to like about Saul's? One of the few real Jewish delis in the Bay Area happens to be owned by a couple of Irishmen who loved the deli food they ate growing up on the East Coast. With the instincts of a seasoned deli man, John Shields, a chef, cookbook writer, and expert on Chesapeake Bay seafood, put together a traditional if versatile menu with something for everyone. Children, vegetarians, sandwich eaters, and big eaters who want big plates of hot food will all be happy at Saul's. Prices for everything are reasonable, especially the hot plates.

Both the spicy pastrami and the unusually moist corned beef, flown in from the East Coast, should be ordered in the "full figured" size for optimum authenticity. Anything smaller means that the filling will be less than twice the width of the rye bread and too skimpy. Either the winning potato salad made with red-skinned creamer potatoes, or crisp coleslaw, can be chosen as a side dish. A bowl of crunchy new pickles, set on the table, complete the meal. Nova Scotia lox and the smoked chub have been first rate, though the freshness of the sablefish, one of my favorites, can be hit or miss.

Everything else is made from scratch: real chicken broth with tender matzoh balls; cold, refreshing beet borscht; a fabulous Middle Eastern salad plate; light ricotta-filled blintzes; and crisp potato pancakes with sour cream and house-made applesauce. Shields shows his cooking genius on dishes like stuffed cabbage that have deep flavor without the usual heaviness. He uses raisins, tomato broth, and lemon like a magician to achieve a perfect sweet-and-sour balance. His brisket melts in your mouth; it comes with potato pancakes and

1475 Shattuck Avenue, Berkeley

Tel: 510-848-3354

Open everyday 8 a.m. to 9:30 p.m.

Credit cards: MC, V

fresh, crisp vegetables. A half roast chicken with golden skin comes with mounds of mashed potatoes and delicious gravy made from real stock. To drink? Cold beer or kosher wine, but the aficionados order made-at-the-table egg-cream sodas of chocolate syrup, soda water, and milk, which for some odd reason goes brilliantly with deli food.

VIK'S KING OF CHAT

726 Alston Way (between Fourth and Fifth streets), Berkeley
No telephone
Open Saturday and Sunday only from 11 a.m. to 7 p.m.
Cash only

Every weekend half the East Bay Indian community stands around this snack counter in the back of an Indian market, slurping down saucy, juicy, vegetarian snacks, or *chat*, out of paper cartons. The lucky ones grab a folding chair at a card table. Others eat at a counter affixed to a wall. The rest just down their snacks out of hand, not worrying about dripping on the cement floor. A variety of snacks, each costing $2.50, are listed on a board. Some are based on crisp, deep-fried hollow spheres called *puri*, which are filled with potatoes, chilies, and onions and sauced with yogurt and tamarind chutney as in *batata puri*. Delicious *sev puri* are flat, crisp disks topped with potato, chickpeas, onions, chilies, tamarind, and mint-cilantro chutneys. *Dokla*, light, airy, steamed chickpea cakes sprinkled with coconut and fresh cilantro constitute another snack category; while *pakori chat* are soft, light balls of chickpea flour that are deep-fried, soaked in water, then squeezed dry and sauced with tamarind chutney and yogurt. A full range of Indian boiled-milk sweets and desserts are freshly prepared and O.K., as Niloufer Ichaporia King, my ethnic-food expert, would say. I like the Indian ice cream called *kulfi*, swathed in cream and clear wheat-starch noodles. The warm *gulab jamun*, fried milk balls soaked in scented syrup, are also nice. At Vik's, you get a little taste of what it's like to eat at snack shops in alleys in Varanasi or New Delhi—without the amoebas.

ULTRA LUCCA

3838 Telegraph Avenue, Oakland
Tel: 510-654-9188
Open Monday through Friday 9 a.m. to 5 p.m., Saturday 10 a.m. to 3 p.m.

4001 Piedmont Avenue, Oakland
Tel: 510-547-7222
Open Monday through Friday 9 a.m. to 7 p.m., Saturday and Sunday 10 a.m. to 6 p.m.

6119 La Salle Avenue, Oakland
Tel: 510-339-9716
Open Monday through Friday 9 a.m. to 7 p.m., Saturday and Sunday 10 a.m. to 6 p.m.

2905 College Avenue, Berkeley
Tel: 510-849-2701
Open Monday through Friday 9 a.m. to 7 p.m., Saturday and Sunday 10 a.m. to 6 p.m.
Credit cards: MC, V

See listing, page 570.

YUNG KEE

888 Webster Street,
Oakland
Tel: 510-839-2010
Daily 9:30 a.m. to 2 a.m.
No credit cards

This small shop is regarded as the best place in Oakland's Chinatown for Chinese barbecued pork, ducks, and chickens. You can eat them with noodles and soup at Formica tables in the store, or take them home, chopped into neat pieces through the bone and packed in white cartons.

BAKERIES/PASTRIES

ACME BAKERY

1601 San Pablo Avenue,
Berkeley
Tel: 510-524-1021
Open Monday 8 a.m. to
noon, Tuesday through
Friday 8 a.m. to 5 p.m.,
Saturday 9 a.m. to 5 p.m
No credit cards

When Steve Sullivan started baking bread at home and then at Chez Panisse, the long organic process overtook him. He became obsessed with bread making, and judging by the huge success of Acme Bakery, which he opened in 1983, a lot of people have become obsessed with buying his bread. Having the right loaf every day is important. I knew that Sullivan's loaves, especially a crusty whole-wheat sourdough round called *levain* and his baguettes, were right for me the moment I tasted them. They have tremendous character and substance without being heavy, which can come only from that long and elusive bread-making process he worked on for so many years. Once you eat these breads you want to have them every day. I do buy other breads and enjoy them, but if I don't have a *levain* on my counter I get edgy, as if I really don't have food at home.

You can buy Acme loaves all over the Bay Area, but the ones you pick up at the bakery next to Cafe Fanny and Kermit Lynch Wines are always the freshest, the most fragrant, the best bread you will find in America. One of the finest qualities of Acme *levain* is that it lasts; it never gets moldy even when it stays in a bag for days. You can take this bread camping: I cart loaves of it to Maui and it lasts the whole vacation. I need my *levain* toast in the morning, and my little boy needs his garlic toast in the evening. As opinionated as we all are in our family, Acme bread is the one food we all agree on.

BREAD WORKSHOP

The Bread Workshop's focaccia buns have provided a landing for some of the best hamburgers in the Bay Area. They're light and flavorful without being oily and make delicious sandwiches. Hundreds of East Bay mothers depend on the Bread Workshop's partially baked pizza dough rounds, which kids top themselves and finish baking. The multigrain bread is substantial and tasty without being tedious. Started by some ex-employees of Acme, the Bread Workshop supplied restaurants early on, unlike Acme, which had a hard enough time meeting the needs of its retail customers and Chez Panisse. Bread Workshop now has a pleasant retail bakery-cafe in a red brick building on meadowlike Strawberry Creek Park, with outdoor and indoor tables where you can drink coffee and eat freshly baked scones.

1250 Addison Street, No.109, Berkeley
Tel: 510-649-9735
Open Monday through Friday 8:30 a.m. to 5 p.m., Saturday until 1 p.m.
No credit cards

THE CHEESE BOARD

See listing, page 548.

LA FARINE

6323 College Avenue,
Oakland
Tel: 510-654-0338
Open Tuesday through
Friday 8 a.m. to 6:30 p.m.,
Saturday 8 a.m. to 6 p.m.,
Sunday 8 a.m.
to 3 p.m.
No credit cards

This authentic French bakery started by Lili Le Coq has been passed on to two generations of new owner-bakers, but the quality of the buttery French tarts and cakes, croissants, *pain au chocolat*, and sweet rolls remains stellar. If there is one pastry associated with La Farine, it's the morning bun, a rich, cinnamony, sugared roll made with croissant dough, which no one can resist. Whenever I drive by this bakery, I have to stop in to buy one. Swiss twinkies, a flat, palm-leaf-shaped sweet roll, have many fans, but not as many as the sublime morning bun. The breads here are soft and delicate; the egg bread makes superlative French toast, and this is also the place to buy brioches. The tarts topped with fresh fruit actually taste as appealing as they look. La Farine is one of the few great French pastry shops left in the Bay Area, and one hopes that the bakers will continue to pass on the secrets of the morning bun to succeeding generations.

KATRINA ROZELLE

5931 College Avenue,
Oakland
Tel: 510-655-3209
Open Monday through
Saturday 9 a.m. to 6 p.m.,
Sunday 11 a.m. to 5 p.m.
Credit cards: MC, V

A clean, modern little shop next door to a Dreyer's Ice Cream store, Katrina Rozelle shows particular strength in old-fashioned crumbly, buttery American-style cookies. Her shortbread rectangles are indeed "simple perfection," to lift the description on the bakery's brochure. Another standout, almond praline cookies, are full of chopped almonds and bits of praline. Their traditional chocolate chip; the Chocolust, one of the few good crisp chocolate cookies around despite the smarmy name; and the bright-flavored ginger cookies please both adults and children. This shop's reputation for cookies keeps the inventory turning over, which keeps the cookies fresh, the most important quality of any cookie. Fine, fancy cakes are baked to order.

SEMIFREDDI'S

A bakery founded on a seeded baguette, Semifreddi's got its inspiration from breads baked at the Cheese Board, where Bob Wax taught many generations of bakers how to make them. Semifreddi's baguettes are on the hard side, very crusty, with a meaty interior. The most popular are thickly coated with caraway, fennel, poppy, and sesame seeds, infusing each bite with a riot of flavors. I think the seeds take over the bread, making it conflict with other foods, but I'm in the minority here. A handsome wood and glass case displays other breads as well, including a whole-wheat walnut-raisin that has both flavor and unusual moistness. On the counter are wrapped slices of tasty fat-reduced lemon pound cake, and whole roasted elephant garlics to squeeze onto bread instead of butter—if you're not going out on a date for twelve hours after you eat it. The bakery also serves espresso.

372 Colusa Street, Kensington
Tel: 510-596-9935
Open daily 7 a.m. to 7 p.m.
No credit cards

ICE CREAM/CHOCOLATES

YOGURT PARK

2433A Durant Avenue,
Berkeley
Tel: 510-549-0570
Open everyday 10 a.m.
to midnight
No credit cards

Gigantic cups of frozen yogurt topped with fresh fruit at the cheapest possible price means that the line never stops forming at Yogurt Park. The Honey Hill Farms yogurt pumped here used to be satisfying when it still had some fat in it. The nonfat mania has ruined most of it, but there's usually a vanilla low-fat option that doesn't taste like chemicals. I have an emotional attachment to this yogurt shop, one of the few remaining, because I used to eat quarts of it when I was pregnant ten years ago. My kid is pretty much made of frozen yogurt.

ETHNIC MARKETS

MILAN INTERNATIONAL

990 University Avenue,
Berkeley
Tel: 510-843-9600
Open Tuesday through
Sunday 10 a.m. to 7:30 p.m.
No credit cards

The smell of spices hits you long before you walk in the front door of this great Indian grocery with aisles and aisles of imported Indian foods, the longest bulk spice section you'll ever see, bulk flours, the best basmati rice being imported at the moment, and a rainbow of dried legumes. One whole wall is dedicated to shiny stainless steel plates, bowls, tiffin carriers and trays, woklike Indian cooking vessels, and utensils. Every sort of jarred chutney, pickle and spice paste, canned fruit, Darjeeling tea, *papadums* (lentil wafers that make the best snack imaginable, especially with martinis), and ever so much more, tempt you to spend hours here imagining how these things taste. Near the front counter on the floor are cartons of fresh items, like ginger, fresh *Kari* leaves, fresh turmeric—which looks like thumb-sized tubers— packaged *chapati* and *nan* (Indian breads), and once in awhile the most flavorful mangoes you'll ever taste in this country. Whoever buys them has flawless taste in this seductive fruit. You can also pick up Indian videos. If being around all the Indian ingredients makes you hungry, you can get a snack next door at Bombay Cuisine.

NEW SAIGON SUPERMARKET

The Chinatown block of Ninth Street between Broadway and Franklin is lined with Asian grocery stores, with produce displays spilling out on the sidewalk, and shelves inside stacked to the rafters with products from all over the East. New Saigon is the largest and most densely packed of them all, with gorgeous fresh gourds, squashes, Chinese eggplants, green papayas, mangoes,

**443 Ninth Street,
Oakland
Tel: 510-839-4149
Open daily 9 a.m. to 7 p.m.
No credit cards**

EATING IN OAKLAND'S CHINATOWN

Good small Vietnamese restaurants have been popping up in Oakland's Chinatown, and several are of note: VI'S VIETNAMESE CUISINE, 724 Webster Street, Oakland (510-835-8375), is a clean and modern dining room that serves excellent Vietnamese noodle salads in a deep bowl topped with shredded vegetables, pieces of grilled pork or chicken, a crisp, delectable deep-fried imperial roll, and a bowl of clear dressing to pour over. VIEN HUONG, at 712 Franklin Street, Oakland (510- 465-5938) is a popular *pho* restaurant, always packed, that specializes in Vietnamese soup and noodles. Other places of interest include NAN YANG, 301 Eighth Street, Oakland (510-465-6924), a Burmese restaurant where I recommend the incendiary sixteen-part ginger salad; and the ever popular JADE VILLA, 800 Broadway Street, Oakland (510-839-1688), for dim sum.

Asian greens, and seasonal delicacies in eye-catching piles. The large meat department is strong in fresh pork, meaty fresh bacon, piles of dewy ground pork, pristine pork liver and tongue, and every other imaginable part of the animal. French-style baguettes, dishware, tofu in bulk, noodles—all the southern Chinese and Southeast Asian cooking necessities are stocked. This is a destination for pork and Asian produce.

OAKLAND MARKET

401 Ninth Street,
Oakland
Tel: 510- 835-4919
Open Monday through
Saturday 9 a.m. to 6:30 p.m.,
Sunday 9 a.m. to 6 p.m.
No credit cards

Roomier and easier to negotiate than New Saigon, the Oakland Market is a modern pan-Asian grocery, with a large section of Asian kitchenware and dishes. You'll see shelves of inexpensive, clean-smelling Panther Peanut Oil in three-liter tins, excellent for deep-frying and more-fragrant Lion and Globe peanut oil in plastic containers, good for salad dressings and cooking. There are refrigerated cases with wonton skins, tofu, and pickled greens. The grocery shelves have items like Japanese seaweed and wasabi, along with Thai, Vietnamese, and Philippine products. The selection of Asian goods is not deep, but it's diverse and comprehensive. Featured in the produce section one day in September were some beautiful-looking papayas for $1.39 each, a great price and probably a loss leader.

G. B. RATTO AND COMPANY

821 Washington Street,
Oakland
Tel: 510-832-6503
Open Monday through
Friday 9:30 a.m. to 6 p.m.,
Saturday 9:30 a.m. to 5 p.m.
Credit cards: MC, V

G.B. Ratto, the East Bay's premier international grocer, stocks hard-to-find items from all over the world, especially from the Middle East, but also from Brazil, the Caribbean, Africa, Portugal, France, and Italy. When you need pâté spice, Ratto's has it, along with hundreds of other specific cooking needs ranging from the most exotic spices in bulk, dried beans, flours, couscous, cooking oils, bottled syrups and pickles, and canned fruits and vegetables. In the deli cases are olives and hummus, Italian cured meats, an excellent imported salt cod from Italy, cheeses, yogurts, house-made vinegar in barrels, *harissa*, filo dough—the variety of foods sold here is astounding. Next door in a large corner space surrounded by windows, Ratto's does a well-attended cafeteria-style lunch every day with deli salads, hot soups, and Italian-style sandwiches. And on the weekends, Ratto's stages wildly popular communal spaghetti feeds with live opera singers. The food is cheap and the singing really good. G. B. Ratto has long been the best international foods store in the Bay Area, and its reputation still stands. If you can't find it at Ratto's, it's probably not available in the United States.

SAM YICK

People love this resonant old-time Oakland Chinatown grocery store with tons of Chinese pottery, dried black mushrooms, packed and in bulk, for good prices and an extensive collection of Asian pantry items and dry goods, as well as a complement of necessary Western groceries like sugar, mustard, and sea salt.

362 Eighth Street, Oakland

Tel: 510-832-0662

Open Monday through Saturday 9:30 a.m. to 6:30 p.m., Sunday until 6 p.m.

No credit cards

PRODUCE

BERKELEY BOWL

2777 Shattuck Avenue,
Berkeley
Tel: 510-843-6929
Open Monday through
Friday 9:30 a.m. to 7 p.m.,
Saturday 9 a.m. to 6 p.m.
Credit cards: MC, V

There are two destination produce stores in the Bay Area, and the Berkeley Bowl is one of them. (Monterey Market across Berkeley is the other.) Your spirits will be lifted when you walk into this expansive former bowling alley turned market and see the amazing variety of healthy-looking produce available under one roof. The organic section alone would fill up most small produce stores, and there is a large representation of Asian produce and tropical fruits. Organic Valencia juice oranges and fabulous organic grapefruits are dead center, and the rest radiates out in waves. Wild and cultivated mushrooms, lettuces, cooking greens, peppers and chilies, and always lots of tropicals such as plantains, tomatillos, chayotes, pineapples, fresh coconuts, mangoes, papayas, *galangal*—all beckon at excellent prices. Also in the produce department are fresh breads, eggs, and dairy, plus a large Asian refrigerated section with noodles and tofu.

On one side of the building is a Japanese fish counter with fresh fish fillets marinated in *sake kasu* (the lees from sake fermentation) or miso, both yellowfin and white-fleshed *tombo* tuna, Pacific halibut, seaweed salad, and some shellfish. The meat and poultry counter isn't as strong. A grocery department takes up the other end of the building with beer and wine, Japanese products, grains, nuts, and spices in bulk, and chips. In essence, the Berkeley Bowl has become a supermarket that sells only fresh foods. If you live near the Oakland-Berkeley border, Berkeley Bowl should be your market of choice.

With two great permanent produce markets in town, why shop at the farmers' markets? Because you can get produce that has been picked hours before, and you also might find some very local crops, grown in such small quantity that they could only be sold by the farmer directly. Produce bought directly from the people who grow it always tastes better, even if you can buy it more cheaply at Monterey Foods. I always make a detour for a farmers' market, if only for the pleasure of strolling down a street lined with fruits and vegetables.

Center Street at Martin Luther King Jr. Way: Saturday 10 a.m. to 2 p.m. Derby Street between Milvia and Martin Luther King Jr. Way: Tuesday in summer, 2 p.m. to 7 p.m. Haste Street at Telegraph Avenue: Sunday 11 a.m. to 3 p.m. May through November

MONTEREY FOODS

This stupendous produce market sets the standard for all others in price, variety, and completeness. There aren't many edible plants grown under the sun that don't show up on one of Monterey Food's tables. Outside in the parking lot is a caged-in area with mountains of the best buys of the season, organic or not, but usually of excellent quality at phenomenal prices. You can't do better at farmers' markets or wholesale markets. Every cook I know periodically checks Monterey Foods to see what's available in the Bay Area and what they should be paying for it. Both big farmers and small producers have established long-term relationships with the two generations of the Fujimoto family who run this market. Bill Fujimoto knows everyone who farms in the northern part of the state and then some. Many farmers come to Monterey Market first because they might not have to go any farther to sell their harvest. Monterey makes its

1550 Hopkins Street, Berkeley Tel: 510-526-6042 Open Monday through Saturday 9 a.m. to 6 p.m. No credit cards

profits on volume, so they buy big and keep their mark-up tiny. When I started my first eight-table restaurant in Berkeley a million years ago, I shopped at Monterey Foods every single morning, and to tell you the truth, I've rarely done better on either price or quality since. The store also has a grocery department with fresh breads, pasta, and a dairy section.

MARKET HALL PRODUCE

**5655 College Avenue,
Oakland
Tel: 510-601-8208
Open Monday through
Friday 9:30 a.m. to 8 p.m.,
Saturday until 7 p.m.,
Sunday until 6 p.m.
Credit cards: MC, V**

A part of the Market Hall group of food stalls under one roof, this large, attractively arranged produce store offers a useful selection of organic and commercial produce at mid-range prices. During a fall visit, fresh, dry, clean chanterelles at a good price of $7.99 a pound, organic apples, baby lettuces, and very pretty whole heads of organic oakleaf, red leaf, red butterleaf, and romaine lettuces caught my eye. Big bunches of arugula and lots of tomatoes cried out to be bought. The produce department also carries Straus Family Dairy organic milk and butter.

OLD OAKLAND FARMERS' MARKET

**Ninth Street at Broadway,
Oakland
Friday 8 a.m. to 2 p.m.**

Next door to Oakland's Chinatown, the Old Oakland market features lots of fresh Asian produce, fresh non-organic fruits and vegetables, and good prices on everything. Asian apple pears, dates, lots of oranges, and the whole spectrum of Asian greens, gourds, and root vegetables are usually represented. Anchored on one side by G. B. Ratto, the great international-food store, and Chinatown on the other, a trip to this part of the Bay Area on Friday could fulfill any number of food shopping goals. The composition of this market is similar to the Civic Center farmers' market in San Francisco.

MEAT AND POULTRY

ALAN'S MEATS

What beautiful smoked and fresh pork this meat stand has! The piles of salt pork, fresh bacon, smoked bacon, ham hocks, smoked ham ends, and fresh, cured, and smoked ham of all sorts make you want to buy some red beans and get cooking. I bought some huge smoked ham hocks, which Alan's sliced, and I made the most delectable split pea soup with them. They were meaty with lots of marrow and gave the soup an honest, clean, smoky flavor. When you visit the Housewives' Market, plan on picking up some bacon.

Housewives' Market,
818 Jefferson Street,
Oakland
Tel: 510-893-9479
Open Monday through
Saturday 9 a.m. to 6 p.m.
Credit cards: MC, V

ENZO

This small high-quality butcher shop carries Harris beef, Petaluma Poultry Company chickens, house-made pork sausage, Grimaud rabbits, osso buco, and some nice-looking lamb from small animals. Enzo is an Italian butcher, so he cuts and grinds for Italian recipes. He also sells big Hebrew National Kosher hot dogs, which are very delicious. For an extra charge of $5 for ducks and $10 for turkeys, Enzo will cook them on the rotisserie for you, so you can pick them up hot and ready to serve.

Market Hall, 5655 College
Avenue, Oakland
Tel: 510-547-5839
Open Monday through
Friday 10 a.m. to 8 p.m.,
Saturday until 7 p.m.,
Sunday until 6 p.m.
Credit cards: AE, MC, V

MAGNANI'S POULTRY

6317 College Avenue,
Oakland
Tel: 510-428-9496
Monday through Friday 9
a.m. to 6:30 p.m.,
Saturday until 6 p.m.,
Sunday 11 a.m. to 5 p.m.

1586 Hopkins Street,
Berkeley
Tel: 510-528-6370
Monday through Friday 9
a.m. to 6:30 p.m.,
Saturday until 6 p.m.
Credit cards: MC, V

Chickens and chicken parts, ducks, turkeys, and other poultry are sold here, though at the College Avenue store the emphasis is on chickens and chicken parts. Of note are the rotisserie chickens, one marinated with Italian herbs, mostly lemon and rosemary, the other in a Japanese teriyaki marinade that is a knockout, especially at $5.75 for a moist, hot, flavorful chicken. The Hopkins Street store is now selling meat as well.

TAYLOR'S SAUSAGES

Housewives' Market,
818 Jefferson Street,
Oakland
Tel: 510-832-6448
Open Monday through
Saturday 9 a.m. to 6 p.m.
No credit cards

In the course of doing research for this book, I've sampled many, many fresh sausages, but the ones I like the best come from this little stand in the old Housewives' Market. Their New Orleans–style *boudin blanc*, a mildly spicy white sausage with rice, is worth a special trip alone without even considering the perfectly seasoned and textured spicy Cajun chicken sausage, the Louisiana hot sausage, the garlic sausage, the Italian— every sausage these people make has balance; melded-together, deep, interesting flavor; and just the right amount of fat to lean to keep the sausages juicy and moist. The prices couldn't be better, the sausages fresher,

One of the most satisfying dishes in the world is red beans and rice. I first ate it in New Orleans, and now I prepare it for football playoffs on television. The best recipe comes from American Cooking: Creole and Acadian (Time-Life Books, 1971), the unsurpassed Time-Life Foods of the World cookbook series. The recipes in these books are so well researched and written that if you follow them carefully, you will always end up with something tasty. You can find these volumes in used-book stores.

The butchers at Alan's will slice their meaty ham hocks for you, which allows the marrow to enrich the beans. You can buy excellent dried beans at the Bean Bag stall in the Housewives' Market near Alan's.

6 cups water, plus more as needed

1 pound dried red beans

4 tablespoons butter or olive oil

1 cup green onions, finely chopped

1/2 cup finely chopped onion

1 teaspoon minced garlic

1 pound smoked ham hocks, sliced

1 teaspoon kosher salt

1/2 teaspoon freshly ground pepper or
   more to taste

6 to 8 cups freshly cooked long-
   grain rice

Bring 6 cups of the water to a boil in a large saucepan. Add the beans and boil over high heat for 2 minutes. Turn off heat and let the beans soak 1 hour. Drain the beans, reserving the liquid, adding more water as needed to make 4 cups liquid.

Heat the butter or oil in a heavy 4- to 5-quart casserole over medium heat and cook 1/2 cup of the green onions, the onions and garlic until soft. Stir in the beans and their liquid. Add the ham hocks, salt, and pepper. Bring to a boil, then reduce heat to low and simmer gently, partially covered, until the beans are very soft, about 3 hours, periodically checking the pot for liquid and adding up to 1 cup of water little by little as necessary.

Remove the ham hocks. Cut the meat from bones and return it to the pot. Taste the beans for salt and pepper and adjust the seasonings as necessary. Put the rice in bowls, cover with beans, and top with the remaining 1/2 cup green onions.

Serves 4 to 6

or the variety more pleasing. No weird ingredients like fruit, curry, or sun-dried tomatoes ever ruin a Taylor sausage. Through several generations of owners, these have always been classic and great. Whoever runs this stand knows they have a good thing in these recipes.

T & S M A R K E T

323 Ninth Street,
Oakland
Tel: 510-268-1155
Open Monday through
Saturday 8:30 a.m. to 6 p.m.
No credit cards

This Chinatown poultry wholesaler also has a retail counter, though most of what they carry is kept in walk-in refrigerators in the warehouse. Just ask for what you need: ducks, chickens, chicken parts, poussins, large squab for $4 each, and exotics like black-skinned chickens. To restore a woman after giving birth, boil up a black-chicken broth with ginseng. The Chinese have been doing it for thousands of years. The results are good. So are the prices here.

V E R B R U G G E M E A T S

6321 College Avenue,
Oakland
Tel: 510-658-6854
Open Monday through
Friday 9 a.m. to 6:30 p.m.,
Saturday 9 a.m. to 6 p.m.,
Sunday 10 a.m. to 5 p.m.
Credit cards: AE, D, MC, V

This successful neighborhood butcher has a long counter filled with moderately priced fresh meat—especially good eastern pork and hams—and a handsome fresh-fish selection. They will cut to order and can get you anything you need if you call ahead.

FISH

BERKELEY BOWL FISH MARKET

See Produce, page 538.

MONTEREY FISH

This is Paul Johnson and Tom Worthington's retail fish store, and it is the best one in the Bay Area. You can't find a fish purveyor with higher standards or more integrity. Anything you buy from Monterey Fish will smell like the sea and stay fresh for several days at least, a tall order when it comes to seafood. The secret behind Monterey's quality is their buying. They seek out sources, cultivate them, and stick with them. If they can't get something in perfect condition, they don't carry it. A mitigating factor is that Monterey sells to a small number of picky restaurants from their wholesale location on the wharf in San Francisco, so they move what they have quickly and always have a fairly large variety of what they deem best at the moment. Monterey Fish is a source for fresh squid, carefully culled live lobsters and crabs in clean tanks, fresh shrimp, outstanding scallops and blue crab from a long-held source in Rhode Island, first-rate small shucked oysters from Washington State, and oysters in the shell from California on up to British Columbia.

Quality and freshness mean everything in seafood, because you don't even want to go near it if it isn't pristine. If you shop at Monterey Market you'll start cooking more and more fish at home and discover that it is the best convenience food you can buy. You don't have to do a thing to a fillet of king salmon, a slice of

1582 Hopkins Street, Berkeley
Tel: 510-525-5600
Open Tuesday through Saturday 10 a.m. to 6 p.m.
No credit cards

red-fleshed Hawaiian tuna, a slab of San Diego swordfish, or a piece of velvet-textured northern halibut except not overcook it. And though some of this fish is expensive there's no waste, and you don't need a huge portion to satisfy. Fish is a clean, flavorful, elegant source of protein that goes with practically any vegetable and starch, so throwing a meal together with it is a snap. If you love fish, buy it at Monterey, and if you've been afraid to cook with it, come here too. You can't go wrong at this fish market; you can trust them. Paul Johnson sells only what he himself takes home to cook.

MOURA'S FISH MARKET

Housewives' Market,
818 Jefferson Street,
Oakland
Tel: 510-444-8784
Open Monday through
Saturday 9 a.m. to 6 p.m.
No credit cards

Next to Monterey Fish, I like this long, immaculate fish counter in the Housewives' Market the best. There are fish bargains to be found here, if you fancy catfish, gaspergoo, buffalofish, and gar. But some sparkling, bright-eyed wild Louisiana red snapper might be available, and if they are, buy one. They are some of the tastiest fish you can find. Moura's will clean it, scale it, and take out the gills, then you can roast it in salt (see recipe, page 67) or barbecue it whole. Its flesh is so juicy and flavorful, it doesn't require a bit of seasoning. If you like your seafood deep-fried, this is the place to find the fattier fish that lend themselves to this kind of cooking. There are also fresh whole sand dabs and rex sole in season, local rockfish and lingcod fillets, and shrimp of all sizes and grades. The cordial people behind the counter know their fish and will be happy to discuss cooking methods with you.

NEW BASEMENT SEAFOOD MARKET

You walk down a flight of worn cement stairs to get to this Chinatown fish market full of ancient wood-framed tanks holding live lobster, crab, lingcod, striped bass, turtles, and more. On a table of crushed ice, clear-eyed local rockfish rest, along with whole sand dabs, rex sole, and whatever has been hauled in that day. As in every Chinatown fish store, you have to look for clear eyes, glistening skin, good smell—but the prices will be excellent and the whole fish will be cleaned and degilled for you. As in most Chinatown stores, most of the fish are whole because savvy buyers like to look a fish straight in the eye.

373 8th Street,
Oakland
Tel: 510-763-8977
Open daily 9 a.m. to 6 p.m.
No credit cards

ROCKRIDGE FISH MARKET

The small fish counter in this popular food shopping hall offers fillets of choice fish like mahi-mahi, swordfish, salmon, and tuna, along with fresh shrimp and live crab and lobsters from a tank. Some good-looking calamari salad, seaweed salad, and a few other fish preparations are also sold. The fish is nicely displayed and well cut. There are no bargains; the emphasis is on high-priced, easy-to-cook fish.

Market Hall,
5655 College Avenue,
Oakland
Tel: 510-654-3474
Open Monday through
Friday 10 a.m. to 8 p.m.,
Saturday until 7 p.m.,
Sunday until 6 p.m.
Credit cards: MC, V

CHEESE

THE CHEESE BOARD

1504 Shattuck Avenue, Berkeley
Tel: 510-549-3183
Open Tuesday through Friday 10 a.m. to 6 p.m., Saturday until 5 p.m.; pizzeria open Monday and Friday 4:30 to 7:30 p.m., Tuesday through Thursday 11:30 a.m. to 2 p.m., Saturday noon to 2 p.m.; coffee service open Tuesday through Friday 7 to 10 a.m.
No credit cards

In its third decade of operation, the Cheese Board not only stocks the largest collection of cheeses on the West Coast (or maybe in the United States), but a full-scale bread bakery and a to-go pizzeria a door away. Once merely a cheese store, the Cheese Board has become an important cultural institution. Over the years, this collectively owned shop has created a wide customer base that regularly makes the pilgrimage to Berkeley to buy cheese. Cheese Board customers have become sophisticated cheese buyers who will try new things. This means that the store turns over enormous volume, not just of common cheeses, but of exotic ones, which in turn means that all the cheeses stay fresh and in perfect condition. The Cheese Board has cultivated this kind of response by requiring every customer to taste every cheese before they buy it. Every cheese is unwrapped in a split second and a taste is shaved off and handed over on waxed paper before you can protest. No one feels constrained to buy a cheese he or she doesn't like. One taste follows another until everyone is satisfied—customer and clerk—that the cheese is right. The cheese sellers taste along with the customers so they intimately know the inventory, which wheel of Brie is at a certain stage of ripeness, which aged Gouda is the nuttiest. They learn the characteristics of every new cheese, how to store, cut, order—and how to serve the customers, some of whom could try the patience of a saint. The clerks know which cheese to pull up for tasting when a customer gives some vague description. They can tell people what to buy for certain recipes; what to serve the day after tomorrow on a cheese tray; what to introduce

kids to; what they personally love and the customer might like, too. The Cheese Board system is an amazing way to sell, unlike any other I've encountered. The end result is that people trust the store and are willing and eager to be turned onto an ever-expanding repertoire.

The smell of warm breads just out of the oven always wafts around the store, which only makes you want to buy more cheese. My favorite is a round loaf called suburban bread, which has the most amazing crisp, thin, but chewy crust and a white, sweet, toothsome interior that's charmingly tender—a bread-baking triumph. Also, people go to the Cheese Board for fine olives in bulk at excellent prices. The pizza sold in a little shop that used to house Pig by the Tail charcuterie is sold slice by slice the minute it comes out of the oven. The bakers can barely keep up with the line. The slices are slapped onto a piece of paper and served on rattan plates. Customers sit or stand outside the store, eating and talking.

I have one bit of advice when visiting the Cheese Board. Take a playing card/number when you walk in and then look around at the breads and cheeses.

Though the clerks are fast and efficient and there are a lot of them, you never know how long the people in front of you will spend tasting, deciding, discussing. This exchange is the glory of the shop, and it has proven that education, generosity, and communal ownership can achieve the highest and best kind of success.

J. WIGGINS CHEESE

6309 College Avenue, Oakland

Tel: 510-652-4171

Open daily 10 a.m. to 6:30 p.m., Sunday until 6 p.m.

Credit cards: MC, V

This tiny international-cheese shop does such a good job of merchandizing that a buyer can choose just by reading the little signs sprouting on all the cheeses. I was led to a fantastic super-aged *rocca* Parmesan—one of the best I've tasted in this country—and a hunk of Gruyère-like Comté from the French Alps, again one of the best I've encountered here. On a wooden cutting board in this densely packed store sat tastes of a goat milk Gouda and a flavorful Cantal, both so good I was tempted to buy those as well. Though the cheeses are prewrapped and tasting can be a bit of an ordeal here, my feeling is that the J. Wiggins people know what they are doing. Their cheeses are carefully selected, well stored and aged, and you can trust them. A deli counter with cured meats and hams, a large selection of olives, and a small selection of breads and crackers, again, are all carefully chosen.

COFFEE

PEET'S COFFEE AND TEA

See listing, page 218.

The perpetual crowd in front of the original Peet's never lets up and neither does the line inside the store. Per square inch, this coffee store must sell more beans and more cups of their intensely brewed coffee than any other, and deservedly so. Peet's has become such a social crossroads that a visit to this model for all the multitudinous coffee store chains in the Bay Area is always an experience. You get a real whiff of old Berkeley milling outside, the maddening, wacky, passionate, political Berkeley that you can walk away from—or join—once you tame your cup of Peet's coffee with half-and-half and sugar.

2124 Vine Street, Berkeley
Tel: 510-841-0564
Open Monday through Saturday 7:30 a.m. to 6 p.m., Sunday 10 a.m. to 6 p.m.
Credit cards: D, MC, V

WINES AND SPIRITS

KERMIT LYNCH WINES

1605 San Pablo Avenue,
Berkeley
Tel: 510-524-1524
Open Tuesday through
Saturday 11 a.m. to 6 p.m.
Credit cards: MC, V

Just as Berkeley has spawned Chez Panisse, the Cheese Board, Monterey Market, Monterey Fish, and Acme Bread, it has also nurtured Kermit Lynch, the groundbreaking wine merchant who brought the wines of Bandol from Domaine Tempier to the United States, along with many other wines from previously undiscovered (at least in the United States) wine-growing areas, which have now become icons of sophisticated eating and drinking. If you read Kermit Lynch's book, *Adventures on the Wine Route: A Wine Buyer's Tour of France*, you'll get a first-hand account of what he was looking for: the quality of the land in the wine, the personality of the wine maker, direct purchasing from the people who make the wines (not *négociants*), and artisanal, not industrial, wine-making techniques.

In his retail store, a cool red-brick room stacked with cases, you'll be able to buy the beautiful wines he made famous in this country, the Rhônes from Domaine Jean-Louis Chave in Hermitage and Auguste Clape in Cornas, plus many of what Richard Olney in his introduction to Lynch's book describes as "inexpensive, clean, refreshing and undemanding ideal daily aperitif and luncheon wines," like Jean Berail-Lagarde's white Roque Lestière and Yves Laboucarie's *vin gris* Domaine de Fontsainte, both from the southwest Corbières appellation. All of Kermit Lynch wines are imported, with particular strength in Burgundy, Alsace, Provence, and the Rhône, and most recently, a bunch of discoveries from the Loire and the Côte de Rousillon on the southeast coast of France. You won't like all the wines; some are very eccentric. But more often than not I've come around to appreciating them, the way you would a brilliant but slightly obnoxious person. When I first tasted the monumental Chablis from Raveneau, a rich, powerful wine aged in oak, a wine that is usually crisp and tart, I began to realize that every wine, even wines from the most traditional wine-growing areas, are as individual as their winemakers, and it is the wine maker's visions that captures Lynch's interest.

Shopping at the store is low-key and interesting. The friendly and extremely helpful clerks have tasted everything; they've traveled to the vineyards and eaten the foods that go with the wines. They are able to give good advice on food and wine matchups. Like the staff at the Cheese Board, they want to turn their customers on to new wines, hear what people think about them, and try to find wines that will please each palate—to be personal wine merchants.

Finally, though some of these wines are found at other stores, since Kermit Lynch is an importer and a wholesaler as well as retailer, you'll find the most complete collection at the best prices at the store on San Pablo.

NORTH BERKELEY WINE COMPANY

Rejuvenated by some ex-employees from Draper and Esquin, North Berkeley Wine Company meets everyday wine-drinking needs with its own-label Merlot, Zinfandel, and Cabernet, inexpensive and very decent, and with interesting imports like Portuguese reds, while also carefully selecting a range of pricier bottles. There are always good closeout specials, especially of Burgundies. The clerks know the wines and will be happy to gab about any of them; they hold special tastings and send

1505 Shattuck Avenue,
Berkeley
Tel: 510-848-8910
Monday through Saturday
11 a.m. to 7 p.m.,
Sunday noon to 6 p.m.
Credit cards: MC, V

out a chatty newsletter with special dinners and wine-tasting events. The East Bay supports a number of small independent wine stores, with years of experience behind their buying, that specialize in first-rate personal service. North Berkeley Wine Company is one of them.

ODD BINS

1025 San Pablo Avenue,
Albany
Tel: 510-526-0522
Open Tuesday through
Friday 11 a.m. to 7 p.m.,
Saturday 10 a.m.
to 5 p.m.
Credit cards: MC, V

The owner of this modest new shop, Morgan Miller, has been in the wine trade for over twenty years. He has a great palate and tremendous knowledge, so he is able to pick up off-year vintages from excellent producers at bargain prices and pass them on to his customers. Wines in the store come from all over the world: Australia, Spain, Italy, small châteaux in Bordeaux. He understands the merits of a good neglected vintage in the middle of two greater ones, like 1987 Burgundies sandwiched between the great '85s and the excellent '88s. As he told me, he finds the wines that have fallen through the cracks of the wine market and offers them at small markups, especially wines wholesaled by Grape Expectations, which has represented and imported some of the best bottles from Europe over the years.

PAUL MARCUS WINES

Market Hall,
5655 College Avenue,
Oakland
Tel: 510-420-1005
Monday through Friday
10 a.m. to 8 p.m.,
Saturday until 7 p.m.,
Sunday until 6 p.m.
Credit cards: MC, V

Service is the thing at this small but very useful wine stall in the Market Hall. The selection of wines here is personal and exciting, with a large section of wines well under $8 and a bunch of more expensive ones, particularly from small California producers and Italy. I spied tasty Rhônes from Château de Fonsalette and some swanky but not outrageous ports, Sauternes, and champagnes. Lots of people walk out with cases. While you won't find the cheapest prices here, what you will find is enlightened selection, a bit of wine education, and a lot of friendly chitchat about what everyone is having for dinner. The vibes are great.

If you're looking for some outstanding buys on imported and California wines, check out Vino, a small store run by longtime wine-seller Mike Higgins. He's got the deals on delicious wines. People in the know go to him for French champagne, a good selection for at least $8 to $10 a bottle cheaper than anywhere else. He's such a savvy buyer that he is able to get his hands on wines at closeout prices. With so much competition for the wine dollar these days and such a mind-boggling collection of wines from all over the world, a small, expertly run, price-sensitive store like this can be a real boon.

6319 College Avenue, Oakland
Tel: 510-652-6317
Open Monday through Saturday 10 a.m. to 7 p.m., Sunday 11 a.m. to 6 p.m.
Credit cards: MC, V

COOKWARE AND BOOKS

BLACK OAK BOOKS

1491 Shattuck Avenue,
Berkeley
Tel: 510-486-0698
Daily 10 a.m. to 10 p.m.
Credit cards: AE, MC, V

This independent bookstore has a large section of new and used cookbooks and an active program of visiting authors. Since it's practically next door to Chez Panisse, you can browse the shelves until it's time for your reservation. Its proximity to the destination food stores and restaurants nearby has raised its cookbook consciousness, so you will always be able to find many books by local authors as well as the classics.

CODY'S

2454 Telegraph Avenue,
Berkeley
Tel: 510-845-7852
Open everyday 10 a.m. to 10 p.m.
Credit cards: MC, V

This may be one of the most complete bookstores in the world, and one with the best service. If Cody's does not have the book you need on their shelves, they'll track it down for you. The clerks know an astounding amount about what is available on any subject. The cookbook section is one of the most complete and up to date because Cody's buyer loves and knows cookbooks. As in so many other areas of culinary interest, Berkeley has the stellar resource, and Cody's is it.

THE GARDENER

1836 Fourth Street,
Berkeley
Tel: 510-548-4545
Open Monday through Saturday 10 a.m. to 6 p.m.,

This enchanting store, constantly recreated by Alta Tingle, has the most unpredictable treasures for the house and garden. They might take the form of certain cookbooks, on rice perhaps; or sumptuous, brightly dyed cotton tablecloths from India, backed with material, trimmed and hand sewn; or market bags; or serving platters in the most arresting shapes and materials. You might find hand-forged iron candleholders or the perfect hand-painted dining room cabinet. There might be an outdoor picnic table and umbrella. The stock is ever changing and every item gives pause. Tingle has an infallible instinct for beautiful, down-to-earth objects that are always useful and well made. Whenever I'm in the neighborhood, having a bite at O Chamé or Ginger Island next door, I stroll through the shop to see what I will be buying for the next year, for my friends and myself.

Sunday 11 a.m. to 6 p.m.

Credit cards: AE, MC, V

Marin County

RESTAURANTS

BISTRO ALSACIENNE

655 Redwood Highway,
Mill Valley
Tel: 389-0921
Open Tuesday through
Sunday 5 to 10 p.m.
Price: Moderate
Credit cards: AE, MC, V

Fritz Frankel, one of the most beloved maître d's in the city, has endowed a number of famous restaurants with European professionalism, elegance, and that warm smile of his. Most recently he opened his own place, Bistro Alsacienne, a cozy wood-paneled restaurant (that used to house Giramonti) with a view of Richardson Bay. Frankel decorated with lace curtains and knickknacks, and the bistro looks exactly like a country restaurant in Alsace. The menu offers some real regional dishes, like the most divine schnitzel, a thin slice of pork or veal coated with bread crumbs and fried in butter to a breathtaking degree of buttery crispness. Served with long-simmered red cabbage and mashed potatoes, it may be one of my all-time favorite plates of comfort food anywhere. Also wonderful is L'Alsacienne's *choucroute*, long-braised sauerkraut full of flavor, topped with white sausages made by a German butcher in Santa Rosa, roast and smoked pork loin, and a few boiled potatoes. The combination of melting cabbage and smoky pork makes for pure pleasure, especially with a bottle of light, fruity German red wine called Ruppertsberger, perfect with the food and very reasonable in price. The house-made pâtés are also tasty.

BUBBA'S

566 San Anselmo Avenue, San Anselmo
Tel: 459-6862
Open Wednesday through Monday 7:30 a.m. to 2 p.m., 5 to 9:30 p.m.
Price: Inexpensive
Credit cards: AE, D, MC, V

Stephen Simmons, who worked with Brad Ogden for seven years, recently left the fold to take over a small authentic diner in sleepy downtown San Anselmo with his wife, Elizabeth. He serves breakfast, lunch, and dinner; the menus for all three meals are listed on the paper place mats. Simmons has pared down his presentations radically, but that certainly hasn't diminished his Zen-like care and skill in the kitchen. There he is behind the counter, meticulously sautéing fresh green beans and corn, tasting a bean for doneness, while cooking pork chops smothered in vinegary cabbage, which he places on a plate next to sublime mashed potatoes. Next to him, his assistant takes apart heads of iceberg lettuce as if he were doing brain surgery, stacking the curled leaves in a pile and drizzling them with an exemplary Thousand Island dressing. A chopped salad turns out to be a colorful pile of grilled vegetables brushed with garlic oil and seasoned with a few drops of vinegar. Fried green tomato slices get a crunchy egg batter and a shot of vinegar for seasoning. It works. Real homemade chicken broth is loaded with diced celery, carrots, soft noodles, and chicken breast—a child's dream. I particularly like the hamburgers, thick and full of flavor, slathered with house-made mayonnaise and served on flavorful whole-wheat buns. For dessert, have a slice of freshly baked apple pie with a slab of ice cream on top; the crust is a classic diner crumbly crust; the filling, long cooked.

This little place, with counter seats and some small booths, is the diner from heaven. The waitresses, in vintage bowling shirts, are as cheerful and efficient as any *Happy Days* walkons. Simmons and his assistant work carefully, keeping their kitchen immaculate and appetizing. With prices at true diner level, this authentic but unusually well-prepared American short-order food is certainly worth a special detour, and the lines are already forming at breakfast and lunch. Everything you ever wanted on a diner menu is offered, but without the usual complement of grease and canned food. This clean approach might be anathema for some die-hard greasy-spoon fans, but Bubba's certainly satisfied me.

LARK CREEK INN

234 Magnolia Avenue, Larkspur
Tel: 924-7766
Open for lunch Monday through Friday 11:30 a.m. to 1:45 p.m., Sunday brunch 10 a.m. to 2 p.m., dinner Monday through Thursday 5 to 9:15 p.m., Friday through Sunday 5 to 9:45 p.m.
Price: Expensive
Credit cards: AE, DC, MC, V

Lark Creek Inn used to be the only culinary reason for visiting Marin, as far as I was concerned, and it still ranks as the most compelling one. This great American restaurant started by Brad Ogden five years ago aims high and delivers on all levels without being stuffy or formal, tones unacceptable to casual Marinites. In fact, visiting Lark Creek is pure fun. Everything that comes to the table, from the basket of warm house-baked breads and corn sticks to the big homey desserts, appeals to Americans' deepest appetites. People devour plates of vine-ripened tomatoes in creamy onion dressing; baskets of crisply fried calamari and clams with a peppery garlic mayonnaise; hearty Yankee pot roast with lots of gravy, airy onion dumplings, and an array of roasted root vegetables; deep bowls of tender braised pork shoulder with white beans and kale; juicy spit-roasted chicken with chive-flecked mashed potatoes and ears of white corn; and plate-sized grilled lamb steaks with fresh peas and irresistible scalloped potatoes and turnips. Even something as esoteric as ravioli stuffed with shredded ham hock in a roasted tomato broth has a down-home side to it. For dessert, expect fresh fruit pies with house-made ice creams; fruit compotes with crème fraîche; shortcakes; butterscotch pudding; and spectacular versions of homemade pastries like a many-layered banana cake with mashed bananas and tons of frosting between the layers.

The cheerful yellow dining rooms, housed in a converted Victorian mansion set among towering redwood trees, are flooded with light from windows and skylights, and the service is both friendly and professional, a rare combination north of the Golden Gate Bridge. One of the nicest sights in the main dining room is the red brick wood-burning oven out of which come aromatic stews, suckling pigs, and roast chickens. Other seating alternatives are an outdoor patio shaded by the gigantic trees, a natural form of air-conditioning necessary in this hot pocket of the bay, and a separate bar-cafe room where you can order from a bar menu or the regular one when you feel like dropping in at the spur of the moment.

All the details here ring true: the all–West Coast wine list with tons of interesting bottles from small producers (no bargains here, but lots of treats); thick, rustic pottery plates and serving dishes that suit the hearty food; thin, simple wineglasses that help you taste a wine; and lots of staff to make sure that everything runs smoothly. Ogden knows what really counts in a restaurant. He's a midwestern boy (raised in upper Michigan) who believes in substance. As a midwestern girl (suburban Chicago), I am 100 percent on the same wavelength. This is one of the few restaurants that both my mother and I agree on. I love it for its inventiveness and charm within an American context; she loves it for the pot roast.

507 Magnolia Avenue,
Larkspur
Tel: 927-3331
Open Monday through
Thursday 11:30 a.m. to 11
p.m., Friday and Saturday
until midnight, Sunday 10
a.m. to 10 p.m.; Sunday
brunch 10 a.m. to 3 p.m.
Price: Moderate
Credit cards: AE, MC, V

Roland Passot, the genial chef-owner of the well regarded La Folie in the city, just opened this vibrant bistro in a historic old hotel in downtown Larkspur, the Blue Rock Inn. To me, the classic, homey bistro fare he's serving here represents his true calling. The food at Left Bank is as straightforward and traditional as the cooking at La Folie is complicated and eclectic. I would be happy to eat every day at Left Bank, driving across the Golden Gate Bridge to sit outside on the covered veranda at a marble table at the center of Larkspur. I'd have a meal like the ones I get in Paris: tender leeks vinaigrette, a savory salad of frisée with lardoons of bacon topped with a poached egg, or a tomato salad in vinaigrette sprinkled with basil; then move on to a steak with *frites;* superb coq au vin served in its own casserole; or *poulet grand-mère,* also in casserole, but braised with tons of julienned vegetables and finished with a little cream. Passot knows the technique behind these dishes inside and out; he can do them in his sleep, and the result is so rewarding, so satisfying, so completely there in flavor, texture, and appearance you want to cancel your flight to France. His portions are huge; his prices very reasonable. Customers get a bargain. Drink a bottle of California Rhône-style red from Qupé; have a warm *clafouti* or some *profiteroles* filled with ice cream in a pool of warm chocolate sauce for dessert; finish with an espresso. Have a cigarette. Just kidding. The whole meal is so French that I get carried away.

The airy interior of the restaurant, with a long bar and several rooms with banquettes and tables covered with white linen and butcher paper, has been cleanly remodeled, but the soul of Left Bank comes from its outdoor terraces. The weather is so clement in this particular part of Marin that you can sit outside on almost any sunny day of the year, especially when the heat lamps are switched on to take away the chill. The oversized French silverware, the little blue bowls of coarse salt on the table, the wicker chairs, the French mustard jars, those marvelous stone pillars supporting the red-tiled roof over the veranda, add immeasurably to the pleasure of eating anything, particularly right here in Marin County.

BRAISED LEEKS

This dish is easy to make in advance and is a good starter. Roland Passot's leek oil adds a glamorous touch.

12 to 16 small to medium leeks
4 cups water
Juice of 1 lemon
1 teaspoon flour
1/4 cup plus 3 tablespoons olive oil
Kosher salt and freshly ground
*   pepper to taste*
1 tablespoon Dijon mustard
1 tablespoon sherry vinegar
Minced fresh parsley for garnish

Trim the ends of the green top of the leeks, then cut 2 inches off the green top and reserve. Slit the leeks lengthwise but leave the very ends attached. Cut off the root and soak the leeks in water for 10 minutes to remove sand. Put the leeks in a large saucepan and cover with the water, lemon juice, and flour. Bring to a boil and simmer until tender, 4 to 6 minutes depending on the width of the leeks. Drain and plunge the leeks into a bowl of ice water to stop the cooking. When cool, drain and dry.

Wash and dry the reserved green leek tops and coarsely chop them. Put 1/2 cup chopped leek greens in a food processor with 1/4 cup olive oil and puree. You should have a bright green liquid. Season with salt and pepper and set aside.

Make a vinaigrette by whisking together the mustard, sherry vinegar, and the remaining 3 tablespoons olive oil. Season with salt and pepper.

In a bowl, gently coat the leeks with the vinaigrette. Place the leeks on serving plates. Drizzle leek oil around the circumference and top the leeks with minced parsley.

Serves 4 as a first course

Note: Chef Passot cuts yellow and red cherry tomatoes of the same size in half and reassembles the tomatoes so they have two tones. He garnishes the plates with these.

1617 Fourth Street,
San Rafael
Tel: 456-1808
Open Wednesday through
Saturday 5:30 to 10 p.m.,
Sunday 5 to 9 p.m.
Price: Moderate
Credit cards: MC, V

The Rice Table has been one of my favorite restaurants for years. The chef, the late Leonie Hool, personally cooked each of the myriad dishes that make up the lush Indonesian rice table with uncommon love and attention. One rarely gets to taste authentic home-cooked ethnic food, but at the Rice Table customers felt as if they had been invited to Ms. Hool's own dining room. The food had the freshness and integrity of family cooking.

Two years ago Leonie Hool died suddenly of a stroke. In shock, her family closed the restaurant, but about six months later her son and daughter-in-law reopened it with an inherited passion to prepare and serve genuine Indonesian food. In fact, they had worked with Ms. Hool for years, learning her recipes and assisting her in the kitchen. Recent visits have produced the same full-flavored, carefully prepared dishes that always have been the hallmark of this unique place. When a family believes in a tradition, they can carry it on. Ms. Hool's love of her native cuisine continues to be expressed in the cozy rattan-lined restaurant she started.

The menu is short and simple. There are only eleven dishes on it, and you get all of them on the Rice Table Special, a bargain at $19.95 for a feast so large that it arrives in waves. The meal starts with three extraordinary *sambals*, or dipping sauces, with shrimp chips. The vitality of the *sambals* tells you right off that everything, including condiments and curries, will be made from scratch. One sambal is a creamy warm peanut sauce spiked with chilies and ginger. The second is a medium-hot, vinegary fresh green chili and onion salsa; the third, a searing-hot red chili paste, completes the hotness spectrum. Then, a bowl of soothing celery-scented *dal*-like split pea soup arrives. The deluge begins with crisp thumb-sized *lumpia*, or spring rolls; fabulous Indonesian coleslaw dressed with tiny threads of orange zest and fresh mint leaves; and a salad of crunchy bean sprouts with chopped peanuts.

Next come the satays: chicken in a complex teriyaki-like sauce; pork in a creamy peanut. Then the stir fries: shrimp with fruity tamarind seeds, an enchanting dish; whole button mushrooms stir fried with hot red chilies, a startlingly good dish. Then braises: a delicious beef stew called *semur* that seduces you with the sweet bouquet of cloves; a mild chicken curry with the subtle richness of fresh coconut milk. When you think the table can't hold any more, a crab and bean sprout pancake, kind of an Indonesian egg foo young in a perky sweet-and-sour sauce, is wedged in. Condiments—toasted coconut, pickled vegetables, cold deep-fried potato sticks coated in hot red chili paste—can be scattered on the curries, stews, and two kinds of fragrant rice: yellow saffron and nutty white basmati. The strategy is to mound a big pile of both rices in the middle of your plate and arrange little piles of the different foods around it. Finally, fried thin rice noodles, lushly sauced and studded with bits of pork and vegetables, banish any remaining hunger at the end of the meal. The problem is that the noodles are so tasty you could make a meal of them alone.

Dessert brings creamy deep-fried bananas sprinkled with powdered sugar; you order a second—even after all that food. Cinnamon-scented Indonesian coffee helps you rise from the table.

I feel almost giddy when I encounter a restaurant that is able to keep up its purity, energy, and spirit year after year, especially when the original chef's passion has been passed on from one generation to the next. Like all the Rice Table's longtime customers, I have been nourished, delighted, and embraced by the restaurant to such a degree that its success and well being feel like my own. As with all great restaurants, the Rice Table's best patrons have become part of an extended family.

CAFES

BOOK PASSAGE CAFE

See Cookware and Books, page 579.

PASTICCERIA RULLI

464 Magnolia Avenue,
Larkspur
Tel: 924-7478
Open Monday through
Thursday 6:30 a.m. to 10
p.m., Friday until midnight,
Saturday 7 a.m. to midnight,
Sunday 7 a.m. to 6 p.m.
Credit cards: MC, V

This authentic, elegant Italian pastry shop and cafe is mentioned in many categories, because Pasticceria Rulli performs every part of Italian sweet and coffee service brilliantly. After a thoroughly French lunch at Left Bank, walk down the street to Rulli for a hit of Northern Italy. Have dessert and coffee at the marble tables, indoors or out, surrounded by hand-painted murals and beautiful dark wood paneling. Many informed clerks—efficient, helpful, smiling true professionals—work the counter, pulling out goodies from a sparkling glass case full of luscious cream cakes with names like Brasiliana (a chocolate sponge cake brushed with espresso liqueur, filled with whipped cream, and covered with chocolate shavings) and San Francesco (baked meringue filled with fresh fruit and pastry cream, topped with whipped cream and crumbled toasted meringue). The most elegant possible versions of *sacripantina* and St. Honoré cakes, the staples of North Beach, are made here with all-butter puff pastry, the tenderest sponge cake soaked with fine wines and spirits, and freshly made custard. You can buy these dreamy cream cakes by the slice or whole. Above the cakes is a shelf of tiny cookies, fresh and crisp, like miniature *palmiers* (palm leaf–shaped cookies made of puff pastry glazed with sugar), amaretti, hazelnut balls, and meringues dipped in chocolate. You need to taste Pasticceria Rulli's version of Italian cookies to appreciate how unique they are, crumbly with bread crumbs or ground nuts, full of interesting flavors, often dense, but meltingly tender. You can choose a little sampler of them to eat with some of the cafe's superb coffee, among the best I've had here or in Italy. When you decide which cookies you adore, you can have the clerks pack an exquisite box of them to take home or give as a gift with a pound of Pasticceria Rulli's house-roasted coffee beans. For ice-cream lovers, house-made *sorbetti* and *gelati*, made with natural essences and fresh fruits, are scooped into tiny cones or glass dishes. Or, you might be tempted by Rulli's satiny hand-dipped chocolates. There's such an embarrassment of riches here you don't know which way to turn. This *pasticceria* was founded by the son of a famous Turin pastry maker, and why he settled in Larkspur, I can't imagine. The place belongs on a chic alley off Union Square. It's a completely first-class operation offering the world of Italian sweets at the highest level of quality. Marin doesn't deserve Rulli. I want them in the city!

BARS

GUAYMAS

**5 Main Street,
Tiburon
Tel: 435-6300
Open Monday through
Thursday 11:30 a.m. to 10
p.m., Friday and Saturday
11:30 a.m. to 11 p.m.,
Sunday 10:30 a.m. to
10 p.m.
Credit cards: AE, MC, V**

There are far, far, worse hours you can spend than those lounging on the sunny deck of Guaymas, right on the water, drinking fresh-lime margaritas and dunking chips into three appealing house-made salsas. This massive, airy restaurant, done in blond wood, red tile, white adobe, and bright yellow furniture, reminds me of dining rooms in Mexican resorts during high season when everyone is on the American plan: three meals included in the price of a room and everyone eating at the same time. The place roars and the kitchen does its best to keep up. Still, the location of this Spectrum restaurant can't be beat, and Guaymas' long menu offers lots of tasty tidbits that go with drinks. If you bike over from the city, which isn't all that difficult, believe it or not, you can take the ferry back to Fisherman's Wharf. It loads on a dock right next to Guaymas.

SAM'S

**27 Main Street,
Tiburon
Tel: 435-4527
Open Monday through
Thursday 11 a.m. to 10 p.m.,
Friday until 10:30 p.m.,
Saturday 10 a.m. to 10:30
p.m., Sunday 9:30 a.m. to
10 p.m.
Credit cards: AE, DC , D,
MC, V**

All the old salts dock their boats at Sam's and climb up the ramp onto the huge outdoor deck with a great view for a cold beer and a hamburger. The food is of absolutely no consequence here, but seats on the deck in this protected corner of the bay are much coveted and feel very good after beating into the wind to get there. After a few bloody Marys, neither the trip nor the food seems so bad. Many sailors like me consider Sam's to be the high point of a typical day on the bay.

DELICATESSENS/TAKE-OUT

ART AND LARRY'S

This is one of the few delis in the Bay Area making an attempt to do it right. Take, for example, the gigantic smoked-fish platter, with big hunks of smoked white-fish, at least one-quarter pound of lightly cured Nova Scotia lox, and a pile of velvety sablefish garnished with cucumbers, onions, tomatoes, and other raw vegetables as befits a Marin County smoked-fish plate, with a big scoop of cream cheese and a very fresh chewy bagel. You need more than one to finish this plate—both eaters and bagels. There's real homemade chicken soup graced with light, tasty matzo balls, and dreamy blintzes, crisply fried and filled with gently sweetened farmer's cheese. The Romanian pastrami in the "Art size" is the way to go on the classic deli sandwich—the smaller size being too skimpy, the larger, ridiculous. You get coleslaw and a whole bowl of pickles. Even the gefilte fish is good here, house-made prim little dumplings that are light and tender, though a little sweet for my taste. Egg cream sodas, thick milk shakes, and satis-fying New York cheesecake made by two sisters from Petaluma all add to the calorie count. The smallish dining room divided into booths is pleasant to sit in, or you can get the above, and many other items, to go. I drive over the bridge for this one.

1242 Fourth Street,
San Rafael
Tel: 457-3354
Open Monday 11 a.m. to 3 p.m., Tuesday through Friday 11 a.m. to 9 p.m., Saturday 10 a.m. to 9 p.m., Sunday 10 a.m. to 8:30 p.m.
Credit cards: AE, MC, V

DAVID'S PRODUCE

See Produce, page 573.

"HAMBURGERS"

737 Bridgeway,
Sausalito
Tel: 332-9471
Open daily 11 a.m.
to 5 p.m.
No credit cards

For those of you taking the ferry ride over to Sausalito from San Francisco, the preferred place to grab a bite is at the nameless hamburger joint with a round charcoal grill in the window and the line out the door. I don't know why or how, but these big, juicy, fire-licked burgers taste better than any others. Get some fries and lots of napkins, and eat in the aquatic park across the street. These hamburgers rank with the best food you can find in this charming, if touristy, little village. You have to take them to go—there are maybe two unpleasant tables squeezed in the back of the room, but the weather in this protected part of the bay is usually mild.

ULTRA LUCCA

107 Corte Madera Town
Center, Corte Madera
Tel: 927-4347
Open Monday through
Friday 10 a.m. to 8 p.m.,
Saturday until 7 p.m.,
Sunday until 6 p.m.
Credit cards: MC, V

For other locations, see page 529.

This very complete and excitingly merchandised Italian delicatessen is one of five branches in the Bay Area, an empire started forty years ago on 40th Street and Telegraph Avenue in Oakland. The Oakland mother ship makes all the salads, pastas, and sauces for the small chain, and I must say they do a rather good job. The fresh, small cheese ravioli have pure white fillings of blended cheeses, and are particularly tasty strewn with Ultra Lucca's well-made bolognese sauce. The cheese department always has some special, non-Italian selections, like a stunning aged Cheddar called Grafton Reserve, as sharp, nutty and buttery as any I've tasted. The real strength of Ultra Lucca is that they stock a full

Italian pantry, starting with wines, waters, and Torani syrups; moving on to real imported buffalo-milk mozzarella balls; Reggiano Parmesan ($10.75/lb); Fontina Val d'Aosta ($11.39/lb), and manchego; tons of salads, housemade sausages, prosciutto from Parma ($25.65/lb), and other cured meats; olives; some first-rate Italian and Spanish olive oils (Lerida, L'Estornell), semolina flour, polenta, Arborio rice, fresh pasta, the highest-quality dried pasta from Rustichella d' Abruzzo (which is made on ancient machines with the hardest-wheat flour), mascarpone, and fresh breads from all over the bay. This is one-stop Italian shopping, and Ultra Lucca stocks the best. In the Corte Madera Town Center store, you can sit at a table by the front window with a made-to-order sandwich or plates of salads and *antipasti*.

The service is extraordinary. When your number comes up, which doesn't take long because the stores are so well staffed, a clerk will spend as much time as you need, patiently giving you tastes of cheeses, cutting the smallest amounts, fixing the most finicky sandwiches, carefully slicing each salami and ham. Though prices are high, you get exactly what you want, in decent condition. As in most other cheese departments, their precut, prewrapped cheeses often take on the aroma of the refrigerator, but we don't live in a perfect world. Nonetheless, Ultra Lucca does make it a better one.

BAKERIES

PASTICCERIA RULLI

See listing, page 566.

ICE CREAM/CHOCOLATES

LYLA'S CHOCOLATES

208 Corte Madera Town
Center, Corte Madera
Tel: 924-6950
Monday through Friday
10 a.m. to 8 p.m.,
Saturday until 6 p.m.,
Sunday 11 a.m. to 5 p.m.

417 Miller Avenue, Mill Valley
Tel: 383-8887
Monday through Friday
10 a.m. to 6 p.m.,
Saturday 10:30 a.m. to 5 p.m.
Credit cards: MC, V

Lyla's luscious handmade chocolates fall somewhere between See's and Godiva, and they earn extra marks for invention. The peanut butter swirls, rich milk chocolate with creamy peanut butter mixed in, or peanut butter frogs with centers of sweetened fresh peanut butter, will make Reese's Peanut Butter Cups pale by comparison. Lyla takes all sorts of American favorites—rocky road, honeycombs, caramels—and makes them with top-notch ingredients in small, rich, beautifully formed pieces, creating a unique line of elegant chocolates at their best. The store in Corte Madera sometimes puts two or three specially made tiny samples on the counter that will get you hooked. This candy shop is worth a special trip for the quality and interesting variety of its chocolates.

PASTICCERIA RULLI

See listing, page 566.

PRODUCE

On one level, David Findlay's large produce market tries to emulate the great-granddaddy of them all, Monterey Produce in Berkeley, with outside tables and huge quantities of commercial and some organic fruits and vegetables, indoors and out. The variety doesn't approach what you can find in the East Bay, but David's features some good-quality produce at moderate prices. The bargains come prepackaged and marked "reduced."

What really sets David's apart are the products he makes out of produce, including a line of fresh juices that go far beyond tame orange and grapefruit to blends of fresh strawberry, apple and pineapple, pineapple and orange, and mango and orange, all pressed daily from fresh fruits. These come in three different sizes and are best drunk immediately to take advantage of their freshness. David also makes some of the nicest Mexican salsas and guacamole around. Sold in half and whole pints, the guacamole tastes mostly of pure, ripe, creamy avocado seasoned with lime, cilantro, and onion, a simple formula that would make purists like Diana Kennedy happy—the only departure being the use of too much lime, which does keep the guacamole fresh and of good color. The tomato salsa is a classic too, just chopped tomato, lime, cilantro, onion, and chilies, and David makes an effort to get his hands on the flavorful tomatoes from local farmers when he can. A hot and a mild version of tomato salsa, a summer fruit salsa, and a sweet corn–tomato salsa are viable as building blocks of a meal. One reason the juices, salsas, and guacamole are so fresh is that they are kept really cold, buried in tables of crushed ice.

Corte Madera Town Center, Corte Madera
Tel: 927-2431
Open daily 9 a.m. to 9 p.m.
No credit cards

Finally, next door to the produce market, David's has opened a busy little taqueria that takes advantage of his salsa and guacamole factory. The integrity of the ingredients in a menu of take-out dishes such as soft tacos filled with grilled chicken, topped with shredded lettuce, salsa, and *queso fresco*; burritos; house-made tamales; and grilled half-chicken plates is high. However, the challenge of using a greater variety of the produce next door in some nonpredictable ways has yet to be taken.

MARIN COUNTY FARMERS' MARKET

**Marin Civic Center,
San Rafael
Thursdays and Sundays
from 8 a.m. to 1 p.m.
year round**

This is one of the most vital farmers' markets in the Bay Area, much frequented by San Francisco cooks who live in the north end of the city until the Ferry Plaza Farmers' Market on the Embarcadero came along. A large market drawing many farmers of both organic and nonorganic produce in different price ranges, the Marin County market is known for its out-of-season, organic, locally raised hothouse Wilgenburg tomatoes (people wait in line at the opening of the market to get them), dates, good medium-priced stone fruit in season, handicraft stalls, and lots of side events for kids. A strawberry farmer not only sells the fruit, but a refreshing strawberry cream sorbet made by his wife; an organic vegetable stand also sells natural wool, gathered from the sheep on the property. Each skein is a different color, ranging from white to dark gray-brown; one could imagine a magical garment knitted from them. The Marin market has the luxury of space, so the stalls are spread out, and the variety and quality is large, concentrated mostly on produce with a little cheese, eggs, and some expensive, highly smoked salmon thrown into the mix.

CHEESE

THE CHEESE SHOP

This tiny, hidden-away shop is worth seeking out if you're a cheese-lover. Owner Forrest Young has collected an eclectic group, which he keeps in top condition. A cheese expert, he knows how every cheese is made. He understands seasonality, the influence of locale, and the increased pleasure of eating cheeses when they are ripe and perfect. His attitude might seem prickly at first encounter, defensive somehow, as if he had had too many run-ins with customers who aren't serious about cheese, but once he sees you're a believer the tastes are offered, the geneologies of the cheese explained. I came away with a Spanish cheese called Mahón, a nutty, buttery, slightly sharp cow's milk cheese made in the Balearic Islands (Minorca) and a wedge of tangy St.-André in perfect condition, both cut to specification. There's no prewrapping here, which keeps the cheese smelling more like cheese and less like plastic and refrigeration. Much information comes forth, if you're interested, with each cheese lovingly set on the counter. Wines, baguettes from Bordenave's, and crackers fill up every inch of the wood-lined store all the way up to the ceiling. But cheese is the thing here, and Young's personal selections make the store interesting.

38 Miller Avenue,
Mill Valley
Tel: 383-7272
Open Tuesday through
Saturday 10 a.m. to 6 p.m.,
Sunday noon to 5 p.m.
Credit cards: AE, MC, V

ULTRA LUCCA

See Delicatessens, page 570.

COFFEE

PASTICCERIA RULLI

See Cafes, page 566.

PEET'S COFFEE AND TEA

88 Throckmorton Avenue, Mill Valley
Tel: 381-8227
Open Monday through Saturday 6:30 a.m. to 7 p.m.,
Sunday 7 a.m. to 6 p.m.
Credit cards: MC, V

See listing, page 218.

SPINELLI COFFEE COMPANY

Corte Madera Town Center, Corte Madera
Tel: 927-0471
Open weekdays 6:30 a.m. to 8 p.m., Saturday 8 a.m. to 7 p.m.,
Sunday 8 a.m. to 6 p.m.
Credit cards: D, MC, V

See listing, page 192.

WINES AND SPIRITS

MARIN WINE CELLAR

This large, air-conditioned wine warehouse behind a locked iron gate (you have to buzz to get in) is stacked floor to ceiling with cases of wine. A small desk with many phones and a wooden rack with some of the most amazing bottles you'll ever see are the only islands in the towering sea. At the back are wine lockers of private individuals. There must be $5 million worth of wine here, and it's traded mostly over the phone like a commodity (which it is, I guess). Harvey Buchbinder, the rotund, bearded, besandled partner of this operation calls wine collecting a rich man's sport. However, he says, certain classics are better investments than the stock market. I asked him if he knew the lineage of some of the blockbuster bottles I saw scattered around—where they came from, how they were cellared and shipped. He shrugged, and it made me wonder about the value of something like a 1918 Mouton Rothschild with an exquisite Art Deco label, listed in Marin Wine Cellar's 1993 fall catalogue at $1,395 (Visa, MasterCard, or American Express accepted). If you open it, what do you have? A dead liquid? A taste memory of the wine in whatever condition it happens to be, a period of anticipation, a trophy in the empty bottle? Displayed on the rack the day I was buzzed in were both 1935 and 1945 Lafites, the 1918 Mouton, and a 1955 Mouton with a beautiful Georges Braque label, a 1954 La Tâche, a bunch of magnums of 1989 Petrus—well, you get the idea. I asked Harvey who buys these wines. He told me that 98 percent of his business is done over the phone, all over the world. He has many private buyers in France, Switzerland,

2138 Fourth Street,
San Rafael
Tel: 459-3823
Open Tuesday through
Friday 9 a.m. to 4 p.m. or by
appointment
Credit cards: AE, MC, V

London, Mexico, and Hong Kong, and most sales involve single bottles—though he recently sent a case of '61 Latour ($8,400) to Barbra Streisand in Las Vegas. Harvey confided that he loves Vegas; that high rollers like big wines. He buys through auction and from private individuals and keeps a one-hundred-year back list for birthdays. When you visit the Marin Wine Cellar, if only to see millions of dollars of wine bottles piled up on top of each other, get a copy of the catalogue, a fascinating document. You can price out a birth-year wine dinner, estimate the value of your own cellar, and actually find some affordable bottles from recent vintages. There's all sorts of fun to be had, but you take your chances here. To Harvey, every bottle is a crapshoot. You have to decide how much to lay down.

MILL VALLEY MARKET

12 Corte Madera Avenue, Mill Valley

Tel: 388-3222

Open Monday through Saturday 7 a.m. to 7:30 p.m., Sunday 9 a.m. to 7 p.m.

Credit cards: MC, V

An adjunct to the popular Mill Valley Market grocery store, this rustic wood-lined, red-tiled, air-conditioned wine cellar is stacked to the rafters with well-chosen California wines, often from such hard-to-find tiny producers as The Terraces and Sky Vineyard, both noteworthy for their Zinfandels, or Abreu Cabernet from Rick Forman. Top-of-the-line imports from Kermit Lynch, Diamond, and Italian wines from Estate are all present and accounted for. This is a Marin County outpost for the Bandols of Domaine Tempier. Finally, the shop has a good selection of specialty booze, lots of fancy tequilas and Scotches.

COOKWARE AND BOOKS

A CLEAN WELL-LIGHTED PLACE FOR BOOKS

2417 Larkspur Landing Circle, Larkspur

Tel: 461-0171

Open Monday through Thursday 10 a.m. to 11 p.m., Friday and Saturday 10 a.m. to midnight

Credit cards: AE, MC, V

See listing, page 95.

BOOK PASSAGE

Anyone who travels should know about this excellent bookstore specializing in travel books and, hence, international restaurant and food guides. If you're going anywhere in the world, you will want to check out the guides, maps, and travel literature on your destination, if only to get an overview. You'll find hard-to-come-by restaurant guides like *Eating Out in Provence and the Côte d'Azur* by Edward Roch, Gaston Wijnen's *Discovering Paris Bistros*, and Faith Willinger's *Eating in Italy*, including restaurants, cafes, outdoor markets, wineries, bakeries, kitchenware shops, and pic-nic spots throughout northern Italy. You can spend hours browsing the huge travel section, concocting trips and adventures you never even knew you wanted to take. When you tire of this, you can have a first-rate Illycaffe espresso or cappuccino and a nice, light, health-foody, Marin County bite at the Book Passages Cafe in one corner of the bookstore near the magazine racks. The cafe gets special

51 Tamal Vista Boulevard (Market Place Shopping Center), Corte Madera

Tel: 927-0960

Open Sunday through Thursday 9 a.m. to 10 p.m., Friday and Saturday until 11 p.m.

Credit cards: AE, D, MC, V

credit for using real plates, glasses, and silverware. Finally, Book Passage publishes a yearly catalogue and newsletter, sixty-four pages long, with all sorts of information on which guides to buy for different parts of the world. If you're an omnivorous, international eater like me, you will find a trip to Book Passage essential before a trip out of town.

JUDITH ETS-HOKIN'S HOMECHEF

329 Corte Madera Town
Center, Corte Madera
Tel: 927-3191
Monday through Thursday
9:30 a.m. to 9 p.m., Friday
and Saturday 9 until 6,
Sunday 10 a.m. to 5 p.m.
Credit cards: AE, D, MC, V

See listing, page 368.

This branch has the advantage of having a large, airy shopping mall site so that the merchandise can be readily seen, examined, and plucked from attractive displays.

WILLIAMS-SONOMA

1802 Redwood Highway, Corte Madera

Tel: 924-2940

Open weekdays 10 a.m. to 9 p.m., Saturday until 6 p.m.,

Sunday 11 a.m. to 6 p.m.

Credit cards: AE, MC, V

See listing, page 175.

The Wine Country of Napa & Sonoma

RESTAURANTS

ALL SEASONS CAFE AND WINE STORE

Open daily 9 a.m. to 10 p.m.; lunch 11:30 a.m. to 3:30 p.m.,

dinner 5 to 10 p.m.

Price: Moderate

Tel: 707-942-9111

See Wine Stores, page 609.

BISTRO DON GIOVANNI

In a modern, barnlike space with tall windows that look out to a sea of vines and mountains in the distance, two expatriates from Piatti, Donna and Giovanni Scala, are cooking up a storm. Their winsome Italian fare includes thin-crusted wood-fired pizzas; fabulous deep-fried matchsticks of zucchini with Parmesan grated over them; and an *antipasto* of broccoli rabe sautéed with lots of garlic and Tuscan olive oil and draped with thin slices of fresh mozzarella. The pastas, like thin, tender ravioli filled with ricotta in a delicate cream sauce flecked with lemon zest; or rustic handmade pappardelle in a juicy

4110 St. Helena Highway
(Highway 29), Napa
Tel: 707-224-3300
Open Sunday through
Thursday 11:30 a.m. to 10
p.m., Friday and Saturday
until 11 p.m.
Price: Moderate
Credit cards: AE, D, MC, V

stew of braised rabbit, sage, and pancetta are the high point of the menu. Focaccia sandwiches filled with grilled vegetables, slathered with lots of aïoli, and served with warm lattice potato chips are dreamy. Summery appetizers of large marinated shrimp grilled in the shell and served with a warm corn salad make for an appealing alfresco lunch on the broad wooden porch that rims the restaurant. Eating lunch outside near the bocce ball court and herb garden is one of the pleasures of visiting the Napa Valley.

BISTRO RALPH

109 Plaza Street,
Healdsburg
Tel: 707-433-1380
Open for lunch Monday
through Friday 11:30 a.m.
to 3 p.m., dinner nightly
5:30 to 10 p.m.
Price: Moderate
Credit cards: MC, V

Ralph Tingle, the chef-owner of this stunning-looking restaurant, happens to be the son of Alta Tingle, the creative genius behind The Gardener (see East Bay, page 556), who in turns happens to be a very good friend of conceptual artist David Ireland. (Ireland's seminal work was the stripping back of layers of paint and wallpaper in his turn-of-the-century Mission District house, treating the wadded-up peelings as art objects, then fixing the raw interior in varnish, making it look like a resonant old Italian villa. Then he took the idea a step farther by using the stripped-away materials to make utilitarian objects like lamps.) Tingle enlisted Ireland's energy in designing her son's restaurant, and the result of their collaboration is one of the most compelling restaurant spaces in all of Northern California. Ireland's deconstructive inventiveness combined with Alta Tingle's intuitive understanding of materials created a room of surprising simplicity and beauty with completely unexpected forms, like a long, undulating wood and metal wine rack behind the counter and an entrance of raw concrete and steel. I like to be in this room at night when everything takes on a romantic Italian-villa glow, although it looks nothing like one.

The cooking can be uneven and quirky, but the whole-leaf Caesar is tasty and pretty, and I am fond of a spicy lamb burger made with local C. K. lamb and Downtown Bakery buns. Bistro Ralph is a destination, if only to experience the restaurant dining room as a work of art.

BROWN STREET GRILL

My favorite spot in the town of Napa, the Brown Street Grill, turns home cooking into restaurant cuisine with a devotion not often found in either place. Formerly partners at the Diner in Yountville, the Brown Street husband-and-wife team of Nickie and Peter Zeller turns out thick, savory sandwiches of grilled ham and cheese, or of juicy roasted tomatoes with mozzarella. Their excellent roast chicken sets a standard, and the fresh, colorful, properly dressed salads sing. I have made a detour for the Gravenstein apple pie a la mode, with its flaky, butter crust, followed by an excellent espresso. The friendly, low-key ambiance may not make this a glittering valley destination, but if you crave lovely home-style food prepared by people who have high standards and good sense about what tastes right, you will want to seek this place out.

1300 Brown Street (at Clinton), Napa
Tel: 707-255-6395
Open for lunch Monday through Saturday 11:30 a.m. to 3 p.m.; dinner Monday through Thursday from 5 to 9 p.m., Friday and Saturday until 9:30 p.m.
Price: Moderate
Credit cards: AE, MC, V

CATAHOULA RESTAURANT AND SALOON

Calistoga, once a sleepy Napa Valley town best known for its hot springs and mud baths, has become the hot spot in the upper valley. The latest evidence of Calistoga's transformation is Jan Birnbaum's Catahoula, a big-city restaurant with the latest in wood-burning ovens in the middle of the dining room, and a menu of updated American dishes that Birnbaum worked on when he was the chef at Campton Place in San Francisco. Catahoula is much more casual and fun than Campton Place, but the

1457 Lincoln Avenue, Calistoga
Tel: 707-942-2275
Weekdays (except Tuesday) Lunch noon to 2:30 p.m., Saturday and Sunday noon to 3:30 p.m.; Dinner Sunday through Thursday 5:30 to

10 p.m., Friday and Saturday
until 10:30 p.m.
Price: Moderate to expensive
Credit cards: MC, V

food is hardly homey. The plates, in many shapes, colors, and materials, are carefully arranged, and the combinations draw on the visual as much as the flavorful. There might be a tasty duck *confit* salad with tangerines and blood oranges, or a tender-leafed green salad made with just-picked Forni-Brown greens in a mild Brazil nut vinaigrette. But sometimes the twists and turns taken to personalize the American menu work against the best interests of the food. Braised short ribs derive smokiness from the wood-burning oven, but they don't get tender enough; and sassafras and chipotle, just two of the flavors on the Sonoma lamb plate, have no real reason for being there. The best-looking thing to come out of the oven is a crusty herbed potato cake, served with an oven-roasted free-range chicken.

A lively scene happens in the saloon across the lobby almost every evening, where people can order from a menu of "small plates": pizzas, crawfish tamales, salads, and richly topped flat breads. The informality here allows for real down-home food and Birnbaum's best efforts. You can sit at the bar or at counters, drink beer from small breweries, and taste local wines by the glass.

DOMAINE CHANDON

One California Drive,
Yountville
Tel: 707-944-2892
Open for lunch daily, May
through October (closed
Monday and Tuesday,
November through April),
11:30 a.m. to 2:30 p.m.;

Philippe Jeanty has been at the helm of this ambitious, very French dining room since it opened over fifteen years ago. As a California adjunct to the famous French champagne house, Moët Chandon, the intention was to bring a high-flying, rather formal French experience along with the prestigious name to the New World. The restaurant has achieved this. You can lunch outdoors on the terrace, sipping cold Domaine Chandon while you gaze at the vines, or dine indoors with sweeping views as

These corn cakes are a snap to mix up. The batter can be held in the refrigerator for 6 hours and then cooked. I top them with yogurt and eat about a dozen, but they are sublime topped with sour cream and smoked salmon, as they are at the Brown Street Grill.

Combine the cornmeal, salt, and boiling water in a medium bowl. Let stand for 10 minutes.

Melt 1 tablespoon of the butter. Beat the melted butter with the egg and milk, and add to the cornmeal mixture. Combine the flour and baking powder and stir into the cornmeal mixture until smooth. Do not overmix. Stir in green onions and corn.

Whisk together the sour cream, lemon juice, cream, dill, salt, and pepper.

In a large skillet over high heat, melt together the vegetable oil and the remaining 1 tablespoon butter. For each corn cake spoon about 2 tablespoons of batter into the pan and fry until the uncooked side starts to show bubbles. Turn. Cook until golden.

Drizzle with the sour cream mixture, top with a slice of smoked salmon, and serve at once.

Makes 8 cakes, serves 4 to 8 as a side dish

GREEN ONION–CORN CAKES

1/2 cup cornmeal

1/2 teaspoon kosher salt

1/2 cup boiling water

2 tablespoons butter

1 egg

1/2 cup milk

1/4 cup all-purpose flour

1 teaspoon baking powder

1/2 cup chopped green onions

1/4 cup sweet corn kernels

1 cup sour cream

2 tablespoons fresh lemon juice

1/4 cup heavy (whipping) cream

2 teaspoons minced fresh dill

Salt and pepper to taste

1 teaspoon vegetable oil

8 ounces good-quality smoked
    salmon, thinly sliced

well. The operation is large and multifaceted, and at its best, the food can evoke a meal taken in a one- or two-star restaurant in Burgundy. Provençal-accented fish and shellfish preparations go with white wines; sophisticated venison, lamb, and beef dishes with reds; and a barrage of sometimes lackluster desserts call for more champagne. The food can be afflicted by a hotel-kitchen inconsistency, especially when wedding lunches are taking place, but the experience can be magical when everything is going right.

dinner Wednesday through Sunday 6 to 9:30 p.m.
Price: Expensive
Credit cards: AE, DC , D, MC, V

Washington and Creek streets, Yountville
Tel: 707-944-2380
Open Tuesday through Sunday from 5:30 to 10 p.m.; prix fixe
Price: Expensive
Credit cards: AE, CB, MC, V

Thomas Keller, a serious French-trained chef from New York, bought this venerable Napa Valley institution from the husband-and-wife team that ran it for years, and is turning it into the Valley's first high-concept destination restaurant. At Rakel, his restaurant in New York, Keller developed a poetic style based on tiny portions of composed dishes inspired by offbeat ingredients. At the French Laundry, the dishes have become even smaller as part of an inventive fixed-price five-course-plus meal that takes about four hours to be served. When you reserve you get a table for the evening, and Keller makes use of every minute of it. He starts sending out food, little bites that precede the five courses you've so carefully ordered. An oversized French tablespoon cradled in a linen napkin becomes the serving vessel for a tiny poached quail egg napped in beurre blanc and fragrant fresh herbs, one ethereal slurp. A martini glass filled with a clear "tomato water" appears with one grilled shrimp hooked onto its side. As you move into the meal you've actually selected, from a menu that offers four or more choices in each category plus a complete five-course vegetarian meal, the serving size hardly gets bigger than a few bites. A cold stew of tiny artichokes, a slice of monkfish in a verbena-scented tomato *coulis*, a round of veal breast layered with root vegetables, a potato-chip sandwich filled with peppery Brie next to a pile of miniature lettuces, and a warm individual chocolate cake that oozed in the middle made up my meal one night. You end up being entertained all evening by a parade of stylish dishes, amazingly unrepetitious when you consider how many ingredients are involved, without feeling stuffed. Keller has mastered the tasting menu by reducing it to edible scale. It's ingeniously put together like a jigsaw puzzle, so that no matter what you order it adds up to a pretty picture. Keller's cooking makes an intellectual as well as sensual statement, but he has advanced in his art to the point where the two support each other.

The setting is as much a part of the experience as the cooking. The French Laundry was always known as a prix-fixe, evening-long destination restaurant where people were encouraged to stroll mid-meal in the garden. The two-story stone building, like a French country house, has tables in two serene dining rooms with windows that look out to vines and greenery. Early in the evening before the chill sets in, you can eat outside on a beautifully manicured lawn enclosed by trees and flowers. The small kitchen, open to view both from the downstairs dining room and the garden, is an intrinsic part of the restaurant. You don't feel a separation between the front and back of the house here, because Keller so consciously molds your experience, from the wooden clothespin with the French Laundry logo holding your napkin at the beginning, to the laundry-list check at the end. Though the list does add up, you haven't been taken to the cleaners: the $49 per meal price does not seem stiff after what has been delivered.

THE GENERAL'S DAUGHTER

A cheerfully and imaginatively converted Sonoma mansion provides the setting for some real country cooking: huge portions of delicious, homey food, deceptively simple and satisfying. You can't eat much better than this if you love things like meltingly crisp onion threads, juicy Caesar salads, Sonoma lamb or rib-eye steaks with huge portions of roasted potatoes and two or three different vegetables, and for dessert, fresh fruit crisps

400 West Spain Street, Sonoma
Tel: 707-938-4004
Daily for lunch 11:30 a.m. to 2:30 p.m.; dinner Sunday through Thursday 5:30 to 9:30 p.m., Friday and

and hot fudge sundaes. The plates look as bright and appealing as they taste, and everything on them is impeccable. The raw materials couldn't be fresher or of higher quality nor the preparations more meticulous. Chef Jaquelyne Buchanan has years of experience with straightforward country-inspired cooking, starting out with Judy Rogers at the original Union Hotel in Benicia and then opening her own small American restaurant in downtown San Francisco. She spent eight years as head chef at the Hayes Street Grill, dealing with fish and salads. She knows how food should taste and doesn't feel she has to fuss around with it to make a statement. Her genius lies in gathering great ingredients and in her sureness of palate, not necessarily invention, and thank goodness for that.

The large multiroomed restaurant feels very much like a stately house, with tall Victorian windows that look out to patios and gardens, which are set up for outdoor dining during the summer. The walls are hung with eye-catching oil paintings of scenes that you might see on your drive through Sonoma. The whole operation strikes an appealing, unified tone: the food, the setting, the decor, the friendly service, the California wine list are all on the same wavelength, and it's one you'll want to be on, too, if you're anywhere in the neighborhood.

Saturday until 10:30 p.m.

Price: Moderate

Credit cards: MC, V

The dining room of this stately Victorian mansion, built in 1881 and refurbished as an inn, trumpets a theme of wine country elegance with a lyrical menu based on locally raised ingredients. Chef Todd Muir takes advantage of the spacious grounds to cold-smoke his own fish, grow his own herbs and lettuces, and cellar an extensive collection of local wines. You can order a four- or five-course fixed-price menu or any dish a la carte. I have had his delicate smoked salmon on blini spread with sour cream, fabulous Bruce Campbell lamb, a pretty salad garnished with a round of warm breaded goat cheese, and a heavenly warm chocolate cake with dried-cherry ice cream for dessert. All of it tasted wonderful in a softly lit parlorlike dining room with Victorian fireplaces and tall French windows, served by a young, enthusiastic staff.

1001 Westside Road,
Healdsburg
Tel: 707-433-4231
Open nightly 6 to 9 p.m.;
Sunday brunch 11 a.m. to
2 p.m.
Price: Expensive
Credit cards: AE, CB, DC ,
MC, V

MUSTARDS

In some ways this first large-scale restaurant to open in the Napa Valley remains its most successful. Mustards is universally loved by local residents and tourists alike for its smoky, tender, spicy baby back ribs; cornmeal-coated fried green tomatoes; tasty Asian-marinated flank steak; Chinese chicken and noodle salad; and of course, Mustards' always-crisp tangle of deep-fried onion threads. The enduring vitality of this place perhaps comes from the fact that this was chef Cindy Pawlcyn's first endeavor and she put all of the dishes she loved on the menu: country dishes transformed by her sprightly offbeat style and sparkle.

Surrounded by a parking lot, the restaurant feels like the quintessential roadhouse with an airy, porchlike

7399 St. Helena Highway
(one mile north of Yountville
on Highway 29), Napa
Tel: 707-944-2424
Open daily 11:30 a.m.
to 10 p.m.
Price: Moderate
Credit cards: DC , MC, V

dining room and constantly busy bar. The very mention of Mustards in the valley conjures up fun. It's the place that launched the other Real Restaurants (Fog City Diner, Buckeye Roadhouse, et al.), and in some ways will always be the guiding light.

NAPA VALLEY WINE TRAIN

1275 McKinstry Street (between First Street and Soscol Avenue), Napa

Tel: 707-253-2111

Departs daily

Credit cards: AE, DC , D, MC, V

Disdain may rain down on me from a certain group of exclusive valley residents for touting the much-opposed wine train, but the slow-rolling, luxuriously appointed dining cars on this resurrected railway line offer lovely views of the valley and pretty decent food during the two-hour journey into the wine country. Wine makers are often in attendance, giving tastes and informal seminars on wine making, while the train staff coddles passengers from the moment they board. Meals begin informally in the wood-paneled club car with tasty pâtés and appetizers, and continue in the romantic dining car with straightforward preparations of salmon, chicken, or red meat. Remember, the food is not the main motivation for a tour, but a context for taking the train through a unique stretch of countryside. You can use your visiting relatives as an excuse to take the ride.

You can always find a good dish on the exuberant menu of this burgeoning Italian chain, which started here in Yountville in an airy wooden building with two outdoor patios and an open kitchen boasting a wood-fired rotisserie and a pizza oven. The menu concentrates on pizzas and pastas, some interesting appetizers, and chicken and rabbit cooked on the rotisserie. Though the noodle dishes have their ups and downs, look for the little ear-shaped pasta called *orrechietti* tossed with cabbage, pancetta, and Fontina; and the satiny, house-made ravioli. Not every dish gets the attention it needs, but a clever orderer can eat well. Ask your waiter for suggestions.

6480 Washington Street, Yountville
Tel: 707-944-2070
Sunday through Thursday 11:30 a.m. to 10 p.m., Friday and Saturday until 11 p.m.
Price: Moderate
Credit cards: AE, MC, V

Until recently, one would not expect to find sophisticated restaurants on the main plaza of sleepy Healdsburg, but in the last couple of years, several have sprung to life to serve the growing number of weekend residents and émigrés from the city. My favorite is the snappy little Samba Java, a spot for breakfast, lunch, and weekend dinners opened by ex-Stars chef Colleen McGlynn and co-owner Jim Neeley. The tall, narrow space has been whimsically designed in a Caribbean motif. Weathered chairs are pushed under galvanized sheet-metal tables. Huge, primitive, cartoonlike paintings hang on concrete and stone walls. Light streams in through skylights and tall front windows.

The breakfast and lunch menus are written on a blackboard by the tiled counter at the back. In the mornings the kitchen turns out homey breakfast pastries like coconut–sour cream coffee cake or muffins

109A Plaza Street, Healdsburg
Tel: 707-433-5282
Open for lunch weekdays 11 a.m. to 2:30 p.m., Saturday 9 a.m. to 2 p.m.; dinner Thursday through Saturday 5:30 to 9 p.m.; Sunday brunch 9 a.m. to 2:30 p.m.
Price: Inexpensive
Credit cards: AE, MC, V

with fresh berries to go with first-rate cappuccino in signature oversized Samba Java cups. At lunch, platters of alluring *antipasti* are set out on the counters, such as grilled summer squashes with sage leaves, beets in caraway dressing, or new-potato and corn salad—whatever is in season. Muffaletta-style sandwiches and juicy hamburgers on Downtown Bakery and Creamery buns, and the definitive bacon, lettuce, and tomato sandwich, regularly show up on the changing card.

Dinner can be a varied treat if you get there early enough to choose among the three or four dishes prepared each night, like a spicy pork stew served over black beans with mango salsa, or Samba Java's tender, velvety grilled chicken served with garlic mashed potatoes and crisp vegetables. Meaty country pork ribs are another triumph, with crisply roasted creamer potatoes and spicy slaw. An al dente vegetarian pasta is always well made.

Be sure to save room for dessert at either lunch or dinner, because they are light, pretty, seasonal, and original. Samba Java knows how to make short-cakes that are exceptionally buttery, crumbly, and perfectly sweetened for once, and slathers them with barely whipped cream and lightly sugared fresh berries. Slices of angel food cake might be splashed with Santa Rosa plum sauce and fresh berries. A tall, unfrosted French chocolate cake melts in your mouth.

This small-scale cafe in the country meets everyday needs with integrity and wit. That Samba Java was the first of a new generation of restaurants to open in Healdsburg and was able to succeed in the off season when the business depends only on locals underscores how appealing it is to everyone in the community. Healdsburg may not have seen anything like it, but now the town can't live without it. Samba Java's casual style, low prices, and delicious food have won everyone over.

STARS OAKVILLE CAFE

One expects something splashy from a new Jeremiah Tower restaurant, but this branch of Stars Cafe in the wine country suits a more conservative upscale contingent in the Napa Valley. The seeming simplicity of the interior of this small restaurant is somewhat belied by a large garden in the back with a dovecote, citrus and olive trees, and beds of herbs that look as if they have been there for years. Rumor has it that the charming landscaping cost nearly as much as the restaurant itself. At any rate, I cannot think of a more appropriate site for a wine country lunch or summer dinner than in the garden of Stars Oakville Cafe. Indoors, the simple white interior, with clay floor and wicker armchairs, is dominated by a kitchen visible behind a plate glass window. I am not sure why diners get to see this clean but technological view of stainless-steel equipment. Though the kitchen has a wood-burning oven, whose smoky aromas waft into the dining room and out the door of the restaurant, you do not actually see it. In fact, you can barely see the cooks, so the windowed kitchen seems like an odd design choice.

However, the food coming out of that kitchen is unfussy, delicious, and cooked and presented with understated style. Many of the dishes will be familiar to San Francisco Stars Cafe patrons. The light fry of calamari and bits of fish is, as always, lightly floured and delicately golden. Two thin slices of house-smoked salmon

7848 Highway 29, Oakville

Tel: 707-944-8905

Open daily for lunch 11:30 a.m. to 5 p.m.; dinner Sunday through Thursday 5 to 9 p.m., Friday and Saturday until 10 p.m.; Sunday brunch 11:30 a.m. to 5 p.m.

Price: Expensive

Credit cards: MC, V

come with a delicious triangle of potato frittata. A nice little salad of frisée sprinkled with sieved egg is flanked by savory chicken liver toasts. Main courses might bring French-style beef stew, heated in the wood oven and presented in a casserole with a dab of mashed potatoes and an herbed biscuit crust to sop up the juices. At lunch a wood oven–roasted chicken and rice salad in a sparkling citrus vinaigrette hits the spot. You can depend on a juicy pork loin sandwich in an ancho chili barbecue sauce, and a Niman-Schell hamburger. At dinner, which has not been as rewarding as lunch, you might find a rib-eye steak with wood oven–baked white bean gratin and aïoli, or grilled salmon with leeks and a rosemary-scented tomato sauce. As always, you can expect the desserts to combine hominess with panache, as evidenced by a luscious, remarkably tender warm chocolate bread pudding made with chocolate brioche. Tower's ideas about what constitutes a civilized restaurant experience are in place: oversized silverware that feels good in your hand; large, thin wineglasses that are only filled up a little bit by the well-trained staff; warm crusty Acme rolls, replaced as they are eaten; a far-ranging wine list that is hardly a bargain, but with bold-face suggestions for interesting bottles. Now Tower has to convince the Napa Valley locals that they want this kind of sophistication, too.

When Hiro Sone and Lissa Doumani opened Terra in a historic stone building in St. Helena, these exiles from Los Angeles' Spago brought to the valley a unique cross-cultural dining experience in a sophisticated package. The offbeat menu includes everything from traditional Japanese barbecued eel to crisp-fried quail with chanterelles and wild rice risotto. Chef Sone goes out of his way to create dishes around unusual ingredients like octopus, sweetbreads, duck liver, and veal shanks, and he has the technique and creativity to make them exciting. His plates don't look or taste fussy, but they often hold at least seven different foods, like a tender, sliced duck breast in a piquant dried-cherry sauce with sweet-potato puree and julienne of raw vegetables, stewed baby artichokes, and sautéed snow peas. The rustic dishes are the most appealing, like braised veal shank served with a marrow fork and the traditional accompaniment of saffron-infused risotto. For the less adventurous there's always a crusty steak served with scalloped potatoes. Hiro's wife Lissa serves as pastry chef and dining-room manager. She whips up gorgeous shortcakes with crème fraîche; a smart tiramisù served in a small earthenware Japanese bowl; and sparkling fresh-fruit sorbets.

The two dining rooms are cool and inviting, with old stone walls, beamed ceilings, terra-cotta tile floors, and large modern oil paintings. A long, reasonably priced local wine list encourages experimentation. Terra continues to be one of my favorite restaurants in the valley for its unique personal vision and unfailing commitment to high quality.

1345 Railroad Avenue, St. Helena

Tel: 707-963-8931

Open Wednesday, Thursday, Sunday and Monday 6 to 9 p.m., Friday and Saturday until 10 p.m.

Price: Expensive

Credit cards: CB, DC, MC, V

1050 Charter Oak Avenue,
St. Helena
Tel: 707-963-4444
Open daily 11:30 a.m.
to 10 p.m.
Price: Moderate
Credit cards: DC , D, MC, V

The tree-shaded courtyard and canopied terrace of this little piece of the Italian countryside in the Napa Valley transform the eating experience here. You can't stay grumpy in this marvelous setting, even if the service is sometimes amateurish or the smell of old garlic overtakes the olive oil set out to moisten crusty country bread. Although the stunning tiled floors have now been covered with utilitarian carpeting and the marvelous faux stone walls have been softened with huge Milanese *aperitivo* posters from the thirties, the lofty, indoor dining room still represents classic eighties Limn design: minimal, but opulent in materials.

The kitchen has always been maddeningly inconsistent, coming up with some real treats from an enticing menu, but disappointments as well. Crunchy, perfectly fried calamari in an Arborio rice–flour batter were delicious one day, if you could fish them out of a pool of sweet mustard sauce, and some delicate Hobbs' prosciutto paired with strong pecorino and fresh cherries, one early summer day, didn't really taste all that good together. At that same summer lunch, a wonderful bowl of tiny, tender spinach-and-ricotta-filled ravioli in a rich, buttery cheese sauce shone, while some overcooked curly strands of pasta suffered in a reduced rabbit and mushroom sauce with soapy-tasting pieces of rabbit. Interesting wines by the glass, like a new California wine made from Tuscan Sangiovese grapes, and some of the best restaurant espresso I've tasted, only make you wonder why the food often misses the mark. In the Napa Valley, however, Tra Vigne remains a destination for its ebullient sensibility and lyrical setting.

The local secret in Calistoga is this small, stylish, home-grown cafe with a wonderful outdoor seating area in a brick courtyard shaded by trees and trellises. During lunch one hot day we stayed cool by ordering a leafy version of Greek salad flanked by tomatoes and tossed with sheep's milk feta, olives, and pine nuts, and a tasty Asian noodle salad topped with grilled chicken. A Mexican plate brought *masa* cakes topped with black beans, strips of sirloin, *queso fresco*, guacamole, and fresh salsa. For dessert during stone-fruit season, look for a pecan shortcake with fresh peaches and cream.

Indoors, the small copper bar offers a long list of beers and generally inexpensive, well-chosen local Italian and French wines. Also fun and refreshing are fresh fruit *liquados* (delicious mango and nectarine), mango lassi, citrus spritzers, and Javanese iced coffee.

1226B Washington Street, Calistoga

Tel: 707-942-4712

Open for lunch Wednesday through Monday 11:30 a.m. to 3 p.m.; dinner Thursday through Monday 6 to 9 p.m.

Price: Moderate

Credit cards: AE, MC, V

BARS

AUBERGE DU SOLEIL

180 Rutherford Hill Road,
Rutherford
Tel: 707-963-1211
Open daily 11 a.m. to
midnight; restaurant
open for breakfast, lunch,
and dinner from 7 a.m.
to 9:30 p.m.
Credit cards: AE, D, MC, V

The best way to take advantage of this tony wine country hotel is to have a bottle of champagne at sunset on the outdoor terrace while you take in the sweeping view of the valley; or go there, perhaps, for Sunday brunch, and have a tasty Auberge bloody Mary made with Absolut vodka and fresh horseradish.

MARTIN'S JOHN AND ZEKE'S

111 Plaza Street,
Healdsburg
Tel: 707-433-3735
Open daily 10 a.m.
to 2 p.m.
No credit cards

Big sports TVs; two good pool tables; hot cashews and pistachios; big microwaved hot dogs with all the fixings; an excellent selection of local wines; a good liquor selection featuring high-end tequilas; tasty margaritas; keno; well-made drinks; friendly people on both sides of the bar; and it's clean and well kept. What more can I say?

DELICATESSENS/TAKE-OUT

CANTINETTA AT TRA VIGNE

One of the most pleasant places to have a bite in the Napa Valley is under a shade tree in the courtyard of Tra Vigne. A glass of wine and a slice of pizza from the Cantinetta, a free-standing adjunct of the restaurant, can hit the spot on a warm Napa Valley afternoon. This delicatessen/wine bar sells prepared food, breads, and wine by the bottle and glass either to have outdoors here at the wrought-iron cafe tables under the plane trees, or to take home. The handsome breads from Pan-O-Rama bakery in Petaluma, an in-house operation that supplies all the bread needs of Real Restaurants, can be paired with chef Michael Chiarello's spicy, dry Calabrese sausage, delicious small oil-cured black olives, cold roast poussin, and green salad for a first-rate picnic. The long wine bar buzzes with activity as visitors to the Napa Valley taste the most interesting local wines. The Real Restaurant people seem to know instinctively what makes a food operation exciting. In the case of the Cantinetta, they cater to every visitor's desire to eat food that goes with wine outdoors in a beautiful setting, without paying restaurant prices for it. Once again, they struck gold.

1050 Charter Oak Avenue, St. Helena

Tel: 707-963-8888

Open Sunday through Thursday 11:30 a.m. to 6 p.m., Friday and Saturday until 6:30 p.m.

Credit cards: DC , D, MC, V

OAKVILLE GROCERY

Early on, the Oakville Grocery knew that the Napa Valley couldn't live without prosciutto from Parma, six kinds of imported olives, goat cheese, aged Italian cheese, French triple-cream cheese, cheese from all over the world, Italian salami and cured meats, Passini baguettes, and a worldwide selection of mustards, jams, pastas, vinegars, and olive oils found in gourmet food

17856 St. Helena Highway, Oakville

Tel: 707-944-8802

Open daily 10 a.m. to 6 p.m.; espresso bar opens at 8 a.m.

Credit cards: AE, MC, V

departments in large cities. To go with these choice foodstuffs, the Oakville wine buyer (one of the partners is Joe Phelps, from Phelps winery) put together a distinguished group of Napa Valley and imported wines. Add a sprinkling of local and organic produce, particularly fruit, and you have one of the most important food resources in the area. Yes, you could find many of these things at stores and delicatessens in San Francisco, but their conjunction in a charming wood-floored store in the heart of the wine country gives everything a fresh context. The store is so well managed, the food so nicely displayed, the inventory of tempting things so creative, that the Oakville Grocery became a destination in its own right. When you rent a house in the valley, the Oakville becomes a regular stop for essentials—the *New York Times*, coffee beans, Clover dairy products, and fresh baguettes. Once you are there, how can you pass up a piece of super-aged Reggiano Parmesan or a pint of that luscious-looking potato salad? Prices were and still are astronomical, but the quality of everything is high. The cheeses are well cared for, the cured meats expertly sliced. Sometimes the produce looks sparse and a little tired, but greengrocer is not Oakville's identity. Its impetus cames from supplying the necessities of civilized life in the middle of the wine country, when no one else was doing it, and doing it better than anyone else, even today.

BAKERIES/PASTRIES

DOWNTOWN BAKERY AND CREAMERY

Kathleen Stewart continues to turn out the perfect desserts of Chez Panisse pastry chef Lindsey Shere, and then some, at this quintessential country bakery, a bakery everyone wishes they had next door. Every morning a seeming army of workers in the open kitchen turns out baskets of warm sticky buns and buttery almond-encrusted sweet rolls, hefty baguettes, and flavorful country breads. The fresh-fruit galettes are dreamy: buttery dark-brown crusts folded over fillings of fresh plums, nectarines, and wild blackberries or rhubarb. They come in a variety of sizes; I eat a small one, still warm from the oven, for breakfast on a bench on the street. The fresh fruit tiramisù layered with berries and peaches has become a birthday classic. Dense, crumbly tea cakes are elegantly glazed with white icing and decorated with tiny tea roses. You can't go wrong with any of the beautiful-looking, simply decorated confec-tions in the case. The main problem is deciding which to pick—and that goes for freshly baked cookies and biscotti and a few choice muffins like the sugar-topped "doughnut muffin." Several days a week the famous Como bread is baked, a rectangular loaf with the most delectable crumb and yeasty flavor, divine toasted and slathered with the bakery's jam. From the creamery department comes a seasonal selection of intensely flavored fruit sorbets and ice creams, which are scooped from a small ice cream freezer between the bakery cases. An espresso machine is constantly at work. In addition to being a pastry chef, Kathleen is notorious for the six hundred rose bushes in her backyard. She brings in huge bouquets of the most exquisite antique varieties to decorate the bakery.

308A Center Street,
Healdsburg
Tel: 707-431-2719
Open weekdays 6 a.m. to
5:30 p.m., weekends 7 a.m.
to 5:30 p.m.
No credit cards

685 South Freeway Drive, Napa

Tel: 707-252-3072

Open daily 7 a.m. to 5 p.m.

No credit cards

I don't necessarily recommend that you visit this retail outlet store in Napa, but I highly recommend the bread, first baked by the Passini family in 1909. In 1972 Sciambra bought the operation, and the baguettes are still fantastic, chewy, sweet (or sour if you prefer), full of character, and denser than most. I discovered Passini baguettes at the Oakville Grocery, but they're distributed all over the Napa Valley, Sacramento, Palo Alto, and Vallejo. You can call the bakery to find out where their nearest retail outlet might be. When I visit the valley, I look forward to making a picnic around them with some olives, cheese, and a bottle of local red wine. The bread makes the meal.

ICE CREAM/CHOCOLATES

The temperature has topped 100° and you can't bear to hear another word about malolactic fermentation. Time to head for St. Helena's old-fashioned A & W Root Beer stand for an ice-cold root beer float served in a frosted mug with huge scoops of hand-dipped ice cream bobbing in creamy draft root beer. If you're feeling particularly indulgent, you could have a bag of A & W's curly fries first.

501 Main Street, St. Helena

Tel: 707-963 4333

Open Sunday through Thursday 9:30 a.m. to 9:30 p.m., Friday and Saturday until 10 p.m.

No credit cards

DOWNTOWN BAKERY AND CREAMERY

See Bakeries/Pastries, page 601.

MARKETS

KELLER'S MARKET

See Meat and Poultry, page 608.

BIG JOHN'S FOOD CENTER

(formerly Vadnais'
Deluxe Foods)
1345 Healdsburg Avenue
(at Dry Creek Road),
Healdsburg
Tel: 707-433-7151
Open daily 8 a.m. to 9 p.m.
Credit cards: MC, V

This large Healdsburg grocery store, which offers the variety of a supermarket with the quality that comes from being independently run, just changed hands, so it remains to be seen if the comprehensive produce section of both commercial and organic fruits and vegetables will still be assembled with a real eye to local availability. The new owner vows that the meat counter will continue on, manned by butchers who cut to order such treasures as like Bruce Campbell's CK Ranch lamb, which is exceptionally sweet, tender, and juicy, never muttony, but full of flavor. Excellent Petaluma Poultry Company chickens and corn-fed pork will continue to be offered. We'll just have to keep our eye on Big John's and hope for the best.

ETHNIC MARKETS

LA LUNA MARKET

All ethnic Mexican needs are supplied at this general store: tortillas, tomatillos, thinly sliced beef for *carne asada* at the butcher counter, white confirmation dresses, high black patent leather boots with pointy heels, piñatas, and videos in Spanish. Vineyard workers order their lunches of tacos and burritos in the morning and stop by at noon to pick them up, hot and ready to go. The house-made tamales, warm from the steamer in their corn husks, filled with spicy pork, taste mighty good with either cold beer or a bottle of soft Napa Valley red wine.

1153 Rutherford Road, Rutherford

Tel: 707-963-3211

Open Monday through Saturday 8 a.m. to 8 p.m., Sunday until 7 p.m.

No credit cards

PRODUCE

HEALDSBURG FARMERS' MARKET

This is one of the sweetest little farmers' markets in Northern California, rife with beautiful, tender, mostly organic produce from a scattering of nearby farms. Before the ring of the opening bell, people line up in front of their chosen booth to grab the few baskets of *fraises des bois* or the limited supply of gold raspberries. Even if you miss the rarities, you'll find lovely things like Howard's Miracles, a large, juicy, yellow-fleshed plum with a skin that makes it look like a nectarine, or old-fashioned fragrant strawberries, both from Malcolm

Just west of the main plaza, Healdsburg

Saturday 9 a.m. to noon, Tuesday 4 to 6 p.m. (Sometimes on Tuesday evenings the market is on the plaza.)

Scott's Middleton Farm. He charges an arm and a leg for them, but they are worth it. However, at the Greenman stand next door, you can find equally wonderful Blue Lake beans for half the price of neighboring Malcolm's, exquisite lettuces, dewy watercress, and chard. Everything is very local—nothing much exotic or trucked in by farmers from outlying areas, but there's a certain charm to this. You eat what comes ripe and wait for it all year. You know that fragile apricots, vine-ripened tomatoes, and strawberries can't travel, making them all the more valued. If you're planning to visit the wine-growing areas around Healdsburg from May through December, try to take in this farmers' market, even if only to taste, and make a stop at the Downtown Bakery and Creamery for bread and pastries.

PALISADES MARKET

1506 Lincoln Avenue,
Calistoga
Tel: 707-942-9549
Open Sunday through
Thursday 9 a.m. to 7 p.m.,
Friday and Saturday until
8 p.m.
Credit cards: MC, V

This rustic wood-frame country store has become a Napa Valley destination for organic produce purchased directly from local farmers. You'll find tiny Forni-Brown Garden salad greens picked with roots intact and packed in green mesh cartons in water. These succulent greens appear in all the upscale valley restaurants. Carefully labeled organic tomatoes, corn, beans, and other seasonal vegetables and lots of fruit, including melons, berries, and stone fruit, fill the long shelves. One time I found some really good English peas in the pod, small and sweet. The variety is amazingly large and surprises pop up, since some of the produce is trucked up from brokers in the Bay Area. The store carries fresh breads and delicatessen items like imported olives, prosciutto from Parma, and cheeses, while the grocery shelves are filled with such essentials as imported Italian pasta and olive oil. With the meat counter at Keller's in St. Helena, cooks in the upper Napa Valley can stay well supplied.

I have found small, fragrant Blenheim apricots here in the spring, and intensely flavored French sugar, or prune, plums at the end of the summer and early fall. This recipe from Anne Haskell puts either fruit to brilliant use in a rustic country tart. I am scared to death of pastry, but I followed this recipe exactly and made a wonderful tart. I know you can do it too.

To make the dough: Cut the butter into the flour and salt until it is pea sized. I use my fingers, rubbing the butter into the flour and working quickly, but you can also use a wire pastry cutter. Stir in the water to form a dough. On a lightly floured board, form the dough into a disk. Wrap in plastic and chill for at least 1 hour.

Preheat the oven to 425°F. To make the filling: Melt the butter in a 12-inch cast-iron skillet over medium-high heat, and stir in the sugar until it dissolves. Turn off the heat.

Starting from the outer edge of the pan, lay the apricots or plums cut-side up around the pan. The fruit should fit snugly, with each circle slightly over-lapping. Cut the remaining apricots or plums in quarters and scatter over the halved fruit.

Place the pan on the stove over low to medium heat. When the fruit starts to release some juice, raise the heat to medium-high and cook for about 25 minutes. The juices will get syrupy and eventually begin to caramelize.

While the apricots are cooking, roll out the tart dough slightly larger than the circumference of your skillet. The dough should be about 1/8 inch thick.

When the apricots are ready, remove the pan from the stove and cover with the dough. I just drape it over the pan and cut off the extra. The dough kind of falls down over the fruit by itself. Bake for 35 minutes. The crust will be nicely browned. Allow to rest 5 minutes.

Have a large flat plate ready. Place it over the tart. Wearing oven mitts and using both hands, flip the pan over so that the plate is on the bottom. If any fruit sticks to the pan, just use a spatula to place it on the tart.

The tart can be eaten warm, or within 3 to 4 hours of baking. The dough doesn't get soggy. Serve with sweetened whipped cream or vanilla ice cream.

Makes one 12-inch tart; serves 8

UPSIDE-DOWN APRICOT OR PLUM TART

Dough

1 cup (2 sticks) cold butter

2 cups all-purpose flour

1/2 teaspoon kosher salt

7 tablespoons ice water

Filling

6 tablespoons unsalted butter

2/3 cup sugar

3 pounds firm apricots or prune plums,
   halved and pitted

Railroad Avenue at Pine Street, St. Helena

Friday 7:30 to 11:30 a.m., May through November

This bustling, all-encompassing market not only offers local produce but farm eggs, mushrooms, Bellweather Farm's sheep's milk cheeses and lamb, and put-up products like jams and vegetable sauces. At a typical late-June market you will find the first flavorful Early Girl tomatoes you've been hungering for all winter, tiny *haricots verts,* Santa Rosa plums, intensely flavored Blenheim apricots, some very nice lettuces, pickling cucumbers, blueberries, and fresh herbs. People know each other at this market, and I have spotted several chefs from Napa Valley restaurants talking up the growers.

MEAT AND POULTRY

KELLER'S MARKET

1320 Main Street, St. Helena

Tel: 707-963-2114

Open daily 8 a.m. to 9 p.m., butcher shop open until 7 p.m.

Credit cards: MC, V

One of the attractions of this useful grocery store in downtown St. Helena is a small but complete independently owned butcher counter that makes its own delicious mild and hot Italian sausages, as well as four or five other kinds. Besides the usual cuts of beef, you will find quick-cooking pork tenderloins wrapped in pancetta for the grill, Fulton Valley and Rocky chickens, and Sonoma lamb. The surrounding grocery gets fresh bread deliveries from Passini and others, and stocks imported pasta, olive oil, and other necessities of life.

CHEESE

OAKVILLE GROCERY

See Delicatessens/Take-Out, page 599.

WINES AND SPIRITS

ALL SEASONS CAFE AND WINE STORE

This wine shop/cafe has put together a wonderful collection of both European and local wines at decent prices. You can buy French and California wines made with the same varietals to compare, or find tiny bottlings from small vineyards nearby to immerse yourself in Napa Valley wine making. One of the best ways to taste wine is with food, which the cafe end of the operation prepares with special attention to seasonal produce and artisanal ingredients. For a $7.50 corkage, you can pick out any bottle, pay the retail price for it (a big savings over wine list prices even with the corkage), and drink it with a charming country meal of one of the house-made pastas, spritely salads, or well-prepared fish and meat dishes that go particularly well with wines. The desserts carry on the fresh seasonal commitment with the likes of summer berry pie with house-made vanilla ice cream; or consider the cheese plate, which makes perfect sense when you're eating in a room full of red wine waiting to be opened.

1400 Lincoln Avenue, Calistoga

Tel: 707-942-6828

Open daily except Wednesday, 10 a.m. to 6 p.m.

Credit cards: MC, V

J. V. WAREHOUSE

Vallergas Market
426 First Street,
Napa
Tel: 707-253-2624
Open daily 8 a.m. to 9 p.m.
Credit cards: D, MC, V

Just as its name implies, wine, beer, and liquor are set out on shelves and you help yourself. The warehouse has lots of Napa Valley wines, including some old vintages. If you know what you want, like all the wine makers and growers in the valley who shop here do, you can find some terrific bargains.

A SPECIAL DETOUR
JOHNNY OTIS MARKET AND DELI

7231 Healdsburg Avenue
(Highway 116), Sebastopol
Tel: 707-824-8822
Open Tuesday through Sunday
at 11 a.m., shows nightly at
8 p.m., Friday 8:30 and 10:30
p.m., Saturday 8 and 10 p.m.;
Saturday breakfast show 8 a.m.
Credit cards: MC, V

Forget about the food part of this operation, because this supposed market is really the most happening night spot in the north bay. Owned by veteran rhythm-and-bluesman Johnny Otis, this former market in a nondescript building in a small strip mall in downtown Sebastopol now is filled with tables and a small stage where the hottest and sweetest live shows you'll ever see take place. Bring the kids. If they play an instrument or can dance, they'll get a chance to perform with the band on the weekends when the Johnny Otis Show takes the stage. Johnny's grown son and grandson play in the band along with a Billie Holiday

See Delicatessens/Take-Out, page 599.

The excellent wine department specializes in hard-to-find Napa Valley wines, which the store will ship. The staff is very helpful.

ST. HELENA WINE CENTER

Lots of local wines at good prices here, along with a few imports. Helpful and knowledgeable owner Dick Graham can steer you to the right wines.

1321 Main Street,
St. Helena
Tel: 707-963-1313
Monday through Saturday
10 a.m.to 6 p.m., Sunday
until 4 p.m.
Credit cards: AE, MC, V

sound- and look-alike called Li'l Bit, and singers Jackie Payne and sexy Dangerous Diva Diane in form-fitting sequins. Three or four other musicians join in on every instrument from sax to trombone. The Otis Show runs through a history of jazz and r & b that gets the house rocking. Johnny Otis brand organic apple juice, sandwiches, beer, and wine are served both during the shows, and during the day when the Johnny Otis Market is just a deli. On weeknights, other acts are booked into the market, but I'd make the detour for the Johnny Otis Show itself.

699 St. Helena Highway
(Highway 29), St. Helena
Tel: 707-963-7888
Open daily 10 a.m.
to 6 p.m.
Credit cards: MC, V

Formerly called Ernie's, this wine store has always stocked high-quality Napa Valley bottles. Now, a good selection from other areas in California coupled with wines from all over the world are included, making this a useful resource for Napa Valley wine growers in search of taste models. The prices are not terribly competitive, but the clerks are competent and enthusiastic. Savvy collectors used to be able to find quirky old vintages of European wines, but, alas, the buyers have caught up with the inventory.

FOIE GRAS IN SONOMA

Sonoma Foie Gras

1905 Sperring Road, Sonoma

Tel: 707-938-1229

This is not a retail operation, but Junny and Guillermo Gonzales produce the highest-quality fresh duck foie gras in California, a product that certainly rivals the fine Hudson Valley foie gras from New York. You can call to find out how to get some (their foie gras is always available at Polarica in San Francisco, see page 462), or to make an appointment to visit the farm. The raw foie gras and ready-to-serve terrines (which will be made upon request) are vacuum packed and stay fresh for shipping. Raw foie gras actually is simple to prepare. Get a cast-iron frying pan really hot and sear slices of the foie gras for just a moment (15 seconds) on each side; any longer and the foie gras will melt like butter. Drape the warm slices on a very lightly dressed salad of haricots verts and baby lettuces in a sherry vinegar–shallot vinaigrette. Foie gras is expensive, but it's one of those ingredients that always seems worth it.

In an unlikely spot on the edge of Healdsburg, a funky, cool cement-floored wine and liquor store offers a surprisingly diverse selection of spirits and wines—a selection that includes all the major growing areas of California and a commendable selection of wines from wine-growing regions all over the world.

90 Dry Creek Road, Healdsburg

Tel: 707-431-0841

Open Monday through Thursday 9 a.m. to 9 p.m., Friday and Saturday until 10 p.m., Sunday until 8 p.m.

Credit cards: MC, V

Some examples: Cacchiano 1990 Chianti Classico for $12.50 a bottle, a good price; fine bottlings from Oregon, like Adelsheim Pinot Noir; an array of Ridge Vineyard wines; representative bottles of one of my favorite Bordeaux, Chateau La Lagune from the Haut Médoc, not to mention a good selection of other Bordeaux. Beware of prestigious labels from off vintages that catch your eye among the current offerings, like a 1986 Romanée St-Vivant from Romanée-Conti at $159, or some over-the-hill, fancy Italian white wines that probably would not be drinkable.

Wine-tasting itineraries have become a conundrum because so many excellent wineries have opened tasting rooms over the last ten years. What used to be a fairly rare service to the public, mounted either by the biggest, most successful wineries able to afford staffing, or by very small wineries dependent on direct sales to visitors, is now de rigueur. So tasters have many, many options. Here are but a few, slightly offbeat, suggestions.

If you are new to the game, you might want to begin your wine-tasting career at ST. SUPERY (8440 St. Helena Highway, Rutherford, 707-944-9707) with its self-guiding wine education installation. The state-of-the-art interactive display includes an illuminating three-dimensional model of the Napa Valley; smell exhibits in which you put your nose into a mask and press a lever to get a whiff of aromas like grapefruit, black cherry, cedar, and wildflowers (typical components of various wines); and a series of photographs showing the natural factors that influence the flavor of a wine, such as fog, soil type, and elevation. The winery is owned by the Skalli family, the biggest sellers of pasta in Europe, and also owners of a large wine operation in the south of France near Languedoc. Their French wines cost under $10 here, a great bargain. The pricier California wines straddle the line between commercial and boutique, with competent bottlings in all major varietals. President Michaela Rodino hired a crack all-woman staff to run the winery, charm the public, and sell the wine.

Tiny CASA NUESTRA (3451 Silverado Trail, North, St. Helena, 707-963-4684) is one of those wineries that sells 90 percent of its production to visitors. The charming owner, an ex-lawyer (Harvard undergrad; Boalt Hall law school) turned grape grower, entertains and charms everyone he welcomes to his rustic piece of paradise, with its picnic tables by the river. He bottles a stunning light red called Cabernet Franc, reminiscent of Chinon from the Loire valley. He bottles some himself and sells the rest in barrels to more famous vineyards.

For the big winery experience, ROBERT MONDAVI WINERY (7801 St. Helena Highway [Highway 29], Oakville, 707-259-9463) offers tours, tastings, and retail sales of its consistently elegant European-style wines. For an art and wine-tasting experience, Donald Hess, the biggest marketer of bottled water in Switzerland, has installed a major modern art collection in an old Christian Brothers classroom-turned-gallery at the HESS COLLECTION (4411 Redwood Road, Napa, 707-255-1144). Along with curating, Hess makes a delicious reserve Cabernet.

In Sonoma County I like to base operations around Healdsburg, near the wineries on the Russian River. Driving down bucolic Westside Road, you'll pass many, but two right next to each other will give you an idea of the best wines from this area.

ROCHIOLI (6192 Westside Road, Healdsburg, 707-433-2305) has achieved spectacular success from one vineyard, which for three years in a row produced the grapes that won the California State Fair Pinot Noir judging. In one of those years Rochioli made the wine, in others Gary Farrell and Williams Selyem made the award-winning Pinot Noirs. Rochioli has won the state twice with its gigantic, grassy Sauvignon Blanc, one year as the best overall wine in the state. This lovely little winery has a tasting room and picnic tables that overlook a vineyard planted with roses.

Next door is one of the most beautiful wineries, HOP KILN (6050 Westside Road, Healdsburg, 707-433-6491), with a historic hops-drying barn built in 1905, now preserved as part of the National Trust. Some of the wines come from ancient vineyards planted at the turn of the century by the once-large Italian-American enclave in the area (whose savings, along with those of Italians on Fisherman's Wharf, started the Bank of America). Hop Kiln has identified many old grape varieties promiscuously planted in their vineyards and makes some monumental wines with them, like their Primitivo (what others call Zinfandel), characterized by a jammy, berryish flavor, and, in old vintages, a spicy black-pepper edge. These wines are made in traditional California style as opposed to the more restrained French claret style, so they are big and chewy. Other interesting wines include a Petit Syrah and a wine called Marty Griffin's Big Red: a big, fruity blend of grapes from these old vines that sells for about $8.50 a bottle and beat out the Mondavi-Rothschild Opus One for the top award at the Orange County Fair one year.

Finally, if you like the idea of tasting wines and exploring the ever-expanding wine country in depth, get your hands on the *Wine Atlas of California* by James Halliday (Viking), an inclusive tome with color photographs, which won both the James Beard and Julia Child awards in 1993. It offers practical information on tasting rooms as well as the wineries.

Indexes

RESTAURANTS

CUISINE

(* *indicates a cafe, delicatessen, or bar*)

BY PRICE

(Inexpensive: food $15 and under; Moderate: food $16 to $29; Expensive: food $30 and up)

FOOD SERVICE AT COUNTER OR BAR

FOOD SERVICE AFTER 10 P.M.

BREAKFAST OR WEEKEND BRUNCH

OUTDOOR SEATING

CHILD FRIENDLY

Anthony's   288

Brennan's Restaurant, Inc.   505

Bubba's   559

Cafe at Chez Panisse   507

Casa Orinda   509

Cinderella   409

Eagle Cafe   101

E'Angelo   206

Ella's   336

House of Prime Rib   380

Il Pollaio   294

Just Won Ton   472

Kate's Kitchen   183

La Felce   295

La Taqueria   231

Lichee Garden   47

Little Joe's   296

Los Jarritos   233

MacArthur Park   143

The Mermaid   515

Mifune   342

Mom Is Cooking   234

Mo's   300

Nob Hill Grille   383

Pancho Villa Taqueria   235

Picante Taqueria   519

San Francisco Art Institute Cafe   304

Sears Fine Foods   154

Taqueria El Balazo   184

Ti Couz Crêperie   236

Tommaso's   306

Ton Kiang Cafe   422

Vicolo Pizzeria   83

Win's   476

Yank Sing   159

BANQUET ROOM

Aqua   130

Bistro Roti   99

Boulevard   100

Casa Orinda   509

Cho-Cho   136

Cypress Club   136

Domaine Chandon   584

Ernie's   138

Fly Trap Restaurant   444

Fournou's Ovens   378

Gaylord of India   103

The General's Daughter   587

Gold Mountain   41

Greens   207

Harbor Village   105

Harris' Restaurant   380

Izzy's   208

Jack's   141

MacArthur Park   143

Madrona Manor   589

Maharani   382

Moose's   301

Napa Valley Wine Train   590

Oliveto   517

One Market Restaurant   107

Oriental Pearl   49

OF HISTORIC INTEREST

Specialty indexes

BAKERIES/PASTRIES

(An asterisk* marks Patty's personal favorites)

BARS

CAFES

CHEESE

COFFEE

COOKWARE AND BOOKS

DELICATESSENS/TAKE-OUT

ETHNIC MARKETS

FISH

ICE CREAM/CHOCOLATES

MARKETS

MEAT AND POULTRY

PRODUCE

WINE AND SPIRITS

RECIPE INDEX

SIDEBARS